Remember
Henry Harris

Copyright © 2019 by Sam Heys
Second Printing, September 2019
Published by Black Belt Books
ISBN: 978-0-57 8-56578-1
Printed in the United States of America

All rights reserved. This book or any portion thereof may not be reproduced or used in any manner whatsoever without the express written permission of the publisher except for the use of brief quotations in a book review or scholarly journal

www.rememberhenryharris.com
www.samheys.com

Cover by: ProfessionalBookCoverDesign.com

Dedicated to my wife,

Patricia Finley Heys

SEC Integration by Year

Here are the initial black players to sign basketball and football scholarships at each of the ten member schools, with the year in which they enrolled.

Year	Basketball	Football
1966	Perry Wallace Godfrey Dillard *Vanderbilt*	Greg Page Nate Northington *Kentucky*
1967		Lester McClain *Tennessee*
1968	**Henry Harris** *Auburn*	
1969	Wendell Hudson *Alabama* Ronnie Hogue *Georgia*	**James Owens** *Auburn* Robert Bell Frank Dowsing *Miss. State* Leonard George Willie Jackson *Florida*
1970	Coolidge Ball *Ole Miss* Collis Temple Jr. *LSU* Tom Payne ** *Kentucky* Steve Williams Malcolm Meeks *Florida*	Wilbur Jackson *Alabama* Taylor Stokes *Vanderbilt*
1971	Larry Robinson *Tennessee* Larry Fry Jerry Jenkins *Miss. State*	Lora Hinton Mike Williams *LSU* five players * *Georgia*
1972		James Reed Ben Williams *Ole Miss*

* - Horace King, Chuck Kinnebrew, Larry West, Clarence Pope, and Richard Appleby integrated Georgia's football program in 1971.
** - Tom Payne entered Kentucky in 1969 but was not on athletic scholarship until the fall of 1970.

Contents

1 April 18, 1974   1
2 Edge of America   6
3 Good Soldiers   11
4 Regardless of Color   18
5 We Are Not Afraid   24
6 A Boy and a Hoop   32
7 The Hope for Years to Come   41
8 Sport v. South   51
9 Send Me   64
10 Forerunners   72
11 Trespassing   79
12 Now It's the Struggle   89
13 The Message and Messenger   96
14 'Watch for Harris'   104
15 Summer 1969   113
16 Change Agent   120
17 Captain America   128
18 Gone   138
19 Ghost Man   145
20 Saving Face   151
21 Hell to Pay   157
22 Workhorse   162
23 Not Who You Think I Am   169
24 'Nigger Corner'   173
25 Everything Is Everything   178
26 Wounded Warrior   188
27 Hero   196
28 The Fight We've Been Looking For   201
29 Systematic Lynching   205
30 Slashed Tires and Fires   211
31 Leaving Alabama   218
32 Summer in Harrisburg   226
33 Milwaukee   232
34 Swept Away   240
35 Big Chill   247
36 A Black Prince Comes Home   255
37 Doubt   259
38 The Weight   266
39 Left Behind   279
40 The Lion in Winter   288
41 Dream Deferred   297

Higher Dreams   305
Epilogue   307
Acknowledgements   321
Endnotes   325
Bibliography   353

Chapter 1
April 18, 1974

The call to the campus police station came at 10:52 Thursday morning. Luann Reblin, a student at the University of Wisconsin-Milwaukee, sounded frantic. She was working the front desk at Green Commons, the cafeteria building that joined the three high-rise towers of UWM's Sandburg Hall. She said a resident on the fifth floor had just called her and told her a body was lying on the roof "outside my window."

Patrol cars 12, 26, and 38 of the Wisconsin-Milwaukee Police Department were immediately dispatched to Sandburg Hall. Twenty-year-old Patrolman Martin Studenec was the first one there. He hurried into the two-story Green Commons building and found Reblin at the front desk. She told him how to get to the roof. He ran up the stairs. On the roof, he quickly spotted the body of a young black man lying face-down near the south tower. He was wearing a brown suit coat, brown trousers, and a navy turtleneck. Studenec rushed to him and checked for a pulse. There was not one. He searched the body for identification. There was not any. Studenec saw that the man wasn't much older than he was.

Within moments, Detective Richard Sroka was standing by Studenec and so was Sergeant Lyle Bliss. They checked the body as well. It was mid-April—April 18, 1974—and still cold on the north side of Milwaukee. The sky was gray and the temperature in the upper 30s. A biting wind was blowing hard off Lake Michigan, only six blocks away. The officers stared down at the prone body. They wondered who the young man was and how he had gotten there.

At the police station, Captain James Breismeister alerted UWM Police Chief William Harvey. After hearing from the officers on the roof, Breimeister called the Milwaukee County medical examiner's office at 11:05. He reached Warren Hill, deputy medical examiner. He told him that a student had "apparently leaped" to his death at Sandburg Hall.

When Chief Harvey arrived on the roof, Sroka was looking up at the south tower, at an open window, high on the north face of the twenty-story building. Its screen was missing. Harvey determined the open window was on the seventeenth floor. He and Sroka headed to the south tower's elevators, leaving Studenec and Bliss with the body.

Upon reaching the seventeenth floor, Harvey and Sroka determined the open window was in Suite S1720. They tried the door, but it was locked. They got a dormitory employee to unlock it and then entered the three-bedroom suite. No one was there. They looked for evidence of foul play but saw none. They tried to open the door to Room S1720-C. It was locked. Again, the dorm employee unlocked it. No one was there. The room was messy, but they could see no signs of a struggle. The room's sliding window, however, was wide open. The officers quickly found personal papers belonging to a student named Henry Harris. Harvey told Sroka that Harris was an assistant basketball coach at UWM. Harvey knew Harris because he attended UWM games. When housing department employees got to the room, Harvey asked them if S1720-C was Henry Harris's room. Yes, they said, Henry Harris, age twenty-four, was the room's legal resident.

Once Hill, the deputy medical examiner, arrived on the roof, he examined the body and pronounced the victim dead. He placed the time of death at approximately eight hours earlier, around 3 a.m. All Hill found in the victim's pockets were $16.41, a key ring with six keys, and a picture of a young woman.

Harvey and Sroka had returned from the seventeenth floor by the time Hill rolled the prone body over.

"That's Henry Harris," Harvey said.

Harris's prone body lay nineteen feet from the north wall of the south tower. He lay on a square-shaped section of roof that covered the walkway between the south tower and Green Commons, named for William T. Green, a local civil rights activist who worked as a janitor in the Wisconsin state capitol before earning a law degree from the University of Wisconsin in 1892.

At 11:55, Hill told ambulance attendants Greg Kamens and John Skipchak to take Harris's body to the Milwaukee County morgue for examination. He then went to Harris's room and met the police department's other detective, Lieutenant Robert Kowalski, a 37-year-old former state patrol officer.

Hill saw that Room S1720-C was a typical high-rise dorm room, only nine by eleven feet. A single room, it had only one bed. A chest of drawers was on the wall next to the door, and a desk was in front of the window. A deflated basketball sat on top of the desk. It was an ashtray, cradling the butts of several cigarettes as well as the very small butts of what Kowalski was certain was marijuana. Four empty Budweiser cans were on the floor, about three feet in front of the door. An empty wine bottle was on the floor next to a book case adjacent to the desk. Another empty wine bottle sat on the floor in front of the chest. On top of the chest of drawers was a Master Barlow pocket knife, a bottle of decongestant, and two undated white envelopes from the UWM Dispensary. Two words were written on the envelopes, "penicillin" and "Henry." In a drawer were three plastic bags of what the men believed to be marijuana. In a leather duffle bag on the desk, they found a bag containing a pipe and more of the substance they assumed to be marijuana. A scented candle in a red glass container burned in the middle of the floor—to disguise the odor of marijuana, Kowalski assumed.

Sergeant Bliss came up to take measurements. He drew a diagram of the room and marked the location of each item found. The window was twenty-seven inches wide and fifty-seven inches high. It was a sliding window, with a four-inch-wide windowsill inside and an outer window ledge of seven inches. The bottom of the window was three feet above the floor. Hill concluded Harris had to step up on the desk and then onto the window ledge to land nineteen feet from the building.

The investigators looked for Harris's wallet but did not find it, only a picture ID from New Cumberland Army Depot in Pennsylvania, issued April 24, 1973. They searched for a suicide note but didn't find one, only some of Harris' writings, the more recent ones expressing how much he missed his girlfriend.

After all the items were inventoried, Kowalski told the housing department to keep the room locked until Harris's family had a chance to come and recover his property, and Hill headed back downtown to the medical examiner's office, where he began returning phone calls. One of his employees, Paul Danko, had already performed an examination of Harris's body in the presence of Kamens and Skipchak, the ambulance attendants. He found compound fractures of the upper left arm and a fracture of the left leg just below the knee. He did not find any gunshot or stab wounds.

Sroka was meanwhile tracking down people to interview. He went to the fifth-floor room of Ben Evans, the student who called the front desk when he saw a body outside his window. When Sroka walked into the room, he could see out the window to the roof where Harris had landed. Evans said he called the front desk as soon as he looked out and saw the body.

"Did you know Henry Harris?" Sroka asked.

"No."

Evans told Sroka he had heard a strange thump outside his window during the night, around four o'clock. He figured it was the room's heater starting up and went back to sleep.

Sroka went to find assistant basketball coach Tom Sager. Sager said he had seen Harris the previous day, Wednesday, about 10:30 a.m. He said he had not sensed that anything was bothering Harris. Sager explained that Harris was a student assistant coach but that his position had been terminated in January, effective July 1. Sager told Sroka that UWM basketball player George Tandy had talked to Harris by phone around 11 Wednesday night, four to five hours before his death, and Harris had not said anything to indicate suicidal thinking or personal problems.

Once back in his medical examiner's office, Hill returned a call from Bill Klucas, UWM's head basketball coach. Klucas told him he wanted to tell Harris's family in person at their home outside Birmingham, Alabama. Hill's office had planned to notify the next of kin, but he agreed that doing so in person would be preferable. Klucas told Hill he last saw Harris three days earlier, on Monday. He explained that Harris had experienced "ups and downs" and was depressed at times but he had never heard Harris talk of suicide. He said Harris had still held hopes of playing professional basketball.

After Klucas hung up, he headed to the airport, but news of Harris's death would precede him to Alabama. As word slipped out of Wisconsin over the course of the afternoon, the death of Harris would be a shocking story in Alabama. The strong, lean young man whose body lay on the roof was a hero back home. He was the first black American awarded a scholarship by any of the Southeastern Conference's seven Deep South universities. He had been captain of Auburn University's basketball team just two years earlier. He was the object of the first Alabama-Auburn recruiting showdown for a black athlete, after decades of both schools refusing to sign African Americans. He was that good, that brave. He was so talented he drew interest from the Dallas Cowboys as a punt returner and so respected by his teammates that they voted him captain unanimously.

Harris was working on a book on his experiences at Auburn, but the end of his very public life was as overlooked as his obscure Black Belt childhood in Boligee, Alabama, his body lying unseen for eight hours on a compact urban campus, seemingly discarded and not discovered until midday. Harris had vanished into the darkness of a long, miserable night. After going one-on-one with old Jim Crow for four years, overcoming the odds again and again, he died unnoticed in a nation he had tried to redeem.

His very presence for four years at Auburn was an act of rebellion, whether walking on to a basketball court, into a dormitory, or into a classroom. He had changed the South just by showing up every day, just by going out every night they tossed a ball up, a lone dark body in a sea of white. In the end, though, he wasn't able to show up for one more day. The same black body he had rendered into a bridge for others to cross—from a black world to a white world in order to create a new world—lay sprawled on a tarred rooftop eight hundred miles from home. An American revolutionary had finally succumbed to his wounds.

Chapter 2

The Edge of America

Wes Bizilia got the first glimpse. It was January 1968, and Bizilia, a graduate assistant at Auburn University, was earning $45 a week teaching physical education and assisting the Auburn basketball team by scouting prospective players.

"We got a game for you to go see," Rudy Davalos, an Auburn assistant coach, had told him. "There's a kid named Henry Harris we want you to look at. It's in Boligee."

Bizilia had graduated from Livingston State, just sixteen miles from Boligee in west central Alabama "You've been over in that area," Davalos said, "so you'll know where it is." But Bizilia had no idea where Boligee was. "I didn't even know Boligee existed," he said.

Bizilia left Auburn in plenty of time for the 180-mile trip across Alabama. He was excited but anxious. The grandson of Ukranian immigrants, Bizilia grew up in Pennsylvania and had never gone into an all-black high school and expected to be the only white person there. When he finally arrived, he couldn't believe it. "Boligee was a God-forsaken place. You drive in there, and you didn't even know it was a town. It was as rural as it gets," he remembered.

Once he found Greene County Training School, Bizilia headed straight to the office of the principal, having called him ahead of time. A. W. Young was expecting him. "Coach, you're going to sit with me," Young told him.

They walked down the hall and into a tight gymnasium. Chairs, not bleachers, lined the court. This would be basketball in the raw, Bizilia thought, nothing but the ball and players and who wanted it the most. A buzz started as soon as Bizilia walked in—the excitement was palpable. Everyone knew why Bizilia was there. He had come for Henry Harris, the pride of the people and the promise of a new day.

Young led Bizilia to their chairs at mid-court. When the Bobcats finally came out to warm up, Bizilia spotted Harris immediately. He was leading them. "When they get to midcourt," Bizilia said, "Henry puts the ball on the floor and goes in and shoots a lay-up."

Bizilia turned to Young and said, "He has a scholarship to Auburn right now."

"But, Coach, you haven't seen him play."

"I've seen enough. He can play."

Young looked at Bizilia in disbelief. "You mean it?"

"I mean it. He can play."

Henry Harris could play. "That first time he shot a layup, just the way he went in, the control of the ball. He exploded when he went up," Bizilia recalled. "He was 6-foot-2, but he had an explosion and quickness about him that you just didn't see every day."

Bizilia was living a recruiter's dream. He could hardly contain himself. Deep in the outback of west Alabama, in the midst of cotton fields and crushing poverty, Auburn had unearthed a marvelous talent. No other recruiters were there. Bizilia was getting a private showing, and the more he watched the more excited he grew. Good body control, he thought. Good control of the basketball. Good shot balance. Tremendous leg spring.

After the game, Young introduced Bizilia to Harris.

"I like the way you play," he said.

Harris smiled, his grin was quick and easy.

"You didn't disappoint me. We're interested. We'll be in touch."

Reporters had discovered Greene County before college recruiters did. Three years earlier, *Newsweek's* Joseph Cumming said he felt he was traveling back in time when he drove into Greene County, calling it "rural, dark . . . out of the mainstream." He described the forty-five miles from "the neon-gaudy highways around Tuscaloosa into lonely and uncluttered Greene County" as a trip from "Technicolor into black and white." But this was the nest from which Henry Harris would fly, a land where large farms were still called plantations and today was always yesterday.

Established in 1819, even before Alabama was a state, the county was namesake of Nathaniel Greene, the Revolutionary War general who drove the British out of the Southeast. Half the county's population had fled since 1900, but its 1869 courthouse and columned hillside mansions still stood tall in the county seat of Eutaw—shrines to the county's onetime cotton kingdom built by enslaved Americans. Blacks in Greene County outnumbered whites eight-to-one, and in Harris's rural postal district, the ratio was much higher, approximately 3,000 blacks to only 169 whites. Greene County was the blackest county in Alabama and one of the six poorest in the United States, its ruling class having turned away industry because it would pay better than farm work, leaving a century-long status quo in place and black Americans still in the fields.

Greene County lay on the western edge of Alabama's Black Belt, a swath of the American South still wrestling time and struggling to catch it. The name—Black Belt—originally came from the soil, a sticky clay that turned to obstinate mud when wet and an impenetrable surface when dry. Once planters figured out how to work it, cotton plantations and slaves followed, creating a density of black dots on population maps from Virginia to east Texas.

The Black Belt was the South's underbelly, a subterranean land for African Americans, who survived under a feudal, caste-like economic system and a self-serving, bully political system that denied them the most basic rights of U.S. citizenship. It was a place of dirt roads and long walks into town, of never looking a white man in the eye and never looking at a white woman at all, a place where white people still owned land and black people worked it, and, in 1968, still a land of outhouses and training schools.

In the Black Belt, rural black high schools were called "training schools," the rationale being African Americans were not educable—they could only be trained—or, perhaps, were *not* to be educated, else they might attain the acumen to flee the plantation. The U.S. Supreme Court struck down school segregation in 1954, and yet, fourteen years later, Harris—the basketball prodigy and high school valedictorian, surviving on the margin in the richest nation in the world—had never sat in a classroom with a white student.

Larry Chapman was the second Auburn recruiter dispatched to see Harris. "Man, he's a good player," Bizilia had told Davalos.

"So Rudy [Davalos] sends me down there," said Chapman, Auburn's freshman coach.

Harris's next game was at West End High School in York, almost to Mississippi, so Chapman and his wife left early for the 185-mile, two-lane trip on history's highway, U.S. 80. They drove through Tuskegee, training site for the black pilots who would quell Americans' doubts about blacks' courage and valor under fire in World War II. They drove through Montgomery, where Rosa Parks birthed the civil rights movement by remaining in her bus seat in 1955. They went over the patch of highway where civil rights worker Viola Liuzzo was shot dead by the Ku Klux Klan. They drove into Selma across the Edmund Pettus Bridge, site of the bloody confrontation less than three years earlier that propelled Congress to pass the Voting Rights Act of 1965. Selma and Montgomery were the seminal bookends of a crusade that had thrust open the gates Chapman was hurrying to find a young man to walk through. His spirits were soaring. He knew Auburn was moving ahead of the other SEC schools in the Deep South. Not one of them had given an athletic scholarship to a black athlete, and now it appeared Auburn could be the first. As the miles dragged and winter twilight approached, Chapman wondered, "Lord, will we ever get there?"

The site of the game was seemingly scripted out of destiny. York was in Sumter County, where Harris's family had struggled to survive for decades and where his mother, pregnant, had to drop out of school at fifteen. Now, a coach was coming to Sumter County hoping to offer her son a college scholarship.

"We go to the high school," Chapman said, "and they let us sit up on the stage. The boys teams come out to warm up during halftime of the girls game. I watch them warm up, and I know this guy is kind of special. And then they start playing, and he is [special]. I don't remember how many points he got; I just know he dominated and was an incredible basketball player. He just instinctively reacted to whatever happened on the court, and that's what basketball is."

Chapman was getting a tinge of the exhilaration major league scouts felt when they found seventeen-year-old Willie Mays playing center field at Rickwood Field for the Birmingham Black Barons in 1948. They had stumbled upon a natural in a closeted, segregated subculture most Americans ignored or didn't even know existed. Chapman couldn't believe his luck, couldn't believe Auburn's luck. He sensed he was watching a "basketball icon" in the making.

"Henry had the ability, because of the grace that had been afforded him and because of practice, to do stuff that other kids could only do a little bit then, because they did not have the quickness and jumping ability," said Chapman. ". . . There was no doubt that, from a basketball perspective, this guy was like someone you would see in a ballet."

But Chapman also saw a larger story—"a story about a black kid in the Deep South who loved basketball. Who was poor. Who lived in a cinder-block home in a part of the state that was pretty desolate. Out of that, rose Henry Harris. It's like he took a wrong turn. He wasn't supposed to be there. But there he was."

Chapter 3

Good Soldiers

Let the black man get upon his person the brass letters 'U.S.,' . . . and there is not power on earth which can deny that he has earned the right to citizenship in the United States.
- Frederick Douglass, 1863

His friends and family never understood the "attacks" or "spells" Henry Harris Sr. had after coming home from Europe after World War II.

Harris Sr. served the United States for four and half years during World War II and its cleanup in Europe and came back home to Greene County as a Tec 4, the relative equivalent of a sergeant for the Army's more technical roles. He entered the Army in 1942 at twenty-one, and after being stationed at Fort Benning during the war, he re-enlisted for eighteen months and was sent to Europe as battle-weary troops returned home. Like most black soldiers and sailors, who were rarely trusted enough for the front lines, Harris served in a supporting role—in the Transportation Corps. When the war ended, however, the Transportation Corps would play an important role in rebuilding Europe. The Army sent Harris to Munich, Germany, as part of the 3457th Transportation Company. A truck driver, he hauled rations, ammunition, and displaced persons, helping put life back together in the devastation left by years of war.

For a man who had dropped out of school before he was a teenager and sweated in the fields all his life, the Army gave Harris a level of self-respect and purpose he had never had. After being honorably discharged in 1947, he returned home, a citizen-soldier in America's victorious army, but back in America, he was still a citizen in waiting without even the right to vote.

He talked with pride about his service in Europe to his buddies back home, who liked to call him Harris, who was 6-foot-2 and 215 pounds, "Big Henry." Harris was soon back in the fields. He met and married Willie Pearl Raymond in Boligee. Their first child was born January 2, 1950, and they named him Henry after his dad.

Later in the year, October 1, Harris Sr. suffered a serious seizure. The ambulance carried him all the way across Alabama, to Tuskegee Veterans Hospital, which was built for African Americans because of the mistreatment black veterans received at veterans hospitals after World War I. It was a long trip. The ambulance left Boligee at 12:10 p.m. When Harris was admitted to the hospital at 4 p.m., he was already unconscious.

For the next four days, Harris would fight for his life under the care of Dr. George C. Branche Sr., a highly respected African American doctor. who went to work at Tuskegee after graduating from Boston University medical school. He performed the neuropsychiatric evaluations of Alabama's "Scottsboro Boys" whose convictions for allegedly raping two white women was twice overturned by the U.S. Supreme Court before they were finally freed. Following his service as a lieutenant colonel in the U.S. Army medical corps in World War II, he was made director of all professional services at Tuskegee.

With Harris, however, Branche was way behind from the start. He immediately tried to lower Harris's blood pressure and treat his kidney failure. Branche diagnosed Harris as having "malignant nephrosclerosis," a hardening of the kidneys that's termed "malignant" because of its rapid progression, with kidney damage occurring within hours as a result of uncontrolled high blood pressure.

Over a four-day period, Branche could never catch up and reverse the kidney failure. Three years after returning home to Alabama, Harris was dead at twenty-nine. His infant son—Henry Harris—was nine months old.

World War II provided a great opportunity for Harris and one million black Americans to prove themselves, their manhood, and their patriotism. They went to war believing their service would change the future. "Those of us who are in the armed services," a black soldier wrote the *New Republic* in 1944, "are offering our lives and fortunes, not for the America we know today, but for the America we hope will be created after the war." The black community talked of the "Double V" campaign—victory at home and abroad.

African Americans returning home with a new sense of themselves, having glimpsed their power and potential, would quickly see no place was set for them at "the table of victory." Seventy-five percent of the returning black veterans would come home to former Confederate states, still ruled by lynch law. Needed desperately by the U.S. to win a war, they were sent to the back of the bus afterward.

Black soldiers often faced more danger in the South than in bloody Europe or the Pacific. The NAACP found that two-thirds of the victims of racial violence in the postwar South were U.S. veterans. In 1946 alone, sixty black veterans were killed by whites in the U.S. On a Sunday afternoon in Georgia that year, twice-decorated veteran George Dorsey was murdered at Moore's Ford along with another black man and both men's wives, one of whom was pregnant. It was a lynching so shocking to a nation basking in peace that President Harry Truman asked for anti-lynching legislation, but southern legislators blocked him, and lynching continued, unabated.

Earlier in the year, Sergeant Isaac Woodard, on his way home from the Pacific, was taken off a Greyhound bus in South Carolina by police officers who beat him with nightsticks until he was permanently blinded. Then in August, veteran Maceo Snipes, a middle Georgia sharecropper, became the first African American to vote in a Georgia Democratic primary and was shot in the back the next day by four members of the Ku Klux Klan. The shooter was a white veteran. He was never convicted, and neither were Dorsey and Woodard's assailants.

The pride and inner strength that made a good American soldier could get a black man killed in the American South.

Thomas Edmonds—Henry Harris Sr.'s half-brother—was eighteen in late 1943 when he reported for duty at Fort Benning. Edmonds dropped out of Greene County Training School after the seventh grade, learned auto mechanics at a gas station, and worked in a Birmingham foundry for $4 a day under the New Deal's National Youth Administration but was ready to fight for his country. During his training, he was designated as a "sharpshooter," but because he was black, he too would serve in a support unit—the Quartermaster Corps.

By Christmas 1944, Edmonds was in France and about to get very close to the battlefront. As a member of the Fourth Platoon of the all-black 23rd Quartermaster Car Company, Edmonds became a jeep driver, transporting officers and couriers of the Ninth Army's XXVI Corps, which spent two months in Belgium during the Battle of the Bulge. By early March 1945, Edmonds was driving in Germany as the XXVI Corps swept the Nazis from the industrial cities north of the Ruhr River. He was close enough to combat to receive battle stars for participation in both the Rhineland and Central Europe campaigns— a rarity for a member of support troops. In October 1945, while in Berlin, he re-enlisted in Berlin for another eighteen months and, like his brother, drove trucks in the Allies' rebuilding of Europe.

Edmonds would return to Greene County in 1947, get married, and quickly have two sons. He was twenty-six on the 100-degree Saturday afternoon he went into Boligee in July 1951. Saturday was always a big day in Boligee, just as it was in small towns across the South. Field work knocked off midday, giving country folks time to go into town to gather their groceries and goods and relax a bit. Blacks would stream off the farmland of western Greene County into Boligee, walking in on dirt roads or riding in mule-drawn wagons or old, dusty trucks. African Americans greatly outnumbered the whites who came to town on Saturdays, but the caste system in effect when Edmonds marched off to war was still in play.

No one can say for sure what happened to Edmonds that mid-July night—not Edmonds' sons or his friends, now old men who don't like remembering the bad old days. Edmonds spent the early part of the day at his uncle's house. He told his fourteen-year-old cousin, Tommie Mae Edmonds, that he would buy her a dress when he went to town that day. He bought the dress that afternoon at Boyd Aman's store in Boligee and sent it home to her with her mother. Edmonds stayed in town, and most accounts of the evening revolve around Boligee's night watchman.

Small towns in the rural South, too small and poor for a police force, would hire a "night watchman" to watch over the town, primarily to make sure African Americans did not break into stores. He wore civilian clothes but carried a gun and could detain suspects until the sheriff arrived to make an arrest. "They hired old men who couldn't work and needed to have a few pennies as night watchmen," said A. L. Lavender, a onetime white mayor of Boligee. Every evening—around nine or maybe later on Saturdays—the night watchman would strike a plow sweep. "He'd beat that plow sweep with a big old ball peen hammer," Lavender said. "Thirty minutes later he'd go beat it again, and it meant all the black people better be out of town."

"At that time, the night watchman was kind of considered a law enforcement person," said Eunice Outland, who taught all three of Edmonds' sons at Greene County Training School. Her memories of his murder were vague. "He was a soldier in World War II who got killed in Boligee by some white men. He was out of the service, and his attitude was not in line at the time with what [white] people thought it should be. 'Uppity' was the term they liked to use. It was a senseless killing."

Edmonds' oldest son, Ernest, has spent much of his life trying to learn how and why his father was killed. He was once told his father and the night watchman got into a fight about the way the watchman talked to a black woman. "They got to fighting, and my father was beating him up and then someone shot my father, blew his brains out," he said.

Both Lavender and longtime black Boligee resident James Cox agree there was a fight and Edmonds was winning. "Edmonds took the night watchman's gun," Cox recalled being told, "and there was a bystander there and he shot him. But the night watchman claimed it, said he had two guns."

Lavender's account came from black witnesses. "They got into an argument, Edmonds jumped on him [the night watchman] and took his pistol away from him. And this other man came out with a .41 stack-barrel derringer, and he shot him [Edmonds] right between his eyes," Lavender said. "He was dead before he hit the ground."

Edmonds' mother, Rose "Showti" Edmonds, was in Boligee that night and rushed to her son's side as he lay in the street.

"Why y'all kill my son?" she screamed.

"Then someone cussed her and told her to shut her mouth," said Tommie Mae Edmonds.

Lavender said the shooter was an "old man," a retired logger who wore a black uncrowned cowboy hat and drove oxen in the 1920s and 1930s to haul trees to an area sawmill. But the night watchman claimed he had a second gun in his pocket and he was the shooter, which would have justified the murder in the 1950s, according to Lavender. "None of the white folks said nothing. I don't know how, but they kept it quiet and said the night watchman shot him," Lavender said.

"They knew but they just wouldn't tell," said Lulu Cooks, who went to school with Edmonds. "Things that went on here in Boligee and roundabout, they had a hush-mouth on it and didn't tell." Cooks said blacks did not talk much about Edmonds' killing either—"if they did, it might have happened to them."

Ernest Edmonds was three when his father was murdered. He never knew exactly how or why. Pregnant with her third son at the time, Edmonds' mother never would talk about her husband's murder, although she knew who the killer was, because she eventually told her son he had died.

Edmonds' death certificate—signed by Sheriff Frank Lee—provided few clues as to how he died. The time of the shooting was left blank, and under "Cause of Death," both "Murder" and "Accident" were checked. There was no investigation and no coverage by the press and no cold case investigation since. "It was a horrible thing," said Ernest Edmonds.

The night he was arrested, Lieutenant Gooden had been drinking. "Lieutenant" was his given name and he was married to Henry Harris Jr.'s maternal grandmother, Pearl Raymond, and a grandfather-figure to the five-year-old boy, living just down the road.

Born in Sumter County, Gooden was a laborer for the Colgrove family, owner of a Boligee dairy farm, and Pearl was their cook. On November 15, 1955, he and two friends, Arthur Cox and Free Manuel, were out drinking when they took the shortcut between Lower Gainesville Road and Boligee. The creek was out of its banks and Gooden ran off the road and was unable to get the car unstuck. "The water was up and he drove into the water and got real wet, and the police came," said Ida Colgrove.

"They might have gotten loud down there," said James Cox, Arthur's brother. "They were all drinking, and somebody might have called in." The deputy told the other two men to go home but took Gooden to the Greene County jail in Eutaw. Going to jail was one of the great fears of blacks who in the rural South. Many knew of men who never came home.

"My brother said he was fine when they took him away," Cox said. And Gooden seemed fine the next day when Harris's mother and grandmother went to visit him. When they returned to the jail the next day, however, they were told he was dead. He was forty-nine.

"He died in jail," said Colgrove. "He stayed overnight and the next night he died. . . . He was such a nice man."

"People around here thought a lot of him," recalled Cox. "He was a nice guy. He just believed in a good time. He was a hard-working guy, but on the weekend he was going to get his drink like everybody else that drank." Cox said he didn't know how Gooden died—"they said they think they could've taken him to jail and beat him up." Educator Robert Brown and Judge William Branch, black leaders in Greene County in the sixties, seventies, and eighties, both heard Gooden was hanged in jail.

Gooden's death certificate was written as ambiguously as Edmond's. The cause of death was written as "overdose of whiskey or cerebral hemorrhage." Next to "conditions contributing to death but not related to the disease or condition causing death" was written: "He was an alcoholic."

When Willie Pearl Harris and Pearl Raymond made it back to Boligee—in shock, grief, and disbelief—they had to tell Henry and his brothers the news.

Lieutenant was dead.

Henry Harris Jr. had not even started school, and his three primary male role models were already gone. Vanished. Father, uncle, grandfather. All dead in a little boy's South.

Chapter 4

Regardless of Color

The band of young black men headed out before dawn. The sons of sharecroppers, tenant farmers, and field hands, they piled themselves into their coaches' cars for a four-hour ride out of Greene County to the black educational center of Alabama—Tuskegee Institute. The trip was Al Young's idea. He had coached Greene County Training School for a decade and knew he had a special team going into the season. And a special player. Wanting to showcase Harris and his teammates, he called a couple of his coaching buddies on the other side of the state and arranged a one-day, two-game expedition into east Alabama.

The afternoon game was at Tuskegee Institute High School, which served Young's players a pregame meal, a custom among black schools, because the South had so few places for blacks to eat on the road, even in 1968. During pregame warmups, Tuskegee coach Ernest Washington started asking, "Which one is Henry?" But no one would tell him. Once the game started, Washington called a timeout—"I know who he is now"—and set his defense accordingly. It made little difference; Harris still scored forty-two points. Afterward, Harris and his teammates traveled another forty miles east, to Phenix City on the Georgia line, to play South Girard. They lost another close game, but Harris again made an impression. "He came over there with a lot of hype as a player, and of course he didn't disappoint anybody. He almost scored at will," said James Patrick, a coach who had led South Girard to the black state championship two years earlier.

By the time Harris and his teammates, sandwiches in hand, loaded back into their coaches' cars and headed out into the winter night and back across Alabama, the trajectory of Harris's life had changed. When they finally arrived back at their Greene County

Training School, it was after 4 o'clock Sunday morning. Harris walked across the road to his home and fell into the bed he shared with his two younger brothers. His one-day basketball odyssey had taken him farther from Boligee than he had ever been in his eighteen years, but the journey was just beginning. By the time Harris and his teammates gathered again Monday afternoon for practice, the race was on. The word was out. He was headed for the big time.

Villanova's George Raveling, the dream maker, called Young within days. As the first black assistant basketball coach at a major college, Raveling excelled at recruiting southern blacks. He subscribed to southern newspapers and built an underground railroad of high school coaches who doubled as talent scouts for him. That's how he had discovered Howard Porter at all-black Booker High School in Sarasota, Florida. The 6-foot-8 Porter was now averaging more than twenty points per game for Villanova's freshman team. Word of Harris's potential was relayed by Patrick, the former South Girard coach who had sent Sammy Sims to Villanova two years earlier. After hearing from Patrick, Raveling wanted to see Harris for himself. He called Coach Young and told him he was coming to Boligee.

Raveling's timing could be extraordinary. On August 27, 1963, he went to Washington with a former Villanova teammate to attend the March on Washington for Jobs and Freedom the following day. When they went to scout out the site that evening, event organizers recruited them as security guards because of their height, assigning them to the podium on the Lincoln Memorial steps. There, they stood sentinel throughout the program, through all the music, all the speeches, and, finally, Dr. Martin Luther King's "I Have a Dream" speech. When King closed with his thunderous "Free at last, free at last. Thank God Almighty, we are free at last," stepping back from the podium, wiping his brow with one hand, and holding the typewritten speech in the other, Raveling impulsively stepped toward him.

"Can I have that copy?" he asked.

King didn't hesitate. He handed him the speech.

Five years later, Raveling took a trip back in time to Greene County, where King himself had spoken, but few dreams had come true. Raveling understood the South despite having grown up in a

Washington ghetto, his dad dying when he was nine and his mom suffering a nervous breakdown when he was thirteen. He received his life break when he went to St. Michael's, a boarding school in Pennsylvania for boys from broken homes. He turned the opportunity into a degree from Villanova. Now, at age thirty, he was coming to Boligee to possibly offer Harris a similar opportunity to escape poverty. Raveling understood the doors sports could open. "Once the whistle blows," he believed, "you're no longer defined by race, but by your skills."

Raveling didn't make it to Demopolis until halftime of Harris's game at U.S. Jones High School, but seeing the second half was enough. He offered Harris a scholarship afterward and invited him to make a recruiting visit to Philadelphia.

Less than forty-eight hours after Harris's game at Tuskegee, Macon County's school superintendent walked into the school system offices in Tuskegee raving about Harris. A basketball fan, he had gone to the game and told system comptroller Jean Howard on Monday morning Auburn should recruit Harris. She said she would tell her husband—longtime Auburn athletic trainer Kenny Howard—about Harris. She did so that evening. The trainer was unsure if Auburn was ready to recruit black athletes, but he told assistant coach Rudy Davalos the next day anyway. That's what prompted Davalos to dispatch first Bizilia and then Chapman to west Alabama.

Davalos was only twenty-eight years old but a born catalyst. Competitive to a fault, he wouldn't let a game of one-on-one end until he had won. He pushed himself and all those around him. As a playmaking guard, he had led Southwest Texas State to the 1960 National Association of Intercollegiate Athletics (NAIA) championship and then married Miss Teenage Texas. As an NAIA All-American, he competed in the 1960 U.S. Olympic trials against African Americans and now welcomed the opportunity to finally recruit blacks. Davalos had tasted the salt of discrimination himself, being banned from the public swimming pools of San Antonio as a Mexican-American child. He found an easy ally in the twenty-six-year-old Chapman. Also intensely competitive, Chapman had never missed a game as a three-year starter at Auburn, and the idea of recruiting black athletes before any other SEC school in the Deep South intrigued him. Both men knew change was coming to the SEC—the 1966 NCAA championship game had assured that with Texas Western's all-black lineup vanquishing Kentucky's all-white team. Davalos and Chapman believed the bold strike of signing Harris would give Auburn a competitive advantage in a region rich in black talent, but they first had to convince head basketball coach Bill Lynn to step up and become the man to integrate Auburn athletics.

Lynn had lived all his forty-three years in Alabama, except for Navy service during World War II, and had reservations about integration. How would his players react? How would Auburn's fans react? How would other SEC coaches react? What would it be like for a black player in the athletic dormitory? What would it be like to coach a black player? What if it didn't work? Would he lose his job? A star center as an Auburn player, the tall, lean Lynn was hardly a social activist, but he depended heavily on Davalos as both a sideline tactician and dynamic recruiter. The idea began to warm on the competitor in Lynn, but he was still anxious. When he ran into university president Harry Philpott while eating lunch at Nick's, a restaurant at Auburn's legendary Toomer's Corner, he sought assurance from Philpott. The holder of a Ph.D from Yale, Philpott said he supported athletic integration, but Lynn wanted more clarity.

"Dr. Philpott, are you saying we can sign the best athletes in the state regardless of color?"

"That's exactly what I'm saying."

"So if we can sign a black athlete, then you're going to allow it."

"Definitely, I want the best athletes in the state of Alabama at this school. I don't care what color they are."

"That's all I wanted to know. We're going to be after them."

Auburn would now recruit Harris as hard as it possibly could.

In Coach Al Young's mind, if Harris was going to integrate athletics in Alabama, the obvious place to do it would be the University of Alabama, the more prominent of the state's two universities at that time and only forty-five miles from Boligee, close enough for Harris to feel the support of family and friends for the challenges he'd face. So in the summer of 1967, Young wrote Alabama athletic director Paul "Bear" Bryant about Harris, although Bryant was still not recruiting blacks for his football team. A reply from Bryant's staff said the Crimson Tide "would be checking" on Harris, but Young did not see an Alabama recruiter at any games until Auburn started recruiting Harris. He would see assistant coach Wimp Sanderson and graduate assistant coach Bob Andrews regularly after that.

Andrews had been watching black high school teams for several weeks by the time he initially saw Harris at Hale County Training School. Bryant had told head coach Hayden Riley he wanted Alabama's first black athlete to be a basketball player. That would give his fan base at least a year to get used to the idea of having a black Alabama football player, while keeping, hopefully, integration proponents and the federal government off his back. Riley told Andrews to locate a quality black player and convince him to come to Alabama. An Illinois native who once scored forty-five points for Riley in an SEC game, Andrews attacked his assignment aggressively. Upon seeing Harris play, he concluded Harris was not only the best prospect available but also an outstanding prospect.

"Here was a young man who could do most everything on the court," Andrews said, "was not at all arrogant, and would represent the university very well."

Early black athletes had to be, first, a super athlete so the team would receive sufficient benefit and detractors could not say the scholarship was based on race. "There was a feeling that if we brought in an African American player, he would need to be a sensational player that was so good everybody would rally behind him," said Joe B. Hall, the Kentucky assistant coach in the 1960s charged with recruiting black basketball players. Black "firsts" also had to be excellent students and even better all-around people. Such credentials would supposedly help the athlete adjust to and be accepted by the dominant white culture. They had to be "the right kind" of black teenager. And "right kind" was written all over Henry Harris.

Harris was a 1960s All-American boy—president of the senior class, president of New Farmers of America, editor of the school newspaper, a Boy Scouts troop leader, and on track to be valedictorian. As an athlete, he was the prototypical country-school boy-wonder—quarterback, safety, and punter for the football team, third baseman on the baseball team, and averaging thirty-four points and seventeen rebounds a game in basketball. He excelled in whatever he did, and his easy-going nature made him a magnet. "You just enjoyed being around him," said his brother James. "Lots of laughter, lots of fun."

"You could have not asked for a nicer, more pleasant young man than Henry Harris," said Auburn's Bizilia. "He was a joy to be around. He had a smile on his face all the time. We never heard anything bad about him. Grades were good. And he was a gentleman."

Harris may have sounded like a rags-to-riches story in the making, but a year earlier neither Auburn nor Alabama would have feigned interest in this black teenager and his forgotten Black Belt family. But the game had changed, and the battle was now on. "Alabama got into a frenzy after Auburn got into it," Young said. And the longer the rivals recruited Harris, the more competitive they became. "You know how Alabama and Auburn are," Young recalled. "It was really a mess."

Auburn had gotten to Boligee first, and with Davalos's recruiting skill, Alabama was behind from the start. With no limits then on how many times a recruiter could visit a player, Davalos was in Boligee a couple of times a week, and Alabama looked for any advantage it could get. When Andrews learned Dianne Kirksey, one of Harris's girlfriends, was a freshman at Alabama, he asked her to help recruit him. She told him, "I would not recommend for any black to come here." Andrews was persistent, though, and tried to set up a Harris-Kirksey double-date with him and his girlfriend, but then his girlfriend refused to go out with a black couple.

Andrews also asked for help from a prominent Alabama fan in Greene County, who suggested a white man in Boligee named Boyd Aman might have influence with the Harris family. Aman told Andrews he was "not really into recruiting niggers" but "understood the necessity" of integration and knew Harris was "top quality." So Andrews scheduled a visit in the Harris home and asked Aman to stop by.

Andrews regretted his decision as soon as Aman sat down. "I don't really remember how long he was in their home, but he was talking down to them the whole time," Andrews said. "All I could do when he finally left was apologize over and over."

Chapter 5

We Are Not Afraid

*The only thing we did that was wrong,
Was stay in the wilderness too long.*
                        - Eyes on the Prize

The Boligee home that recruiters invaded in 1968 was a squat, concrete-block rectangle that hardly looked like a house, more like a store or even a juke joint. It had been both at one time or another. But it had been a home ever since the September day Willie Pearl Harris stood up to Boyd Aman.

James Harris, Henry's younger brother, saw it happen. His mother was standing on the front porch of their three-room frame house, the one with a hole in the kitchen floor. The bathroom was out back, but the rent was cheap, only $10 a year. The cost was high, however—all the cotton she and her sons could pick from the fields of white enveloping the house.

For decades, the black schools of the rural South did not start classes until sometime in October, so black children could work the fields of white land owners. By the mid-1960s, though, Greene County Training School was starting classes in early September although land owners' expectations had not changed. "You were not to go to school until that crop was in," James said. Willie Pearl had always allowed Henry, James, and Robert to work in the fields the first two weeks of school, but this year Aman wanted them to work more than two weeks. "Just stay out there and work. A month or month and half," Robert recalled.

A large man and a powerful man in the small-town segregated South, Aman was owner of a general store in Boligee. He leased the property where the Harrises lived and the fields surrounding it. "He had a lot of cotton," said Robert. "But my mom said, 'Nope.'"

Willie Pearl was a serious and bright student before she had to drop out of school when she became pregnant in the ninth grade. She was determined her children would finish high school and—in her dreams—go to college, and she would not let Aman control their education. "I recall, almost verbatim," James said, "her telling this man that her kids were not going to stay out of school to pick cotton, and if he wanted his cotton picked, he'd get out there and pick it himself or get his children to pick it."

"I guess you'll have to move," Aman told her, issuing the choice black Americans had faced for a century in the South: cross the man and leave the land, run off like medieval serfs. Little had changed.

When word of Willie Pearl's confrontation with Aman reached Johnny Snoddy, however, he said, "Well, I can fix that." Snoddy was a rare black land owner. He had farmed for a white family while working for the railroad and U.S. Steel in Fairfield, Alabama, saving enough money to buy forty acres. The Snoddys' home was a mid-century halfway house for anyone needing a hand. They were their brother's keeper.

A quarter-mile down Lower Gainesville Road from the Harrises' home, the Snoddys owned a vacant cinder-block building where they once operated a small store. Before that, the squat structure with a flat roof was a "juke joint" that came alive on weekends with "fish frys" and dancing to a Rockola.

Snoddy offered the building to Willie Pearl rent-free, and she accepted. "She didn't have no place to live," he explained. The building had only two rooms—a dance floor and a kitchen across the back. Henry and Robert helped Snoddy divide the front room into two bedrooms. Willie Pearl and her daughter, Glenda, took one side, and her four sons still living at home took the other. That's how it had been for years—Willie Pearl and her kids, on their own, surviving in the Black Belt.

Months after World War II ended, Willie Pearl Raymond moved to Boligee from Emelle, only twenty miles away in Sumter County, to start a new life for her and the baby she was carrying. She was fifteen. Henry would be her third child before age 20. She would then have two more sons and a daughter. The Harrises owned neither a car nor a telephone, and they had no indoor plumbing.

"We were an extremely poor family, but we were a close-knit family," James said. "It seemed like kids from the community were always at our home and my mother shared what we had to eat. We raised just about everything we ate. You name it, we grew it. There must have been many nights my mother cried, wondering how she was going to feed us, clothe us. Raising the number of kids she had with the income she had blows my mind."

Willie Pearl received a small monthly Social Security check for Henry as a result of his father's death and worked in the fields as well as the school lunchroom. She was a woman of great inner strength, refusing to go on welfare. She didn't even drink sodas, and she stopped smoking the day James told her he would start smoking if she didn't quit. But her greatest gift to her children was likely the mantra Henry and the others heard frequently:

"You are the descendants of kings and queens."

Despite living in a time and place structured to force black Americans to feel inferior, Willie Pearl understood her African legacy more than a decade before *Roots* was published. "You are just as good as anybody else," she'd tell her kids. "It doesn't matter what color your skin is; it's what you've got inside you."

"My mother wasn't a racist, but I always felt she believed black people were superior. She made us feel superior," James said. "Within my family there was never any desire to be white. We were proud to be black people."

The humiliating irony of Aman entering the Harris home on behalf of Alabama symbolized the hypocrisy of the college recruiting process. The world Harris had known for eighteen years was suddenly turned upside down.

"I resented these white folks coming in. It was patronizing. I resented it tremendously. I still get angry just thinking about it," said James, a precocious fourteen-year-old then. Most irritating to James were the boxes of steaks sent to their house—a staple gift of Roy Sewell, a west Georgia clothing manufacturer and Auburn's major athletic benefactor. "I felt we were being bought with steaks. It was just insulting," he said. "We were poor, we weren't ignorant."

For Willie Pearl, the ultimate insult was the offer of a new car from an Alabama booster. She told her son Robert, "We're staying in this hellhole and this man says, 'This car is yours if you let him go to Alabama.' What good would a car do if I don't even have a house?"

The recruiting process contradicted nearly every custom of Harris's heretofore circumscribed life. His postgame introduction to Bizilia was likely the first time he shook hands with a white man. And when Davalos entered the Harris home, that was another first—white folks didn't venture into "black folks' shacks," said James.

"Everything was separated," Robert said. "They had the land, they had the stores, and they had the money. We didn't associate with them. We were the consumers and workers. We worked in their fields, cleaned their houses, cooked for them, and raised their children."

The 1954 *Brown v. Board of Education* ruling and the Civil Rights Act a decade later had hardly dented Greene County. By the time Harris started school in 1956, the Alabama legislature already had passed a law allowing local school boards to close schools rather than integrate them. The law denied the state had a responsibility to provide public education at all, but voters still ratified it 104,000–68,000. Not until 1963 did black students integrate any Alabama public schools, and only twenty-one students did so.

In 1965, four black parents courageously sued the Greene County school system seeking a permanent injunction against denying their children entrance to white schools. When finally forced to issue freedom-of-choice enrollment forms, the county told black principals and teachers anyone encouraging integration would be fired. When black students tried to enter the white high school, state troopers turned them away, as Klansmen watched. The principal eventually enrolled a dozen black students, telling seventy-five others there wasn't "any more room."

Greene County Sheriff Bill Lee bragged to *Newsweek* that the day the Civil Rights Act was signed "I carried a bunch of colored folks into the only two eating places here in town [Eutaw] and sat down and ate with them. Yes sir. And I carried colored children at a rate of four a day, twenty-seven of 'em all count, in there to the picture show and sat down and watched picture shows with them." But when black children went to the county's segregated swimming pool, whites arrived with chain saws, bats, and shotguns. Lee told the blacks to get out of the pool and the whites to leave. The pool closed for good soon afterward. When Davalos recruited Harris, he learned to leave him in the car when he wanted to buy him dinner. "I would go in and buy a sack full of hamburgers and fries and milk shakes" and then take the food back to the Harris home. "I probably violated some NCAA rule by buying food for his brothers, sister, and mother," he said.

It would take the Voting Rights Act of 1965 to change Greene County and the Black Belt. Eliminating so-called literacy tests and expensive poll taxes, the new law finally gave African Americans a fighting chance. After the march from Selma to Montgomery in March, the Student Nonviolent Coordinating Committee sent two workers into Greene County and other volunteers into other Black Belt counties. By summer, the Southern Christian Leadership Conference would send volunteers into Greene and 111 southern counties.

SNCC and SCLC organizers found long-suffering black people waiting to be mobilized. Once organized, they marched day and night in Eutaw, amidst its antebellum and Victorian homes, many already on the National Register of Historic Places. The Ku Klux Klan burned crosses and paraded through black neighborhoods, but they didn't stop marching. Even Governor George Wallace couldn't stop the marchers, asking the U.S. District Court to stop the demonstrations. In his suit, Wallace charged Dr. King, SNCC leaders John Lewis and James Forman, and SCLC field director Hosea Williams with encouraging "Negro students to withdraw from the public school" to participate in mass street demonstrations.

The marches were often part of the economic boycott of white-owned businesses, organized by SCLC to create economic pressure on the power structure to meet demands. "They'd have mass meetings, getting people riled up and getting more and more people involved. Usually, they would target certain businesses to do things that we wanted to get done, like removing whites-only and blacks-only water fountains or entrances," said Robert Brown, one of Harris's teachers and a leading civil rights activist. "Most of the whites who operated stores were put out of business. No black would dare go into a store and shop. There would be other blacks on the outside watching, and they'd take their groceries or do something to their cars." African American families survived the year-long boycott by banding together for a purpose. They carpooled to Demopolis or Tuscaloosa to shop or sent one person to shop for several families.

SNCC eventually sent twenty-five staffers into Greene and four other Black Belt counties. Greene County pushed back by closing its voter registration office two days a week and requiring applicants to show proof of age, in an era when many blacks had been born in their homes and did not have birth certificates. By October, U.S. Attorney General Nicholas Katzenbach sent in voting examiners.

The Voting Rights Act scared even decent landlords to death. *Time* reported that when attendees at one church meeting were asked to move to the left if they had been evicted from their home for trying to register to vote, "it seemed like the whole church moved to the left." In Tishobee, a tent city arose of those banished from the land.

In early 1966, Lewis announced that SNCC was helping to create an African American political organization in Greene and Lowndes counties so black candidates could get on the ballot for the Democratic primary in May. Because of Alabama's high illiteracy rates, state law required any party appearing on the ballot to have a symbol by a candidate's name. Lewis said the symbol of the new National Democratic Party of Alabama would be the black panther, indigenous to the area. Eight months later, Bobby Seale and Huey Newton would adopt the Black Panther name for the militant, black self-defense organization they founded. One of its future leaders, Stokely Carmichael, had worked a year for SNCC in Lowndes County. "When I talk about black power," Carmichael told *Face the Nation* that spring, "I talk about black people in the counties where they out-number them [whites], to get together to organize themselves politically and to take over those counties from the white racists who now run it."

When voting day finally arrived May 3, 1966, Americans who had never been allowed to vote in their seventy-odd years dressed in white shirts and Sunday hats to cast their ballots. Whether in a dilapidated schoolhouse or black juke joint, America was finally fulfilling its promise to them. The most important race was for Greene County sheriff. "Everybody focused on getting rid of the sheriff. They called him Big Bill Lee," Brown said. Greene County's decades-old us-versus-them culture finally had a face and name—Thomas Gilmore v. Bill Lee.

Gilmore was a twenty-five-year-old Greene County Training School graduate who had tired of Alabama's meanness and moved to California for two years before returning with his family in 1965. Not long afterward, he accidentally hit a puddle pulling into a gas station and splashed muddy water on an Alabama state trooper's car. The trooper made him wash the car—Gilmore understood what could happen if he didn't. Understanding that segregation was not just a system of separation but a means for keeping blacks "in their place," Gilmore joined the movement.

But Lee vowed he would not lose to a "cotton patch nigger," believing the job was his birthright. His father and brother had alternated as Greene County sheriff for thirty-two years, and Lee had held the job for another dozen, taking over in 1954, the year before Lieutenant Gooden died in jail of a cerebral hemorrhage. Running Greene County was the family business. His brother Frank, who signed Thomas Edmonds' death certificate in 1951, was now the state prison commissioner.

Lee liked to brag he did not wear a uniform or carry a gun, ruling by size, personality, and the ponderous weight of history. He was a tackle for Curly Lambeau's NFL champion Green Bay Packers in the 1940s and wrestled professionally during the offseason. Cauliflower-eared and red-cheeked, he considered himself a moderate on race. "I don't think no more of walking into one of those nigger joints without a gun, and a hundred liquored-up niggers in there, than I would think of walking into a church. Because they know ol' Bill's gonna be fair with them," he told *Newsweek*. ". . . We never really had a problem here with our colored people. . . It's just the best place in the world for a colored person to live. . . . They know the law's not gonna bother 'em here."

With black voters out-numbering whites nearly two to one by 1966, Gilmore looked like a certain winner on election day, a day whites had been dreading for years. "It would be hard to exaggerate the harrowing implications . . . for the rural white southerner of a black running for sheriff of his county. The sheriff was kind of absolute totem image of all authority and order out in the southern countryside," wrote *Newsweek's* Frady. Dr. King understood whites' fears and arrived in Eutaw four days before the primary. Speaking to a crowd of 1,000 in a Eutaw church, he proclaimed simply: "We are not Bill Lee's children. We are no white man's children. We are God's children."

The day before the election, the U.S. Justice Department sent more than two hundred observers into Greene and six other Black Belt counties in Alabama to ensure registered blacks would be permitted to vote, making it the first election watched by federal observers since Reconstruction. Still, Greene County poll workers prevented observers from watching as they marked the ballots of illiterate blacks and asked one black woman if she wanted to vote for "Sheriff Lee or Bill Lee." Because of a failure to purge voting rolls, more white adults were registered to vote than lived in the county.

Yet, Gilmore led late into the night, until the absentee ballot box was hauled into the courthouse, which was a replica of the white stucco courthouse that mysteriously burned down with one boom in 1867, conveniently destroying federal indictments against local Klan leaders.

When the two hundred absentee votes were counted, only one was for Gilmore. Big Bill Lee was still sheriff. The white man had won again.

Chapter 6

A Boy and a Hoop

While others marched and voted, Henry Harris practiced jump shots, even as a little boy. Anyone driving down Lower Gainesville Road would see him there in the front yard of the little wooden shack. A boy and a hoop, framed against a white canvas of cotton. No backboard, just a bicycle rim nailed to a pear tree, on a court of overcooked Alabama earth, swept clean with a brush-broom. Summer or winter, day or dark, there he was, unless chores or his mother beckoned. "He always had a ball," said his brother James. "Every spare moment he was playing ball."

Greene County Training School was 150 yards away so it was easy to dream of playing there. He was in the gym by the time he was eight. His best friend, Gary Pettway, was the son of Patrick Pettway, the athletic director, and he'd open the school for summertime pickup games in the stifling gym and let the little fellows shoot until the big kids got there. By the time they had finished the seventh grade, Harris and Pettway were playing against the older boys. Harris made the varsity at fourteen. As a skinny 5-foot-11, 140-pound freshman, he averaged twenty points per game. As a sophomore, he scored forty points in a 78-77 victory over Tuscaloosa's powerful Druid High School, and his legend was on the make. By his junior season, he was averaging more than thirty points per game.

Harris's easy smile belied a steely competitiveness, sharp elbows, and dead-set seriousness about the game. Basketball was his life, his anchor, his bridge from the fields to the future. He practiced every chance he got. For a young man granted a scant chance in the Black Belt, basketball was rebellion. Each dribble on hard-baked dirt, each shot taken under stars, seemed to cry out, "I will not confine myself to your limitations. I am going to learn this American game and learn how to play it really well, better than even the white boys." Basketball, it turned out, was more than rebellion; basketball was black power.

Auburn was ready when Harris made his recruiting visit Wednesday, March 6, 1968, exactly a week before SEC schools could begin signing high school seniors to basketball scholarships. Auburn President Harry Philpott had forewarned the board of trustees during a luncheon at his home that Auburn expected to sign its first black athlete. "Oh, we can't do that. This state is not ready for that," said trustee Frank Samford Sr., a generous patron of education in Alabama and benefactor of Birmingham's Samford University. But other trustees spoke up quickly, arguing the integration of college athletics was inevitable. Redus Collier, a trustee from Decatur, Alabama, said he had taken another black high school star, Isaac "Bud" Stallworth of Hartselle, to dinner to help coaches recruit him. A surprised Samford replied, "All right. I won't say anything more. It probably is time."

Harris's visit to Auburn was timed for the season-ending Auburn-Tennessee game, the final basketball game at the Sports Arena, a small, antiquated gymnasium known lovingly as "The Barn." Beforehand, he attended a reception for donors and players' families and was treated with respect by white Alabamians for the first time in his eighteen years. He wore his Sunday shoes and flashed his magnetic smile. "He seemed genuinely humble, but awestruck, much like you would expect a black athlete would be at a white cocktail party," said Bill Perry, brother of Auburn star Tom Perry.

At the game, the only other black person Harris could see in the 2,500-seat arena was custodian Bennie Carter, who swept the floor before games and at halftime, usually to wild cheering by the crowd. The more he pranced, the more the crowd hollered.

Two days before Harris visited Auburn, Bear Bryant announced he had accepted the resignation of basketball coach Hayden Riley, who had closed out the 1968 season over the weekend by losing to Auburn for the twentieth time in their previous twenty-four games. Bryant said Alabama's new coach would be C. M. Newton of Transylvania College in Lexington, Kentucky, hardly a well-known name in the SEC. When Bryant had called Newton over the weekend to offer him the job, Newton asked if he could sign any player he wanted. Bryant told him there would be no restrictions on recruiting.

"Just get the youngsters who will go to class and help us win and project a good image for the university," Bryant replied. "But if you cheat, I'll fire you."

Newton knew if he were not allowed to sign blacks, he would be fired for sure because Alabama had a new 15,500-seat arena he'd be expected to fill. Only winning could do that, and he couldn't win without the state's best players. So after the press conference, when Alabama assistant coach Wimp Sanderson told him, "Look, we need to recruit Henry Harris," Newton got in Sanderson's car and said, "Let's go."

Newton was immediately impressed with Harris's "speed and quickness," but he also was impressed by Harris himself. "A quiet, respectful, nice young man, very bright," he thought. The impression stuck—"he was a great player and a great person in every way," he recalled forty years later.

Charles Martin Newton had played basketball for Adolph Rupp at Kentucky during the same era Bryant coached football there. He had worked as a graduate assistant coach at Alabama in the mid-sixties, so Bryant knew what he was getting. He also knew Newton had already integrated Transylvania despite Rupp telling him "he was ruining basketball in Kentucky." As a pitcher in the New York Yankees' farm system, Newton had learned black and white could win together. Nino Escelera, a black Puerto Rican who was hitting .374, was Newton's first black friend.

On the eve of signing day—Wednesday, March 14, 1968—Auburn coach Bill Lynn and graduate assistant Wes Bizilia moved into a motel in neighboring Sumter County. They wanted to get to Boligee quickly the next morning. But Bob Andrews, Alabama's graduate assistant coach, got there first. He woke up Harris and his family and told them he had the paperwork to sign for a scholarship to Alabama. Harris said he wasn't ready, that he'd sign later in the day.

When Lynn and Bizilia arrived at Greene County Training School, they took Harris into an empty classroom. Bizilia said Harris told them he wanted to go to Auburn, but when the coaches saw

Alabama's Sanderson drive into the parking lot, they took Harris out the window of the one-story building. "I guess this really wasn't legal," said Bizilia, "but we put Henry in the car and said, 'We'll go get a hamburger.'"

Harris told him, "Coach, there's no place in this county I can go and get anything to eat."

"Well, Henry, we'll find a place, and we'll get some hamburgers and French fries."

With Lynn's nephew driving the car, the three white men took off with Harris. "Wimp was running all over the place trying to find him and calling me," recalled Coach Young. "I said I don't know where he is.'"

"We kept riding around waiting until Henry signed that paper," Bizilia said, "because he told us he was coming to Auburn. But he wouldn't sign it until he got home and talked to mama. So we said, 'We'll go home.'"

Sanderson was already there.

"I want to talk to Henry," he said.

"Well, he's already signed, he's already signed the paper."

"I want to see it."

"Well, you're not going to see it, but he's already signed it."

Sanderson started talking directly to Harris.

"Henry, did you sign that thing?"

"Yes, I did," Harris replied.

Sanderson, who had watched George Wallace stand in the schoolhouse door from an upstairs window in Foster Auditorium, had worked hard to recruit Harris and believed he had convinced him to become Alabama's first black athlete. "I thought I had him and lost him," Sanderson said.

"Wimp just fussed and fumed," Bizilia remembered. "But he left [the house]. And then we went in and signed it. And Henry's mama said, 'I am so happy.' His mama wanted him to go to Auburn. She was very happy about it, and we felt good about that."

The *Atlanta Journal* understood the paradigm shift Harris represented. In an article stripped across the top of its March 14, 1968 sports section—"Auburn Signs Negro Athlete"—executive sports editor Jim Minter reported Auburn was "the first Deep South SEC school to make an athletic crossing of the color line." The signing of black athletes by Kentucky in 1965, Vanderbilt in 1966, and Tennessee in 1967 had been significant, but Harris was breaking a barrier in the old Cotton Belt that many thought might not budge for a long time. In addition to reporting Harris's senior averages of 34.5 points and seventeen rebounds per game, Minter wrote Harris had already passed the ACT and "is all set up to get into school." He quoted Lynn saying Harris was "the kind of ball player we must have. He's a real good long shooter, an excellent ball handler, has great speed and quickness, and can jump out of the gym. . . . He is one of the finest one-on-one players I have ever seen."

The following day, Benny Marshall, the well-respected sports editor of the *Birmingham News*, reported Harris could have gone to the University of Houston, ranked No. 1 in the country at the time, and had a 3.33 academic average. "He's just the kind of boy who's good at everything," principal A. W. Young told Marshall. "He's got a good temperament. He won't say much. He just gets at whatever he has to do, like his lessons."

Three days later, *Mobile Press* sports editor Dennis Smitherman reported more details on what he termed "a real stiff fight" between Auburn and Alabama "to see which would be the first to announce the signing of a Negro athlete." He wrote that Auburn coaches believed they had Harris ready to sign with them—until Wednesday, when Auburn "found they had a confused youngster on their hands." Whether he was wavering or not, they were not sure, but Alabama was applying the pressure," Smitherman wrote, adding that Alabama had badly wanted to be the first state school to sign a "Negro athlete."

All Harris's signature had done, however, was eliminate Alabama or any other SEC school. The SEC letter-of-intent had no bearing on Villanova or any other college outside the South. With national signing day still more than four weeks away, many more coaches were about to hear of Harris.

The last week of March, Harris and Coach Young flew to Pittsburgh for the prestigious Dapper Dan Classic, the era's only major high school all-star game. It pitted the Pennsylvania all-stars against a ten-member "national" team that Harris was chosen for on the strength of George Raveling's recommendation. "I was able to sell them on the idea that here was an extremely talented kid out of the South that nobody knew about that could make an immense impact on the game," Raveling said.

It would be a big week for Harris. He'd be playing, practicing, and living with whites for the first time in his life. Coach Young flew up with him. So did Davalos and Bizilia. Davalos knew he could not keep Raveling and other coaches from talking to Harris in Pittsburgh, but he wanted to be talking to him too. "There were a lot of people talking to Henry in Pittsburgh," said Bizilia.

Harris's big-name teammates were Chris Ford out of New Jersey, Detroit's Ralph Simpson, New York's Tom Riker, and Tom Parker from Illinois. Even the all-stars' practice was covered by the press. The *Pittsburgh Post-Gazette* reported Harris showed "some dazzling footwork" and made "a crackling, one-handed pass, fired on the dead run without breaking stride or dribble" that surprised some of his teammates. The game drew 13,266, the largest crowd to ever attend a sports event at Pittsburgh's Civic Arena. Harris came off the bench and scored two points, making only one of six shots. "Henry didn't stand out, but he belonged," Bizilia said. "They didn't have enough basketballs for those guys."

Iowa offered Harris a scholarship before he left Pittsburgh, and once he was back in Boligee, Young's phone wouldn't stop ringing. "They were calling every day," he said. But if Harris had any second thoughts about going to Auburn, he did not say so. "He was sick of recruiting anyway," Young said.

National signing day would come and go, and Harris would keep his word. He was going to Auburn.

A couple of days after Harris signed with Auburn, George Raveling spotted Davalos and Larry Chapman outside Louisville's Freedom Hall, where all three men were scouting players at Kentucky's Sweet Sixteen state tournament. "Why would Henry Harris want do go to a school like A-a-u-u-b-u-u-r-n?" bellowed Raveling in his best fake southern drawl. Like Sanderson, Raveling was disappointed, believing he had struck up a good relationship with Harris.

"Everybody was surprised we signed Henry," Chapman said. "If Henry hadn't wanted to sign with Auburn, his mama would have never said okay. That was a matter of relationship and trust. Back in those days, there wasn't much trust [by blacks of whites], and there's no reason there should have been. What we did was develop a relationship with Henry and his family."

"I think Henry felt extremely comfortable with me and Larry," Davalos said, "and I think his mother felt confident that her son would be fine with us. Henry had a very classy mom, a great mom. We established a good relationship." Davalos was at ease most anywhere—he had coached successfully in Australia for two years—and for the Harrises, his warmth belied a lifetime of contact with white people. "I felt I had a great relationship with Henry," said Davalos, estimating Auburn coaches saw Harris and his mother fifteen to twenty times. "You can't build relationships with players like that anymore in recruiting,"

The personable Raveling visited Boligee about five times and also struck a good relationship with Harris. "We aggressively recruited him and, for a long time, I thought for certain that he was going to go to Villanova, but down toward the end, Auburn was able to convince him he should stay closer to home," he said. "One disadvantage we had was distance. We couldn't see him as frequently as Auburn, and I think that probably helped Auburn a lot."

When Newton saw the closeness of Harris's single-parent family, he was confident he would not leave the state, that Villanova and Philadelphia would be a bridge too far. His brother James believed his mom wanted all her kids "close under hand," primarily because she had them at such a young age and rearing them had been a struggle.

"We [Auburn] were very lucky to get him, with the close proximity to Tuscaloosa," Bizilia admitted. "But Alabama didn't get on him until late, much after we did." Sanderson claimed Auburn was already "dug in." Davalos didn't disagree, saying, "C. M. Newton got down there and went after Henry. But we had him locked up by then."

Sanderson told a reporter in 2013 that Auburn took the Harrises "more groceries than the A&P has." And Andrews, the Tide coach who got Harris up on signing day, said he came home with Lynn and Bizilia in new clothes. "I felt like they [Auburn] bought him," he said.

Frank Morrow, a teacher who worked with the basketball team, said Harris told him a couple of years later that Auburn coaches had taken his mother "to Meridian, Mississippi, or somewhere. I don't know what they did down there." Eunice Outland, a neighbor of the Harrises also heard about the Meridian trip. When she asked why Harris was going to Auburn, his twelve-year-old sister, Glenda, replied, "The man was nice to us that came down from Auburn. He took us all shopping and bought us all some clothes." Forty years later, Glenda said she had no memory of a shopping trip to Meridian but admitted she had forgotten a lot of past events.

Although against NCAA rules and done in secret, paying star players was not uncommon at the time. The greatest dynasty in basketball history—UCLA, with nine NCAA titles between 1964 and 1975—would eventually be found to have violated NCAA rules by helping players financially through wealthy alumni and friends of the program.

If Auburn did "buy" Harris, it may have gotten him on the cheap. "We didn't have anything," said Glenda, "so to us anything would have been a lot." James said he does not remember any offers. "Knowing my mother, it would not have been anything she countenanced. That just wasn't my mother," he said. "I'm not saying those things didn't happen. I don't believe they happened or I am not aware of them happening. As tight as my mother was with a penny, I am pretty sure if any serious money had changed hands, our living situation would have been different." Older brother Robert also said he had no memory of inducements from Auburn that would have violated NCAA recruiting rules. "Maybe," he said, "someone at Auburn gave someone something to give to her."

Robert said his mom "wanted Henry to go where he wanted to go, and she depended on the coaches to guide her," but neither Young nor football coach Paul Pettway believed Auburn was the best place for Harris. "He didn't pay too much attention to what I said anyway," Young said.

James Harris recalled his mother primarily sought counsel from Young's father, principal A. W. Young, who lived next to the school. Willie Pearl had cleaned and cooked for the family for years. Because Young was retiring as principal that year and moving to Tuskegee to be closer to family, he felt he'd be able to see Harris play fifteen miles away. "My dad was swaying Henry that way," said Coach Young, who thought Tuscaloosa would be better for Harris emotionally. "People would have been up to see him or he could run home. Over at Auburn, you're jumping off in the middle of nowhere almost." But it was obvious to Coach Young that Willie Pearl did not want Henry at Alabama. "He was sort of dating Dianne Kirksey then, and she was already up there. For whatever reason, Henry's mother was saying, 'I don't want him up there with Dianne,' Why she thought that way, I don't know." Kirksey's father, Peter Kirksey, was a school principal and would eventually become county school superintendent.

Although Tuscaloosa was much closer to home than Auburn, its proximity was counterweighted by history. Alabama's image among blacks in the 1960s was not dissimilar to that of South Africa's national rugby team, Springbok, during apartheid. Because white South Africans reveled in Springbok's success, blacks rooted against the team that represented the oppressive power structure. And the longer Deep South colleges continued to field all-white teams, the more they represented the subjugation of segregation. So blacks pulled against State U. throughout the Deep South, but nowhere more than in Alabama, where Wallace had blocked the door and Bryant had once told his statewide television audience in the mid-1960s, as well as *Look* magazine, that he had no plans to recruit blacks. Young African Americans took Wallace and Bryant's stands personally, that they weren't good enough, not just as a student or athlete, but as a human being.

Alabama, not Auburn, represented the state's ruling class, particularly in Greene County where the most powerful and feared man was Sheriff Bill Lee, "Big Bill" Lee, one of the University of Alabama's best football players ever. As an All-American tackle, Lee lined up beside Bryant himself. As seniors, they helped lead Alabama to a perfect season, a Rose Bowl victory, and national championship. Lee was captain of the team.

Chapter 7

The Hope for Years to Come

We were ignorant. We were afraid.
- Rosie Carpenter'

A week after Harris signed with Auburn, Dr. Martin Luther King Jr. returned to Greene County during a two-day blitz to drum up support for his Poor People's Campaign in Washington that summer. It was Wednesday, March 21, 1968. King had started the week in Memphis, speaking at a rally supporting the city's striking sanitation workers, promising to return. On Tuesday, he spoke seven times in Mississippi, hurrying from one small town to the next. By the time his plane landed in Hattiesburg, it was after midnight, but 800 people were still waiting for him at a local church.

King reached Greene County late Wednesday afternoon. He gave the clapping, singing crowd at Eutaw's First Baptist Church details about the Poor People's Campaign. A mule train would leave Jackson, Mississippi, April 27 with shacks on flatbed trucks and pick up participants as it wound through the South. King wanted to demonstrate the living conditions of thousands of blacks in the Deep South by setting up the shacks on the Washington mall for marchers to live in. He intended for them to stay in Washington until something was done by the federal government. He told the packed church, "All ye who are tired of segregation and discrimination, come unto us. All ye who are overworked and underpaid, come unto us."

When the rally was over, King asked Thomas Gilmore, the would-be sheriff, to drive him and other SCLC leaders to stops in nearby Greensboro and Marion. With King and Ralph Abernathy in the front seat and Hosea Williams, Dorothy Cotton, and Bernard Lee squeezed into the back, Gilmore's 1963 two-tone green Chevrolet headed east into the dwindling daylight of Alabama Highway 14. Already behind schedule, Gilmore got stuck behind a tractor trailer on the curvy road. When he finally saw an opening, he passed the eighteen-wheeler. But as soon as another straightaway appeared, the truck driver pulled up alongside the Chevy, edged ahead of it, and veered into its lane, forcing Gilmore off the road and into a service station. He slammed to a stop a few feet from a gas tank. The truck pulled off too, and its angry young white driver began walking toward Gilmore's window. Hollering:

"Nigger, get those lights out of my rearview mirror."

Suddenly, a clear, powerful, and familiar voice boomed out the Chevrolet's window.

"Young man," King bellowed across the front seat, "get in your rig and go ahead now. You're starting trouble, and you don't need that." Recognizing King, the driver shut up and backed away.

As Gilmore pulled onto the highway, King talked of how troubled America was, how the sickness was almost palpable.

In Greene County, however, the early spring saw welcomed progress in an old murder case. In 1962, an all-white jury convicted Johnnie Coleman, a young black man, of murdering John "Screwdriver" Johnson, a white Eutaw man, sentencing him to death. The U.S. Supreme Court eventually ruled Coleman was denied a fair trial because Greene County's majority black population was not part of the jury pool. When Coleman was retried in 1968, the defense struck all white males on the jury roll and the prosecution struck all the white females, so an all-black jury heard the case. It delivered its verdict April 4—not guilty. "Everyone was jubilant and shouting," Gilmore recalled.

The celebration ended just after dusk when word came that King was dead, murdered in Memphis, gunned down while trying to help garbage collectors, assassinated by "a reactionary attitude that was afraid of change."

"You can't imagine the range of emotions we felt," Gilmore said.

When Harris walked across the road to go to school the next morning, students were standing around outside. They were hurt, confused. The loss of King was personal. He had cared enough about their future to come to Greene County, had walked among them. They had felt his leadership. He was their inspiration. They were heartbroken. And they were terribly uncertain. What would happen next? It seemed the white man had won again.

As the news had seeped out of Memphis and across America that Thursday evening, hurt turned to anger. Riots and protests erupted in 110 cities and lasted for days. Twenty-two thousand federal troops and thirty-four thousand national guardsmen were called up to maintain peace. Thirty-nine people died. America was on fire.

In May, as Harris was graduating as valedictorian of the Class of '68, the U.S. Civil Rights Commission held hearings into "Negro living conditions" in Greene County and fifteen other Black Belt counties in Alabama. Five days of impassioned testimony in Montgomery revealed that a "lack of adequate nutrition, clothing, and shelter" and "poor and segregated schooling" still existed in the Black Belt. "Young people are growing up without real hope," the commission concluded. A century after emancipation, Greene County and the Black Belt were still laboring under slavery's stain. The Civil War had settled only a few things, like the sovereignty of the union, but the issue of race was left to be reckoned with by the ages.

The Black Belt was a uniquely American creation, carved from the backs of enslaved Americans and prospering on their misery. Slavery had shackled the South with a costly labor system that did not spare enough capital for industrial development, so economic advancement meant more land and more slaves. After emancipation, blacks were slow to leave the land, as they had no other way to earn a living, and the agricultural economy stumbled onward. In a nearly cashless economy, wages were quickly discontinued and the standard contract for black Americans became a share of the crop. But by design, sharecroppers could rarely stay out of debt to the landowner's "farm store," the ball and chain of involuntary servitude that could reduce blacks to beasts of burden.

Slavery's most lasting and damaging scar, however, was the notion of white superiority, promulgated to rationalize slavery itself, and all interaction was structured so both blacks and whites behaved in a way to support that notion. By the time Alabama enacted laws in the late 1800s to enforce segregation, they were not needed in the Black Belt. Habit, poverty, and fear had already institutionalized separation.

The result was a society so odd few outsiders could comprehend it. From Reconstruction until World War II, few outsiders ventured into the rural South, further protecting its peculiarities, and the U.S. government ignored the region as some sort of outback. Black Americans were on their own for survival. They had nowhere to turn.

"It was just like slavery," said Rosie Carpenter, a local civil rights organizer in Greene County. "They paid sometimes fifty cents a day, from sunup to sundown."

"It would have been more than oppressive to be black in Greene County," said historian Leah Rawls Atkins, co-author of *Alabama: The History of a Deep South State*. "It was another world. They were isolated culturally and economically."

"We didn't own anything," said Harris's best friend, Gary Pettway. "Everybody worked for somebody white. They owned the county, and they could buy and sell you, and you knew the Klan was out there. They [whites] were over there, and you were over here. You knew where the line was, and you didn't cross that line. You hit them and you go to jail."

Harris's safety zone was Greene County Training School. It was always the biggest thing in Harris's vision field, the only thing he could see except for acres of cotton. School was a nurturing nest. "The teachers made you want what they had to offer. Everyone had good values, everyone wanted you to be something," Pettway said. Teachers doubled as guidance counselors, girding students emotionally for a Jim Crow adulthood and prepping them mentally for something more. They were community leaders and modeled sacrifice. One Greene County Training School teacher, William McKinley Branch, studied law at the University of Illinois and had job offers up North, but when he asked God what he should do, saw a vision of a hand pointing to Alabama and heard a voice saying, "Go back to Alabama." He eventually became a principal in Greene County but was fired when he helped organize the county's economic boycott. "That was the worst thing they [whites] could have done," said Coach Young. "That gave him time and even more motivation."

Robert Brown, who taught math, chemistry and physics, had earned four Purple Hearts as a turret gunner in the famed 761st Tank Battalion, an African American unit that fought in the Battle of the

Bulge, through the Rhineland, and into Austria. Yet, he could not register to vote until he found a white voter to "vouch" for him. It took him a year. The judge asked the white man to sign his name as Brown's supporter. "This man told the judge he couldn't write," Brown said. "The judge asked him if he could make an X. He licked the end of his pencil and made an X and threw the pencil down and said, 'Damn it, there it is.'"

Brown later earned a PhD from the University of California at Berkeley, but when he became a leader in the movement, he was exiled to a small, dilapidated junior high school in Tishobee. "They sent me there, I guess, as a form of punishment, hoping I would leave. But I didn't leave," he said. Brown came home from WWII confident and determined, before being banished to the back of America's bus again. He would continue the struggle, however, and inspire the next generation to finish it. That's why he taught children.

Education was more than a possible avenue to a better job, it was a right withheld by the South's ruling class as a way to control black Americans by leaving them often illiterate and thereby trapped in poverty. That's why education was so important to Willie Pearl Harris. "She made sure her kids studied. She had high expectations," said Eunice Outland. "And she took those kids to Sunday school."

The civil rights movement was birthed in the black church, blossomed in its nourishment, and Harris and his family were there every week, walking less than a mile down the road to St. Paul Baptist Church, organized in the 1890s by Americans born into slavery. "We were raised in the black Baptist church," said Harris's brother James. "You went to Sunday school every Sunday."

Whether in missionary zeal, to control their slaves, or to absolve their conscience, whites had unknowingly given black Americans the key to unlock their liberation—the Bible. African Americans found the Bible laced with emancipation messages, whether from the Old Testament—"I am the Lord. I will bring you out from under the burdens of the Egyptians"—or the New Testament—"He has sent me to proclaim that captives will be released, that the blind will see, that the oppressed will be set free and that the time of the Lord's favor has come." Ministers were vanguards of a movement biblical in its undertones, and blacks were safe in the House of God, out of reach of landowners. No one had to go into the fields on Sunday; it was a day of rest. Church members could cling together and summon the sustenance to walk into another week. Isolated on farms, they learned what was happening in town and how to look out for one another. "The church was kind of the cornerstone of our community—a lot of skills training," James said. "We participated in a lot of activities in the church that translated into paying off later on, little speeches you would do." The black church, black schools, and black parents had been preparing young people for integration seemingly forever, and now the kids were leading the revolution so long coming.

College students led the sit-in movement at lunch counters in 1960. They boarded busses for the Freedom Rides in 1961. "It was like a wave or wind that you didn't know where it was coming from or going to, but you knew you were supposed to be there," said Pauline Knight-Ofsu, one of the Nashville, Tennessee, students who refused to let the rides end following a bloody spring Sunday in Anniston and Birmingham, even when they were warned someone could be killed. "We signed our last will and testament," responded Dianne Nash, one of the leaders. "We know exactly what we are facing."

Then in 1963, children, not even teenagers, took center stage in Birmingham, marching with American flags before they were pelted by fire hoses and attacked by snarling dogs. Seven hundred children willingly went to jail that day. The South was their Egypt, and they did not scare easily. They had less to risk than their parents, who had jobs to keep and children to rear. Hurriedly trained in non-violence, they took to it quickly because they were so conditioned to never step out of line. Black children did not need to be told how to act. They just knew. Their survival depended on it. More than 2,000 were arrested during the May "Children's Crusade"—third-grader Audrey Faye Hendricks stayed locked up seven days.

Black adults who had lived in fear saw young people defying the system that imprisoned them for decades and rebuke the myth of black powerlessness. The power structure redoubled its resistance, but mass meetings chased fear, and black Americans who had never given up on the promise of America seized a new spirit.

"I appeal to all of you, to get into this great revolution that is sweeping this nation," said SNCC chairman John Lewis, the son of

Black Belt sharecroppers, in 1963. It would be a volunteer rebellion, driven from the bottom up. A black man or woman would stand up, saying, "I'm tired of this mess. I will not accept this anymore." Common folks, one by one, would exterminate Jim Crow—from courtrooms, restrooms, hotel rooms, even locker rooms.

Surrounded by its flashpoints—Tuscaloosa, Birmingham, Selma, and Philadelphia, Mississippi—Harris understood the story. His brother Robert had figured out the "key for getting out of Alabama" was to read, so he took the *Tuscaloosa News*. When he heard about the *Pittsburgh Courier*, the national black weekly, he got a mail subscription, and he and Henry read it "religiously."

As a high school freshman, Henry had seen Robert and at least a dozen other students stay outside school one morning "just upset and mad" and then get hauled off to the Greene County jail. "They put us all in a cell," said Robert. "The man said, 'We can kill y'all or do anything we want to with y'all.'" When SNCC volunteers held classes that summer, Robert went. "They tried to teach us how to protect ourselves and never to go anywhere alone. They said, 'They killed Viola Liuzo, and they'll try to kill you, so stick together,'" he said, referring to the mother of five shot dead that year by Klansmen as she drove black marchers back to Selma.

No one could live in Greene County from 1965 through 1968 and not be touched by the hope and determination of the brave young civil rights workers. "When you see something and you can make a difference," Robert said, "you should do what you can." In the winter of 1968—"the year that rocked the world"—Henry Harris got a chance to make a difference. It was his turn.

"Maybe there's something in the universe or the environment or in the spirit of history, and you have sort of allowed yourself to be used," said Lewis, the future congressman. "Sometimes you have to put yourself in harm's way."

It was the 1960s and it was America, where the president said, "We choose to go to the moon," not because it's easy but because it's "hard."

Boligee burst with overwhelming pride when Harris signed with Auburn. "It was jubilation," said Boligee teacher Severe Strode, "just a joyous feeling to know that he had been chosen to be the first one." The faculty and staff of Greene County Training School understood how important it was for an athlete to integrate Auburn or Alabama, to be judged good enough to wear the school's colors. "It reflected well on the community, on the school," said James Harris, and that would have been "a great influence on Henry," according to his good friend, Jerome Roberts, president of the Class of 1967. "We had tremendous respect for those teachers."

If history is mankind's best source of identity, then making history, if ever granted the chance, was imperative for most black Americans. "No one had ever had this opportunity before, so of course you take the opportunity," said C. B. (Chuck) Claiborne, Duke's first black basketball player. "It wasn't a hard decision at all because it was what I was expected to do."

"You have to go . . . ," said Bill Garrett in 1947 when given the chance to go to Indiana University and finally crash the Big Ten's basketball color barricade for good. "You're good enough to prove blacks are worthy. You have to go for all those who wanted to prove it, and could have proven it, but never got the opportunity."

Harris had an opportunity. It was an honor. People had been waiting for this chance for a long, long time. Hopes had gone unmet, dreams unrealized. Now, after so much waiting, the window was flung open. For Harris, it was hardly a choice at all. He was the chosen one. He had a gift so great that even white people took notice, a gift so great it could punch his ticket into mainstream America and even make reservations for others to follow. If you and your race have been told forever you're inferior, not good enough for the white man's school, the decision was obvious for any idealistic eighteen-year-old willing to be used for something greater than himself.

At a mass meeting during the Children's Crusade. Dr, King said, "There are those who write history, and those who make history."

The coaches offering Harris a college education were not the first recruiters to venture into the Black Belt promising a better life. A half-century earlier, fear and destitution made southern blacks easy prey for labor recruiters, who slipped into the South seeking factory workers to supplant soldiers leaving for World War I. Courted for the first time in their lives—with the offer of a train ticket and vision of a better life, one with electricity and running water—they were part of a generation unconditioned by slavery and less willing to accept the violent South of their parents. Because they knew how to work hard, they knew they could find jobs and then send for family to follow. They became American pioneers in the truest sense, departing in the silence of night with the moon as their witness, leaving it all behind—friends, relatives, bad times. They squeezed into overloaded jalopies, with a cardboard suitcase on the roof, a basket tied to the rear fender, and a dream on the other side of the windshield. They took one-way tickets to the promised land. Out of Alabama and bound for Ohio and Michigan. Or, up out of the Carolinas and on to Philadelphia or New York. Or, on the Illinois Central, escaping Mississippi's Delta for Chicago.

"Once the drift started, it just picked up momentum, and they flooded the highways and byways," said Brown, the teacher, tank gunner, and activist. "Get a loaf of bread and a stick of peppermint candy and grab that freight train."

Between 1915 and 1940, more than one million black Americans fled the South, forever reshaping the lives of their descendants and the sociology of a nation. They were chased out in part by two natural disasters—the Mississippi River flood of 1915, which left thousands homeless, and the boll weevil, which destroyed 90 percent of America's cotton crop, the staple of an already impoverished region. The hard times spawned a resurgence of the Ku Klux Klan and lengthened its evening shadow on southern shacks. Mothers worried whether sons would ever see adulthood. Would they one day speak their mind and vanish by the next dawn? If parents could not even protect themselves, how could they possibly protect their children? The KKK's American terrorism was so unchallenged that thirty thousand of its five million members were allowed to parade down Pennsylvania Avenue in Washington in 1925, not even bothering to wear hoods, just their robes and coney hats.

More than half the African Americans living in the South before the Great Migration, however, did not leave. Some didn't want to, others couldn't. Southern states worked frantically to halt the exodus of the cheap labor their economies ran on. State legislatures cooked up ways to ban recruiters and empowered police to act like the old slave patrols, scavenging train stations and arresting blacks for holding a ticket. Many blacks, however, didn't want to leave family in the South, and others were made to believe the farm was the only place they could survive, preferring the devil they knew to the one up North. "It's so cold up there, you'll freeze," landowners would tell them. "It's better here than it is up there." Other landowners would threaten to throw the entire family off the farm if one member left.

But staying was a defiant decision for many, a courageous choice to stand their ground. Without ever owning an acre, they knew intuitively the South was their land too, theirs by days of sweat and blood and long nights of tears. It was home and no one would run them off. They would stay and fight for their rights as Americans where their ancestors had toiled and died hoping that one day their children or grandchildren would become full American citizens.

Willie Pearl Harris—seeing her family as descendants of kings and queens—stood fast. Her younger brother, James, moved to Chicago and offered to help her family move there. But Willie Pearl did not want to abandon her mother. She would take her chances on raising her six children in Alabama. It was an American response to hardship—"hope in the face of difficulty, in the face of uncertainty, that dogged faith in the future that has pushed America forward even when the odds were great," as Barrack Obama would say four decades later.

Like others left behind by the Great Migration, Willie Pearl would make a way out of no way. So would her kids. And the old folks would be there pushing them onward, like the black farmers in overalls who crowded around static-filled radios in country stores on Saturday afternoons, listening for Jackie Robinson to come to bat, to swing at a white man's pitches. Like Robinson, Harris would represent what they could not attain.

For black Americans who had stood their ground in Greene County, who did not flee, Henry Harris was their hope, the hope of the left behind.

Chapter 8

Sport v. the South

*No man can keep another man in a ditch
without staying in the ditch with him.*
                        - Booker T. Washington

Henry Owens worked fifty acres of Tennessee Valley bottomland near Oakdale, Alabama, for Big Jim Cannon, a fox-hunting Irishman who had bought Owens' debt to the "farm store" owned by Albert Owens, a white man whose family had enslaved Owens' father before the Civil War. Battered and bowed by a sharecropper's life, Henry Owens once told his tenth child, James, "It don't do a colored man no good to get too high, because it's a helluva drop back to the bottom." But Owens's wife, Emma, was weary of watching her children nearly starve in north Alabama, so she sent Owens and their two oldest sons to Cleveland to find work. James watched his father pack and noticed how his hands were shaking. But Henry Owens made it to Cleveland and found a job, and James and the rest of the family followed. In Cleveland, James Owens found a track to run on, a scholarship to Ohio State, and a new name—Jesse. In 1936, he went to Berlin and ran the Germans off their feet, winning four Olympic gold medals and decimating Adolph Hitler's theory of Aryan supremacy.

On the eastern edge of Alabama's Black Belt, in Chambers County, Lillie Reese Barrow was a farming legend. Weighing more than two hundred pounds, she could plow a mule all day. Her husband, Munrow, suffered from epilepsy and would be committed to Searcy State Hospital, never to come home, so she managed the two-horse farm planted in thirty-five acres of cotton. After birthing her seventh child in 1914, she even tried sharecropping for a decade to support her family but never could make it work. She started dating Pat Brooks, who moved to Detroit and found a Ford factory job. Lillie Barrow and her kids followed. By then, Joe Louis Barrow was twelve and still walking to school barefooted. In Detroit, free from farm work, he started going to the gym. He dropped Barrow from his name so his mother wouldn't know he was boxing and became Joe Louis. He eventually became the "Brown Bomber" to America and Superman to his race.

Jerry Robinson was earning $12 a month working dawn to dusk as a field hand when he approached the owner of the Sasser plantation deep in the southwest corner of Georgia, asking to become a sharecropper so he could more adequately support his five children. The landowner reluctantly agreed, but the pressure was too much for Robinson, and in 1919 he fled with a neighbor's wife. That left Mallie Robinson with five mouths to feed and a vengeful landowner, who held her responsible for her husband's request. Evicted, Mallie Robinson packed her kids' sparse belongings and slipped out of Georgia late one night on Train 58, headed for the West Coast. The train took the Robinsons to California, where her brother lived in Pasadena. She found a job washing and ironing and raised her family on a little house on Pepper Street. That's where her youngest son, Jackie, learned to play ball so well that UCLA gave him an athletic scholarship, and then Branch Rickey and the Brooklyn Dodgers gave him a chance to change America, one embattled ballfield at a time.

Jesse Owens, Joe Louis, Jackie Robinson—the triumvirate of black sport in the 1930s and 1940s—would walk into American history only after walking out of the American South.

In the spring of 1954, Nat Peeples was to become the Jackie Robinson of the South—as an Atlanta Cracker. "Earl Mann told me my job would be harder than Jackie Robinson's, because he played up North and I would have to play in the South," Peeples said, referring to the Crackers' owner. Mann had decided to integrate the Class AA Southern Association. "I thought it was time they were given a chance. I didn't know of any earthly reason why a black man should not be allowed to play," he said.

In 1949, Mann had confronted segregation and the Ku Klux

Klan by scheduling three exhibition games against Robinson's Brooklyn Dodgers. Robinson's appearance at Ponce de Leon Park would mark the first time blacks and whites had competed in organized sport in Atlanta. The Klan's grand dragon threatened that Robinson would not set foot on the field, but Mann said that if he was in the lineup, he would play. And he did. The games went on without incident, and the Sunday game drew a record, standing-room crowd of 25,221, which included 13,885 African Americans, hungry for equal participation on any stage. Folks got along; everyone wanted to see the game. That was the power of sport.

Seeking to affect change everywhere, Brooklyn general manager Branch Rickey brought the Dodgers through southern cities annually for exhibition games—Macon, Mobile, Montgomery, Nashville. He saw racism as the South's physical and emotional bully, keeping blacks and whites alike from "stepping out of line." For that reason, he believed integrated competition in the South would come at a greater cost to its pioneers and take longer to accomplish than it did in the rest of America. He was right. Despite Robinson's 1947 debut, segregation still held firm in the 175 southern cities and towns in the South's twenty-four minor leagues for four more seasons.

It would be 1951 before the southern minors started integrating with two Class D leagues outside the Deep South. The next year, pitcher Dave Hoskins integrated the Class AA Texas League, ignoring death threats to draw huge crowds and win twenty-two games. When the Hot Springs Bathers signed brothers Jim and Leander Tugerson in 1953, the Cotton States League threw them out of the league before their first game. However, five players successfully integrated the Class A South Atlantic League in 1953 despite intense fan opposition, and nineteen-year-old Henry Aaron was one of them.

The Southern Association, however, was the South's premier minor league and included its largest cities—Birmingham, Mobile, New Orleans, Memphis, Nashville, Chattanooga, and Little Rock—so the signing of Peeples was big news. The twenty-seven-year-old former Negro Leagues outfielder hit six home runs in only forty-eight at-bats during spring training. In the season's first two games at Mobile, he did not hit the ball hard in any of his four at-bats and did not play when the Crackers returned to Atlanta to open their home season.

By the end of the season's first week, facing continued league pressure, Mann dispatched Peeples to Jacksonville, making him the first and last African American to play in the Southern Association. Choosing death over integration, the league folded in 1961 without a black base hit, as major league clubs began breaking off working agreements because their black prospects could not play in the league.

But by bringing integrated competition to the South, baseball's minor leagues created cracks in the wall of white supremacy. Courageous young players were breaking down a system that black Americans had been unable to touch and warned to stay away from. They were making an impression on a region, one fan at a time. Every time a black star stopped to sign an autograph for a white child, an opinion might change. Future Hall of Famer, Willie McCovey was a scared seventeen-year-old from Mobile when he reported to Sandersville in the Class D Georgia State League in 1955. By the end of the season, he was named the team's most popular player. Over four days in April that year, Montgomery hosted six major league teams featuring some of the best black players in baseball—Jackie Robinson, Hank Aaron, Willie Mays, Roy Campanella, Roberto Clemente—and the crowds that came to see them play were huge. Patterson Field became an experiment station for social evolution, and the "Cradle of the Confederacy" caught a glimpse of a new day. Eight months later, seamstress Rosa Parks went to jail rather than sit in the rear of a city bus, and a revolution began.

The turning point in the integration of southern college sports occurred in 1954 when the Supreme Court's *Brown v. Board of Education* outlawed the 1896 "separate but equal" doctrine of *Plessy v. Ferguson*. *Brown v Board* signaled an end to the U.S. government's largely hands-off policy toward the South's racial policies, unleashing a fear that spread like a contagion.

Segregation in graduate schools and professional schools was outlawed by federal courts during the postwar years, but one southern state after another had dodged integration by sending black graduate school applicants to northern schools, spending taxpayer money for out-of-state tuition rather than bending on tradition. But *Brown v.*

Board banned segregation not only in grades 1-12 but also in undergraduate college education.

Segregated schools were the result and instrument of white superiority—"You are not even good enough to sit in a classroom with us. We'll give you our hand-me-down books." So integration represented social equality and a crack in the underpinning of all Jim Crow laws and southern life itself. Viewed as the tool to force southerners to finally live and work together, *Brown v. Board* provoked the South's basest fears about "race-mixing," politicians' code for miscegenation. School integration was the South's Trojan horse, and walls were constructed quickly to keep it out.

Just as the South responded to emancipation with Black Codes, the KKK, and laws named for blackface actor Jim Crow, it retaliated to *Brown vs. Board* with "White Citizens Councils," copious local legislation, and the vilification of black Americans. Once seen as reliable and hard-working, black Americans became demonized, to be kept away from whites at all costs, even it meant closing public schools, as one Virginia county did.

More than one hundred southern senators and congressmen adopted the Southern Manifesto in opposition to *Brown vs. Board*, openly saying they would resist any form of integration in schools or other public places. The Supreme Court's directive to integrate with "all deliberate speed" was re-interpreted as "proceed when you're good and ready." A battle line was drawn over education, and college sport would become a casualty. Rather than advancing integration and racial harmony, as Robinson, Owens, and Louis would do, southern college athletics would become part of the South's resistance. When the Ole Miss basketball team was to play Iona in 1957 in Owensboro, Kentucky, its starters walked on the court for the opening tipoff only to walk off before the ball was tossed into the air, intentionally humiliating Stanley Hill, Iona's lone black player, on orders from Mississippi governor James P. Coleman. The forfeit never entered the Ole Miss record books, as if it never happened.

The SEC's all-white teams would evolve into statewide symbols of racial purity, a reminder of contemporary defiance, and instruments of the South's "Lost Cause" mythology when the Civil War's celebrated centennial collided with the civil rights movement in the early 1960s. As the South was dragged through the national news nightly, its football teams became the most visible symbols of its pride and valor, and its racism.

No school owned a deeper legacy of mixing southern culture and sport than Ole Miss—the plantation name for the "old master's" wife. A massive Confederate battle flag became part of its football halftime show after the 1948 Dixiecrat political revolt against the national Democratic Party. In 1959, with integration closing in, Ole Miss cheerleaders began passing out small Confederate flags at games. By then, though, Rebel flags and *Dixie* were part of the fanfare at colleges throughout the South.

In a region that had struggled educationally for so long, state universities carried the pride and aspirations of the South. They were beloved castles of white privilege, where traditions and power were handed down from generation to generation. If professional baseball was America's pastime, made for the masses, college football was the country club of southern sport. Men still wore coats and ties to games in the 1960s, perhaps with a flask in their coat pocket. College sport was the South's pride and great joy, and the Lost Cause blended in seamlessly. It was still a poor province in the world's richest economy. It had lost a war in a nation with great military success. And it practiced inequality in a democratic society. But on autumn Saturdays, its football teams and their fans believed they could take on anyone. When the home team took the field, its band blaring "Dixie," fans could swear they were back at Gettysburg for Pickett's charge.

Such a panorama, however, left scant space for black Americans, whom the war had been about in the first place. Anyway, blacks already had longtime roles on southern teams. They were water boys and mascots.

A black man, Clegg Starks, was the longtime water boy for the University of Georgia's football team. Dressed in shiny black pants and a red jacket, he would lead the team onto the field as a sort of a mascot-like figure. (Tulane dressed its black mascot-water boy in green and white.) When Starks died, Squab Jones took over as water boy. Like Starks, he had worked for the Georgia football program since he was a young boy.

The "trainer" for Robert Neyland's overpowering Tennessee

football teams from 1926-1940 was J. M. Forgey, an African American mute known to fans as "Dummy" Forgey. When he died in 1941 after being hit by a truck while crossing a street in downtown Knoxville on a Saturday night, the *Knoxville News-Sentinel* reported the accident under the headline "'Dummy' Forgey, Veteran U-T Trainer, Hit By Truck." Because of his disability, Forgey was seen as a benign black man at a time when black manhood was feared, not unlike "Blind Jim" Ivey, the longtime unofficial "Dean of Freshmen" at Ole Miss. An ordained Baptist minister, Ivey was accidentally blinded as a young man when he got paint or creosote in his eyes while painting a bridge over the Tallahatchee River. He took to singing for pennies and eventually sold peanuts and candy at Ole Miss, becoming a beloved fixture at Ole Miss athletic events, home and away, until his death in 1955. "He showed the students and faculty how a Negro can live as a Negro without resentment . . . ," wrote the *Jackson Clarion-Ledger* at his death. By then, Ivey was not hanging around campus as often, telling one student friend that other students had started saying mean things to him. By then, *Brown v. Board* was on the books and a siege mentality was settling in.

Southern universities could have helped resolve a major issue confronting their populace. That's what universities do, solve problems with the best minds and resources available, but most were state schools and their administrators, faculty, and funding lived in fear of segregationist state legislatures. Not one of the seventeen southern states practicing segregation integrated higher education until forced to do so, by litigation within their states or by the Supreme Court. The greatest confrontations occurred at SEC schools in the Deep South, and athletic events or arenas were at the center of the drama.

Charlayne Hunter and Hamilton Holmes were admitted to Georgia under court order in January 1961. Within a week, following an overtime basketball loss to Georgia Tech, Lumpkin Street in front of Hunter's dormitory became the scene of a riot orchestrated by state legislators, students, and the Ku Klux Klan. For two hours, a "mean, angry, loud, very emotional, and out of control" crowd of 2,000 threw bricks and bottles at the windows of Myers Hall, set fires in adjacent woods, and fought with police before being dispersed by fire hoses and tear gas. The next day Georgia suspended Hunter and Holmes "for their own protection." They were eventually reinstated by a federal court.

In 1962, during halftime of the Mississippi-Kentucky football game in Jackson, Ross Barnett, Mississippi's grandstanding governor, jumped in front of a microphone and conflated sports and racial politics to a degree unmatched by southern demagogues before or after. It was two days before the mandated enrollment of James Meredith as Ole Miss's first black student, and Barnett was not thinking about football, urging the crowd and the state not to give up, to resist, and never to change. "I love Mississippi," he cried. ". . . I love our way of life." The next night, inspired by their governor's defiance, Ole Miss students, Klansmen, and anyone else flooding into Oxford looking for a fight attacked federal marshals in what was called "the last battle of Civil War." The insurrection continued into the next day and night before being put down by 30,000 federal troops. Two people were killed and thirty-five federal marshals were shot, but Meredith, an Air Force veteran, became an Ole Miss student.

Nine months later, June 11, 1963, Governor George Wallace made his stand in the door at Alabama's basketball arena, Foster Auditorium, the site of registration for summer classes. He was keeping an inaugural promise made earlier that year when he pledged, "Segregation today, segregation tomorrow, segregation forever," calling forth the KKK motto of "Here today, here tomorrow, here forever." Wallace was playing university registrar to block the enrollment of Vivian Malone and James Hood, but he stepped out of the way when confronted by federalized Alabama National Guardsmen. However, the integration of southern colleges had finally forced President Kennedy's full attention on human rights in the South. Hours after federal marshals escorted Malone and Hood to their dormitories, Kennedy addressed the nation via television, announcing major civil rights legislation would be submitted to the Congress to guarantee equal access to public facilities, end segregation in education, and provide federal protection for the right to vote.

Wallace's play in the schoolhouse door would be dubbed Dixie's last stand, but it was hardly that. The next night a member of the White Citizens' Council would assassinate Medgar Evers, the

NAACP's Mississippi field secretary, who participated in the D-Day invasion of Normandy and applied unsuccessfully to the Ole Miss law school in 1954.

The Civil Rights Act was two months old the Saturday night Archie Wade, Joffre Whisenton, and Nathaniel Howard, three black men, went to Denny Stadium to see Georgia and Alabama open the 1964 football season. Whisenton, a professor at historically black Stillman College in Tuscaloosa, was a Ph.D student at Alabama, and in an effort to integrate the stadium, Alabama president Frank Rose gave him three tickets. Whisenton asked Howard and Wade, an assistant professor at Stillman, to go with him.

Their seats were on the first row behind the band. "We could hear people calling us names throughout the first half," Wade said, "but what got pretty bad was when the band took the field for halftime. We were sort of sitting ducks." Wade and the other two men were suddenly much more visible to the fans around them. "They could see us and they could throw things because they wouldn't hit anyone else, because the band was on the field. They threw cups with ice and bottles and, I guess, anything they could get their hands on."

Howard got up and found a security guard. "Howard asked him if he could provide us with some kind of protection or find us another location to sit," Wade said, "because it was too dangerous for us just to keep sitting there." The guard told him no.

"I think I will just leave," Wade told the others, "because I'm not going to sit here and be subjected to this. I'll read about the game." Howard and Whisenton decided to leave too. "We all got up—they were still throwing things," Wade recalled. "We just went home."

The desegregation of southern colleges would be conceded grudgingly. Racism would not only block black Americans from enrollment but also limit their college life once admitted. Integration would have to occur in program after program on campus after campus, with every school having its own timeline, its own resistance, its own forgotten pioneers. But nowhere would black exclusion persist more publicly than in athletics.

College athletics could have driven change within the university and throughout southern society much earlier than it did, but most coaches were hardly wild about the idea themselves. In 1963, Kentucky's campus newspaper, *The Kernel*, polled SEC members about integration. No athletic directors or coaches would say they would not play against an integrated SEC team, yet only Kentucky said it was ready for black athletes on its teams. Coaches, who preached leadership and loved players who jumped in the front of the line to start a new drill, were back-of-the-line guys on integration. Uncertain of their footing, they were like southern politicians, worried about their constituency.

The SEC did take action in 1963, however, that would slow integration, although the move slipped in under other pretenses. In an effort to raise "academic standards"—in the same year Tulane and Georgia Tech announced they were dropping out of the league because of other members' low academic standards—the SEC began requiring its athletes to have 750 on the SAT or a 17 on the ACT. Intentional or not, the new rule would hand coaches more stalling time by complaining they could not find any black athletes who could qualify academically, while never mentioning the South's separate-and-unequal school systems or the emerging studies finding the SAT was racially biased. The Atlantic Coast Conference—also staring down the barrel of integration—had made a similar move in 1961 and then upped the SAT score to 800 in 1965.

If the SEC had any conversations about integration, they were private. It was the elephant in the room and never discussed formally at SEC meetings in the mid-1960s. The league itself had little control over its members as it was run by college presidents who were skittish about jeopardizing state funding by stirring up state politicians. Only Kentucky presidents Frank Dickey and John Oswald pushed publicly for integration.

If a Southern Manifesto-type, go-slow pact existed among SEC coaches, it would not have been the first time a gentleman's agreement kept a league white. Baseball got rid of blacks in 1891 when no one spoke up otherwise, and then integrated in 1947 only because Brooklyn's Branch Rickey spoke up. A gentleman's agreement in the Big Ten Conference barred blacks from basketball for decades, even after they were accepted on league football teams.

Racial progress was slow in sports even when black athletes proved their ability convincingly. Starting with Robinson, black players were selected the National League's Rookie of the Year nine times in thirteen seasons and were voted the league's Most Valuable Player seven straight seasons starting in 1953. Yet, only half of all major league teams were integrated the season before *Brown v. Board*—seven years after Robinson broke the color line.

By the mid-1960s, though, things were even changing in the Deep South. An exhibition pro football game was moved in 1963 from Mobile when local officials and Governor Wallace refused to budge on Ladd Stadium's segregated seating. The Oakland Raiders paid the cancellation fees and the New York Jets' travel expenses to Oakland. Only a year later, minor league baseball returned to Birmingham, with blacks now on the team and the chicken wire used to segregate Rickwood Field's seating ripped away. But every night that season when the lights went out at Rickwood, Bert Campaneris, a cautioned Cuban shortstop, would *run* the two blocks to his apartment. Two years later, 1966, the Milwaukee Braves moved to Atlanta with Hank Aaron and a bevy of other black stars. Black and white fans from all over the Southeast would come see the Braves play, drawing full houses on Sunday afternoons and creating the South's most integrated hours. Pro sports brought the outside world into the South, and those Sundays in the summer of 1966 helped begin the birthing of an Olympic city, as thirty years later, the 1996 Summer Games would come to, of all places, the American South.

The Atlanta Falcons, Miami Dolphins, and New Orleans Saints would begin play with fully integrated rosters in 1966 and 1967, and change was even occurring in neighboring conferences. Maryland integrated Atlantic Coast Conference varsity football in 1963 and then basketball in 1965-66. Even high schools would host integrated competition before the SEC.

The dominant professionals of the 1960s—Jim Brown in football, Bill Russell in basketball, Aaron and Willie Mays in baseball—were all southern-born African Americans. But the surplus of untapped talent could not sway even the competitive coaches of the SEC. Twenty future members of the Pro Football Hall of Fame played at historically black colleges in the South before the SEC was fully integrated. In 1968 alone, Harris's senior year in high school, the NFL drafted eleven players from Jackson State.

The SEC was the South's final citadel of segregation. Busses, theaters, restaurants, even swimming pools would integrate before the SEC. And when it did integrate, teenagers—like the young soldiers being packed off to Vietnam—would be the ones charged with clearing the quagmire left by generations.

In 1955, the University of Texas admitted five black male students in a proactive response to *Brown v. Board*, but when one mentioned wanting to play football, Texas threw all five out school. In 1961, when Holmes, Georgia's first black male student, said he was interested in playing football, administrators quickly dissuaded him for fear that opponents, or his own teammates, would try to harm him.

Unlike at Texas and Georgia, though, no one tried to stop Darrell Brown from going out for football in 1965 as a freshman at the University of Arkansas, then a member of the Southwest Conference, although the dozen other black students at Arkansas did tell him he was crazy. Brown had never played football because Sevier County Training School didn't have a field or team. But Brown was an outstanding athlete, weighed 190 pounds, and had listened to Martin Luther King Jr. on an old Philco radio growing up in Horatio, Arkansas, becoming so inspired that he felt he had a personal relationship with King, who stressed "doing your part." Brown believed his part was integrating southern college sports.

The Arkansas equipment manager issued Brown a uniform, and no one really asked any questions. Then practice started. At some point, Brown was given the opportunity to return a kickoff. He was so excited he didn't even notice he had no blockers. It was eleven-on-one football. But Brown got back up and said nothing. The drill was repeated often. And there was a post-practice wrestling match against a player who weighed sixty pounds more than Brown and spontaneous chants from teammates of "get the nigger" when he ran the ball.

Throughout his season on the freshman team, Brown did not complain. "I never had a playbook, was never taught a play. I was placed on the field without knowing any part of the system," he said. Brown said no one ever spoke to him that season, certainly not varsity coach Frank Broyles, on his way to a hall of fame career. His silence condoned his players' chants. "It all came down from the power that Broyles possessed," Brown said. "I remember him being up in the stands when I was running back kicks against eleven of them, and he'd shout out, 'Why is it that you can't catch that nigger?'

Chapter 9

Send Me

*And I heard of the voice of the Lord saying,
"Whom shall I send and who will go for us?"
Then I said, "Here am I. Send me."*
— Isaiah 6:8

When the Boston Braves sent a frightened eighteen-year-old from Alabama, Henry Aaron, to Eau Claire, Wisconsin, in 1952 to play his first season of minor league baseball, they made sure he had a couple of black teammates. They understood the road would be hard and he would need companions.

Henry Harris, however, would integrate Auburn athletics alone. Two other African American teenagers passed on the opportunity Harris seized.

One was Joby Wright, a seventeen-year-old from Savannah, Georgia, who was a second-team Parade Magazine All-American as only a junior. Six-foot-seven and already 220 pounds, Wright had thighs nearly the size of the waist of some high school opponents. After repeated visits to his home in Savannah, during the summer of 1967, Auburn coaches Rudy Davalos and Larry Chapman invited Wright and his family to the Kentucky-Auburn football game in October. "They loaded it up to say, 'We want you here.' They went full-barrel after me," said Wright, who met with the university president, was interviewed by a sports writer for the campus newspaper, and went to a party at Phi Gamma Delta, a white fraternity. "Everybody at the party knew who I was. I said, 'Now wait a minute, they had to prep them on this.' It was very impressive because I grew up in the segregated South and went to an all-black high school."

The only incident that gave Wright pause was the football game.

"There were state troopers stationed north, south, east, and west of me," he said. Blacks were still an oddity in the stands of Cliff Hare Stadium in 1967, black fans being previously sequestered in rickety end-zone bleachers they called "the hole." (At Georgia, the segregated seating at the top of Sanford Stadium was called "nigger roost." At Clemson, "nigger hill" overlooked the stadium.) "What you were taken aback by," recalled Wright, "was all these people from the university coming at you in the direct opposite manner than George Wallace saying, 'No, we ain't going to integrate.' Everywhere we went, people had open arms," Wright said. "My daddy couldn't believe the effort they put in trying to convince me to come there, to convince him they would take care of me. He felt, 'These people really want you here, and these are some good people.' It was a great trip and I would've seriously considered it if I had stayed in the South."

Since Wright was thirteen, he had spent every summer in Harlem and Washington, D.C., staying with his dad's brothers and learning to play basketball on playgrounds and at the Lenox YMCA in Harlem. In Washington, he played on the playgrounds against Notre Dame's Austin Carr, who would finish his career in 1971 with the highest scoring average ever in the NCAA tournament. Carr and a couple of his teammates discouraged Wright from being the first black player at a southern school. "We had a conversation about not wanting to be the first, being concerned about safety," recalled Wright.

Wright had plenty of options anyway. Villanova recruited him hard for Villanova, as did Kentucky—Coach Adolph Rupp told him his hands were as big as "meathooks." Wright's top choice, however, was North Carolina, where he would be the second black player. "No one recruited me harder than Dean Smith," Wright said. But when Wright failed to make the Atlantic Coast Conference minimum 800 on the SAT, Smith wanted him to spend a year in prep school first, so Wright turned to the Big Ten, where his father had dreamed of playing football. "When I was a little boy, my daddy made me recite all the teams in the Big Ten, and he was so proud I could do that," said Wright, who had his pick of Big Ten schools. He chose Indiana, which also gave Wright's teammate Ed Daniels a scholarship. "We would have taken two of their players to get Joby too," said Joe B. Hall, the Kentucky assistant who recruited Wright.

The other black player Auburn recruited—Bud Stallworth, valedictorian of Morgan County Training School in northwest Alabama and the first trumpet in the school band—decided to go the University of Kansas. The previous summer, the 6-foot-5 guard had attended the Midwestern Music and Arts Camp at Kansas, where his sister Harriet was already a student. Kansas basketball star JoJo White spotted Stallworth playing pickup games during the camp and soon had him playing games with Kansas's varsity players. Back in Hartselle, Alabama—fifteen miles from where Jesse Owens grew up—Stallworth averaged 35.3 points and 23 rebounds a game as a senior.

On his recruiting visit to Auburn, Stallworth and his parents, both educators, attended a game at the Sports Arena unescorted by state troopers. When the Stallworths visited Alabama, however, and attended a game in which LSU's Pete Maravich scored fifty-nine points, troopers were all around them. "If they had to have state troopers for a recruiting visit," Stallworth said. "I can't imagine what it would've been like to try to travel and play in that conference."

Stallworth met with several university administrators in Tuscaloosa. "They knew about my academic background," Stallworth said. "But I didn't meet anyone on the basketball team, and to me, that was a little strange. So the visit was me meeting with leadership people and with Bear Bryant. It was a short visit with Coach Bryant, but what he said was that I should come to school there. What I said to him was, 'I don't play football.'"

Stallworth considered his decision to go to Kansas a "no brainer." "I just didn't think it [staying in the South] was a good fit for me, to have to worry about academics, sports, and, then, where you would end up if you wanted to go get something to eat at night or if you were hanging out with some friends at night. I had enough coaching from my parents, especially my dad, about safety, where you wanted to go and didn't want to go. For me, it was whether I wanted to have to worry about being physically or mentally harassed, or did I want to go to college and enjoy my college career?"

Although it took a lawsuit to get them in the game, Harris and Stallworth were voted the "outstanding players" of Alabama's two annual basketball all-star games on August 8, 1968. Many state high schools had integrated in some fashion by 1968, but two state basketball tournaments were still in play, one operated by the black Alabama Interscholastic Athletic Association and the other by the Alabama High School Association. A lawsuit by the AIAA seeking fully integrated competition had prompted a federal court to order the two organizations to merge by July 1, 1968, meaning the AHSA's annual all-star basketball and football games at the University of Alabama would be the dawn of a new day in high school athletics. One black player was placed on each all-star team.

One of them was Travis Grant from Clayton, the home of George Wallace. At seven, he had cut the bottom out of five-gallon can, nailed it to the front of his block house on Peanut Lane, and shot at it year-round with any ball he could find—rubber balls, tennis balls, dime-store bouncy balls. Folks eventually told his mom her son should be working, but she let him keep shooting. A domestic, his mom worked as a domestic for whites who threatened to fire her if her children joined the local civil rights movement. Despite the warnings, Grant marched once in a demonstration. He could see the hatred in eyes of the white bystanders. "They're angry," he thought, so when integration finally arrived and he was recruited by a white high school before his senior season, he stayed instead at Barbour County Training School. He averaged forty-two points per game as a 6-foot-6 senior, but the only white schools to recruit him were small. He signed instead with historically black Kentucky State.

Sam McCamey, the fourth black all-star, was one of the initial black students to attend the white high school in Scottsboro, site of the notorious 1931 "Scottsboro Boys" case—its convictions overturned twice by the U.S. Supreme Court before the nine black men accused of allegedly raping two white women were freed. McCamey, his mother, and younger brother chopped and picked cotton, moving nearly every six months to another sharecropper shack. At Scottsboro High School, he fell under the care of a coach who told him, "Don't worry about what they call you. Just play basketball," and an English teacher who tutored him three nights a week and kept reminding him, "Anyone can accomplish anything if they want it bad enough." "I wanted it bad. Nothing could be harder than picking and hoeing," said McCamey, who earned a scholarship to Middle Tennessee State.

But Harris was the player reporters wanted to talk to; he was the athlete who would integrate major college sports in Alabama. "He was the talk of the all-star games, and he was very good," Grant said. "He was kind of low-key and modest, not a big talker." Harris told the *Birmingham Post-Herald* he did not anticipate any issues at Auburn. "I can't see where I'll have any more problems than the minor ones I had in high school," he said after a practice. He maintained that the decision to go to Auburn was his own, although admitting, "My mother was real pleased I signed with them because it was so close to home." He said what "convinced me was the atmosphere at Auburn," echoing Wright's experiences at Auburn. "Coach Lynn along with other coaches and the players were pleasant people to talk with, and they made you feel like you were wanted."

Harris made good on his press clippings in the game, running the South's offense, scoring on both drives and jump shots and finishing with twenty points and seven rebounds. "He was very tough, very physical, a heck of a player," said McCamey.

With one Alabama sports barrier broken, Harris went home to Boligee and began the five-week wait for the next barrier on the horizon. In 1968, however, every step forward was often countered by one step backward. America's summer seemed to be one long inner-city riot, the product of racial oppression and economic deprivation, according to a study by the Kerner Commission. At times, the rage enveloping America reached all the way into the homes of teenage athletes preparing to integrate a southern university. Upon signing Harris, Auburn coaches and even university president Harry Philpott received letters of protest, one to Philpott saying, "The desire to win a ball game at any price is a terrible thing." It was "typical stupid, bigoted stuff," recalled Davalos.

In the summer of '68, Florida hurriedly signed Ron Coleman to a track scholarship after the U.S. Education Office reported the school was not in compliance with the Civil Rights Act, but not everyone was happy about Coleman becoming Florida's first scholarship athlete. Although track was a minor sport, the reaction was virulent, with one concise letter reading:

Dear Nigger,
    Prepare to die. You will never make it to Gainesville.

Two other members of the Class of '68—Ernest Cook of Daytona Beach, Florida, and Calvin Patterson of Miami—received racist, threatening mail when they signed scholarships to become the first black football players at independent Florida State. It seemed to Cook to be an organized hate mail campaign. "They were the meanest—with the n-word, with expletives, signed by supporters of FSU," said Patterson's childhood friend, Javan Ferguson. Cook decided to go to Minnesota.

In late August, Harris received a letter from Auburn coach Bill Lynn telling him what to bring to campus

1. Socks – 6 to 10 pair
2. Undershirts and shorts – 6 or 8 sets
3. 2 pair pajamas
4. 1 dress suit
5. 1 sport coat
6. 1 raincoat
7. 2 pair shoes
8. Pants for school
9. Shirts for school
10. 2 dress shirts
11. Shaving supplies
12. Toothbrush and toothpaste
13. Handkerchiefs
14. Jacket and sweaters (2)
15. 2 or 3 ties
16. 1 umbrella
17. Towels and wash cloths
18. 1 pair bedroom shoes

Lynn's specificity was atypical of letters he sent to incoming freshmen, perhaps itemizing items because of Harris's socioeconomic background. Yet, he offered no ideas on how the Harrises could afford so much clothing. He continued the letter by saying:

> I believe the above list is all the necessities you will need. However you might buy any other clothes or a radio, etc., if you should want to. As far as sheets, pillow cases, blankets, and a pillow, etc., I will take care of this for you. Let me know as soon as you get in town, and I will come to the dormitory and help you get situated. . . .
> I require all boys to dress neat at all times, short hair and clean shaven at all times. Keep your room neat and make bed daily. Be on time for all classes and practice sessions, live a happy but clean life. Basketball players are recognized as one of the best groups of the people on campus.

As Harris prepared to leave for college, Willie Pearl and his three younger siblings prepared to leave Boligee too. They were moving to Bessemer, a Birmingham suburb, to live with Willie Pearl's older sister, Mary Alice Sipp, a widow who owned her own house. Willie Pearl had wanted to leave Greene County after her mother died eighteen months earlier, but Henry wanted to finish high school in Boligee. The timing of the move—after Harris signed with Auburn—created suspicion that Auburn had found her a job in Bessemer or given her enough money to buy a house. After the move, however, Willie Pearl worked at a grill in Bessemer and then in a school cafeteria, just as she had in Boligee. Her sister was a domestic who had to make timely bus transfers daily to reach the houses she cleaned in affluent Mountain Brook on the other side of Birmingham. Neither woman owned a car.

The move provided an escape from Black Belt oppression, a better opportunity for her children, and a chance at financial improvement. "The thinking of my aunt was that the two of them working together could affect that type of change," said Henry's brother James. "I think a lot of her thinking was very apropos—the pooling of resources, getting a larger home, an extended family. They had come from a large extended family, and I think that is what my aunt was trying to get back to."

Harris's September 17, 1968, pilgrimage across Alabama was marked as much by disbelief as hope. A year earlier, his dream was playing ball for a historically black college, but after decades of little headway, integration was advancing quickly. The window was suddenly thrown open, and Harris had been stolen away for the fight.

Going to Auburn, however, defied deep-seated impulses, ingrained by what Harris had heard all his life—you can't trust white people, they will take advantage of you. Now he was going to live with whites and go to class with them. His world had turned upside down. The change was long overdue but mandated breaking free from the cycle of fear crafted to entrap black Americans.

Harris had chosen new hope over old fear, but he was still by himself. He would have to be his own weapon, and his implement of change would be showing up, again and again. The Freedom Riders, so young and determined, had no weapons; they would not strike back. It was the American way, the quintessential means of correcting democracy. First displayed *en masse* in Montgomery thirteen years earlier, nonviolent change would ride through the same city on the shoulders of Harris, an eighteen-year-old going off to college—like his neighbor's castle, the one that had always been off-limits.

Harris believed in the future in a way that had pushed Americans past rivers of doubt for centuries. At the end of Jackie Robinson's 1947 rookie season, *Time* placed a drawing of Robinson on its cover. The artwork's caption credited Robinson and Brooklyn general manager Branch Rickey with having taken "a chance."

Now it was Harris's turn to take a chance—his life's roll of the dice. It was his opportunity, his time. King was dead, and someone had to go live out his dream. The bold experiment was on. The cotton fields of Boligee, Alabama, and the sleepy academic village of Auburn were on a collision course, the Old South and the New South crashing together in the life of one American teenager.

Chapter 10

The Forerunners

Time and need snatched Greg Page out of Middlesboro, Kentucky, a hilly town in the mountainous confluence of Tennessee, Virginia, and Kentucky. He was the son of a coal miner, Robert Page, a proud man who survived growing up as one of ten black children in Depression-starved Mississippi and then gone to war for America. For two years he fought through the jungles of the Pacific to finally reach Japan, only to return home to a land of restricted freedom. His son, Greg, courageously helped integrate Middlesboro High School and appeared bound for football-proud Oklahoma when the governor of Kentucky came calling, asking Greg to help give African Americans a chance to represent their state university. For his dad, it was powerful, humbling moment, making the long wait for redemption seem worth it. This was the American dream.

As a meeting ground of the South and North, Kentucky was a decade ahead of other SEC states in integrating high school athletics, and Governor Ned Breathitt thought Kentucky should have the distinction of integrating the SEC because its athletes were accustomed to integrated competition. It was something Kentucky could do for the league, he thought, and as chairman of the university's board of trustees, he was determined to make it happen.

By late 1965, with seventeen years having passed since the integration of the university, Breathitt was frustrated with Kentucky's lack of progress. For two years, the school had claimed it was trying to recruit black athletes. In 1964, it had gone after Louisville's Wes Unseld, possibly the best high school basketball player in America, but Unseld received death threats when word of his recruitment leaked out and doubted the sincerity of longtime coach Adolph Rupp. The following year Rupp put more effort in recruiting Butch

Beard, again the best player in the state, and again the player's family doubted Rupp's sincerity, so Beard joined Unseld at the University of Louisville, where blacks had played since the mid-1950s.

With Rupp continuing to strike out, university president John W. Oswald, chosen partly because of his willingness to integrate athletics, began putting pressure on football coach Charlie Bradshaw, an unlikely candidate for a morality play. An Alabamian, Bradshaw was a Marine drill instructor during World War II and also fought in the Pacific. Afterward, he played on Bear Bryant's first three Kentucky teams and was one of his top assistants at Alabama before being hired by Kentucky following Bryant's first national title in 1961. A disciple of Bryant's hard-nosed style of play, Bradshaw quickly got in trouble with the NCAA for his offseason training program—his first Kentucky team being dubbed "The Thin Thirty" after fifty-eight players surrendered their scholarships rather than endure Bradshaw's brutal regimen

Eventually, Oswald came up with an offer so enticing it rendered Bradshaw color-blind: If he would integrate his team, he could have lifetime employment with the university. Following a 6-4 season in 1965, Bradshaw signed a "contract of indeterminate length after the season," guaranteeing him "a position of equal standing if and when he decided to quit coaching," according to Russell Rice, then Kentucky's sports information director.

When Kentucky failed to sign any blacks in December 1965 during the SEC's early signing period, Governor Breathitt promised an "immediate all-out effort" to integrate the university athletically. Within a week, Kentucky brought Nate Northington, a black halfback from Louisville, to campus for an initial visit. The son of a domestic who moved from Mississippi at fourteen, Northington was pictured in Kentucky newspapers the following day signing a scholarship, surrounded by three powerful white men—Breathitt, Oswald, and Bradshaw. After signing, he left a fancy lunch at the governor's mansion with a promise from the three that he would not be alone.

Two months later, Kentucky began to recruit Page, a defensive end, ostensibly to provide Northington a black roommate and help shoulder the pressure. A chiseled 6-foot-2 and 220 pounds, Page was urged by local fans in Middlesboro, as well as Breathitt, to attend

Kentucky. It was an arduous decision, though, as he could go to Oklahoma and not worry about integration. Like his father, Page became a patriot. He would do something for his state and country.

After starring on the freshman team, Page and Northington were both competing for playing time on the 1967 varsity when preseason practice started. On the third day with players still not even in full pads—wearing shorts, shoulder pads, and helmets—the team was running a half-speed, seven-on-seven defensive reaction drill. The offense would snap the football, and the defense would move toward the ball carrier and stop his momentum by surrounding him and bumping him around rather than tackling him. Page was the defensive end on the side away from the flow of the play, so he was trailing the ball carrier. When the other defensive end stopped the ball carrier, he knocked him back into Page. Although the drill was usually run with no one ending up on the ground, this time it resulted in a pileup of players. And Page was on the bottom of it. He didn't get up. He was unconscious and not moving. Practice quickly stopped, and a large group of white players, coaches, and trainers surrounded a strong black man lying on the ground. Page was having difficulty breathing.

Trainers performed mouth-to-mouth resuscitation and carried him to the training room. An ambulance was called and took Page to the emergency room, where a tracheotomy was performed to help him breathe. He was paralyzed "at least temporarily."

A week into practice, Page was still in intensive care, paralyzed from the neck down, and breathing by machine. His father and mother, a head nurse in Middlesboro, were at his side constantly. Bradshaw came to visit nearly daily, and if he didn't, Page asked where he was. Robert Page even went to practice and spoke to his son's teammates, magnanimously telling them not to feel bad about the injury, to play all the harder because of it. If he had any bitterness, he refused to show it, accepting what everyone told him, that it was a freak accident, that his son's head had been "up," in the wrong position for contact.

"Greg was coming from the back side [of the play]," Bradshaw recounted in 1980, "and when the combined weights came back through him, his face was up and it just went right back through him. The irony of it was it was just kind of a half-speed situation. It was a complete freak accident."

Robert Page believed Greg, who regained consciousness, would have somehow communicated with him if he felt someone had tried to hurt him. "He told us he didn't know what happened, and he didn't," Robert Page said. Because X-rays showed no fracture and the exact location of the injury was not determined, doctors were never certain if the injury was a bruise to the spine or a partly cut or completely severed spinal cord.

Thirty-eight days after a pileup that wasn't supposed to happen, Page died at University of Kentucky Medical Center, still unable to breathe on his own. It was late Friday night, September 29, the eve of the first integrated SEC football game, between Kentucky and OleMiss in Lexington. The Pages told Bradshaw to go on with the game, that's what Greg would've wanted. The next day Northington integrated the SEC in a game preceded by the playing of Dixie, a Kentucky gameday staple. On Sunday, in a memorial service at Stoll Field, Page was called a "credit to his race." His funeral two days later at the white First Baptist Church in Middlesboro drew seven hundred people, including the governor. Some 1,200 people signed the guest book, and Page was buried in the Kentucky travel blazer he never got to wear.

Perry Wallace of Vanderbilt was the quintessential candidate for integration. He was valedictorian of the 441-menber senior class at Nashville's black Pearl High School, a basketball power that had won three National Negro High School Championships. In 1966, Wallace led Pearl to a perfect 31-0 season and into the finals of the first integrated Tennessee state basketball tournament, ironically played on the same night Texas Western beat Kentucky in the NCAA finals. Pearl won its championship by beating a white team from Memphis's Treadwell High School, vanquishing decades of indignity and oppression in a methodical fury.

Wallace was a prodigy, recruited out of the band to play basketball. He taught himself to dunk a basketball—at age twelve—by doing thousands of squats while watching 1950s sitcoms on television. But like so many black southern athletes before him, Wallace seemed headed to the Big Ten before Vanderbilt, the upper-crust white school two miles away, started recruiting him. "It was such an unusual thing," he remembered, "to have spent most of your life with people saying, 'You stay over on this side of town,' and 'All of you stay together.' Then all of a sudden somebody's saying, 'Come over and play basketball with us.'"

Integrating athletics was the idea of Vanderbilt chancellor Alexander Heard, and Coach Roy Skinner did not protest. When Wallace asked them if he would be heckled on the road, they said "probably, but just at Alabama and Ole Miss." Besides, they told him, most of his time would be spent at Vanderbilt, which had already "moved past prejudice." Wallace's parents hid the threatening hate mail from him, and Wallace, admittedly naïve, tried to ignore the pioneering factor. "I felt, 'Well, they say this is a good thing and I would like to do a good thing by integrating the SEC,'" Wallace said. "I was seventeen or eighteen, and there's only so much a guy can know at that time." He eventually chose Vanderbilt because he thought it would be hard not to obtain a good education there and because of his parents. "It was going to be nice to have these poor black people who had worked very, very hard, to have people in the city that they had worked in and struggled in show them the respect they deserved," he said.

If Wallace could not fully understand what he was getting in to, he quickly did after moving on campus for the summer semester. Deeply religious, he attended University Church of Christ, a white church across from his dormitory, until several members drew him aside one Sunday and told him that, although they weren't prejudiced, they feared his continued attendance would affect contributions from older members. "I was in a world I didn't understand," Wallace said, "but I had to try to be effective in it, so all you could do is sort of act. And there was no script written."

Ole Miss canceled its two freshman games with Vanderbilt although Wallace was never told exactly why, Ole Miss telling *Sports Illustrated* it was because of "school work." The cancellations, however, did not spare Wallace a trip into Mississippi State's Quonsenhut-like New Gym. Fortunately, he did not have to go there alone. Vanderbilt had also signed Godfrey Dillard, a black guard from Detroit, whose father had served America in four European countries as a mechanic for the Tuskegee Airmen.

Sitting almost on top of the court, Mississippi State fans jeered and hooted and pelted Dillard and Wallace with racial epithets—and spit or threw Coke on them if they got too close to the sideline. "The business they were about was trying to destroy you," Wallace said. "They said the most hateful things I have ever heard in my life." The two teenagers wondered if they might die. They knew it was Mississippi and it was the 1960s so anything was possible. At halftime, they sat next to each other. "We held each other's hand just to develop the strength to go back out and play well," Wallace said.

Somehow, Wallace—despite being only 6-foot-5 and hearing "We're going to lynch you!" on the road and "Jump, boy, jump!" at home—averaged a phenomenal twenty rebounds and eighteen points a game for the freshman team. The following season, he became the first African American to play SEC varsity basketball. Because Dillard missed the season with an injury, he traveled the Dixie highway alone.

Tully Gymnasium at Florida State University was packed December 1, 1966, with fans curious to see how well a black man could play basketball. Lennie Hall left them with no doubts. Florida State's first black player scored the game's first basket by taking a rebound and slamming it through the rim before returning to the floor. He got another basket on a twenty-foot bank shot. He also had two rebounds and two assists in a furious first four minutes. And then it was over. He tried to block a shot, fell over a player, and blew out his knee. He was done that quickly. Because he was a senior, having played junior college ball and sat out a couple of seasons, his first game was his last. Hall, however, never forgot those few minutes when he returned home to New Jersey, nor the letters he received. "The Klan sent quite a bit of mail," he said. "Some of the letters told me to go back to the North and let some decent white kid from Florida get that scholarship."

Hall entered college the same year Page, Northington, Wallace, and Dillard did but got to play varsity ball immediately because he was a transfer student. As challenging as his ordeal was, Florida State was an independent in the 1960s. Without conference membership, southern independents had no "gentlemen's agreement" to break and no racist league brethren. In 1967, after Georgia Tech and Tulane left the SEC, both Florida State and Memphis State were reportedly rejected for SEC membership because they had already integrated.

Tulane's Steve Martin actually integrated SEC varsity competition in 1966, but few noticed, as baseball was considered a minor sport and Martin did not receive an athletic scholarship. He played on the freshman team in 1965 and then became the varsity center fielder in 1966. With Tulane leaving the SEC months later, he received little recognition.

Regardless of what Martin achieved, or what Page, Northington, Wallace, and Dillard accomplished, another barrier remained. One of the SEC's seven Deep South schools had to sign an African American to athletic scholarship in a major sport, football or basketball. Some wondered if it would ever happen. The students who became the Freedom Riders were on schedule in 1961, rolling through Virginia and the Carolinas with only minor antagonism, and then they hit the Deep South, where all hell broke loose.

Joe B. Hall, the Kentucky assistant basketball coach hired to recruit blacks, attempted to bring one of his Central Missouri State players to Lexington in 1965. "He was good enough to play at Kentucky—he was in the Olympic Trials," Hall recalled. "And even though he became a good friend of mine, he wouldn't come with me to Kentucky. He said, 'Coach, I know what it's like in Mississippi and Georgia and Louisiana and Alabama.' He said, 'I don't want to lead that crusade through the South.'"

The Deep South would be Henry Harris's crusade.

Chapter 11

Trespassing

We walk into that which we cannot yet see.
- Elizabeth Alexander
January 20, 2009

Carrying few belongings, yet the baggage of centuries, Harris arrived in Auburn Tuesday afternoon, September 17, 1968, five years to the week the Birmingham church bombing killed four girls and precipitated the Civil Rights Act. He checked into Sewell Hall, a modern three-story brick building on the edge of campus, named for Auburn athletic benefactor Roy B. Sewell, the west Georgia clothing manufacturer. Sewell Hall was the nicest dormitory on campus—its bedroom doors opening onto an exterior walkway, like a motel. It was home to 135 athletes, and 134 of them were white.

"Can you imagine being the only black kid to walk into Sewell Hall?" said Larry Chapman, who would be Harris's freshman coach. "If you'd asked some of those players on that Auburn team when Coach Lynn, Rudy, and I brought in Henry Harris, a lot of them would've said, 'What are you thinking? What are you doing?'"

And that was just the basketball players. Most of Sewell Hall's residents were football players, many from small towns in Alabama and Georgia. Football players were the ringleaders in the verbal abuse directed at Perry Wallace when he played the previous two seasons at Auburn. For segregationists, Harris represented more than the collapse of a wall; his presence heralded that more were coming. He was the "other"—the black American—when he entered Sewell Hall's dining room that first evening. There he was, living with white boys, who were perhaps as fearful of the unknown as he was.

"I thought there was a lot of animosity there at first," said Tim

Ash, another freshman. Ash, from Indiana, and Bobby York, a small-town Georgia guy, were the first players to meet Harris when he arrived. "I got to the dorm, helped Ash and his whole family move his stuff into his room. Henry arrived about that time, and I remember meeting him and talking to him, just talking normal basketball talk, getting-to-know-you-type stuff." When freshman Greg Austin arrived from Lexington, Kentucky, Harris's smile made an instant impression. "Henry had a great big toothy grin that was disarming," Austin said. Harris seemed to always be smiling, Ash recalled, "kind of like a Magic Johnson. He was very friendly."

Tom Bardin, the 6-foot-10 son of a North Carolina sheriff, was the fifth freshman on scholarship. "The first night we were there, we all got together," Ash said. "Henry knew his place, very discreet, just acted like one of the guys. And everyone got to treating him that way once they got to know him. He stuck with us pretty much—the five of us hung together because none of us knew anybody."

Harris was assigned a room on the third floor with the other basketball players. Like everyone in Sewell Hall, he would live in a double room in a four-bedroom, eight-person suite. Harris, however, didn't have a roommate. The prevailing belief in the southern college athletics then was that whites would more easily accept blacks as teammates than roommates. Many colleges signed two blacks initially to solve the roommate dilemma, including Kentucky, Vanderbilt, and Tennessee, the three SEC schools that preceded Auburn in athletic integration. Blacks and whites living together was at the heart of "race mixing."

Harris was supposed to have a roommate, according to Dan Jacobs, the student team manager from 1967-1969, but no one can remember if he did. "My recollection is he did have a roommate and it [the choice] was done on purpose to help him in settling in, because everybody knew it was going to be difficult," Jacobs said. "The attitude I remember being shared with me [by the coaches], is that we all wanted to make him successful because he would help make the team successful, so the key was to make him comfortable. The key would be the interaction with the other players." Ash sensed there wasn't "too much bigotry among the players." "A lot of them didn't want to room with him, but they were friendly with him," he said

Harris may have lived alone, but he was not as isolated as Harold Franklin was four years earlier. Auburn's first black student was given an entire three-story dormitory wing to live in, by himself.

Although it was Agricultural and Mechanical College of Alabama initially and then Alabama Polytechnic Institute until 1960, Auburn was always known simply by the small town from which it grew, its name coming from Oliver Godsmith's poem *The Deserted Village*—"Sweet Auburn, loveliest village of the Plain." Like many southern colleges, its earliest history was linked to the Civil War. Classes were held in "Old Main" until most students and faculty left to join the Confederate army, with the campus becoming an army training ground and "Old Main" a hospital for wounded Confederates. History would not die quickly.

In 1948, Auburn received its first African American applicant—William Bell a former Army master sergeant with four years of overseas service to the United States in World War II. Bell wanted to major in architecture at Auburn but was dissuaded by Acting President Ralph Draughon, who paid a black man, Jim Israel, to convince Bell to withdraw his application. Two months after applying, Bell did just that, in the midst of what he called a "nervous attack" prompted by reaction to his application.

After the Supreme Court's *Brown v. Board* ruling in 1954, Auburn's Board of Trustees instructed Draughon not to integrate until forced do so by the federal government. For the next decade, Auburn dodged admitting blacks by withholding requested admission forms or by not processing applications from qualified blacks until enrollment was full or by contending they did not have the necessary qualifications. Following Governor George Wallace's failed theatrics in Tuscaloosa in 1963, Draughon received a telegram from President John Kennedy inviting him to the White House to discuss integration with other educators. Draughon would suggest to the Board of Regents that Auburn go ahead and admit a black student who was "less bad than the others" but again was told not to desegregate unless ordered by the courts.

When U.S. District Judge Frank M. Johnson Jr. ruled in Montgomery that Harold Franklin must be admitted, Auburn appealed, lost again, and decided fighting further would only sully the image of a college growing rapidly in both enrollment and stature.

A month before Franklin enrolled, Draughon called a meeting of all students, faculty, and staff in Cliff Hare Stadium and outlined rules students had to follow or face expulsion, including turning in all guns. "You young people seem to have been born into a time of change and crisis," Draughon said. ". . . You are going to have to learn to live with change and crisis, for it appears we will have them with us for a long time."

When Franklin, a lanky, thirty-one-year-old Air Force veteran, arrived on campus to register for winter quarter on Saturday, January 4, more than one hundred state troopers were in place, and the campus was mostly quiet, with about 150 onlookers herded across the street from campus. Having already saved face at Tuscaloosa, Wallace stood down on Auburn at Draughon's request to prevent federal troops from coming on campus. Order was maintained and Auburn became the next-to-last SEC school to integrate, but it had done so without the student riot that occurred at Georgia, the fatal gun battle at Ole Miss, or the governmental revolt at Alabama.

Auburn refused Franklin a dormitory room until Judge Johnson ordered the school to house him like any other student. Whether to protect Franklin or other students, Auburn isolated him in a small wing of Magnolia Hall. "I had a whole wing of a dormitory to myself," said Franklin, who had a key to the front door and all three floors to himself. Franklin departed Auburn just a year later, having completed his master's coursework. Faculty members had rejected the first draft of his thesis on civil disobedience, suggesting he instead write on the history of Alabama State, and Franklin doubted he would ever receive a degree. Three weeks after he left, the firearm ban was lifted.

"You can legislate rights, but you can't make people accept them," said Willie Wyatt, a black freshman who entered Auburn later in 1964 with Anthony Lee, another black freshman. They were placed in Magnolia Hall next to Franklin. "We were on the first floor, and as people came through the quadrangle and if our windows were up, you'd hear things you didn't really want to hear," Wyatt recalled. When the trio went to the lobby to play ping pong, a crowd would gather. "People would stand around and watch and laugh, like we were some sideshow," Wyatt said. "If I had six ping-pong balls, the game was over by the time the sixth one hit the floor because they would step on them."

The abuse Auburn's first blacks endured was similar to that at other southern universities. James Hood, who integrated Alabama with Vivian Malone, left after one quarter to "avoid a complete mental and physical breakdown," he said. Ole Miss emptied an entire first floor of a dorm for James Meredith to live in. In the room directly above Meredith's, students took turns bouncing a basketball around the clock. Harold Black, one of Georgia's first African Americans, saw his dorm windows broken regularly and his room set afire twice. The university bookstore refused to sell him textbooks initially, and the first time he went swimming, the pool was drained afterward.

Wyatt and Lee were accompanied by state troopers at Auburn's home football games. "We had our own little seating area," said Lee, "because no one was sitting around us. And the state troopers had to protect us from them." (Interestingly, when Billy Graham preached at Auburn in 1965 following the Selma marches, thousands of blacks and whites sat side by side in Cliff Hare Stadium—by Graham's decree.)

Wyatt left Auburn after a year, but in May 1968, Lee became the first African American to graduate after enrolling as a freshman. Growing up in Tuskegee, Lee had dreamed of integrating Alabama, but with that option gone, he enrolled at Auburn. "I was very proud to do that," he said. "That was my privilege." When Harris arrived four months later, only fifty-six of Auburn's 13,877 students were black, and most of those were daily commuters who would disappear as soon as their classes were over, dodging dormitory expenses and a hostile habitat both day and night.

Harris expected to be the only black in his fall-quarter classes—U.S. history, college math, and intro to business—but quickly noticed he was one of three black males in the large, auditorium-style history class. The instructor noticed too. "The guy [instructor] comes into class and slaps his desk and says, 'All men are not created equal,'" said Charles Smith, one of the blacks in the class. "And it looks like he is looking at me. And Henry thinks he's looking at him."

Like Harris, Smith was coming from a rural black training school. "I'm shocked already when I go to class—all these white people. I've never seen so many whites in one place in my life," he said. "And I've been told all people are created equal, and this guy comes in and shoots it down. I didn't remember much after that." Harris, Smith, and Donald Williams, the other black student, said nothing to the instructor. "When you've got to get a grade, you keep your mouth shut," said the normally voluble Williams. They all flunked the course. "That was my first encounter with Auburn," said Smith, "and how it was going to be."

Smith and Williams were also breaking racial barriers at Auburn. Smith was a walk-on player on the freshman football team, and Williams was integrating the Auburn band. Three days after classes started, he understood fully what a big deal that was. That's when Auburn opened its football season.

When the band marched into Cliff Hare Stadium, "you could see them [fans and students] nudging each other and pointing at me, because I was pretty damn conspicuous," Williams said. Eventually, he realized the fans were paying more attention to a black man on the field. They kept referring to him as "Leroy," a racial slur used by whites in the latter half of the sixties. "Leroy" was really Jerry LeVias, an exceptional wide receiver and kick returner for Southern Methodist University.

Although Alabama had yet to play an integrated team in Tuscaloosa or Birmingham, SMU was the third integrated team to play in Cliff Hare Stadium. Wake Forest wide receiver Kenneth "Butch" Henry and linebacker Robert Grant were the first blacks to play at Auburn in 1966. On the team bus to the stadium, they knew to sit in aisle seats to thwart a possible attack, having played already at Clemson, Florida State, and South Carolina. Still, their reception at Auburn stood out. "It was pretty rough down there," Henry said. "They hurt their own team by piling on."

When Nate Northington played his second SEC game—at Auburn in 1967—Kentucky was refused accommodations at its usual Auburn motel. On the field, Northington played cornerback and tried to return punts, but Auburn consistently kicked the ball away from him. Off the field, the state troopers along the sidelines had little Confederate flags stuck in their holsters. "We heard the n-word over and over and over and over again," said white teammate Phil Thompson, who particularly remembered the racism from state troopers and fans close to the field when Northington was on the sidelines: "Put Leroy in. Let's kill Leroy."

It was October 7, 1967, four days after the funeral of Northington's black roommate, Greg Page, killed in football practice.

Harris was also in Cliff Hare Stadium to hear the reaction to LeVias, who had become a lightning rod for the outrage many Texans felt over the social change they believed was being forced on them. In 1966, as a sophomore, LeVias and Baylor's John Westbrook integrated varsity football in the Southwest Conference, a rough-and-tumble league that took football about as seriously as the SEC.

A phenomenal high school player in Beaumont, Texas, LeVias was recruited by Coach Hayden Fry, who came to SMU under the condition he could recruit blacks. Fry had grown up around blacks in Odessa, Texas, and determined then he would help them one day if he could. He practiced full disclosure, telling LeVias's family he "could not fail." Once LeVias arrived in Dallas, Fry realized LeVias's life would be worse than even he imagined.

LeVias's white roommate moved out after his parents threatened to pull him out of school. In anthropology, a classmate asked the professor if blacks have smaller brains than whites. In his first scrimmage, LeVias was blindsided by a teammate, cracking three ribs. Athletic department secretaries screened his mail, and late-night obscene and threatening phone calls prompted Fry to get him an unlisted number. That didn't stop the phone call to the SMU dean's office in 1966, the week SMU was to play at rival Texas Christian in Fort Worth. The caller's message was crisp: "We're going to shoot that dirty nigger LeVias on Saturday." Fry told LeVias he could sit out the game, but LeVias played anyway, with his teammates huddling around him on the sideline and the SMU offense running from a quick-snap count.

After downplaying the cheap shots LeVias had caught all season, Fry finally challenged other SWC coaches to better police their players. Texas Tech coach J. T. King told a reporter that the only way to stop

LeVias was to "put a 'Whites Only' sign over the locker room door." By the end of the season, though, LeVias was Southwest Conference player of the year and an Academic All-American and had transformed a team that was 1-9 two years earlier into an 8-2 league champion.

Over the offseason, the conference even issued a statement urging its players to show better sportsmanship toward LeVias, but that would not halt the unnecessary roughness that referees refused to call. LeVias just kept getting back up. He didn't quit and he didn't transfer—Fry had told him leaving would "handicap the program for other people."

LeVias's experiences in Texas were so horrid that he acted unfazed about playing in Alabama, joking, "I'm not worried, man, those rifles don't scare me none. I've got my equipment with me, bulletproof vest and all." During pregame warmups, an Auburn assistant coach who knew Fry handed the SMU coach a sheet of paper that was supposedly the stadium's bylaws. "There was all this legal stuff on it," Fry said, "and down at the bottom, it said blacks weren't allowed to play in the stadium." It was a joke, sort of.

Fry, however, had his players ready to play. Twelve-point underdogs, they jumped to a 20-0 lead. When Auburn finally scored, "everybody was singing, screaming, and clapping, but instead of playing the Auburn fight song, they play *this* song 'Dixie,'" Smith recalled. "How negative can it be?" By the end of the game, LeVias had one hundred yards on five catches in a 37-28 upset. It was the most points SMU had scored in seventeen years and the second most Auburn had allowed in fifteen.

In the SMU locker room, LeVias had a busted lip, swollen foot, and bruised shoulder, but he was on his way to an All-American season. He would catch fifteen passes at Ohio State the following week, lead the nation with eighty catches for the season, and finish fifth in Heisman Trophy voting. He had given the state of Alabama a fleeting glimpse of the future, and now he was moving on. Harris, however, having witnessed it all, was just getting started in the Heart of Dixie.

Three days after the SMU game, Auburn coach Bill Lynn wrote a letter to Al Young, the Greene County Training School basketball coach, to assure him Harris was adjusting well to his new home.

"Henry has not had a problem at all," Lynn wrote. "He has fit right in and is now part of Auburn and our ball club. He seems to be as happy as can be and is liked and respected by not only the basketball players but all the athletes in the dormitory."

Lynn's letter was in response to a letter from Young asking how Harris was doing socially. Young understood the adjustment Harris faced socially, as the area surrounding Boligee was ninety percent black and Harris could go days without seeing a white person other than in a passing car. "Henry had never spent that much time around white people," said Fred Hughes, one of his high school teachers. "Our students did not have that much interaction [with whites]. You went to a store to get what you wanted, and you got in and you got out of there." Boligee's white teenagers lived "away from us," said Harris's friend Jerome Roberts. "We never came in contact with them."

In closing his August 19 letter to Harris, Lynn had acknowledged the door Harris was walking through:

> Henry, I want you to come here and feel you are a part of Auburn because you are, and you are wanted here. I want you to excel not only in basketball but in the classroom and on campus. I will assure you again that we here at Auburn will help you. Looking forward to having you with us.

Harris had trusted the sincerity of Auburn's coaches, just as Joby Wright did. "Both of those guys [Davalos and Chapman] had a way with them that impressed me in terms of the sincerity," Wright said. "And then meeting Coach Lynn, he was a very down-to-earth, sincere guy. He really impressed me, telling me how sincere they were in recruiting me, but also in the manner they spoke to my dad, in making a commitment they would take care of me."

But on campus, Harris and other black students struggled to know who could be trusted. Whereas protestors in Greene County and across the South had one another, Harris figured out early he would need to rely on himself. That's what he did during a basketball hazing ritual that fall. All freshmen players had to choose whether to be paddled—it was called "boarding"—or blindfolded and taken on a "road trip" and left in the woods. "We didn't cut Henry any slack. He had to do the same thing everybody else did," said Jimmy Walker, a sophomore. "Henry said, 'Ain't nobody boarding me.' We said, 'Okay, if you don't get boarded, you get blindfolded and we take you off somewhere, and you've got to find your way back.' He said, 'All right.'" Harris was left in Chewacla State Park, about five miles from campus. "There wasn't nothing out there. So we dropped him off, and then we went out fooling around," Walker recalled. "Well, when we got back to the dorm, Henry was already there."

Like other southern universities, Auburn was not an easy place to live in 1968 for anyone who was "the other." Three attacks were reported on hippies during fall quarter, and the Alabama Department of Public Safety was spying on students who favored integration— or opposed the Vietnam War.

Except for Williams and Smith in his history class, the only blacks Harris saw regularly were the three Sewell Hall custodians who cleaned the athletes' rooms. They became his friends.

Harris quickly gravitated to the black residential and business area just north of campus, where he could be himself. It was known as "going across the tracks." "No matter what town you live in, if someone tries to tell you where the black section of town is, at some point in the directions they say, 'Then, cross the tracks,'" said Ralph Foster, a black businessman in Auburn and owner of Duke's Barber Shop. "Harold Franklin spent every day at the barber shop." Lynn had asked Foster to call Harris when he arrived in town. "They say the barber shop is the black man's country club," Foster said. "Henry's first two years, he was over here all the time."

Chapter 12

Now It's About the Struggle

Recruited into a society for which he has no cultural preparation, and isolated by its unwritten codes . . .
— Jack Olsen, Sports Illustrated

A month after Harris arrived on campus, basketball practice finally started. In a state where black masculinity had been so often crushed, Harris would get to compete with young white men step for step. He had been playing afternoon pickup games and impressing his new teammates since he arrived—"he is an even better ball player than I expected," Bill Lynn wrote Al Young.

Preseason practice began October 15, and Harris quickly earned the respect of his teammates on the freshman team. He was quiet, easy-going, and the type of basketball player they all wanted to be— a "stud" as they called him. Older varsity players were less sure. "Even though he may have externally been smiling, Henry had to be scared to death—maybe not about his safety but about what tomorrow brings," said team manager Dan Jacobs. "Because—even though they might say, 'We welcome you'—a lot of people's upbringing was such that they were not as accepting of integrating the team as they might have been showing outwardly."

"Many were trying to find fault with him," said freshman coach Larry Chapman, "but I don't think it was about Henry. I think they treated Henry very nicely, and I'll tell you why. Henry was very polite, very nice, and very, very conscious of what was going on. That had a lot to do with how he was raised and all those things that manifested themselves into a kid who, as painful as things were at that time, was able to cope. Coping is what he had to do."

But just a day after practice started, the headway Harris had made in building the trust of his varsity teammates was abruptly eroded when Tommie Smith and John Carlos took off their shoes, mounted a podium in Mexico City, and raised black-gloved fists after winning gold and bronze medals in the Olympic 200-meter dash.

Born on June 6, 1944, the day Americans went ashore to free Europe from a bully's grip, Smith also was the offspring of the cotton fields of the American South, the son of east Texas migrant farm workers who moved to northern California in 1950 to give their dozen children a better shot at the American Dream—from a small cabin in a farm labor camp. Smith could not get used to being around white kids but eventually learned to work twice as hard as the kid next to him because he was afraid to fail. He earned a track scholarship to San Jose State, and there he met sociology professor Harry Edwards, a 6-foot-8 former discus thrower. Edwards became founder of the Olympic Project for Human Rights, which carefully considered a black boycott of the Olympics until six weeks beforehand, when the athletes decided they had worked too hard not to compete and would express their protest on their own. Smith decided he would raise his fist only if he won the gold medal, which he did in world-record time, but he turned "scared" waiting for the medal ceremony. Then, he realized, "Why should I be scared now? I've been scared all my life."

Although nonviolent, the raised black fists of Smith and Carlos symbolized black anger in a way a boycott never could have and touched a long-held fear of many whites, that black Americans would one day rise up in rebellion. The reaction nationally was instant and livid. The cover of *Time* cried out: "Angrier, Nastier, Uglier," mocking the Olympic motto of "Faster, Higher, Stronger."

The Mexico City protest, however, was more about dissent by black college athletes than black Olympians. Magazine articles during the summer of 1968 reported increasing revolt by black athletes at U.S. colleges—athletes at thirty-five schools had made demands for change. In *Sports Illustrated*'s groundbreaking five-part series, "The Black Athlete: A Shameful Story," author Jack Olsen wrote: "Recruited into a society for which he has no cultural preparation, and isolated by its unwritten codes, the typical Negro athlete discovers an immense gap between himself and the college community."

Smith and Carlos had served notice that integration itself would not be enough and the coming years on college campuses would be difficult. Black militancy versus white backlash would become the background noise of Harris's four years at Auburn, and just one month after his arrival, he would be seen with increased suspicion in Sewell Hall. "Everyone is looking at you different now, whether they say so or not," said Edwards. "Now, it's not about basketball, it's about the struggle."

Three weeks later, Republican Richard Nixon narrowly won the presidency over Democrat Hubert Humphrey. Former Alabama governor George Wallace, taking his hate nationally and preaching "law and order," won 13.5 percent of the popular vote as a third-party candidate. Often whining that blacks were taking "our jobs," moving into "our neighborhoods," and going to "our schools," Wallace won four SEC states, plus Arkansas, and many northern votes in the conservative tide sweeping America after eight years of liberal leadership. Nixon represented a return to the "good old days" in a violent year full of protest by a generation seemingly born to rebel and create a new America.

In February, two months before Dr. King's murder, three students at historically black South Carolina State College in Orangeburg were killed and twenty-seven wounded or injured when police opened fire on a campus protest. Later that month, the National Advisory Commission on Civil Disorders blamed "white racism" for 150 riots or major disorders between 1965 and early 1968, concluding, "Our nation is moving toward two societies, one black, one white—separate and unequal." Its report warned that without drastic measures "continuing polarization of the American community" would occur, as well as "the destruction of basic democratic values."

President Lyndon Johnson decided not to seek re-election, his decision driven by the growing unpopularity of the Vietnam War, ignited by waves of student protests. Ten weeks later, Robert Kennedy was assassinated in Los Angeles after winning the California Democratic Primary, and much of young America's idealism died with him. "Is our country coming apart?" wondered network newscaster Dan Rather. But what was happening in America in 1968 mirrored confrontations globally between new thought and old ways.

In April, students at Columbia University took over five campus buildings and held them for a week before New York City police cleared them out in bloody battles. In May, students in France occupied universities and factories, inciting a two-week nationwide strike by 11 million workers that shut down the French economy. And student protests were the energy spawning the "Prague Spring" that saw Czechoslovakia experiment with free speech before two hundred Soviet tanks rolled down Prague's streets in August.

The following week, street fighting broke out in Chicago during the Democratic national convention, as student protestors squared off with police night after night in class warfare. At issue was the Vietnam War, spiraling out of control in 1968, starting with North Vietnam's Tet Offensive in January and ending with 16,000 young Americans dead in just twelve months. Even in Mexico City, where the world was to come together in peace, more than three hundred students, protesting human rights abuses, were massacred by police with machine guns just weeks before the Olympics.

One of the biggest American stars to emerge from Mexico City was Spencer Haywood, a little-known 6-foot-8 junior college basketball player who led the U.S. to the gold medal. Haywood had accepted a scholarship to Tennessee just a year earlier but failed to meet the SEC's 750 SAT requirement. He moved to Knoxville for the summer and Tennessee sought to get him tutoring for the test, but SEC commissioner Tonto Coleman forbade it.

Haywood's childhood was as country as Harris's. He grew up in the Mississippi Delta, hungry every night. He started working in the cotton fields at six and got his first pair of shoes at seven. He fled to Chicago at fourteen to live with his sister after spending a day and night in jail for trying to take a quarter from an older black man who nailed it to a counter as a set-up. He finished high school in Detroit after being rescued by an outstanding high school coach and disciplinarian, who took him into his home and found him a willing tutor in a young guidance counselor named Wayne Dyer. The eventual author of more than forty books on self-help, Dyer made Haywood his Eliza Doolittle, preaching positive thinking and self-esteem.

Playing for the University of Detroit after the Olympics, Haywood led the NCAA in rebounding, scored thirty-two points per game, and became the linchpin in a court case striking down the NBA rule prohibiting drafting college underclassmen. Had he played SEC freshman basketball in 1967-68, he would have been so dominant that every SEC basketball program might have been integrated by the fall of 1968. But Harris ended up being the only black basketball player signed by SEC teams in 1967 or 1968, and he continued to prepare for his SEC journey by showing up at six every morning at the Sports Arena for freshmen practice.

By November, having seen how well Harris played defense, how well he rebounded, how well he drove to the basket, Chapman could not believe Auburn's good fortune. "Here is a player with a great work ethic, who is well liked and has an easy manner," thought Chapman. "What a great person to integrate Auburn athletics." Chapman believed God's handiwork had put Harris there. He could not think of any other explanation for Auburn's luck.

A southeast Georgia farm boy, Chapman had started every game during his three-year Auburn career and been chosen for the 1964 U.S. Olympic trials. By his own definition, he was a "hard-nosed" guy. "The only thing I ever said to Henry after he came to Auburn is that—sometimes he would go into the lane and they would hit him and knock him down. And he would be slow getting up," said Chapman. "Finally, I called him into my office and I said, 'Henry, we have talked about how you might be perceived. Let me tell you something, the next time you happen to get knocked down, unless you get carried off the court, you need to pop up, or else whatever people say about you will probably be justified. That doesn't mean it's right, but that's the way it is. You are too precious and too good a person, you don't need anybody to be able to accuse you of anything. You need to get your rear end up and get to that free throw line.' As far as I know, I don't think he ever lay on the floor again. That might not have been a fair thing to say to Henry, but it was the right thing for Henry in view of the time he lived and the problems of transforming athletics into what it is today."

Forewarned, Harris was ready for his opening tour of the American South, at least hustle-wise. The Civil Rights Act had been law for four years, but finding a meal in the Deep South still put black athletes in their greatest peril.

Just six weeks earlier, Kentucky football players Houston Hogg and Wilbur Hackett, two black sophomores on their first SEC road trip, ran a mile from a Baton Rouge restaurant to their motel to escape police. It was nearly midnight, and Kentucky had lost to LSU a couple of hours earlier. With the motel's restaurant overflowing, Hogg, Hackett, and three white teammates walked to a small restaurant for a meal.

"The waitress told the other guys at our table that she could serve them but that me and Hack would have to go around back and order something," Hogg said. "One of our teammates got mad. One thing led to another, and I guess she called the police."

Chairs and tables were flipped over. "We had to get out of there, and we didn't get up politely. We got up with furniture. Then all we did was just run," said Hogg, who was running so hard that he tore the wooden screen door off its hinges. "I can remember running up the highway with the restaurant screen door in my face. I was scared."

When the players, black and white, reached the motel, "it looked like a riot almost. Cops and dogs," according to Hogg. "The dogs were fine until they saw me and Wilbur. Coach [Charlie Bradshaw] told them to get us into the room and don't let us come back out. I couldn't understand why we couldn't sit down and eat. I didn't know people were like that. The further we got down South, they changed your name down there. They'd call you anything. The n-word, that's all we were to them."

During the basketball season, North Carolina's team was refused service at an Atlanta restaurant when the owner saw Charlie Scott, a U.S. Olympic gold medalist just months earlier. Scott was UNC's first black player, and his young coach, Dean Smith, was furious, storming out of the restaurant after giving the team managers money for the players to eat on their own.

Harris arrived at his first game, in Atlanta, without incident. His challenge came at Georgia Tech's Alexander Memorial Coliseum, a round, domed arena adjacent to the downtown freeway. The name-calling started during warmups. Although only a scattering of fans arrived early enough to watch the preliminary freshman game, the emptiness of the arena only made the epithets echo. "Nigger."

"Coon." "Leroy." When the Georgia Tech band played "Dixie," fans got up and started clapping. For an eighteen-year-old from Boligee, the experience was surreal, as evidenced by Harris's play. "The first six times I had the ball, I threw it away—into the stands, everywhere," he said. "I was in a daze. It's something I can't explain."

Harris settled down enough to score twenty points. A week later, he scored twenty-eight against Gordon Military College in Barnesville, Georgia, and seemed more than prepared, at least physically, to embark on his odyssey through the SEC two days later.

In trying to reassure Savannah's Joby Wright, Auburn's initial black recruit, Coach Lynn had written a letter saying: "If you come to Auburn, you will have complete respect from myself, my coaching staff, my administrators, the student body, and most of all your teammates." He closed, however, by saying, "I would be the first to tell you it will be tough at first. We will go places where things are not so pleasant."

Chapter 13

The Message and Messenger

With a schedule seemingly ordained by the devil himself, Harris took his first SEC road trip straight into the vast unknown of Mississippi.

Auburn was supposed to play two games—Ole Miss on Saturday night and Mississippi State two nights later. Harris, however, caught a break when State canceled both its freshman games with Auburn rather than play against him.

Mississippi State had hosted Vanderbilt freshmen Perry Wallace and Godfrey Dillard in a raucous, racially hostile arena two years earlier. But with Harris, State used the tactic Ole Miss did in canceling its freshman games against Wallace and Dillard. It was the strategy both schools had used during segregation when faced with possibly playing an integrated team from another region—just don't play. Freshman coach Larry Chapman viewed the cancellation as "kind of like a victory for us." "We were ahead of everybody in the Deep South," he said. "We felt it [integration] was the right thing to do."

Right or not, Auburn coaches had to face the reality of taking an integrated freshman team to Oxford, Mississippi, where Harris would be both the message and the messenger of change. Harris knew Auburn's freshman football team did not take his friend Charles Smith, the black walk-on, to Ole Miss although he traveled with the team to Florida and Georgia—Smith believed the coaches were protecting him. He also knew state troopers had accompanied his friend Don Williams at Jackson's Memorial Stadium when the Auburn band went there for a game against Mississippi State.

When Ole Miss had played its first integrated football opponent on campus in 1967—the University of Houston and its star black tailback Warren McVea—security surrounded the field a year. A year earlier, Rebel fans had pelted Houston players with rocks and empty beer cans in Memphis, forcing even coaches to wear helmets.

In February 1968, Ole Miss hosted its first integrated basketball opponent, Vanderbilt and Perry Wallace. It was a long-dreaded trip for Wallace, who grew up reading everything he could about black pioneers. His mother warned him to put on the "full armor of God" in hostile surroundings, but nothing could have prepared him for Oxford. Even during warmups, fans cheered when he missed a shot and booed if he made one. When the game started, they hooted and hollered. "We're going to kill you, nigger." "We're going to castrate you, boy." When the game started, fans listening on radio in Nashville could hear the name-calling. When Wallace grabbed a rebound in the first half, a Rebel player poked him in the eye. As the other players ran down the floor and Wallace stood by himself, holding his hands to his bleeding eye, the referees refused to call an injury timeout. During halftime, Vanderbilt's trainer doctored Wallace's eye and was still working on it when his teammates returned to the court. When Ole Miss fans saw Wallace was not among the Vanderbilt players, they whooped with glee, believing they had vanquished the black man.

In the locker room, as the trainer continued to work on his eye, Wallace wondered what might happen in the second half. It was the 1960s, and he knew anything was possible. Some eighteen months earlier, a would-be assassin had shot James Meredith on a Mississippi highway as he made his one-man "March Against Fear," trying to prove blacks had no reason to fear registering to vote.

When the trainer was done, Wallace began his long walk through the tunnel to the court—by himself. No players stayed in the locker room to walk with him. No assistant coaches, no administrators, no one. He walked the gauntlet of hatred, catcalls, and Confederate flags alone. The cacophony was deafening. It seemed as if all the frustration of not being able to stop integration was raining down on Wallace. But the bravery he summoned to walk back on the court carried him through the second half. He grabbed rebound after rebound and, once on a fastbreak, made a behind-the-back pass left-handed—"I had never done that in my life." As Vanderbilt's lead widened, the crowd gradually quieted. Wallace had shut them up.

Harris arrived in Oxford ten months later knowing nothing of

Wallace's trials—racial harassment was not a story sports writers reported. He would play in the Rebels' new coliseum, adjacent to a Confederate cemetery, and confront the ghosts of the South's past. All eyes would be focused on him. He was easy to spot and he was in the Rebels' den. As the Auburn freshmen trotted out of the locker room past the Ole Miss students, someone hollered, "Nigger, get out of our gym."

The reaction of some whites to the social change of the 1960s was: "I've got to hate somebody," and within a crowd, that hatred could become anonymous, contagious, even energizing, making a basketball game an outlet for all that had to be repressed during the work week. The shadow of lynching not only enveloped black Americans, it also affected young whites, spawning a desensitization toward blacks passed from generation to generation, converting a person into an object that no longer had a name or unique identity. While many southern whites had moved past race by 1968, too many still feared ostracism and kept quiet. "It wasn't minorities that the southern majority feared as much as the stigmatization of their own tribe," wrote Pulitzer Prize-winning author Diane McWhorter. Such was the bully of racism.

Harris was "scared to death" at Ole Miss, according to Coach Lynn. He had never been exposed to such open hostility. "Somehow my mother sheltered us from all that," said Harris's brother James. Angry whites yelling at him instinctively meant danger, but he had to trust the situation. Yet, he had to wonder if he could trust his new teammates—the quiet son of Georgia mill workers, the son of a North Carolina sheriff, a Kentucky guard, a handful of walk-ons from Georgia and Alabama. He liked them, but could he count on them in a confrontation? Nothing in Harris's eighteen years had told him he could trust whites, but now he had to. Eventually, Harris realized his teammates were catching hell too. The crowd was calling them "nigger-lovers." "I sat down on the bench by Henry," said Greg Austin, "and someone behind us hollered, 'Hey, Austin, you like that nigger shit, don't you?'"

Like Wallace—and Jackie Robinson before him—Harris figured out he could fight back only by doing well, proving he belonged right where he was. Despite playing in abject fear, he finished with twenty-five points and twelve rebounds and led his new teammates to victory. It was one of the most courageous performances by an eighteen-year-old in SEC history.

Harris's second SEC game—in Athens, Georgia, January 6, 1969—came eight years to the day a federal court ordered the University of Georgia to admit Hamilton Holmes and Charlayne Hunter, who would become national newscaster Charlayne Hunter-Gault. The Ku Klux Klan helped instigate the riot that followed a Georgia basketball game the following week, and the local KKK would resurface again in 1964 with a murder that shocked America.

On the lookout for "outside agitators" during Freedom Summer, the Klansmen believed they had found some when they spotted three well-dressed black men in a Chevrolet Impala with an out-of-state tag an hour before dawn. Northeast of Athens, they pulled along the Impala and fired a shotgun at Lemuel Penn, the driver. Hardly agitators, Penn and his passengers, Charles Brown and John Howard, were U.S. Army Reserve officers on their way home from two weeks of summer training at Fort Benning in southwest Georgia. A lieutenant colonel and World War II veteran, Penn supervised five vocational high schools for the District of Columbia. He was buried in Arlington National Cemetery, a soldier killed by hostile fire in his own country.

In the eight years since the integration of its student body, the University of Georgia had repeatedly turned its back on the state's black athletes, as had Georgia Tech. "I would've given my four fingers to go to one of those schools," said Augusta's Emerson Boozer, who would carry the football ten times that week in Super Bowl III for the New York Jets. Georgia Tech told Decatur's Clarence Scott in 1966 his "talent didn't warrant a scholarship," although he would become an All-American at Kansas State and play thirteen seasons for the Cleveland Browns. That same year, Don Adams, an A student, so wanted to attend college close to his Atlanta home that he took his basketball scrapbooks to the *Atlanta Constitution* sports department to plead his case. His efforts were futile, although he was good enough to return home with the NBA's Atlanta Hawks.

Even after the Braves and Falcons came to Atlanta, drawing huge crowds to integrated competition, nothing changed in nearby

Athens. "We were just cautious. We were just not sure how it would work out," said Georgia athletic director Joel Eaves. "We were in a section that was slow in integrating." In 1968, Georgia had failed to recruit both David Hall, who led Savannah's black Beach High School to victory in the first integrated state basketball tournament in 1967 and had thirty-seven rebounds in the 1968 state semifinals, and Joby Wright, the first-team Parade All-American. Georgia coach Ken Rosemond, who primarily recruited the East Coast, told Wright, "You know, I just don't believe black boys from the South can play basketball." A black student had attempted to try out for Georgia's freshman basketball team during fall quarter, but freshman coach Major Joe Bradley told him "an alumni discussion had decided it was not the time to integrate the major sports."

The turned-away student was Maxie Foster of Athens, who was already on a track and field "performance scholarship" covering just his tuition and books and only as long as he made academic progress. Getting to track practice on time, however, was a bigger obstacle than academics, as Georgia's football players would not allow Foster to enter the locker room. "They were quite open with it. They didn't want me over there at all," Foster said. Georgia track coach Spec Towns, a gold medalist in Hitler's 1936 Olympics, had to intervene once when several football players were harassing Foster.

One of Foster's white high school teammates, Bob Bowen, was a walk-on guard on the Georgia freshman team Harris faced in Athens. "Henry was at the point of their zone defense," Bowen said. "I threw a pass that I had probably thrown a thousand times in my life, reversing the ball to the other side of the floor, and he intercepted it and took it down and laid it in the basket. And I'm sitting there going, 'How did he do that?' I had never seen anybody that quick. He was one of the first guys I ever ran into that I knew I could not check. He was quick and very strong. He could go wherever he wanted to go on me. He was on another level physically."

Bowen was the only Georgia starter from the South. "At some point after a whistle had blown, one my teammates referred to Henry as a 'nigger,'" Bowen said. "My recollection is that he called Henry a 'f---ing nigger' or something like that. I went over and grabbed him by his shirt and said, 'We don't use that word around here.' But the main thing I recollect was Henry's reaction. He had a kind of shocked look on his face. I just had a sense that he was surprised a guy was standing up for him." Bowen sensed Harris's appreciation. "Henry was not a real talkative guy. I think as a defense mechanism he kept his mouth shut and just played hard. But he would talk to me, on jump balls, after timeouts. You get knocked on the floor and he helps you up."

Harris scored twenty-six points, leading Auburn to victory again.

Harris finally got to play a game at Auburn four months after he started attending classes there. It was January 11, 1969, and Auburn's new Memorial Coliseum was finally ready and would be filled with 11,000 fans because the opponent was LSU and Pete Maravich, who was averaging more than forty points a game and playing to capacity crowds wherever he went. Auburn's new arena would likely hit capacity by the second half of the freshman game, as if scripted for the debut of Harris, who wondered how fans would react to him. Would he hear some of the same hatred he had heard on the road? Surely not, but how could he be sure? He had lived at Auburn long enough to feel the ostracism from students and professors. He had heard about how fans treated Perry Wallace at the Sports Arena. And he had attended Auburn football games.

Ten weeks earlier in Auburn, the University of Miami's first black football player had to sleep with an FBI agent guarding his motel room door the night before the Miami-Auburn game. Miami officials had received a death threat against Ray Bellamy, a 6-foot-5 sophomore wide receiver who had grown up in Florida's migrant farm camps, warning that Bellamy would be killed if he played at Auburn. The FBI took it as a serious threat, but Bellamy made it through the night. On gameday, however, as he was entering Cliff Hare Stadium for warmups, he was struck on the head by a rock. Injured enough to urinate blood, Bellamy turned more determined than anxious and played anyway, catching eight passes for 121 yards in the finest game of his career.

As Harris's week wound toward Saturday, the pressure mounted. What if he made a stupid mistake? What if he threw a pass into the seats or air-balled a free throw? It was the same pressure black fans felt when they went to see Jackie Robinson play. Whenever he stepped to the plate, kids could see their parents' anxiety—"Please don't let him strike out." The same pressure rode with the first black Greyhound bus driver. "Please don't let him run into something." African Americans lived through those who earned the first chance because so much depended on them. If they stumbled, the whole race failed.

The sun had already set in the Alabama sky when Harris went on the court for the opening tipoff at 5:45 p.m., a black man dressed in Auburn's shiny white home uniform for the first time. A group of black custodians were clustered at one end of the court. A smattering of black students and townspeople—still unsure how emotionally safe it was to attend a game at Auburn—were scattered among the crowd. Harris did not disappoint any of them, and every time he made a shot, or leaped high for a rebound, or stole the ball and broke on a fastbreak, he gained a few more fans. He finished with twenty-four points, and the Auburn freshmen, playing as a cohesive unit, won again.

Four days later, Harris scored twenty-four again and got eleven rebounds to lead Auburn over despised Alabama, his tenacious defensive play and full-court hustle endearing him to blue-collar Auburn, where athletic grit had always counted more than talent. He then scored twenty points against Georgia, giving the Auburn freshmen three victories in ten days in their new arena. Harris was averaging twenty-four points and ten rebounds per game for an undefeated team. Integration was working, and more and more students were coming to watch. "Everybody would go and see the freshmen play," said Ralph Foster, owner of Duke's Barber Shop. "They saw some moves they had never seen before."

"God blessed Henry tremendously," said freshman coach Chapman. "He had moves. He could get into people with his dribble and then get around them real quick. He could run forever. He was phenomenal."

After the Georgia game, a photographer asked Harris to pose with a cheerleader's megaphone. When he picked it up, the student section erupted in cheers. Harris was already a crowd favorite. The media was impressed as well. "It's not rare to see him [Harris] go up, steal a rebound from a taller opponent, fight off interfering arms and legs, and bank an arching jump shot. All this in one jump," wrote Ed Ruzic in the *Auburn Plainsman*.

In a column headlined "Henry the First," *Columbus Enquirer* sports editor Paul Cox wrote, "Young Harris is not a crusader. He is simply one of the boys. He might easily be the most popular basketball player at Auburn. Students cheer his every move, and he makes a lot of them." Yet Chapman, his coach, still felt the need to remind fans Harris was no showboat, telling Clyde Bolton of the *Birmingham News*, "He's a good ball-handler and can go either way, but he's not a fancy player, just a good solid player. You never see him put it behind his back or anything like that, although he could if he wanted to."

Like Perry Wallace, Harris had already figured out he had to play with little flash and lots of control. "The last thing I wanted," Wallace said, "was for people to be able to accuse me of playing 'nigger ball.' I didn't want to reinforce those stereotypes." Harris also understood what he needed to say off the court. Asked by a local reporter how fans at Ole Miss had treated him in December, he replied, "I don't think they noticed me."

Chapter 14

'Watch for Harris'

Even if it was just a freshman game, the meeting of Auburn and Kentucky on Monday night, February 3, 1969, was full of promise. Kentucky's guards—Stan Key and Kent Hollenbeck—would be varsity starters most of the next three years, and forward Tom Parker would be the SEC's "Sophomore of the Year" the following season. With Parker and Harris, the game would feature two of the ten players selected to the Dapper Dan national all-star team. Even the coaches were both up-and-comers. Joe B. Hall would coach Kentucky to the 1978 NCAA championship, and Auburn's Larry Chapman would win more than 700 games in four decades as a college head coach. Even the venue was special—Memorial Coliseum in Lexington, probably the most historic on-campus arena in America, where four NCAA championship banners hung on the wall, all won in an eleven-year span. By the start of the second half of the freshman game, more than half the 11,500 seats would be taken. Kentucky fans cane out by the thousands for freshman games to evaluate their own young players and scout future SEC stars. Many had already heard of Harris. His reputation was spreading as the league's most talented freshman.

As knowledgeable as Kentucky fans could be, they could also be very hard on black players, but Harris responded to the hostility with grit, just as he had at Ole Miss. He had twenty-one points at halftime, and, by the end of the game, had forty-three.

Kentucky's Hall had structured his defense to run Auburn out of its patterned "shuffle" offense, creating numerous one-on-one opportunities for Harris, and Kentucky had no one who could stay with him. Harris hit pull-up jumpers inside fifteen feet and used his quickness to get open inside for layups.

Kentucky's up-tempo offense would beat Auburn, 98-75, but Harris could have run with Kentucky all night. "Henry was a flow player," Chapman said. "The more space, the better he could move." He scored another twenty-two points in the second half despite being knocked off balance while in the air and landing hard on his knees, shoving both kneecaps out of position. Chapman was not convinced it was an accident. "Henry jumped so high, they used to knock him down," he said.

Harris made sixteen of thirty-two shots and eleven of fourteen free throws, a remarkable performance on a big stage. The *Lexington Herald's* game story was headlined, "Kittens Win, But—Watch for Harris," and reported Kentucky's freshmen had gotten "a glimpse of a guy who may be lots of trouble in the seasons ahead." "Harris is an excellent ballplayer," Hall said afterward. ". . . You can't leave him open." Chapman agreed: "He's a good player all right. He's played great all year."

As well as Harris was scoring, he was playing in handcuffs. On many of his steals and breakaways, he could have dunked easily, but the NCAA had banned dunking a year earlier in reaction to the increasing number of dominating black players, specifically Lew Alcindor, who led UCLA to the 1967 national title as a sophomore. Kentucky coach Adolph Rupp was influential with the NCAA rules committee and lobbied hard for the ban, his 1966 team the victim of Dave "Big Daddy" Latin's historic power dunk early in the NCAA finals. The following season, Rupp saw Vanderbilt's 6-foot-4 Perry Wallace throw down a dunk over his own star freshman, Dan Issel, a future Basketball Hall of Famer.

Meanwhile, the freshman team that faced Harris was as white as Kentucky's varsity the night it lost to Texas Western in 1966. Since then, Kentucky had been either unable or unwilling to sign a black player, despite pressure from university president John Oswald and his hiring of Hall to recruit blacks.

Kentucky had attempted to recruit at least one black player in the high school class of 1968—Savannah's Joby Wright, the 6-foot-7 strongman recruited by Auburn. Wright spent an entire weekend at Kentucky but got only fifteen minutes with Rupp. "I'll never forget it," he said. "We shook hands and he [Rupp] said, 'Your hands are as big as meathooks.'" When Wright played at Kentucky as a sophomore at Indiana, "I was blown away, like 'Wow!'" he said. "I never got called the n-word so much in my life. They called me everything but the son of God."

Despite being the first SEC school to sign an African American to an athletic scholarship, Kentucky had achieved minimal racial progress since December 1965.

Three weeks after the 1967 death of Kentucky football player Greg Page from a half-speed practice injury, Nate Northington packed his bags, told teammate Phil Thompson, "I can't take this shit anymore," and slipped out of Lexington in the gloom of night. His guilt almost palpable, he told a reporter he could not live up to everyone's expectations: "I just couldn't make it. . . . I know I'm letting a lot of people down."

Before Northington left, though, he found Wilbur Hackett, Houston Hogg, and Albert Johnson, Kentucky's three black freshman football players. He told them he was packing up but *they* couldn't leave, that integration had to work. So they stayed, even on nights they wanted to leave. "Houston, Albert, and I had our bags packed more than once. On many nights. But we told Nate we would stay. He was fervent about it," Hackett said.

Hackett and Hogg did not see Page's injury occur and often wondered what had really happened. "I don't believe anyone tried to kill Greg, but I'm not sure someone didn't try to hurt Greg," Hackett said. "We did have some mean-spirited players that did not want us to play. You can tell when people don't like you."

"I don't know if it was an accident or someone did it on purpose," Hogg said, "but it shouldn't have happened. It was a non-contact drill—shorts, shoulder pads, and helmets." Neither player ever heard anyone talk much about Page's death. "To me, it was kind of hush-hush," Hogg said.

Chris Patrick asked about Page's death when he became Kentucky's new trainer in 1968. "Nobody would ever talk about it. I'd bring it up a couple of times for a learning experience for myself. It fell on deaf ears," said Patrick, who would go on to serve forty-two years as Florida's trainer.

The media accepted Kentucky's explanation that it was a freak accident, an account the administration had to repeat often because of Coach Charlie Bradshaw's reputation for brutality and Kentucky's legacy of racism. The *Louisville Courier-Journal*'s David Kindred reported the most widely held account: "The defensive line was to surround the quarterback, moving at half-speed with no intentions of making a tackle. But Greg stumbled. Someone shoved the quarterback. They bumped together. And the instant Greg's neck was snapped back by the collision, he suffered a paralyzing injury to his spinal cord."

Northington's departure came a dozen days after his game at Auburn. He was depressed, discouraged, and still living by himself, with Page's clothes still in the room. Even playing football reminded him of his roommate, and if any counseling was available, no one told him. Northington skipped some classes out of his despair. As a result, assistant coach Charley Pell took Northington's meal ticket away and suggested he eat at friends' homes, inferring that any African American would know other blacks in town.

But Northington's greatest emotional wound came the evening after Page's funeral in Middlesboro. He and the other twenty-six sophomores served as honorary pallbearers, but when their bus returned to campus, they learned they would pay for missing practice. They were put through a three-hour practice under the lights of Stoll Field that was classic Bradshaw and Pell, also a Bear Bryant protégé. By the time it was over, two starters and a third player had quit, and a fourth had gotten in a fistfight with a coach.

Three weeks later, having counted every block on the walls of his dorm room more than once, Northington became the eleventh player to leave the team in two and a half months. He would transfer to Western Kentucky and not talk publicly about his days at Kentucky for the next forty-five years. They were just too painful.

The final two stops on Harris's SEC welcoming tour were Baton Rouge, Louisiana, and Tuscaloosa, both loathsome sites for "firsts." "There was a lot of bigotry, a lot of talk at ball games, especially when we went further down South, down in Mississippi and Louisiana," said Tim Ash, from Shelbyville, Indiana. "They would call Henry names and use the n-word all the time on him. He took a lot of verbal abuse and shook it off like it was nothing and let his basketball ability speak for itself."

Ash was Harris's roommate on the road and recalled Harris being turned away from restaurants "more than once." "I said, 'Well, if he's not going to eat, I'm not going to eat.' So we left," Ash said. "Sometimes we'd talk them into it. 'Hey, we're from Auburn, we're playing here in town. We need to get something to eat.' Sometimes they'd say, 'Well, OK, that's fine.' Other times, they'd say, 'Sorry but we don't serve their kind.'"

At LSU, three years had passed since Press Maravich, Pete's father, became the coach and announced he wanted to recruit blacks before LSU President John Hunter quickly rebuked him, claiming, "My coach was misquoted." Maravich had even asked John Sibley Butler, a black LSU student, to walk on the team before giving up on the idea. Despite the pro basketball talent growing up in Louisiana in the 1960s—Willis Reed, Elvin Hayes, Bob "Butterbean" Love, Don Chaney—Maravich would wait five years to integrate his program, but he still would be ahead of the LSU football program.

LSU was a puppet of Louisiana state government, which had been the South's most virulent state in reaction to *Brown v. Board*. When Southwestern Louisiana signed three black players in 1966, the state board of education withheld their scholarships, prompting Coach Beryl Shipley to get the local black community to pay the players' tuition, room, and board, which landed the team on probation with the National Association of Intercollegiate Athletics.

In Tuscaloosa, Harris would play before friends from Boligee. He knew, however, the atmosphere would be quite different than when he was MVP of the high school all-star game seven months earlier. When Duke's first black player, C. B. Claiborne, played there the previous season, Alabama fans clustered behind the backboard when he shot free throws and waved Confederate flags. Harris had his lowest point output of the season.

Every time Harris showed up in a different arena, the message was the same, "Like it or not, here I am"—even if the band played *Dixie* as if he was invisible. Unlike Jackie Robinson who heard the same hatred on the road but also the appreciation of the thousands of African Americans there cheering him on, few blacks were in the seats awaiting Harris's arrival, save for a few custodians scattered around. The fans were white, the referees were white, the sports writers, all his teammates, and all his opponents.

Fear was the South's critical tool in controlling black Americans for a century, but Harris, like Wallace, felt the fear and walked onto the court anyway. They were rebels, revolting from everything southern society had tried to teach them, that they were inferior, not good enough to be on the same court, or classroom, with whites. What Harris was doing for two hours a night in basketball arenas were the latter steps of the civil right movement. But unlike marchers or protestors, he was alone in this traveling American morality play.

Harris knew all the myths and could never forget them on the court. He had to play with constraint. He couldn't look like he was out of control. He had been invited to the big dance, he had to behave. No pushing, not even pushing back. Anger from a black man was an American fear. "Never make America feel threatened," said Dr King. Yet, Harris had to play hard, harder than anyone else, or he would be written off as lazy. And he had to do it all on a racially charged stage. Harris was not playing the Tide or Bulldogs as much as he was taking on mythology, that African Americans lacked the intelligence, poise, and teamwork necessary for athletic greatness, or so it was thought, an unyielding myth that not even Texas Western could obliterate.

Harris heard enough of SNCC teachings in Greene County to understand anger was weakness in a nonviolent movement—it took more courage to stand down than hit someone. Nonviolence forced moral issues on the conscience, with Harris claiming the higher ground by playing on, no matter the tumult around him. Dr. King told Jerry LeVias, "A lot of things are going to be happening to you, but the one thing most important is that you always keep your emotions in control."

When Auburn's Wally Tinker intentionally hit Vanderbilt's Wallace in the back in his first varsity home game and no foul was called, Wallace wondered how he should react. He wondered if Vanderbilt fans would support him attacking a white player and how Auburn's fans would treat him at Auburn later in the season. (Tinker was captain of Auburn's varsity during Harris's freshman season. He would apologize to Wallace many years later.) Wallace decided to get even by playing his best to beat Auburn, which Vanderbilt did, but some blacks considered his response weak. "You had to walk a very fine line," Wallace explained, meaning Harris had to play assertively enough to prove he belonged in the SEC, yet under control. Somehow, he had pulled it off. When a game was over, he had his points, his rebounds, and his assists, and no one on the court had played tougher defense.

Harris heard the same hatred and ugliness that black minor leaguers had heard on their tours of the South in the 1950s, and swallowed his dignity, like they did. "If it was about dignity, there wouldn't be any blacks in baseball," said Frank Robinson, who moved on from a season in the South Atlantic League in 1955 to a Hall of Fame career and then history as the first black manager in the major leagues. Not everyone could play on. The New York Giants sent eighteen-year-old first baseman Bill White to their team in Danville, Virginia, where he was the only black in the Carolina League in 1953. White was talented enough to have a long major league career and wise enough to become the first black president of the National League, but he was only eighteen and unprepared emotionally for the hatred. He responded by shouting at his hecklers—before being removed from several games for his own safety.

The verbal abuse heaped on Harris and other pioneers went as unacknowledged by administrators, coaches, and teammates as physical violence historically had in the South. No one brought it up, so Wallace often wondered, "Am I crazy?" "You'd hear someone say they were going to lynch you or castrate you. Nobody else heard it, for some reason," he said. "People would say, 'You're too sensitive,' so I decided to keep it to myself. I felt if you're going to be a pioneer, there are certain situations you're going to have to handle in-house [on your own]." Racism was still the South's dirty secret, rarely mentioned in public. Sports writers didn't report what they were hearing all around them. They were unaccustomed to covering race, and most were part of the same social order Harris was challenging. Even Page's death received relatively little coverage outside of Kentucky.

Coach Chapman did not remember any slurs—"I think if anyone had said anything, I would have been fighting"—and neither did many of Harris's teammates, at least the ones from the Deep South. Acknowledging epithets, however, would have carried a challenge for whites. What are you going to do about it? Wallace longed for a teammate just to say, "Hey, you're not crazy. I heard those people out there calling you 'nigger' and threatening to hang you, and I just want you to know I'm with you."

For the season, Harris led the team in scoring with twenty-one points per game and rebounding with ten a game, as well as in assists and seven other offensive statistics even though the kneecap injury at Kentucky limited him the final month of the season. After leading Auburn in scoring in eight of its first nine games, he did so only once in the final nine.

Harris had created a great first impression. He had blown away any doubts of his coaches or teammates. He had disproved myths at Auburn and around the SEC. He had passed all the tests, passed them at Ole Miss, passed them at Kentucky, passed them night after night in arena after arena. He had done his job. He had proven blacks could play and fit in on Deep South teams. He defied all the stereotypes southerners had heard for so long, all the lies. Harris was a game-changer. He had proven he could play on the college level in spite of all the distractions, all the attention, and all the hostility.

"He was a natural, gifted, graced athlete, and he had in him that nature that you can't give a person," Chapman said. "Henry was like a sponge. He wasn't a guy who thought he was God's gift to basketball. He was just Henry. He was like a lot of kids in those days. There wasn't all kinds of visibility, a lot of publicity, and people whispering in your ear telling you how good you were. It was just basketball. Henry knew who he was." And he now knew why he was at Auburn. If he had not fully comprehended his mission at eighteen, he did after his tour of the SEC. His game was bigger than basketball.

On the Saturday afternoon in 1966 when Perry Wallace and his Pearl High School teammates were getting ready to head over to Vanderbilt to play in the finals of Tennessee's first integrated state basketball tournament, one of his teammates—Walter Fisher—was stopped on his way out by a teacher.

"Do you know what you're doing today," he asked Fisher.

"Yeah, I am getting ready to go play for a state championship."

Not satisfied with Fisher's reply, the teacher said, "Let me tell you what you're playing for. You're playing for every black face in the state of Tennessee."

Taken aback, Fisher finally asked, "What are you talking about?"

Fisher loved to play basketball, was really good at it, but this, he began to realize, sounded a lot like civil rights.

When he arrived at Vanderbilt's 10,000-seat Memorial Gymnasium, he saw lines of fans, black and white, already on the sidewalks, wrapping around the arena, waiting to get into a game they wouldn't dare miss. When he got inside, Fisher saw the stands were *already* full, and he finally comprehended the brief conversation he had with his mother that afternoon.

As he was leaving the house, Fisher had told her, "Mom, I'm getting ready to go to play for the championship. Is there anything you want to tell me?"

"Yeah," she said, before pausing for several seconds before speaking again. Finally, she said, "Win."

Now, three years later, no one had to tell Harris whom he would be playing for when he put on Auburn's varsity uniform in eight months. He had already figured it out—every black face in Alabama.

Chapter 15

Summer 1969

On the fifth anniversary of the signing of the Civil Rights Act, Harris was back in the news. While taking classes during a sleepy summer semester in Auburn, his name popped up at the top of a lawsuit. A group of nine former and current students at the University of Alabama filed suit July 2 in U.S. District Court in Birmingham against Paul W. "Bear" Bryant for failure to integrate the football team. The class-action suit listed fourteen recent black Alabama high school athletes as the "class" Bryant had not signed. Despite being a basketball player, Harris was second on the list, behind only James Owens, a nationally recruited running back from Fairfield who had signed with Auburn in December.

The lawsuit against Bryant and his assistant coaches originated within Alabama's student-led Afro-American Association. It was funded by the NAACP and filed by U. W. Clemon, a Birmingham civil rights attorney. "What we are contending," Clemon said, "is that the University of Alabama, a state school, has not pursued black athletes with the same determination that it has pursued white athletes and thereby has denied blacks equal protection under the law. . . . We contend that the state has a responsibility under the Fourteenth Amendment to treat all citizens equally."

Clemon compared the percentage of black athletes at Alabama with the large percentage of blacks playing high school sports in the state. "It is quite unrealistic to think that no blacks can be found to play football for the Crimson Tide," wrote the campus newspaper, the *Crimson White*.

Clemon, a twenty-seven-year-old attorney, had seen racism up close growing up in Birmingham. He, his brother, and a friend were once walking down a city street when a squad car pulled up beside them. The policemen made Clemon's friend get in the car and drove off. They eventually stopped the car and made the youth urinate on himself. Their entertainment over, the officers took him back to Clemon and his brother.

After Clemon enrolled at Miles College, he helped organize the successful 1962 Miles student boycotts of downtown Birmingham stores, which created the momentum Dr. King tapped into in 1963. Clemon then used the state's policy of paying for blacks' out-of-state graduate education to attend Columbia Law School, graduating in 1968. He returned home with a degree in hand and started filing suits that would "shake the cultural foundation of Alabama."

Black student leaders, meanwhile, formed the Afro-American Association in 1968, with Dianne Kirksey, Harris's onetime girlfriend in Greene County, helping to write the charter. After two more years of seemingly futile discussions with Bryant, the students filed suit.

Black students at Alabama had threatened Bryant with a lawsuit in 1967 but backed off when Bryant allowed five black students to participate that year in spring practice—Doc Roane, Antonio Pernell, Art Dunning, Melvin Leverett, and Jerome Tucker. But Pernell was the only one of the "Alabama Five" still around for the 1968 spring game. A 5-foot-8, 150-pound receiver, Pernell had not even wanted to attend Alabama. "I knew I wasn't wanted there, but I felt like I had to go. . . . We said the Pledge of Allegiance to the flag every single day. The pledge said 'justice for all,' and I figured that included me too," Pernell said. Alabama's players were "distant" but less rude than a professor who joked in class that he was "more tired than a field nigger."

But when Pernell returned to Tuscaloosa for 1968 preseason practice, Bryant told him he had to give up his scholarship from the United Presbyterian Church. Bryant explained the NCAA limited schools to having 125 football players on scholarships of any kind and that allotment was already full. The choice was obvious. Unable to complete his education without a scholarship, Pernell quit the team, and the Crimson Tide was all white again.

Harris spent the summer of 1969—the summer of the moon shot and Woodstock—in Auburn, taking biology, economics, and some easier courses to maintain his athletic eligibility. He played pickup basketball every afternoon. He was still trying to learn how to survive at Auburn. He had been there nine months, but nothing was telling him he belonged there. If he had any doubt, it was vanquished in April when the *Auburn Plainsman* published its April Fool's spoof edition. On the front page was a headline: "Commies Incite Auburn Nigras to Riot, Loot." "I picked up a paper, and there it was as big as day," said Charles Smith, Harris's friend and fellow freshman.

Smith had also graduated from a rural "training school" and likewise was struggling with culture shock. "I was ready to go, and then in April of '68, Dr. King was killed. What a blow! Riots and fighting and confusion. It's just a mess," he said. "And you're just eighteen years old and soaking all this in. What's life going to be like now? So I ended up at Auburn trying to figure out what it's going to be like dealing with these white people. I've never seen so many white people in one place in my life."

Harris, a first-generation college student from a small community, should have been an ideal fit for Auburn, a school without pretension and a motto of "a spirit that is not afraid." Auburn was loved by its students and alumni because it felt like family, its overall friendliness and spirit perhaps unmatched by any other large southern university. But the family feel that appealed to Harris during recruiting and should have made integration easier for him was two-edged. Blacks had never been part of the family. "Everyman's school" had always been every white man's school. It exemplified the "left-out" anguish of southern society itself.

No effort was made by Auburn or any social organization to assimilate Harris into university life. University administrators, whether by naiveté or intention, did nothing to help Harris, Smith, or any black student navigate the culture gap, but Auburn was no different than any large southern university in the 1960s. Courts had ruled all students should be treated equally, and administrators followed the law by simply treating blacks and whites the same, being still years away from realizing the needs of students from all-black schools or predominantly black communities. That's why it was determined Harold Franklin, Auburn's first black student, should walk from his dormitory to the library without a safety escort on his first day on campus. Many whites were on the lookout for any sort of preferential treatment of African Americans, so if no white student would be given an escort, why should Franklin? The Auburn athletic department followed the same mantra with Harris—"we treat all our athletes the same."

But Harris's experiences, past and present, differed from those of his teammates, although they rarely thought about it because most had never had a black friend. Separation of the races had bred ignorance. Few whites knew what blacks were going through, and they didn't have to. Privilege entitled them not to have to understand African American life, so myths and stereotypes filled the vacuum. White-owned media had ignored blacks' day-to-day challenges in the South to such a degree that in 1957 a thousand paratroopers had to enter a U.S. city—Little Rock—so American kids could go to school.

Although he may have been invisible to whites in Boligee, Harris was not at Auburn. White students parted like the seas when Harris walked across campus and stared at him when he entered a classroom as if to ask, "What are you doing here? Are you the janitor?" He was, in fact, more at ease around one of Sewell Hall's black custodians, Willie Pitts, than he was with most of its residents. "We got along together real good," Pitts said. "He'd come by my house." But when Harris returned to campus, he was back on, essentially, racial probation, always watching himself, how he appeared, what he might say.

Author Ralph Ellison believed history had conditioned young black Americans for such challenges. They had to learn early to watch themselves around whites, he said, to hold themselves in check, to never ask for exception. "The child is expected to face the terror and contain his fear and anger precisely because he is a Negro American," wrote Ellison a decade earlier. "It is a harsh requirement, but if he fails this basic test, his life will be even harsher." Elizabeth Eckford, one of the Little Rock Nine who integrated Central High School, knew being a pioneer was "going to be rough, but knowing it and experiencing it are two different things," she said. Black teenagers who had lived all their life in the South's separateness could only guess what "rough" might look like. "The culture shock of a kid coming from the Black Belt to Auburn would have been huge," said Leah Rawls Atkins, an author and historian who was an Auburn history instructor then. "He [Harris] would have been a lost ball in high weeds."

Like many black men, Harris used a depilatory to shave. He'd mix Magic Blue powder with water and then cake it on his face for a minute or so until it burned off the whiskers, which he could then scrape off easily with a spoon. Because it was summer quarter and fewer athletes were on campus, Harris and his roommate, Pat Cowart, lived in a suite with football players. "Henry may have left a little mess in the bathroom, and somebody—they didn't holler but they were talking between themselves, I guess it was loud enough to hurt Henry's feelings. It didn't need to be said. He kind of quietened up," said Cowart, speaking in a soft, regretful tone decades later.

Lynn had assigned Cowart, a junior college transfer, to be Harris's summer roommate. "I grew up in Huntsville [in north Alabama], and we had always played and competed against black kids," Cowart said. "Henry and I got along well." When Harris said he wanted to sleep with the lights on, Cowart didn't push the issue or ask any questions. Dormitories could be scary places for early black students at southern universities. Wake Forest's first three football players awoke once to smoke pouring through the crack under the door. A note said, "Next time we're going to bring the matches, niggers."

Harris and his friend Gary Pettway had slept with the lights on when they spent the night at Bryant Hall on a recruiting visit to Alabama. "We were brought up to understand that when the lights went out, we had no help," Pettway said. "They [parents] literally let you know, 'We can protect you in the light, but we can't protect you in the dark.' Even though we knew change had occurred, we were mindful we were not full players. I think we all had the same intrepidness of what new world we were going into and what could happen." Harris had slept with the light or TV on while rooming with teammate Tim Ash at motels on freshman team road trips. Neither Ash nor Cowart ever wondered if Harris might feel safer with a light on. "That never crossed my mind," Cowart said.

Cowart and Harris got along well that summer. "There wasn't a lot of people in school," he said. "We'd go to class and play basketball every afternoon." The pickup games were making an impression on varsity coach Bill Lynn, who wrote star guard John Mengelt that Harris was working hard and had "improved more than seems possible."

Laid back for a college coach, Lynn had a fatherly relationship with Harris. When asked by a friend why he chose Auburn and Lynn as a coach, Harris responded, "He was just like a father." Lynn knew what it was like to be poor in the rural South. He had grown up on a dirt farm in north Alabama, near Cullman, one of ten kids trying to survive the Depression. He was barely eighteen when he joined the Navy to go to the war in the Pacific.

Realizing Harris's economic situation, Lynn occasionally invited him to his house to do odd jobs to earn spending money. "Henry would come over to the house, and Daddy would give him jobs to do, because he never had any money," said Bill Lynn Jr. "I can remember him putting together a set of twin beds for us." Lynn's payment of Harris violated NCAA rules, and even if charitable, his actions smacked of Harris as a hired hand, the South's typical white-to-black experience.

Lynn's four children really liked Harris. The family's dog did not. "We had a dog that didn't let anybody in the yard," said Bill Lynn Jr., a teenager at the time. The dog was a German shepherd, the breed police used to attack protesting children and teens in Birmingham in 1963. "One time the dog got after Henry, and Henry climbed up on top of the car," Lynn Jr. said. "He was on top of my dad's car, on the roof." Six years after Birmingham, 6-foot-3 Henry Harris—high school valedictorian and the most prized basketball player to come out of Alabama—was on top of his coach's Chevrolet, essentially treed like a slave running for his freedom a century earlier.

While white Americans walked on the moon in late July, black Americans in Greene County went to the polls for the most important election of their lives.

The National Democratic Party of Alabama, with its Black Panther symbol on ballots, qualified more than a half-dozen blacks for Greene County's November 1968 general election, but probate judge Dennis Herndon disqualified them. The party had filed suit and appealed the case to the U.S. Supreme Court, which ordered Herndon to put the blacks back on the ballot. He refused, knowing that the long-dreaded black rule would follow. The NDPA went back to court, and the Supreme Court ordered a new election with everyone's name on the ballot.

When voting day arrived July 29, Greene County's black Americans again dressed up to go to the polls. When the ballots were counted that night, four black farmers—Frenchie Burton, Vassie Knott, Harry C. Means, and Levi Morrow Sr.—were elected to the five-member county commission. And Robert Hines and J. A. Posey Sr. were elected to the school board, creating another black majority.

To even consider that blacks would rule Greene County politically was "unthinkable, a nightmare to whites," according to Jonathan Sokol, author of *There Goes My Everything*. But for African Americans who had toiled in Greene County and survived in the feudalistic Black Belt for decades, it was the culmination of a rebellion birthed when they formed carpools to buy groceries in other counties and then nurtured by courageous SNCC volunteers and Dr. King himself. It was, at last, Independence Day.

Chapter 16

Change Agent

A life is not important except in the impact it has on other lives.
- Jackie Robinson

When Harris returned to Sewell Hall for his sophomore year in September 1969, he found that Coach Lynn had assigned eight of his best players to one four-room suite. Harris was to live in Room 303 with Tim Ash, who had roomed with Harris on freshman road trips at the request of Davalos, because Ash was from Indiana and the rest of the freshmen were southerners. But a week or so into fall quarter, Ash moved in with Greg Austin, who had a vacant bed, and Lynn didn't assign anyone else to live with Harris. "There was a bunch of switching around going on," remembered Ash decades later. "I roomed with Henry for a while. I roomed with Greg for a while. I don't think I roomed with Henry that long."

"There was nothing sinister about it. It just turned out that there was an extra space and that's where Tim went," said Bill Perry, the team's student manager that year. "My perception at the time was that it had nothing to do with race. They were just good friends, listened to the same music. I didn't sense that there was any rejection of Henry at all."

Perry lived in Magnolia Hall but preferred staying in Sewell Hall and often ended up sleeping on Harris's spare bed in 303. Lynn had asked Perry "to keep an eye" out for Harris to ensure he wasn't having any difficulty in the dorm or on campus. Having grown up in middle Georgia, Perry had heard all the racist stereotypes about African Americans, but the more he got to know Harris, the more he realized "everything you've been told is a lie." "I felt real comfortable around Henry," he said, "to ask him anything, to talk about anything."

Room 303 actually looked like no one lived there. "I went in his room a bunch of times, but he didn't have anything in there," said Dan Kirkland, a freshman that year. "You see," said Jimmy Walker, a junior teammate and friend. "Henry wasn't prepared socially to live in that kind of environment. They furnished you with the bed, but you had to have the sheets and whatever else, and he didn't have any sheets. He just slept on the bed."

Knowing the Harris family might not be able to afford linens, Lynn had told Harris in a letter before he enrolled that he would provide linens. If Lynn actually followed through on his promise, Harris could have sold them for spending money or money to send home.

"I don't recall there being any pictures on the wall, any attempt at all to make it home," Perry said. "The rest of them [players] would take their room and fix it up with posters and pictures. Henry's room was empty, really sparse. He kept it really hot. He kept the heat on all the time."

Even if Sewell Hall still wasn't home, Harris knew his second year at Auburn would be better than his first, for he was no longer alone. The arrival of James Owens, Auburn's first black football player, made Harris's freshman year seem worth the ordeal. He had held his position long enough for reinforcements to start arriving.

James Owens was a fast, strong running back and one of the best football players in America in the fall of 1968, a third-team Parade All-American. He had offers from Ohio State, Nebraska, Oklahoma, and more than fifty other schools. For the first time in his life, he felt special. He was a marvelous athlete—an all-state basketball player and sprinter who placed third in the state in the high jump. He even had pioneer credentials, having integrated football at Fairfield High School, a blue-collar school near the massive U.S. Steel complex in suburban Birmingham.

Owens started high school at Fairfield Industrial, the all-black school Willie Mays dropped out of in the late 1940s to play professional baseball. To get there, he had to walk past Fairfield High School. "We'd get talked about, rocks thrown at us," Owens said. About a dozen black students had integrated Fairfield High that fall, 1965, and Owens decided to join them the next year, although he was not allowed to play football as a sophomore. Coach Red Lutz told him he didn't want to be responsible for protecting him at road games and he should play intramural football—"I was the best touch football player you'd ever want to see," he recalled. Others thought so too because Lutz found a place for Owens as a junior even if he had to make all his players wear their helmets on the sidelines at road games. "They'd say, 'Whatever you do, don't take your helmet off.' And people would holler at you and call you all sorts of names and throw stuff at you from the stands, using all sorts of racial epithets. 'Get that coon.' It was kind of scary," said Virgil Pearson, a black teammate. When Lutz moved Owens from receiver to running back as a senior, "they [opponents] couldn't tackle him," Pearson recalled.

Owens wanted to go to Tennessee because it already had black players, but his mother thought Knoxville was too far. He was offered a scholarship to Alabama, even shook hands with Bear Bryant, but Auburn assistant coach Jim Hilyer developed a close relationship with Owens's parents, appealing to their faith. Owens felt Hilyer was "gentle and Christian" and showed respect for his parents at a time when many whites still spoke to black adults like children.

At Auburn, Owens and Harris quickly became friends—once they met each other. Because football and basketball players were on different practice schedules, lived on different floors, and rarely intermingled in the dining hall, Harris and Owens were naturally isolated from each other, and Sewell Hall's resident supervisor, Brownie Flournoy, tried to ensure it stayed that way. "When I got there," Owens remembered, "Brownie told me Henry was a gangster, a thief, was this and that. That was to keep us away from each other. So I was kind of afraid of Henry. I'd go the other way when I saw him coming. Then one day he sat down with me and we started talking, and I found out he was all right."

Harris would thrive as a mentor to Owens, always attempting to find something positive to focus on. "If Henry had not been there, I probably wouldn't have stayed at Auburn my freshman year. He talked to me about all the things he had been through and made it sound like things were a little better than when he was a freshman," Owens said. "We were together all the time. He always tried to find things for us to do."

The signing of Owens by the Auburn football staff had been even more shocking than the signing of Harris. Football coach Ralph "Shug" Jordan had complained to university president Harry Philpott about Lynn signing Harris, saying it created pressure on him to integrate football. "He [Jordan] was cautious. He grew up in Selma," Philpott recalled later. "I would say when I came [in 1965] if I had told him he had to [recruit blacks], he probably would have resigned. As we went along, he very definitely, on his own, saw this [integration] was something that was going to take place and he might as well take advantage of it."

Jordan warned Hilyer there could be pushback from fans and he, Hilyer, would be the recipient. A Catholic, Jordan was discriminated against when seeking high school coaching positions after graduating from Auburn and before going off to war. He took a shrapnel wound at Utah Beach and then participated in the Okinawa campaign in the Pacific. He was lured back to Auburn in 1951 to save a ship going under, but he did more than that, constructing a power where one had never really existed, winning the 1957 national championship and creating one of the South's toughest teams.

The athletic director who brought Jordan back to Auburn was Jeff Beard, an Auburn alumnus who, by 1969, had been AD for eighteen years and was so well respected that he was chairman of the SEC's athletic directors committee. Following Kentucky's loss to Texas Western in the 1966 NCAA finals, Beard wrote his friend Adolph Rupp to congratulate him on a fine season. "Those of us at Auburn still feel that you have the best team and should be the national champions," he wrote. "I certainly feel that your team is the Caucasian national champions to say the least." Beard received hate mail when news circulated that Auburn was recruiting Harris, with one fan writing: "It is beyond me why Auburn, in particular, and any other Southeastern Conference school, thinks they have to join the parade and go out and recruit Negro athletes. You will probably have enough trouble with that without going out and looking for it. It seems to me you should be concentrating on how to avoid the situation rather than plunging ahead to embrace it." Beard replied: "I share many of the thoughts expressed in your letter, however, some I do not. . . . I do not know what the future holds for our athletic program."

The belief among the Auburn coaches in the mid-1960s had been that when integration finally arrived, "Auburn would probably follow the lead of the University of Alabama," said longtime track coach Mel Rosen. "There were some differences of opinion about recruiting African Americans, some tense moments." Rosen wanted to recruit black track athletes long before he was finally allowed to in 1971, but "if I had pushed the administration, I probably would have been fired." Basketball and football integrated first because of "more pressure to win," Rosen said. "If we didn't recruit black athletes, we couldn't compete successfully against schools that did."

If a desire to be competitive was a carrot, federal financial pressure was a potential stick pushing all SEC schools toward integration. In 1965, presidents of universities receiving federal funding had to start certifying annually that their college adhered to the Civil Rights Act. The following year the American Civil Liberties Union filed a discrimination complaint, saying the importance of athletics in the SEC "cannot be overemphasized," and the U.S. Office of Education soon began collecting data on athletic scholarships, threatening that noncompliance could lead to funding cuts. And whether coincidence or not, the signing of Harris came six months after a 1967 visit to campus by Department of Health, Education and Welfare representatives. An August 15, 1969 letter—from the chairman of the Auburn faculty committee on athletics, Charles F. Simmons, to his counterpart at Alabama, Willard F. Gray—detailed the visit:

> Approximately two years ago [late summer 1967], we had a team from the Department of Health, Education, and Welfare visit us in regard to the matter of Negro athletes on the Auburn campus. The meeting was cordial and seemed to be mostly in the nature of a visit to get information about the status or future status of Negro athletes on the Auburn campus. It was explained to the team that Negro high school athletes had been scouted by our coaches and that we were sure that when they found Negro athletes who had good athletic ability and were reasonable risks, academically, they would be actively recruited.

The presence of Harris did little to change long-held beliefs of some members of the athletic department. "Daily meal attendance reports" sent to Beard from Sewell Hall still broke down the number of meals served into five groups—students, coaches, guests, staff, and "colored employees."

The athletic department, however, largely mimicked the university, which continued not to pursue black students, faculty, and administrators. And progress was just as tardy in the Auburn community. When the Atlanta Hawks and Chicago Bulls came to Memorial Coliseum for a regular-season game in the fall of 1969 as part of a doubleheader featuring the Harlem Globetrotters, Lou Hudson tied a Hawks franchise record with fifty-seven points. Yet, he and his black teammates were, at least initially, unable to eat a meal at the Heart of Auburn Motel. And when football players were made to get their hair cut by Coach Jordan, Owens asked his teammates where to go. "They said there was a barber shop in downtown Auburn, so I went in there and said, 'I need to get my hair cut,'" Owens said. "And the guy said, 'No, we can't cut your hair. You're going to have to leave here.' He went on to say, 'Please don't get my business in trouble, go on and leave if you will.' I said, 'Okay.' So Henry told me about the guy across the tracks, and I went there and got a haircut."

Outside of Auburn, however, Harris was having a major impact. Of the SEC's other six Deep South schools, four followed Auburn's lead and integrated their football or basketball programs within a year of Harris's signing. Alabama and Georgia signed a basketball player, and Florida and Mississippi State signed two football players each. Any gentleman's agreement was finally torn asunder, and Harris was the catalyst. Only Ole Miss and LSU remained all white in both football and basketball, and both would integrate their basketball teams the following year. Additionally, three other major Deep South colleges—Georgia Tech, Clemson, and South Carolina—also integrated their athletic programs within a year of Harris's signing.

Although Harris was changing the rules everywhere else, he had to wonder if he was just a token black at Auburn. His coaches chose not to sign a black player to follow Harris in 1969. The closest they came was a questionable—in their mind—6-foot-6 prospect out of Birmingham's inner city who Davalos thought was too skinny for SEC competition and needed to go to junior college first.

Parker High School, Birmingham's huge downtown black high school, won Alabama's first integrated state basketball tournament in 1969, and one of its stars was 6-foot-6 Wendell Hudson. Yet the only colleges interested in him were junior colleges and historically black colleges—and Alabama, whose coach, C. M. Newton, was still looking hard for his first black player. After a month of hesitation, he offered Hudson a scholarship. "Wendell was the most unsung player on the team, but he was in the top ten percent of his class," said Newton, who knew a more publicized recruit might make integration easier. "But after a while, our staff felt like, 'Let's go with our instincts.'"

When Lester McClain signed a football scholarship with Tennessee in 1967, his mother cried because it was the greatest thing ever to happen to the family, but when Hudson decided to go to Alabama, his mom cried because of fear, convinced her son would be killed. At the signing, she anxiously asked Newton how he would be treated. He replied: "I don't know. I'm a middle-class white guy who works there. All I can promise you is how he will be treated by our staff."

Like Harris, Hudson was friendly and easygoing, and his urban family was similar to Harris's rural one—a teenage mom, no father figure. He lived near Dynamite Hill and so close to the Sixteenth Avenue Baptist Church that he felt the bomb blast that murdered four black girls in 1963. One of his teachers at Parker was the mother of one of the girls. Founded in 1899, Parker was the primary source of the participants in the 1963 Children's March.

Newton and Hudson both got plenty of hate mail, but Hudson's was from blacks—"I can't believe you're going to Alabama. You sold out." But Hudson knew he was getting an opportunity people had died for and refused to forsake it. "If you want to play basketball, you have to take some chances somewhere down the line," said Hudson, who did not turn anxious until he started packing. "All of a sudden, I went from being in my neighborhood, which was all black, to the only black player in a dorm with 160 to 170 other people. . . . It was scary."

As Hudson moved in, Bryant Hall was quiet, but by the time he went to dinner, the football players were back from practice. "I walked through the door and the cafeteria is all athletes, it's all noise, everyone's talking, plates clanging. By the time I got to the front of the line, it was quiet . . . ," Hudson remembered. "There was a little wall where you got your food. I turned the corner and the people serving behind the counter were black, and they were smiling. I had more food on that plate than I could eat."

Eventually, Hudson began to tell himself, "I don't care if you want me here or not. I'm here. I didn't do anything wrong. The system was wrong. I have a right to be here." He would walk out of a freshman history class and take an "F" rather than listen to the professor talk about the joys of the Old South life for both races. Newton, meanwhile, kept his promise to Hudson's mom and treated her son like everyone else. He assigned him a white roommate.

Chapter 17

Captain America

In the foreboding dark days when the Nazis were rolling through Europe and the Japanese were building ships of war and slaughtering their neighbors, a hero arose from the thin pages of an American comic book. He came to slay evil, to vanquish the villains. It was 1941, and he was hope for a threatened nation. He was Captain America.

Three decades later, for black Americans sitting by radios across Alabama, for the black custodians and groundskeepers huddled at the corner of the court, and for all the people who needed him and had awaited him so long, Henry Harris—his black skin stark in Auburn's white-white uniform—was Captain America. He had come to slay the notion of white superiority, and like Robinson, Owens, and Louis, would shoulder the dreams and validation of a race, as the struggle for freedom through sports marched on.

Harris was the tip of a spear heaved by his forebears—the kings and queens his mom talked about, all the slaves who had lived and died between them and him, the field hands who persevered in the South for decades, waiting for a chance to prove themselves. It was as if they had ushered him out of the cotton fields, a basketball in hand, to meet this appointed hour. He was an ideal face of the revolution because he represented the abject rural poverty that had imprisoned blacks across the Deep South. He was the Old South. But he symbolized African Americans' ability to compete with whites on a level playing field, and thereby, in life itself. He was a young black man playing free on a basketball court in Alabama with young white men—no wonder he was always smiling. It might have been just a basketball game to his teammates, but Harris was playing the enemy every game. A year into the experiment, he knew what was at stake.

The South needed him. America needed him, especially at Auburn, deep in the Heart of Dixie, where some children had grown up and never heard a positive word about a black American, a family tradition shoved down through the ages. Harris was taking all that on, changing one mind at a time with his composure and competitiveness, possibly transforming a family for generations forward. By applauding Harris, Auburn fans did not have to take a stand on school desegregation or interracial dating. They were just cheering their team, their guys. Using his God-given talent, work ethic, and countenance, Harris enabled southerners to see what black and white cooperation looked like.

By simply wearing the Auburn uniform five times during the first fifteen days of December 1969, standing side-by-side with white players, Harris became part of history. Not the history he was making, but all the history that had gone on so long. Auburn history, significant southern cultural history. The uniform did that. When black Americans marched to war for their country in the 1940s, their uniforms were more celebrated by black communities than by the soldiers and sailors themselves. They were a badge of being good enough, of making the team. On April 15, 1947, before his first game in Brooklyn's Ebbets Field, Jackie Robinson stood looking at himself in the mirror, looking to see if the uniform fit, *really* fit. It was a challenging view even for him to accept. Now, a basketball uniform that had excluded, embodying racial purity, suddenly included. Henry Harris, in Auburn navy and orange, was the New South.

When Auburn opened the season December 1, the lights were turned off in Memorial Coliseum for the pregame introductions and spotlights found each starter as he trotted onto the court. Harris received the largest applause, a testament to the impression he made as a freshman and the number of whites ready for athletic integration. His first game was against the No. 1 team in America, South Carolina, top-ranked in both preseason wire-service polls even though an all-white team had not won the NCAA championship in eleven years. Harris was a natural to defend Carolina guard John Roche, the cover boy of *Sports Illustrated's* college basketball preview issue, but instead, because of his strength and leaping ability, helped defend against South Carolina's massive front line of Tom Owens and Tom Riker, 6-foot-10 New Yorkers, and John Ribock, a 6-foot-8, 235-pounder. He scored only six points in a lopsided loss before fouling out.

"Playing an unfamiliar position [forward], Harris couldn't get the ball," wrote *Birmingham News* sports writer Clyde Bolton, who reminded Harris afterward he had received the most applause before the game. Harris smiled but said, "I doubt if I will next time, though. I don't think I did anything tonight." Bolton asked Harris what he was thinking about as he became Auburn's first black varsity athlete. "It didn't have that much of an effect," he said. "The only thing I was thinking about was a winning effort—which I didn't provide." Harris told Bolton integration was going without incident. "The only problems I've had are the problems ordinary students have." He remained evasive when asked why he chose Auburn, replying, "I've been asked that question a thousand times, and I've given a thousand different reasons."

Coach Lynn bragged to Bolton about Harris's assimilation. "He's liked by the students and he is popular in the dormitory." Then, as if suddenly realizing Harris was living by himself, Lynn said, "I don't have a boy who wouldn't room with Henry as quickly as anybody else. . . . I didn't sign Henry because he was colored, I signed him because he was the best guard in Alabama." Lynn called Harris the perfect pioneer. "The first one had to be the right kind of boy. We told him we couldn't go into this blind. It was a critical time here."

What Lynn did not tell Bolton was that he was having difficulty assimilating Harris into the offense and blending together the most talent he had ever coached. Junior guard John Mengelt had averaged nineteen points per game as a sophomore, and co-captain Carl Shetler was back at point guard, so Harris became a forward as Lynn tried to put his best five players on the floor at one time. But before Auburn headed to Clemson later in the week, he told reporters he planned to move Harris to guard. "We feel like we need to get the ball to Henry. He can score and we've got to shift things around so we can get it to him," Lynn said. "It's hard for a good player to play without the ball. And Henry's electrifying."

Only two months earlier, most of Clemson's seventy-five black students had fled campus because of racial tension, before eventually returning. Among the students' complaints were the use of a Confederate flag at sporting events and the racial taunting of visiting black basketball players. When the ACC's first black football player, Maryland wide receiver Darryl Hill, was scheduled to play at Clemson in 1963, longtime coach Frank Howard threatened first to withdraw from the ACC and then to not allow Hill in the stadium. But Hill made it inside, although ticket-takers denied admission to his mother until she was rescued by Clemson's president, who invited her to sit in his private box. During warmups, Hill looked for other blacks in the stadium but could only spot some outside on the dirt slope that whites called "nigger hill." His anger so motivated him that he broke the ACC single-game record with ten pass receptions.

Clemson's football and basketball teams were still all white, and Harris heard plenty of taunts and again scored only six points. Two nights later, he finally faced a black opponent when Wake Forest came to Auburn with its two talented guards, Norwood Toddman and Charles Davis. Harris responded to the more fast-paced tempo by scoring nineteen points. When Auburn hosted Ole Miss, Harris struggled again, scoring only four points.

Mississippi State, which refused to play Harris a year earlier, came to Auburn December 15. Harris was ready. He scored twenty-one points, made eight of thirteen field goal attempts, and stole the ball five times. "He might have scored thirty or forty if Lynn had felt like leaving him in. He was that good," wrote the *Atlanta Journal's* Kent Mitchell. He received an ovation when he left the game. "Harris trotted over to the Auburn bench," Mitchell wrote, "put on his warm-up jacket and sat down, trying to control the shy smile that kept flashing on and off his face." Lynn pulled Harris out with ten minutes still to play—only two nights after letting Mengelt stay on the floor long enough to break the Auburn single-game record with forty-seven points.

By early January, Harris was back at forward for good. After he scored thirteen points against Florida and twenty-one in a loss to Georgia, Lynn continued to tell reporters what a great player Harris *would* be. "Henry Harris is coming along real good. He's a good ball player, but believe me, he can be a great one," he said. "We're playing him at forward, but he'd probably be better at guard. We believe in playing the five best boys we have, and Mengelt and Shetler are proven guards who played together all last year."

Auburn went to LSU next, held Pete Maravich to 37 percent field goal shooting—he still scored forty-four—and everyone who played for Auburn scored in double figures, except Harris, who took only seven shots. In the locker room afterward, the team was told John Retseck, the brother of freshman Jim Retseck, had been killed in Vietnam. "It put some things in perspective. Here we were worried about some stupid ball game," said Dan Kirkland. "It was a funny time. Here we are bitching about how we didn't get to play when all the guys we went to high school with, who didn't go on to college, were over there getting killed."

Two nights later in Tuscaloosa, Harris took only nine shots but scored twenty points and made eight of nine free throws. At one point, he stole the ball, scored, and then scored again, completed a three-point play moments later, and, after two baskets by teammates, made another steal and basket.

Harris got six points and nearly a broken jaw in a loss that ended in a melee in Athens. The primary combatants were Georgia's 6-foot-11 Bob Lienhard and Auburn co-captain Bill Alexander, a muscular, 6-foot-6 center from north Alabama, the epitome of the Auburn work ethic. Lienhard took a swing at Harris—"if he had hit Henry, he would have broken his jaw," Lynn said—but Harris dodged the blow, and Lienhard's fist landed on his shoulder. Then, as the game ended, Lienhard flattened Mengelt in a charging/blocking collision and was last seen running up the tunnel toward the locker room with Mengelt in pursuit.

On January 24, Auburn and Vanderbilt made history in Nashville by playing the first SEC basketball game between integrated teams. The only two blacks in the SEC, Harris had fourteen points and Perry Wallace twelve. The next week in his debut on the SEC Game of the Week, Harris took only five shots but made four in a victory over Tennessee. Mengelt shot eighteen times for twenty-two points.

Three factors were affecting Harris's ability to score—the "Auburn shuffle," playing forward, and John Mengelt. The shuffle was a motion offense that stressed player and ball movement and high-percentage shots. It had been so effective it was on the cover story of *Sports Illustrated's* 1961-62 basketball preview issue. Created in the 1950s by Auburn coach Joel Eaves, he used it to win the SEC in 1960 with no starters taller than 6-foot-3, setting an NCAA season record with a 51.2 team field goal percentage. When Harris was a freshman, the varsity ranked second nationally in field goal percentage at 50.2, but Auburn players had been running the shuffle so long that some opponents were now beating them to their assigned spots.

"It was just a constant motion offense. You're just constantly moving, you're going here, you're going there," said guard Bobby Nix, who ran the shuffle on the freshman team that season, one year after leading all Kentucky high schools in scoring. "I came out of a system that was fastbreak, get it down the floor and produce something."

"As talented as he was, Henry sure got frustrated—a lot of us did—trying to run that dadgum Auburn shuffle," said Parks Jones, who played on the freshman team with Harris. "It wasn't a natural offense for athletic basketball players, but they insisted that was the plan, probably been done for centuries." Teammate Bobby York compared harnessing Harris with the shuffle's patterned movement to putting a "plow on a racehorse." "At the time of integration, black athletes were racehorses. There was a lot of catching up to do with a lot of these coaches," he said.

Although the shuffle made offensive positions interchangeable, playing forward defensively affected Harris's scoring ability. "The guy was out of position," Mengelt said. "When you're playing defense and you get caught underneath the boards, you really can't get out on the fastbreak, and that was more his game than anything else." When Harris was scoring in high school and on the freshman team, he consistently had the ball in his hands. "He kind of needed the ball to do his thing," Mengelt said.

Mengelt was a small-town Indiana star who chose Auburn because he liked the school's slower pace and the fact the SEC did not have the quicker black guards he'd have to face in the Big Ten. An all-state quarterback who could have gone to Notre Dame, Mengelt had an explosive jump shot and averaged twenty-seven points per game for the Auburn freshmen long before the NCAA adopted the three-point shot. As a sophomore, he scored a school record forty-two points at Kentucky. Shetler, the point guard, believed it would have been difficult for anyone else to become a significant scorer. "It would've been real tough," said Shetler, who considered Mengelt a shooter and Harris "a scorer, a slasher." "They were different players," Chapman said. "Mengelt was an offensive-minded player. Henry was a strong, competitive, and athletic guy."

Ironically, Harris, the black American, was more liked by his teammates. "He [Mengelt] didn't get along well with anybody," said teammate Tim Ash. Wes Bizilia, the graduate assistant who was the first to scout both Harris and Mengelt, said, "John was so cocky about himself. And that is sad. Good looking physically. Talented kid. Good smarts. Not liked by his own team." "You got the impression that John came first," Perry recalled. "He had his goals [to play in the NBA]. When he got it, he pretty much shot it."

Mengelt was notorious in SEC arenas, drawing technical fouls for scolding referees. Fans catcalled and booed him. "He was mean, he was nasty, and he was really good," said Georgia guard Tom Brennan. Mengelt seemed to relish the bad boy image. "Hey, those fans had some bad words for the man tonight, didn't they?" Mengelt once told the *Atlanta Journal's* Lewis Grizzard after a game. "They didn't like me a bit. I love it, though."

Watching from the bench that season as manager, Perry wondered why Harris never "turned loose." "He played hard but he was kind of going through the motions in a sense," Perry said. Daily practices at Auburn produced incessant verbal sparring that often erupted into scuffles. "It was a rarity that you didn't see a fight in practice," Perry said. "Henry wouldn't fight, which says to you he didn't turn loose." But Perry, and probably Harris's teammates, didn't understand what Harris was going through as an Auburn sophomore while everyone else was playing basketball. Harris couldn't fight; he had to stay under control. He knew he couldn't mess things up for his would-be successors.

Auburn dropped out of SEC title contention in early February by blowing a late seven-point lead at Florida, with Harris held to only six points in Alligator Alley. He scored only four against Mississippi State, the same team he scored twenty-one on in December, but this was his first game in State's Quonset-hut gym, where fans rang cowbells and beat plowshares against rafters. They started unloading on Harris during warmups but could not rattle his defensive intensity. He held high-scoring guard Jack Bouldin scoreless in the first half before being assigned to forward Randy Hodges, who had nine first-half baskets but would get only one against Harris.

On Valentine's Day, Alabama came to Auburn, and C. M. Newton was angry before the game even tipped off. During the freshman game, Auburn football players sitting behind the Alabama bench harassed Wendell Hudson, the Tide's first black athlete, saying, "some stuff that was just unbelievable," according to Newton, who went to athletic director Jeff Beard to clear out the players. "It was the most racial slurs I had ever heard," Hudson said. "'Nigger, go home. Nigger this, nigger that.'" By the end of the varsity game, however, Newton was furious. The final score was 121-78—the most points ever scored by Auburn and the most ever allowed by Alabama. Newton, starting five sophomores in his second season, was angry that Lynn subbed little until late in the game and allowed Mengelt to score sixty points, more than half of them coming in the second half. Mengelt took forty-four shots and did not leave the game until 4:09 was left. "John had fifty-eight points when he [Lynn] pulled John out," said Perry, who was keeping the scorebook on the bench. "I eased over to Coach Lynn and said, 'Coach, John has fifty-eight.'" Mengelt asked Lynn for a chance at sixty. "You can have one more shot and you'd better hit it," Lynn replied. Mengelt re-entered the game, got the ball, and scored in twenty seconds. Harris, ever the team player, had only ten points but eleven rebounds and six assists.

Lynn would have been better off backing his players off against Alabama—they made only 27 percent of their shots two nights later and lost at home to LSU. Harris had twelve points and ten rebounds. Maravich scored forty-six. By week's end, Auburn had lost again at home, to Vanderbilt. Harris got six points and Mengelt forty. Wallace had a big game, as if to say farewell to Auburn forever—eighteen points and nineteen rebounds.

At Tennessee, Harris hit a jumpshot to put Auburn ahead and had a game-high twenty-one points and eleven rebounds. At one point, an angry Chapman had to be restrained from going on the court. "I got really upset because something happened in the game, and it looked like they tried to hurt Henry," he said. At Kentucky two nights later, Auburn was blown out 102-81, its third loss in four games since running up the score on Alabama. Harris had fourteen points and eleven rebounds and was applauded loudly when he left the floor after fouling out.

Harris still had one more trip to make, to Ole Miss. Just six days earlier, Hudson had played in Oxford with the Alabama freshmen and gotten in immediate foul trouble. "I may have played eight minutes," he said. "It was a joke. We knew what was going on." Ole Miss students were right behind Alabama's players. "I'm sitting on the bench, the rebel flags are waving, and they're calling me every name in the book." Again, football players were the ringleaders. And again, Newton complained to the athletic director, Tad Smith, about "a hell of a lot of abuse." As soon as the Alabama team bus crossed the state line headed home, Hudson asked to stop; Newton thought he was sick. But when Hudson got out, he fell to his knees and kissed the ground, saying, "I've never been so happy to be back in Alabama."

The Ole Miss fans would again harass Harris. "Henry and I were sitting together," said Greg Austin, "and they were calling Henry, 'Nigger this and nigger that.'" Harris scored thirteen points and Auburn won to finish with a 15-11 record, but that was too many defeats for Harris. "Every time we got beat, it was a little tough on him," said co-captain Shetler.

Over the summer, Lynn had written Mengelt that "no one man can handle" Harris in the team's daily pickup games, yet Harris finished the season only third on the team in scoring. Years later, Newton broke down the problem by saying simply, "There's only one ball." Mengelt averaged twenty-seven points per game.

Still, Harris averaged 12.5 points and 7.5 rebounds per game and made the SEC's all-sophomore team. Perhaps more importantly, he passed a huge test by fitting in on a Deep South varsity basketball team. "Henry did very well with us. He got along fine with the players, the coaches, and never was a disruption," Shetler said. "Henry was a real good guy, you know, good to be around, good teammate. He was fun to be around."

During the season, Lynn became adept at discussing stereotypes without mentioning race. "Henry's never been a problem. You tell him something and you don't have to worry about it again. And he has gotten to be a good student, although he had a hard time with his school work when he started out," he said. Lynn told another reporter, "Before he leaves here, Henry will be a great one. He will be a great scorer too. We're playing him out of position as a forward. He needs to have the basketball. But we have had to play him as a rebounder and defensive man, covering bigger people every time he plays." Lynn said Harris would "definitely be a guard next season."

"I think we had a good year, all things considered," Lynn said. "We're fairly pleased." That was not a majority opinion on the coaching staff.

Chapter 18

Gone

Rudy Davalos and Larry Chapman, Auburn's assistant coaches, had hit their limit. The season was over, but the twenty-one-point loss at Kentucky was still reverberating in their heads. Auburn had come within a point of beating Kentucky a month earlier, so the blowout loss in Lexington was infuriating, indicating, to them, the program's direction.

It was a disappointing season. In a letter to the team in September, Lynn had called the group the most talented he had ever coached. Both Davalos and Chapman believed Lynn needed to be more demanding. "We had a lack of discipline. We felt like we should be way better than we were," Davalos said. The fatherly Lynn and his young lion assistants were on a collision course. The season was over, but the tension in the Auburn basketball office was palpable.

Davalos and Chapman were Type A personalities who had gotten the absolute maximum out of their ability as players, both being invited to the U.S. Olympic Trials, Davalos in 1960 and Chapman in 1964. Although loyal to Lynn, his college coach, Chapman was drawn to Davalos's competitiveness and vision for what Auburn basketball could become. "Rudy was a big influence in my life," Chapman said. "He was not a typical yes-guy about anything."

Davalos had worked as a graduate assistant coach at Kentucky and observed Coach Adolph Rupp's absolute commitment to the game and developed a similar focus as a coach. After leading Auburn's freshman team to an 18-0 season in 1963-64, he spent the summer coaching national teams in Australia. He dreamed of building a program that could compete with Kentucky for SEC titles. "He was a climber, a great politician, very cunning. He struck me as a street fighter," said Bill Perry, the Auburn manager. "I felt like he was about to explode to take over. I have no idea how he and Coach Lynn peacefully coexisted, but I don't remember Davalos ever disrespecting Coach Lynn." Davalos had all the right stuff—strategist, motivator, determined recruiter, master salesman. "He'd do or say anything to get you there," said sophomore Tom Bardin.

"A lot of people had problems with Davalos—I didn't," said Jimmy Walker, who would captain the 1970-71 team. "I liked him and the kind of coach he was. He didn't put up with a lot of crap." And even players who didn't always care for Davalos's ego liked having him on their bench. When an opponent would reel off a run of points, Lynn would turn and ask Davalos, "What do we do?" Davalos always had an adjustment. "Rudy did everything," said Carl Shetler. "Whatever decisions were made, I think Rudy was writing them out. We were his boys. I thought Coach Davalos and Chapman really did a good job, and Coach Lynn was smart enough to listen to them."

The 6-foot-6 Lynn was as unpretentious as his rural roots in north Alabama. He drove a white, standard-issue government car—with the Alabama state seal on the door—even on recruiting trips, but his unassuming nature built trust with families. Chapman's father trusted Lynn more than any other coach he met. "I knew Alabama was a long way away, and if you were going to leave, I wanted you to be around people I trusted," he said.

Harris picked up on the same easy vibe—"he seemed like a father," he told Perry, the manager. "I think Henry felt Coach Lynn's kindness and sincerity," Chapman said. "Coach Lynn had a great heart. Bill Lynn's heart was good. His nature was very caring."

After playing basketball in the Navy, Lynn earned a scholarship to St. Bernard Junior College in Cullman, Alabama. As a sophomore, he was second highest scorer in college basketball and earned a scholarship to Auburn. An athletic center, he led Auburn in scoring as a junior and senior. The following year, Coach Joel Eaves made him Auburn's freshman coach and, later, assistant varsity coach. When Eaves had a heart attack and could not coach the final two weeks of the 1962-63 season, Lynn filled in. So when Eaves resigned eight months later to become Georgia's athletic director, only weeks before the start of the season, Auburn quickly promoted Lynn.

Lynn's best seasons were his initial ones, prompting an attractive offer from Florida that he turned down. He was deeply loyal to Auburn, although his salary was so meager he supplemented it by building homes. "They didn't pay basketball coaches anything back then," Bill Lynn Jr. said. "We moved thirteen times before I left home. He was always building a house." The father of four, Lynn also owned a furniture store, and his responsibilities at Auburn even included recruiting football players during the offseason and teaching a physical education class at 7 a.m. Basketball was hardly a high priority. "If you won only ten games and beat Alabama, that would be okay," Perry said. Lynn clearly understood the importance of beating Alabama, having done so fourteen times in sixteen games as coach.

A paradigm shift was occurring in the SEC, however. "When Pete Maravich hit the world, basketball in the Southeast ratcheted up about ten notches," Perry said. "The crowds were so huge that the programs began to stand on their own financially, so there was more pressure to win." And more seats to fill. Maravich's arrival coincided with the construction of new arenas throughout the SEC. Auburn, Alabama, Georgia, and Ole Miss all moved into new, much larger arenas from 1964-1968, and Tennessee expanded its capacity.

Davalos and Chapman liked the increased pressure, and, in their mind, everything was coming together for Auburn. They were bringing in better and better recruiting classes every year. "We had signed great players. We had signed Jim Retseck, we had signed Dan Kirkland, we had signed Gary England, we had signed Bobby Nix, who transferred to Minnesota," Chapman said, referring to the 1969-70 freshman team. "What was happening after their freshman year was parents were starting to ask, 'Why isn't my child playing?' Bobby Nix was a helluva player. He didn't leave because he couldn't play. He left because he felt he wasn't going to get an opportunity to play."

It had reached a point where Davalos and Chapman preferred that Lynn not accompany them on recruiting trips. "He was not dynamic in any way as a recruiter," Chapman said. But recruiting had grown increasingly difficult for another reason. "Part of Coach Lynn's problems were being used against us in recruiting," Davalos said.

Bill Lynn was an alcoholic.

What had been a whispered but widespread secret had become louder the previous summer when Lynn wrecked his Volkswagen late one night in the middle of Auburn. He said he had fallen asleep. He also said he was "dodging some kid at three in the morning," recalled Chapman. "He had stitches in his head, had to shave his head, and was in the hospital." Prompted by opposing recruiters, high school players began asking Chapman and Davalos if Lynn was an alcoholic.

"My dad did have a drinking problem," said Bill Lynn Jr. "Dad swore he never drank before a practice or a game or anything like that, but I don't know. When you're an alcoholic, you're an alcoholic, and you're going to drink."

Lynn was a "periodic" alcoholic, or "binger," according to his son. "It wasn't like something that he did every day. He wouldn't even drink every week. He'd go two or three weeks and then he'd get drunk," said Bill Lynn Jr. "We didn't even have alcohol in the house. I didn't even know he drank. I saw him drunk for the first time when I was in the seventh grade, and that was the first I had ever heard of him drinking. And I was around him all the time. Sometimes he'd go two or three months without drinking, then he'd always end up drinking for some reason. It was very clear that he was an alcoholic."

Lynn had held on to his job because the Auburn athletic department at that time was run like "a mom and pop grocery store, a place that took care of its family and overlooked its transgressions," said Richard Hyatt, who covered Auburn for the *Atlanta Constitution*. "Auburn was isolated and stayed that way longer than most places. That would have made it harder for blacks to exist, because it was such an isolated, old-school place. Henry Harris was probably left to fend for himself." Auburn's isolation also shielded Lynn, as did the fact that "Alabama sports writers didn't give a rip about basketball," said Hyatt.

Harris would tell his friends he once came out of a game for a breather, sat down next to Lynn, and reached for the Coke he'd left under his chair. He mistakenly picked up Lynn's spiked Coke, took a sip, and immediately spit it out.

"Bourbon," Harris would tell listeners when retelling the story.

Auburn players occasionally smelled alcohol on Lynn's breath at practice, going back to the early 1950s, and by the time Harris arrived at Auburn, Lynn was drinking Old Crow regularly on road trips. The morning after Harris's first game at Ole Miss as a freshman, the team's student manager, Dan Jacobs, had to drive the varsity to the airport. "Coach Lynn was not feeling well that morning, and I took the team on the aircraft to Mississippi State and Coach Lynn came later by car," Jacobs said. A loss at LSU later that season turned particularly ugly when three players did not make curfew. Drunk, the 6-foot-7 Lynn sat up blocking the stairway, waiting to catch the trio. When they came in, he got up to go after them. The ensuing hallway shouting match woke up Bobby York, one of Harris's freshman teammates.

"I opened the door, and [Wally] Tinker was screaming at him [Lynn]," York said. "I saw him [Lynn] holding on to the wall, looking like he was going to fall, and my natural reaction was to run to grab him before he hit the floor." When York reached him, Lynn slapped him to break free. "It didn't knock me out, it probably hurt my feelings more than anything. I was coming out of a sleep, and all of a sudden my coach is backhanding me and cussing at me, saying he's going to take my scholarship away. I kind of backed off and went back in my room." Lynn didn't remember the incident the next day.

On the flight home from Florida in January, when Auburn lost on a twenty-five-foot shot at the buzzer, Lynn disappeared into the plane's restroom and "stayed in there forever," said Walker. "Finally, Coach comes out, and Henry had the most unusual laugh you've ever heard. Henry was sitting by me and kind of hit me to look because the back of Coach's shirt was hung up on the bottle he'd sucked dry in the bathroom and then stuck in his back pocket. So as Coach continued up to the front, everyone was looking and dying laughing."

The season's low point, though, came on the trip to Tennessee and Kentucky. As the players loaded the bus Sunday morning in Knoxville, Lynn was not there. They waited about an hour for him. "The players are making comments about it," Chapman said. "Finally, Kenny Howard [the trainer] goes and gets him and brings him out."

Chapman had tried to help his old coach but was overmatched by the disease. "I felt it was my place to look after him. I would never leave him," he said. "We didn't understand alcoholism like we do now." Viewed then as a weakness and moral failing, alcoholism carried a deep social stigma, especially in a small town. Yet, Lynn, a steward in the Methodist church, had the plain-faced courage to attend

Alcoholics Anonymous meetings in Auburn. "My mother had read up on it and they went," said Bill Lynn Jr. "Dad wanted to do the right thing, but it's a disease."

Days after the season ended, Davalos and Chapman went to see athletic director Jeff Beard. They asked Beard to make Lynn get help—or to make Davalos the head coach.

Not everyone believed their motives were so noble. "They tried to pull a *coup d'etat*," said Bill Lynn Jr. "They tried to get Daddy fired, so Rudy could take over as coach. My dad did have a drinking problem, but you're supposed to have a little loyalty."

During the season, Davalos had arranged for the *Constitution's* Hyatt to have phone interviews with Auburn players, hoping to expose what was happening in the basketball program. "He hooked me up with several players. They told me stories of Coach Lynn missing practices," Hyatt remembered. "He wanted to help those guys, but he also wanted that job."

After the postseason meeting with Davalos and Chapman, Beard met with the team's co-captains, Shetler, Bill Alexander, and Ronnie Jackson. "They called us in and asked us about the situation, who we supported," recalled Shetler. "When it came down to it, we all supported Coach Lynn. Of course, my loyalty has always been to the head coach."

Whether Davalos and Chapman resigned or were fired depended on whom one talked to—Chapman said in 2008 he resigned—but either way, they were gone. The athletic department wanted to issue a news release, but university president Harry Pillpott stopped it, so word of their departures drifted into the press and made little sense—both assistants were leaving simultaneously and neither had another position. Beard finally announced they had "resigned."

For all his astuteness, Davalos, the outsider, had misjudged his surroundings, misreading the significance of Auburn loyalty. The actions of Davalos and Chapman were seen as a "revolt." "Daddy was Auburn through and through, 100 percent Auburn, wanted what was best for Auburn," said Bill Lynn Jr. "Coach [Shug] Jordan and [football coaches] Paul Davis, and Gene Lorendo—Mel Rosen [track coach] lived next door—they were Daddy's friends and they still were until the day he died. Davalos was kind of an outsider. He was never accepted by that bunch. He wasn't Auburn."

Lynn and the Auburn athletic family were willing to forgive Chapman, the former Auburn player, believing he was unduly influenced by Davalos, and tried to convince him to stay. But Chapman told Lynn, "Coach, I can't do this anymore. I just can't be a part of bringing kids in here anymore. We talked a minute and I said, 'Coach Lynn, my mind is made up. I didn't want it to happen this way, and I wish you didn't drink.'"

Upon losing their jobs, Davalos and Chapman went to Sewell Hall and called their players to the lobby, telling them, "We asked Coach Beard to make him get help. We gave him instances." "But Beard called them disloyal," said Bobby York. "They had tried to talk to Coach Lynn until they were blue in the face. It [alcoholism] affected them too." None of the players went to Beard. "If they were fired, what would he do to us [for speaking up]?" asked York.

Nix, the freshman guard who had led all Kentucky high schools in scoring with 30.4 average per game a year earlier, came to Auburn because of Davalos and Chapman. "I just packed up and left. I didn't say anything to anyone," he recalled. Freshman Dan Kirkland, a high school All-American, was also recruited by Chapman and Davalos. "They ended up getting fired for reporting Coach Lynn's drinking," Kirkland said, "and that left all of us who were close to those guys kind of in the lurch."

But no player would miss Davalos and Chapman more than Harris, who was already living on an island at Auburn. He would play his final two years without the team's best coaches and without the men who most wanted him there. They were gone, vanished, just like his father, just like his uncle Thomas Edmonds, and just like Lieutenant Gooden, who went to jail one night and was dead two days later.

Chapter 19

Ghost Man

On Saturday night, March 7, 1970, in his final game at Vanderbilt, Perry Wallace got twenty-nine points and twenty-seven rebounds, received a plaque and platitudes at halftime, and drew a five-minute ovation when he left the game. Wallace was voted team captain by his teammates, chosen All-SEC by coaches, and elected "Bachelor of Ugliness," the highest honor on campus, by fellow students. He was on track to graduate in the spring with a B average in a double major of electrical engineering and engineering mathematics. As the first African American to complete an athletic career in the SEC, Wallace had written a resounding success story for racial progress. But that was not the story on Wallace's mind when he talked to *Nashville Tennesseean* education reporter Frank Sutherland for two hours the day after his final game.

"It is ironic to be elected Bachelor of Ugliness because I have been a very lonely person at Vanderbilt," Wallace told Sutherland in his deep, deliberate voice. " . . . I know some people will say I am ungrateful, but that's the way it's been. If I don't say this at some time in my life, it would be too much unbearable pressure." Wallace said more students wanted to celebrate him than actually know him. "They respected my basketball ability but they still considered me as a person who sweeps floors . . . ," he said. "The last year I lived in a dorm, there were guys right across the hall from me who made an effort *not* to speak to me."

Wallace knew he was writing his ticket out of his hometown, that there would be no local job opportunities despite his Vanderbilt degree, but he needed to speak his truth. Not doing so would be like—in the words of Andrew Maraniss, his biographer—Lewis and

Clark touring America and telling no one about the trip. "An institution would like to be able to say we took the risk and everything worked out fine. And I wanted to too," Wallace explained years later. "That's why I never really said anything about it until it was over, and I began to realize there would be others coming along, and if they didn't find out, they could be traumatized coming into that experience. I was the only one who knew how harmful that sort of experience could be to a young person."

The article appeared on the front page Monday morning. Calls flooded the *Tennesseean's* office all day. Subscriptions were canceled.

Wallace had also spoken openly as a junior when asked to address Vanderbilt's Human Relations Council. His seven pages of remarks were forthright and eloquent, yet poorly received. Days later, an athletic department administrator suggested to Wallace that if he was unhappy, he should leave. Wallace replied, "Sir, it isn't my job to leave. It's not my job to get up and leave injustice in a country that claims to have justice. I have a right to be here like anybody else, and I'm not going to leave Vanderbilt."

Harris, like Wallace, was a revolutionary, assigned to live behind enemy lines and not free to leave. He had two assignments—hold his position until reinforcements could arrive and, in the meantime, blow up every negative stereotype teammates, classmates, and anyone else around Auburn had heard all their lives about African Americans. He was to accomplish his missions however he could. He had no manual. By his sophomore year, though, his strategy was apparent—show up, try to fit in, and then disappear.

Dianne Kirksey, the Greene County girlfriend Alabama tried to use to recruit Harris, thought he was "fitting in" when she visited Auburn as a member of Alabama's dance troupe and Harris introduced her to his teammates. "They were his friends, and he was very comfortable with them. You know, jocks, a whole lot of beer, a whole lot of drawl. You know, horsing around, kidding around. He seemed to be part of the good ol' boy network," said Kirksey, who placed third in voting for Alabama's homecoming queen and made network news as the first black Bama Belle, a weekly honor chosen by the campus newspaper.

Harris would interact with his teammates in Sewell Hall. "I remember him coming down to our room a lot. Just to talk, cut up, and laugh," Bobby York said. "We congregated a lot in our room and [Greg] Austin's, laughing and cutting up. We played cards a lot, but I think Henry did more watching than playing. I remember he was always going around and picking at people [teammates], and when he did that to me, I'd grab him, and we'd go to wrestling. He was pretty aggressive, but the matches were friendly. He laughed and cut up. We'd talk about stuff, and I guess Henry was comfortable."

"From an interaction standpoint, I thought Henry's ability was very, very positive. He liked to interact with people," said Dan Jacobs, the team manager the previous year. "I can picture Henry now, telling stories about his life. Because he had a very difficult upbringing—I thought I was country. He was really from the country. I'm sure there was no one on our team that could relate to what he had been through, both personal life and being in the schools he had been in."

Auburn's basketball players threw parties at a nearby farm owned by teammate Dan Kirkland's family. "Henry would come. He'd bring a date. Everybody was fine," said Kirkland, who considered Harris quiet but always cordial. "Being nineteen or twenty years old, you're not very empathetic. I never mistreated Henry that I know of. None of the players did. I think most of the pressure was from the outside, from people he knew—the 'Why would you go to a white school?' type of thing. That's the impression I would get whenever he would get to talking. He didn't talk much, but he certainly did seem to think he was out of place. Especially at a place like Auburn. It was one of the most conservative student bodies in America. We only had about ten hippies in the whole school." In Kirkland's mind, Harris was "friends with everyone when we were playing a game or in practice." But as far as socializing away from Sewell Hall or the parties at the farm, "it just didn't happen," said Kirkland.

So the barren walls of Room 303 became a testament to Harris's nomadic lifestyle. "Henry didn't stay there any more than he pretty much had to," said student manager Bill Perry. Harris had to make room check on weeknights but not on weekends. "If he didn't have to be somewhere, he'd disappear. He'd get dressed and leave, and he'd stay gone. He had made friends and would probably sleep at some friend's apartment or down in the neighborhoods where the black people stayed. He never made Sewell Hall home."

Black children in the segregated South were taught not to call attention to themselves. As Sewell Hall's most conspicuous resident, Harris understood the best way not to draw attention was to disappear. "You didn't see much of Henry—and understandably so," said Wes Bizilia, who would go to see Harris after he returned to Auburn to replace Davalos. "I'd never find him at the dorm. But who was he going to hang around with at Auburn? We had a dining hall. He was the only black kid sitting in there for a year or so. If I was to go to Russia and nobody spoke English, I couldn't understand them and they couldn't understand me. I kind of thought that's where Henry was. Here's a kid from Boligee, Alabama. He's thrust into a university with some thirteen thousand students, and he's the only black [athlete]. Here's a kid from a very poor family, with no money and no access to any money. I thought Henry was a very lonesome kid."

"We were close," Perry said, "but nobody was really close to Henry." Tim Ash, another good friend, considered Harris "a loner, to himself." "It was like he was scared all the time," said Carl Shetler, the co-captain. "You'd see him around the dorm. He was always by himself. Some of the white people didn't care for him being there."

Friends never could "get much sense" where Harris went, likening him to a cat, disappearing in an instant. "I'm not sure what Henry did in the evening time," said Larry Chapman. "My guess is he gravitated to the black community in Auburn, and I understand that."

"He went off on his own,' said teammate Gary England. "That's no slap on him. That's the way society was then." He usually fled on foot. Or a bicycle, the old one Gary Pettway gave him before they went to college. "You're watching white guys riding around in brand new cars," said James Owens. "You're watching [John] Mengelt riding around in a nice car [a Malibu SS 396], and Henry's got a bicycle."

"It's probably very difficult," Mengelt said, "when you go to college and don't find a lot of people to run around with. As teammates, we got along real well, but his really good friends were the black people in the Auburn community, because there weren't many on campus. So he had to go outside the college community for his friends, and I don't know if that was the best thing that ever happened to him."

Harris never had to worry about how he talked or acted "across the tracks." "He came on this side of town often," said Rush Tanner, his barber. "He was a friendly guy. Talked a lot of trash—had good lies to tell you, how he could fake an opponent. He was no troublemaker. He was real friendly. Everybody liked him when he came over here."

He was particularly popular at Van's, a cinder-block black night club that sold beer and bootleg whiskey. "Van's was the first place Henry took me," Owens said. "I'm a little ole freshman fellow, and I'm scared to death. We walked in, and we never had to buy a drink. Everybody was glad to buy us a drink." At eighteen and nineteen, Owens and Harris were heroes, toasted by grown men who had lived a lifetime in the Jim Crow South and could glimpse tomorrow in a couple of fresh-faced Auburn students. Van's was "the fraternity we had to go to," Owens said. The cost of membership, though, was socializing with folks twice their age in a place that, according to one black student, "looked like someone got killed there every night."

Harris would also escape to Tuskegee Institute [now Tuskegee University], just twenty miles down Highway 29 in a town that was a fountainhead of civil rights history. When attorney Fred Gray filed suit to integrate Tuskegee High School in 1963, Governor George Wallace got the state board of education to close it. "He said, 'Don't send your child to that school. We will start a private school,'" Gray recalled. "And they started Macon Academy right down Highway 29, and he got the state paying to support it. And that was the beginning of the private school movement in the United States." In 1964, Macon County High School integrated and was quickly burned down. Then, in 1966, Tuskegee undergraduate Sammy Younge was murdered for using a service station restroom marked "Whites Only." A Navy veteran who participated in the blockade of Cuba, Younge had gone into the restroom to intentionally integrate it two years after the Civil Right Act was passed. The station attendant who shot him was found innocent by an all-white jury.

Historically black colleges were a source of social life and survival for many young black men integrating southern colleges. C. B. Claiborne, Duke's first black basketball player, spent so much time at North Carolina Central that he bought a meal ticket. Wake Forest's early black athletes would socialize at North Carolina A&T.

At times, though, Harris and other black Auburn students could find little sanctuary even at Tuskegee. Students there would accuse them of trying to be white or not being "black enough." Early black students elsewhere heard the same thing—"Aren't black colleges good enough for you?" SMU's Jerry LeVias was called a "white nigger," and even the seven blacks who led Texas Western to the NCAA title were called Uncle Toms by blacks, which hurt them more than being called "niggers" by whites.

"On one hand, we were trying to integrate this institution in the South, and we were catching hell from whites," explained Wallace. "But on the other hand, black America was becoming separatist, and we were catching hell for being something like Uncle Toms."

Chapter 20

Saving Face

The balky integration of athletics at SEC schools was such an issue by 1970 that FBI agents were tracking the class-action lawsuit against Alabama football coach Bear Bryant. The FBI regularly monitored possible civil rights violations and often monitored public figures under FBI director Herbert Hoover, who had to approve the monitoring because of Bryant's high profile.

Two weeks after the lawsuit was filed in 1969, the Christian church finally jumped into the integration of southern college athletics. Although well suited for taking a stand, the South's white churches had usually looked the other way or, at best, worked behind the scenes on civil rights. But the United Presbyterian Church put Bryant under a national spotlight with an article in *Presbyterian Life* about walk-on Antonio Pernell not receiving a football scholarship. Bryant was also feeling pressure from the U.S. Department of Health, Education, and Welfare. Three months after the lawsuit was filed, associate athletic director Sam Bailey had to send HEW a letter listing all the predominantly black schools Alabama had contacted or visited during recruiting.

Harris was one of the fourteen athletes named to represent black high school athletes in Alabama in the lawsuit, and in a pretrial sworn deposition, Bryant said Alabama spent fifty hours recruiting Harris. When the lawsuit was finally heard July 8, 1970 in federal court in Birmingham, Bryant was questioned under oath by U. W. Clemon, the plaintiffs' attorney. Two weeks later, lawyers for both sides met with federal court Judge Frank McFadden and agreed to a delay in hearing the case. "The university felt a trial, regardless of the outcome, would hinder its ability to recruit blacks in the future," said Clemon. "The plaintiffs, after talking with some black athletes, tended to concur. We also felt it was likely the judge would rule against us, thereby necessitating an appeal, so we agreed to a postponement until May 10, 1971. If Bryant signed a substantial number of blacks before then, we would drop the suit. Otherwise, it would be heard." When pressed by a reporter to define "substantial," Clemon replied, "Around five football players."

Bryant had already signed an initial African American player to a scholarship—Wilbur Jackson of Ozark, Alabama, who would start practice with the freshman team in August. He would need to sign only four more black players in his next signing class, and the national spotlight would be off him and he'd be back in control of his program.

Control was important to Bryant, who twice rejected overtures from the NFL, fearing star players might usurp his power. No one would tell Bryant what to do on or off the field. That was one of the several reasons he was slow to integrate, once telling a writer he "damn sure wouldn't stand" for a black signee "showing up with a bunch of photographers and some big-talking civil rights leader trying to get publicity." In the end, however, college students and a NAACP-backed civil rights lawyer trapped Bryant in a corner he couldn't escape. He could, however, punt and play defense a little longer.

Bryant was a football coach, an exceptional one, who believed his responsibility was to win games and develop young men, not lead social change. He had repeatedly expressed anxiety about how Alabama fans might react to blacks. Would they be hard on them? And would that undermine the integration process? (University of Georgia president O. C. Aderhold blamed athletic boosters for blocking integration in 1967.) But Bryant may have been more concerned about image than his fans' prejudices, his image being the cornerstone of his control. Never appearing weak on race was a sixties mandate for southern politicians. When Mississippi Governor Ross Barnett knew he'd have to admit James Meredith to Ole Miss, he asked Attorney General Bobby Kennedy to instruct U.S. marshals to point guns at him to create the impression he was forced to relent. Similarly, George Wallace's posturing in the schoolhouse door in Tuscaloosa was about symbolism.

But at least one other factor affected Bryant's foot-dragging. "Coach Bryant had to work through a personal bias," said Alabama basketball coach C. M. Newton. "He had problems with it."

Bryant caught a break, however, when the NCAA voted in early 1970 to allow football teams to play an eleventh regular-season game. Bryant quickly used the new rule to schedule a season-opening game in Birmingham against Southern California. If his goal was to expose his base to a racially mixed national power and illustrate the need to integrate the Crimson Tide, he chose the ideal opponent. Southern Cal would field an all-black backfield, and Bryant had to suspect his "skinny white boys," as he liked to call them, would be overmatched.

Birmingham, the city of bombs and Bull Connor, would host an integrated bigtime college football team in the midst of black housing projects west of downtown, in a football-crazy atmosphere that only Birmingham could generate. The stage would be Legion Field, the so-called "Football Capital of the South." It was marvelous theater, and Bryant got what he may have expected, a 42-21 beating from Southern Cal.

No one could have been too surprised. Bryant's teams were already getting routed regularly in bowl games by integrated teams from the powerful Big Eight Conference, losing 35-10 to Missouri in the 1968 Gator Bowl and 47-33 to Colorado in the 1969 Liberty Bowl. Alabama fans had of course watched those losses on TV, so they could have hardly been surprised. Yet, history has tried to portray the game as some crucible in southern sport, as the night the South got religion. More accurately, the game's storyline is compelling and satisfying—to a white audience at least—but a vast over-simplification of SEC integration, ignoring the roles played by courageous young black Americans like Wilbur Jackson, Wendell Hudson, and Henry Harris and, for that matter, by a lawsuit or the HEW.

The point made by the Southern Cal game was essentially a moot one—Jackson was already on campus in Tuscaloosa, a solitary, eighteen-year-old living out Dr. King's dream one day at a time. The game would not be a "catalyst" for integration but rather, in the words of author Michael Oriard, a "rationale" for it. It enabled Bryant to be both a hero and a victim of integration, just like George Wallace. Bryant, the hero, had held out as long he could—until it became obvious that he had to surrender, had to integrate—deepening the mythology already surrounding his cult-like shadow.

Lost in history was the fact that after Southern Cal left town, Alabama proved it was not a very good football team, losing to Ole Miss by twenty-five points and to Tennessee by twenty-four.

From 1961-66, Alabama had won three national championships and arguably should have won a fourth. Its won-loss record was easily the nation's best during that time, reinforcing Governor Wallace's segregation stands and giving white Alabamians a respect they were not receiving on the nightly news. But ever since an undefeated Alabama team had lost out on the 1966 national title because of the state's racist image among voters in the wire-service polls, the Tide's record had declined steadily, falling to 6-4 in 1969 with a loss to Vanderbilt. By 1970, Alabama had lost four straight games to rival Tennessee, and Georgia and Tennessee had each won two SEC titles since 1966. New powers were on the rise, and Bryant's ability to motivate young men appeared to be waning with the mop-haired jocks of America's hippie years. Whether he knew it or not, Bryant needed a new group of athletes to coach.

Ole Miss football coach Johnny Vaught once told the SEC's annual preseason tour of sports writers that he was recruiting black players. After getting the satisfaction of seeing the writers' shocked expression, he quickly added he was only "joking." That was September 1966, the same month Greg Page and Nate Northington entered Kentucky and Perry Wallace and Godfrey Dillard entered Vanderbilt as the SEC's first black scholarship athletes. Vaught did admit to the media that his coaches feigned recruitment of African Americans to comply with "some sort of act to get federal funds." "We fill out a form to show we have looked at one," he told them. "We have not found one good enough yet. By the time we find one good enough, I'll be gone."

In May 1969, however, with Vaught still coaching, Ole Miss signed J. T. Purnell, running back at Jackson's all-black Brinkley High School, to a football scholarship. It was an event that even surprised Purnell. His coach, the legendary Tyree McBeth, came to get him out of class. He introduced him to two men from Ole Miss. Purnell had never seen them before. They asked him if he would like to sign a football scholarship to Ole Miss. Believing and wanting to prove he was good enough to play for the Rebels, Purnell said he wanted to sign. "Well, let's go find your mother then," the men told him, needing her signature on the scholarship. Purnell's mother was a custodian at Murrah High School, Jackson's premier white high school. When she was summoned to the principal's office, he introduced her to the Ole Miss recruiters and told her, "Don't come back until they are through with you." Later that day, Purnell signed with Ole Miss. But Purnell would never play for Ole Miss.

Because the southern letter-of-intent for an athletic scholarship was not binding nationally, Southern Illinois continued recruiting him and flew him to its campus, where, under his mother's direction, he signed a scholarship. Vaught, meanwhile, after nearly a quarter-century as Ole Miss coach, retired following the 1970 season. He had college football's best won-loss record at the time, six SEC titles, and three national championships—and he had kept his word. He never coached a black player.

A year earlier, in one of the most baffling SEC coaching changes ever, longtime Florida coach Ray Graves also retired without ever coaching an African American. The move was made following Graves's best season, 9-1-1, and with the nucleus of his offense returning for two more years. Graves's retirement was announced simultaneously with the hiring of Tennessee coach Doug Dickey, who had just won a second SEC championship. More importantly to Florida president Stephen O'Connell, Dickey had successfully integrated the Tennessee program.

Florida had been under pressure from the federal government to integrate athletics since early 1968, and Graves was the subject of at least two NAACP complaints. But Gainesville was not Knoxville. "People had a hard time with it [integration] at Florida," Dickey said. "The people in East Tennessee were not as vocally troubled by integration." Gainesville's Alachua County was the site of twenty-one documented lynchings between 1891 and 1926 and was one of the counties that went to the Supreme Court to contest desegregation.

Nowhere was resistance greater than in varsity football programs on SEC campuses in the Deep South. Not until 1972 would black Americans play varsity football at Georgia, LSU, or Ole Miss.

Ten years passed between admission of a black student and signing black football players at Georgia and Ole Miss and sixteen years passed at LSU. Georgia actually signed its first black player—John King of Huntsville, Alabama—in early 1971 but couldn't get him to sign a national letter-of-intent. He would go instead to Minnesota and become an All-Big Ten fullback.

Chapter 21

Hell to Pay

When Harris returned to campus in September for his junior year, he was, again Auburn's only black basketball player. Alabama coach C. M. Newton, meanwhile, had signed two more black basketball players—Ernest Odom and Raymond Odums—just one year after signing Wendell Hudson. So Alabama suddenly had three times as many black players despite Auburn's one-year headstart.

Rudy Davalos said he was never discouraged from recruiting more African Americans after signing Harris, but Wes Bizilia, his replacement as assistant coach, remembered, "You didn't hear much about recruiting black players. We didn't pursue anywhere what we should have at the time." Bizilia recalled that a popular stereotype among white coaches then was "if you've got one black athlete, you're all right. If you've got two, they segregate themselves."

Some Auburn coaches apparently had those concerns in the fall of 1970. Two full years after Harris moved into Sewell Hall, the athletic department segregated all three of its black athletes in single rooms. Harris would again live alone in a double room, as would James Owens and freshman football player Virgil Pearson. As former Fairfield teammates, Owens and Pearson were obvious roommate candidates. Owens had a white roommate as a freshman, and Virgil had roomed with a white player during the summer, but both would spend the 1970-71 school year living by themselves.

"I thought I was special—a big old room by myself," Owens recalled, laughing loudly. "The thing you realized was that they didn't want a group of black men together, because it represented strength. If you can keep them separated, you can control them better." The single rooms echoed "separate but equal," fed feelings of inferiority, and kow-towed to many whites' objection to the races living together.

In 1967, Reggie Jackson, while looking for a place to live during his season with the Birmingham A's, stayed briefly with three white teammates also bound for the major leagues—Rollie Fingers, Dave Duncan, and Joe Rudi. But when the landlord threatened to evict the others for letting a black man stay with them, Jackson left quietly. During a 1969 road trip to Auburn, Kentucky junior fullback Houston Hogg had a pistol pointed at him by the white teammate assigned to room with him. "Yeah, I went on to bed that night," Hogg said, "but I didn't go to sleep for a while." A year later, Auburn football coach Shug Jordan, perhaps fearing a similar incident on his own team during Owens' first varsity season, offered walk-on Roger Mitchell a scholarship if he would room with Owens on the road. He accepted Jordan's offer and was put on the traveling squad even though he was being redshirted as a transfer student and thereby ineligible to play. Owens heard about the offer years later—"he [Jordan] said, 'Roger, I need you to go on the traveling squad, but you have to room with James Owens.'" Mitchell recalled in 2016 Jordan told him, "We want someone who will room with James who can take care of any situation." "Coach Jordan was looking out for him. I did not see color," said Mitchell, admitting no one understood how alone Owens felt. "We did not know what he was going through. We were so into ourselves. We were eighteen or nineteen."

As a junior, Owens would room with Gossom, who was redshirted and ineligible but, again, inexplicably landed on the travel squad. (When Gossom moved into Sewell Hall that fall, resident counselor Brownie Flournoy warned him to stay away from Owens, that he was a "bad influence"—the same instructions Flournoy gave Owens two years earlier in telling him to avoid Harris.)

Blacks and whites living together intimated equality of the races in a region where even blacks and whites eating together was viewed as an encroachment on white superiority. Whites' fear of blacks and whites living together, however, was founded on their dread of blacks and whites cohabiting. Many historians and sociologists believed fear of interracial dating and sex was the bedrock of segregation. Responses by whites to a 1940s survey of their greatest fear related to integration were very consistent—that whites and blacks would eventually date and create an amalgamation of the races, according to *An*

American Dilemma by Nobel laureate Gunnar Myrdal. Whites believed sharing a lunch counter, a bus seat, or a classroom with an African American would be just the start.

Harris arrived at Auburn only a year after the U.S. Supreme Court legalized interracial marriage so interracial dating still carried great risk in the Deep South. Regardless of the region, dating whites had long been a great no-no for early black athletes at traditionally white universities. Junior Coffey was third nationally in rushing in 1964, until University of Washington coaches learned he had a white girlfriend. He never started another game. Duffy Daugherty, the Michigan State coach who recruited blacks out of the South, forbade future All-America Bubba Smith from dating whites. Baylor coaches warned John Westbrook, who integrated the Southwest Conference football with Jerry LeVias, not to date whites, although Baylor had only seven black students. And Wake Forest coaches suspended freshman William Smith from the team for hugging white female members of his Baha'i congregation at a freshman game at Clemson.

Wide receiver Ray Bellamy, Miami's first black athlete, was arrested in Miami for riding in a car with a white woman. He used his one call to dial university president Henry King Stanford, a south Georgian who had pushed hard for athletic integration. By the time Stanford rolled into the Miami police station, he was furious. Before taking Bellamy out the door, he shouted at the officer on the desk:

"This shit has to stop."

But "this shit" had been going on for a long time.

During the summer of 1969, Harris became friends with Susan Warley Hales, a freshman art major and the daughter of parents so true-blue Auburn that they married at historic Toomer's Corner in the center of town. Harris was playing pickup games every afternoon at Memorial Coliseum and Hales would be waiting for a friend to get off work. They would talk after Harris finished. "I really had a crush on him," said Hales, who couldn't understand why Harris rebuffed her advances. "I didn't get it. He'd say, 'Susan, as long as I am on this court, life's fine, but I cannot walk out this door without there being trouble.' I said, 'Come on.' He said, 'No, I'm sorry. That's just the way it is. I can't date a white girl.' I do believe he had been cautioned or was wise enough to know. Henry knew better than I did that there would be hell to pay."

Young women, black and white, would continue to pursue Harris. "There were a lot of girls interested in him," said Hales, who called Harris "the most gorgeous thing I'd ever seen in my life. He was a human specimen like nobody you've ever seen. But he was also very personable, very nice." "He was beautiful," said Dianne Kirksey, the first black Bama Belle.

In high school, his buddy Gary Pettway would get his dad's old truck or the family's 1955 Chevy, and he and Harris would head out to see their girlfriends. "Henry didn't go with anybody. He was a ladies man, he was everybody's boy," Pettway said. "Henry never got his fill of that stuff. It's like any star."

"He had a way with the ladies," said Auburn teammate Tim Ash. "He was really a charming guy." But whereas Harris had a school full of girls to date in Boligee, his freshmen class at Auburn included only two African American females. So he dated blacks from Auburn or Opelika. "There were many nights he was over in Opelika partying and couldn't find a way back [to the dorm]," said Ash, who would go pick Harris up in his purple Plymouth Barracuda. "He was a character. He could go all night long and not sleep, go to school, come out and practice, and drop twenty points on somebody."

Harris had at least one white girlfriend while at Auburn, early in his junior year, but he "kept it under control," according to Gossom. "He could get away with it if he didn't flaunt it." Seeming discretion, though, didn't mean no one noticed. "He [Harris] dated white girls and that made it a little worse [on him]," said Carl Shetler, the 1969-70 co-captain. "We were not used to seeing that."

By the time his junior season began, Harris was dating Debra Threatt, a black high school senior whom he met at a "block party" in downtown Auburn. She had been one of the first black students at Auburn High School, so they made a quick connection. "We both had our challenges. We'd talk about the racial things that went on at the high school," Threatt said. Forced desegregation that year had increased racial tension. "We used to exchange stories of what had happened to me that day. He'd tell me things that had happened to him, some of the encounters. It was really a struggle for him."

Threatt and Harris had something else in common—wanting to help their mothers. "He'd say, 'I want to do something for my mother. I'm going to play basketball, and I'm going to do something for her one day.' He was going to help his family out and bring them out of their situation," Threatt said. "I think he had big hopes for his mom. I think everything he did was for her." Threatt liked Harris's friendliness—he used to say, "I'm from B-o-l-i-g-e-e, Alabama. You ever heard of Boligee?" "Everybody liked him. He was an easy-going person who got a long with everyone. He was a beautiful person."

On November 5, 1970, the *Birmingham News* reported that Greene County was under "complete black power." Thomas Gilmore was elected sheriff the day before, beating incumbent Bill Lee, and William McKinley Branch, the black educator who lost his job for leading protests, was elected probate judge, defeating Judge Dennis Herndon. With the sweep of the county commission in 1969, blacks now held all major Greene County offices. Eutaw mayor William Tuck described the white community as "stunned," "hurt," and "humiliated." "We thought we had a lot more colored friends," he said.

The new school superintendent, appointed by the predominantly black school board, was Harris's former teacher, Robert Brown, PhD, the World War II tank gunner. Justice had finally arrived in Greene County.

Chapter 22

Workhorse

"I need you here tomorrow," Bill Lynn told Wes Bizilia after Rudy Davalos and Larry Chapman left Auburn. After completing his master's degree at Auburn in 1968, Bizilia had returned to coaching high school basketball in Mobile. He sensed real urgency in Lynn's voice during the early March phone call. "They fired both Davalos and Chapman," Lynn told him. "I don't want to go into it, but I need to know something tonight." Bizilia talked to his wife and kids that night. He was in Auburn the next day.

When Auburn's graduating players heard Bizilia had taken the job, they warned him what he was in for. "Carl Shetler and Bill Alexander and Ron Jackson said, 'Coach, what in the hell are you doing?' I said, 'What are you talking about?' They said, 'You're not going to win.' I said, 'Well, nobody else in the SEC has offered me a job. Maybe I can do some good.' They said, 'Coach, you ain't got a prayer.'" A teetotaler, Bizilia was aware of Lynn's drinking but did not realize he was an alcoholic. "I said, 'All I need to do is keep him straight. Take care of him. Keep him out of it.' They said that was impossible."

Lynn wrote Harris a late-summer letter promising, "I am determined to do a better job than I have ever done," but Davalos's in-game adjustments would be missed the first week of the season when Auburn played third-ranked South Carolina at Carolina Coliseum—the ACC's most hostile arena for black players. Fans there started cussing Olympian Charlie Scott, North Carolina's first black player, during warmups. They threw coins at him in a 1969 game in which officials had to clear the floor of students carrying a Confederate flag around the court. Afterward, victorious UNC coach Dean Smith and an assistant went into the stands when they heard a fan call Scott a "big black baboon." It took a half-dozen ushers and policemen to hold them back. By the time Harris got to Columbia, the Gamecocks had a black player on the bench, sophomore Casey Manning, but their star was still John Roche, whom sports writers twice had voted ACC Player of the Year even though Scott averaged twenty-two points and seven rebounds per game both years. Five voters had left Scott off their ten-player 1969 All-ACC ballot altogether.

Harris and Mengelt held Roche under twenty points, but Auburn still lost by seventeen. Two nights later, Auburn beat defending ACC champ North Carolina State, which was captained by its first black player, Al Heartley, who was much loved by fans for his hustle. Like Harris, though, he struggled with State's pattern offense and was primarily a defensive stopper.

After exams, Auburn traveled to Ole Miss, where the Rebels' first black athlete, Coolidge Ball, played in the freshman game and was cheered by fans. But when Harris came out for warmups, the crowd unleashed its usual hostility toward him. Bizilia couldn't believe it.

"You goddamn nigger."

"Kill that nigger."

Bizilia jumped up from the team bench and spun to confront the fan several rows behind him. "You've got a black kid out here now. How can you call him that?" he asked loudly.

"He's our nigger," the man replied.

Tim Beavers, a freshman from Indiana, heard "things that were pretty shocking" on the road throughout the 1970-71 season. "I can remember certain places where Henry went through a lot. I heard it in every arena, and I have no doubt he [Henry] heard it. You heard it everywhere, and certainly at Kentucky," Beavers said. "I would like to say it was from only a handful of every crowd. But things were very, very different then, and Henry never outwardly showed any reaction to any of that." Nor did he talk about it. "He didn't bring it up, we didn't bring it up, because we were very supportive of him and he knew that," said Beavers. "I just don't think there are many people—white or black—that could go through what he went through and still be the kind of player and individual that Henry was."

With Perry Wallace having graduated, Harris was the SEC's lone returning black varsity player, but three black sophomores had joined the league—Wendell Hudson at Alabama, Ronnie Hogue at Georgia, and Tom Payne at Kentucky. So, four years after Vanderbilt signed Wallace, only four African Americans were among the SEC's more than 130 varsity players. Hudson and Hogue had talked to each other as freshmen about the arenas they had played in. "Both of us had traveled to the same places with no one else [on our teams] to understand what was being said and done. At certain schools, it was almost ridiculous," Hudson said.

Losing five of its nine games in December, Auburn hardly resembled the team sports writers had tabbed as the second best in the SEC. That prediction was based on a backcourt of Harris and Mengelt, but by the new year, Harris was back at forward. Lynn would explain to reporters that he saw early on he did not have a natural floor leader, so he moved 6-foot-3 senior captain Jimmy Walker from forward to guard, and Harris, a better rebounder, returned to forward. Meanwhile, sophomore Gary England, a good outside shooter, would play increasingly as a third guard or when both Walker and Harris were at forward.

Although Mengelt considered Harris an adequate ball-handler, making Harris the playmaking guard was apparently not discussed. "I don't think it ever dawned on him [Lynn] that was what Henry could do," said Bizilia. If Auburn was not ready to have a black American dribbling the ball up the court, it was no different than teams throughout the SEC and ACC—Heartley was the only "first" in either league to play point guard. According to the era's stereotypes, "black athletes, one, can't or don't think; two, choke; and three, can't be trusted in key positions," according to Perry Wallace. A more natural position for African Americans then was "workhorse," as detailed in *Sports Illustrated's* 1969 "Black Athlete" series—rebound, play great defense, set up others to score.

To Harris's friends, his supporting role reeked of racism, holding not only Harris back but also his race at a time when blacks were striving to prove their worth. But if Harris could not be a star, he would wait until his senior season to show the NBA he could score. Until then, he would disprove another stereotype as the consummate team player on an otherwise all-white team. "He could get you your shots better than anyone else could," said forward Dan Kirkland. "He was a special talent, I'll tell you that. He could get a shot any time he wanted if you let him. He could've gotten his shot better than the one you gave him after sitting in that shuffle for ten minutes." Even Lynn admitted, "He does many things better than Mengelt." Lynn was a defensive coach and that's what he loved about Harris. "Henry is a fabulous defensive player," he once told a reporter. "I didn't say he was going to be a great. I said he's already a great defensive player. . . . He's a boy who gives everything, all he's got." That's why Lynn would continue to assign Harris the opponent's second biggest player. "Sometimes that means Henry, who is 6-2, is covering a man who is 6-8 or 6-7. But he does a good job of it. He overcomes his disadvantage in size with his quickness." "That was what was important to Daddy," said Bill Lynn Jr., "being tough."

Chapman, however, saw another attribute that made Harris a great defender. "His passion to be a kid that pleased the coach made him what he was," Chapman said. "Henry wanted to please you. Coachability was his forte."

Harris and his teammates came back to Auburn after the holidays with nearly 90 percent of their SEC schedule still ahead of them and an opportunity to salvage their season. But after losing at Florida, they went to Athens and beat Georgia by twenty-one. Mengelt took twenty-three shots and scored forty points; Harris took five and scored six. Alabama came to Auburn the following week, still angry about Mengelt's sixty points a year earlier. This time Alabama's defense held him to twenty, enabling Harris to take more shots and score twenty-three. The game's high scorer, though, was Hudson, the black Alabama sophomore whom Auburn had passed on. Georgia came to Auburn a week later determined to shut down Mengelt and held him to two-of-fourteen shooting. Harris was again the beneficiary, taking thirteen shots, making eight, and scoring twenty.

In a blowout loss at Vanderbilt; Auburn gave up more than one hundred points for the third time in eight SEC games. Mengelt had thirty-six points, Harris had one. Auburn then yielded ninety points to slow-tempo Tennessee, losing by twenty-two. Two nights later at

Kentucky, it gave up 114, losing by thirty-eight a year and a day after its valiant one-point loss to the Wildcats. In the 366 days since, the wheels had fallen off, and Auburn had now lost six straight SEC games. "We are really struggling. . . . It's going to be a long season," assistant coach Larry Phillips wrote a recruit.

Auburn's inept defense was emblematic of a team in turmoil. The abrupt and poorly handled departure of Davalos and Chapman disappointed and disillusioned most of the team. Not only did point guard Bobby Nix leave, so did Bobby York and Greg Austin, two of Harris's good friends. Auburn had recruited great scorers, but there was only one basketball, and the mix of players eventually bordered on toxic. "It was a mess. We had more trouble that year than you could throw bricks at," Bizilia said.

During the losing streak, columnists wrote that Auburn's players could not work with Mengelt because he was not a team player. "Mengelt wasn't held to the same restrictions as the rest of us," Kirkland said. "If he wanted to break the shuffle and do something else, that was okay. He could miss four or five shots and stay in, because then he'd make five or six in a row." "Mengelt was a one-man show. I don't know why Coach Lynn let that go," said Walker, who was elected captain. "Our junior year, he wasn't that bad. But, boy, by our senior year, all he cared about was getting his average up and what he could do to help himself [in the draft]. I think Chapman and Davalos would've reigned that in." Over the summer, Mengelt had played for the U.S. team at the World University Games in Italy, and Lynn made it clear that he was "our offense," said England.

The dissension was so obvious the *Atlanta Journal* reported on it in a midseason article. "We told them [the *Journal*] about some people getting extra tickets and the coach drinking," said junior Tim Ash. "The drinking problem affected every one of us. So when they asked me about it, I told the truth. 'People want to know why this team can't do anything, that's the reason why.' It was anonymous, but when they [the coaches] found out about it, they raked us over the coals. I didn't play much more after that."

As captain, Walker made the room assignments on the road and always chose to room with Harris. "Henry and I were already pretty close as ballplayers, and I didn't want to put anyone else in a position where they would have to room with a black person," he said.

An odd couple for sure, Harris and Walker had a complex friendship crafted by the time and place in which they grew up. Walker was a 6-foot-3 physical player who averaged only four points per game as a senior but conveyed leadership through his toughness. He had played against blacks in high school in Atlanta and liked Harris. "I thought a lot of Henry. He was part of the family as far as I was concerned." Walker double-dated with Harris and also let Harris use his 396 Chevelle SS. "Henry thought that [car] was the greatest thing in the world," said Walker.

But Walker also teased Harris about reading *The Autobiography of Malcolm X*. "We'd call him the philosophizer and make fun of that too. He'd start spouting off all this stuff." By that time in his college career, Harris, according to Thom Gossom, "would and could rap about anything under the sun."

Harris would often tell Walker, "Everything is everything." Walker would ask him, "Henry, what in the hell does that mean?"

"He never would explain exactly what it meant, but that was his number one saying," Walker said. "I'd cut up with him all the time about that. I aggravated all of them, and I didn't cut Henry any slack."

Harris bantered with Walker, according to teammate Pat Cowart, because "around us Henry wanted to be one of the guys." "Walker would call him 'Brother' and kid him about his afro, Black Power, and stuff. Henry wouldn't call him a cracker, but he'd stand his ground. It was all in fun." The tightrope of trying to fit in on an all-white team was emblematic of the entire pioneer experience and had to be walked by many young black athletes. Arkansas football players joked loudly about sending John Richardson—the first black player on scholarship—to the back of the bus.

One thing Walker didn't tease Harris about was sleeping with the lights on. "I got ready to cut the light out," Walker remembered, "and Henry said, 'No, we have to keep the light on.' I said, 'What? No way, Henry. What's your problem?' He said, 'Ghosts.' He said, 'There's ghosts all around, and I just can't sleep in the dark.' There wasn't any way he was turning the light off. I didn't argue with him over it because I knew he was serious."

But the real challenge Harris and Walker faced on the road was eating. "Most of the time if you won, you got to go somewhere decent to eat [as a team]. If you lost, you got $5 or $6 each to have at it," Walker said. "When we lost and we were in places like Starkville or Oxford—or, hell, any place, LSU—Henry and I would say, 'Well, let's go eat.' So we'd go into white restaurants, and they wouldn't let us in. So we'd go to black restaurants, and they'd say, 'Naw, you got to go.' So we'd just bounce around until we would find a place that would accept us. We were on foot and this was just the two of us." Walker estimated he and Harris were refused service in three or four different college towns. "I remember one night we went to two white places and two black places and had to go to the fifth place to get served."

It could be a scary situation, but one Harris was accustomed to. As freshmen, he and teammate Greg Austin once borrowed Mengelt's car and stopped at "a little place along the side of the road somewhere between Atlanta and Auburn," according to Austin, a Kentuckian. "We walked in and sat down, and the waitress came over and said, 'You can't sit in here.' I said, 'What do you mean we can't sit in here?' She said, 'This is whites only.' I said, 'Okay.' Henry got up and I got up. She said we had to go outside for Henry to be served. We both went around back, and the black people wouldn't let me in. I think we may have ended up going somewhere else, and I went inside and ordered for both of us."

But now in 1971, seven years after passage of the Civil Rights Act, the SEC's racial pioneers—or at least those playing for coaches oblivious to the lingering peril of being black in the New South—were still being turned out of restaurants. In Baton Rouge, Florida basketball player Steve Williams found himself surrounded at a bar while seeking a post-game meal with three white teammates. He left. So did Florida's first black athlete, track sprinter Ron Coleman, when he was informed in a small restaurant outside Tuscaloosa, "We don't serve nigras in this here restaurant." Coleman retreated toward the door, praying silently until he reached the door.

Chapter 23

Not Who You Think I Am

Auburn went to Tuscaloosa in mid-February to play Alabama in the SEC's Saturday afternoon TV game of the week. Off camera before the game, Alabama coach C. M. Newton promised TV commentator Bill Justus that the Tide would make the game physical. "Coach, I think that's the last thing I would do with Auburn," Justus told him. "I don't think you're going to win that game." But Newton was ready to make a statement: Alabama basketball would no longer be bullied by Auburn.

Newton went 4-20 his first season and then integrated the program in the offseason, later admitting, "I was not a popular coach." His record improved only marginally his second season, but now in his third season, Newton could see clear progress. Alabama was 6-6 after losing at Auburn in January, but then Wendell Hudson broke his wrist. Athletic Director Bryant had seen the program's improvement and, knowing there would be more losing without Hudson, had given Newton a new contract in the past month to take some of the pressure off him. Newton was 0-5 against Auburn, and Alabama had also lost its past two football games against Auburn and was looking for something to cheer about. Alabama might not win, but Newton would make sure Auburn didn't score 121 points as it had a year earlier when Mengelt had sixty.

With Hudson out and the Tide's other two African Americans on the freshman team, Harris was the only black on court, and Alabama's football players would harass him in retaliation for the treatment Hudson received at Auburn as a freshman. The Alabama fans sitting behind the Auburn bench, meanwhile, focused on Coach Bill Lynn once they spotted a whiskey flask in his back pocket. As he got up and down on the bench, his coattail would catch on the flask, leaving it exposed.

"Hey, Bill, how bout a drink?" they hollered.

"Hey, Bill, you got anything in your pocket?"

Auburn assistant coach Wes Bizilia could hear every word. "The whole ballgame they got on him. I was embarrassed for him," he said.

Newton also had something to say to Lynn, walking down to the Auburn bench in the second half and standing in front of him.

"Bill, what's the matter? Hasn't he gotten his average yet?" he asked, referring to Mengelt.

Alabama's physical play did not produce victory but did get the crowd involved in the game, and the referees. They called fifty personal fouls and six technical fouls and ejected two players. Two technicals were called on the crowd for throwing paper on the court to protest a technical foul on Newton late in the game. A minute and a half later, Auburn's Jim Retseck and Alabama's Alan House were both ejected from the game for fighting. "They [Alabama] had some very physical players then, and anytime Auburn and Alabama get together, it's going to be a knockdown, drag-out," said Auburn assistant coach Larry Phillips.

But Auburn won 92-76, and Harris played well for the folks who drove up from Boligee—nineteen points and ten rebounds. His performance was made more impressive by the fact that he had played through a painful knee injury he sustained when a larger player fell on him in the football-like atmosphere. "Henry got hurt, Mengelt got hurt," Bizilia said. "They were both limping pretty good."

Debra Threatt, Harris's girlfriend back in Auburn, was watching the game on TV. "I remember when he fell. Oh my god, I remember that. I was crying," Threatt said. "He went down and did something to his knee and they were talking about it on television. The announcers said, 'He's down, he's down. That's a bad fall.' Seems like he had gone up for a shot and then came down."

Harris called Threatt after the game, before he and his teammates headed to Baton Rouge for the final LSU basketball game at Parker Agricultural Center. The largest arena in America when it was built in 1937 with 12,000 seats, the pride of Governor Huey Long, it was now a downsized, outdated "Cow Palace" that still hosted livestock shows on its concrete floor and smelled like it. It was here—with clouds of dust rising from the cracks between the court's floor boards and following the bouncing basketball—that Harris went out for the opening tipoff only forty-eight hours after injuring his left knee. "Henry said some big guy fell on him. He said they had another game two nights later and they shot him up with something and shipped him back out onto the court," recalled friend Henry Ford.

Despite limping, Harris managed to get a basket, a rebound, and two assists in the first ten minutes before the pain grew intolerable. When he left the game, Auburn was leading 28-19. With Harris gone, LSU would win 114-94. "You just can't imagine how much he [Harris] means to our ball club," Lynn said afterward. Later in the week, Lynn told the *Huntsville Times* Harris had torn cartilage in his left knee and it was "highly doubtful" he would play in Auburn's final four games. "He's probably the best kid we've got too . . . most valuable to the team, I know that," Lynn said. But Harris had torn more than cartilage in his left knee; he had also torn two ligaments.

Yet, when Vanderbilt came to Auburn Saturday, Harris was on the court warming up. "He told me after he took a few shots, he was ready and he is the kind that if he tells you he can play, you can count on him," Lynn said. Harris played thirty-four minutes, got five rebounds, and made three of his four shots. Mengelt took thirty-one shots and scored forty-eight points.

A week later, Harris played thirty-nine minutes in a home loss to Tennessee, making four of seven shots. Two nights later in Auburn, he played thirty minutes in a loss to Kentucky, getting seven points, five rebounds, and two assists. Mengelt had thirty-eight points and afterward took the blame for Auburn's losing season. "Maybe it was my fault. I should have helped provide more leadership," said Mengelt, who averaged twenty-nine points a game. In its final game, Auburn beat Ole Miss by a point to finish 11-15 overall and 8-10 in the SEC. With a promising season evolving into disaster, reports circulated that Lynn would not be back for another season. He had known he was fighting for his job the last month of the season, so players played and surgery waited.

"Any player would have done the same thing, and any trainer would have allowed the same thing back in those days," Beavers said. "It was entirely different back then. Players, particularly those with the constitution that Henry Harris had, were going to try to play."

With his left knee taped so tightly he could hardly straighten it, Harris had started five games. "Henry was motivated to win, and he wouldn't give up," Walker said. "He was a team player." If the whole ordeal had been a test of toughness, of commitment to State U., or of simply seeing whether blacks could "take it," Harris passed his exam, his answer a resounding, "I'm not who you think I am."

"Henry Harris would have continued to try to play because of his desire as an athlete," Beavers said. "Whether there was more to it than that, I was not mature enough to realize."

"He'd hurt after a ballgame," Lynn said. "Sometimes he could hardly walk. But when it was time to play, he'd play." After each of the final four games, Harris would retreat to his single room in Sewell Hall and cry. "There was nothing he could do," Ford recalled, "the pain was so bad."

Chapter 24

'Nigger Corner'

Before Harris got to the operating table, he watched the NCAA basketball tournament on television. In the Mideast Regional semifinals, he saw Western Kentucky, with five black starters, rout Kentucky, 107-83, in a watershed game for the state and longtime coach Adolph Rupp. Western's three top scorers were all recruited by Kentucky, but none were interested in being its first black basketball player. "Jim McDaniels, Clarence Glover, Jim Rose, we recruited all of them," said Kentucky assistant coach Joe B. Hall.

Western advanced to the Final Four, where it played Villanova, the school that recruited Harris so hard. In a classic semifinal, Villanova finally prevailed, 92-89, after two overtimes, with All-American Howard Porter, the forward George Raveling recruited out of Sarasota, leading the way with twenty-two points and sixteen rebounds. Two days later, Villanova lost to UCLA in the finals by six points.

Back in Auburn, Harris had to wonder what might have been. Villanova's guards were Chris Ford, his Dapper Dan teammate, and sophomore Tom Inglesby, but its roster lacked depth—four starters played the entire game in both the finals and semifinals. Harris knew he would have been a starter if not a star. "He [Harris] would have played a lot," Raveling said. "I'm certain that by that time he would have been a star. He was a player who was multi-talented. It was just a question of getting him in the right set of circumstances. He had stardom written all over him. That was the thing I tried to sell him on. He had a chance to come and play a style of basketball that was conducive to his talents."

While Harris hobbled around on crutches with a white cast all the way up his thigh, two dozen of his black classmates, including James Owens and Thom Gossom, took over the Auburn president's office on a late-May afternoon. They had been sitting at the Haley Center, the new student center, in their usual spot near the door, the area other students called "nigger corner." As they were playing cards and dominoes, they began talking about things "we didn't have that we needed, that should have been there, because we were part of Auburn University," Owens said. "We were upset. 'We're tired of this,' we said. 'We don't have a [black] history course. We don't have a black counselor. We don't have anybody to go to.'" Since integrating, Auburn's leadership had not pursued black faculty, staff, or additional black students.

The students at the Haley Center decided they would go talk to President Harry Philpott. They had made requests a year earlier but nothing had come of them. So they walked up to Samford Hall, the red-brick administration building constructed in 1887 on the site of Old Main, which was Auburn's original classroom building as well as a Confederate hospital during the Civil War.

"We said, 'We want to see President Philpott,'" Owens recalled.

"He's not here. You can see the vice president,'" they were told.

"We don't want to see the vice president. We want to see Philpott.'"

"Well, he's not in town."

"Well, that's okay, we'll just sit in his office until he gets here and play dominoes.'"

The students went into Philpott's office, got out their dominoes, and waited. When Philpott eventually walked in, they told him what they needed.

"We need to be treated better. We need a black counselor. We have problems, and we can't even go and talk to anybody about our problems. We have history, but black history is not being taught. . . . We had a list of things we read to him," Owens remembered.

"Give me until next year," said Philpott.

The students agreed. "He listened to us," said Owens. "He could have easily had the police arrest us."

Owens and Gossom may have escaped arrest but not assistant head coach Paul Davis. He called them into his office the next day.

"We don't do things like that," he told them.

Owens and Gossom replied that they were part of not only Auburn's football team but also Auburn's black student body.

"We are giving you a free scholarship," Davis replied. "Auburn University is paying your way, and you're marching on the university? You can't boycott a place that is paying your tuition."

The message was clear. "You can't be a football player and a black student," thought Owens. For Gossom, it was: "When you're a black athlete, you weren't really black and you weren't really white."

When University of Florida students held a sit-in that spring in President Stephen O'Connell's office, seeking to discuss policies they considered "unfriendly" to black students, more than seventy were arrested, prompting some two thousand students to march to O'Connell's house, leading to more arrests. One-third of Florida's black students withdrew from school in protest of the arrests. Football pioneer Willie Jackson announced black athletes would stay, however, because "there's got to be somebody left here to keep the pressure on so changes can be made."

The spring of 1971 was a time of racial unrest for black students on numerous southern campuses. Protests also occurred at Alabama, Georgia, LSU, and Ole Miss, which had expelled eight African American students for protests during the winter. At Alabama, more than forty students took over the president's office for five hours, demanding a black studies program and better conditions for black university employees. Five students were arrested.

Foot-dragging was the watchword by administrators throughout the South. In their rush to comply with the law and "treat everyone equally," most southern colleges tried to "treat everyone the same," which would significantly slow the assimilation of black students on white campuses. Few administrators understood or considered issues facing black students, who were fed up with the racism they faced daily on campus. "We all were a little militant. You're forced to get into that sort of thing when you're put into certain situations," said one of the Auburn marchers, Charles Smith, Harris's friend. Smith always kept an iron pipe in his dorm room in case trouble arose and finally used it that year when a drunk student repeatedly called him a "nigger" while he studied in a common area of his dormitory. "I was there alone, studying. It was kind of bloody, but they didn't call the police. They took him out of the area and grabbed me and put me in my room," he said.

Protection was needed on other campuses as well. That winter three Georgia football players followed two black students and attacked them in a university parking lot—just weeks after the Bulldogs had signed their first black football players. The two students testified against their attackers in magistrate court, but when the case was called in August in state court, the black students reportedly "couldn't be found," and the case was dismissed.

"My freshman year, every day I went on campus I had a reason to quit," recalled Alabama's Wendell Hudson. Quarter after quarter, Owens would enter an Auburn classroom and see the same routine. "You'd get to a seat and sit down, and everybody would start scooting a little bit. They didn't want to get too close to you," he said. And that was just fellow students. "We had instructors who had the reputation of having never passed a black person in a class, and that would be their badge of honor," said Henry Ford.

Even some academic advisers resented having to work with blacks. Rufus Felton, a pre-med major who had marched to Philpott's office, was given an eighteen-hour first-quarter course load that fall—chemistry, physics, algebra, zoology, English, and world history. "A normal course load was twelve to fifteen hours. I had no one to tell me, 'You might not want to do this.' They pumped me up. 'Aw, you can handle it,'" said Felton, who turned down a scholarship to Morehouse to go to Auburn. "They needed me at Auburn—my guidance counselor, my mother, and, in their words, society. They needed good black students to help integrate Auburn University. I never saw myself as getting an education at Auburn. I saw myself as making a statement. I felt I always had to prove something to someone other than me."

When Felton showed up early for biology lab one day, he walked in on a conversation between two instructors. "I was the topic of discussion. They were discussing 'the nigger' in the class," Felton said. "At that point, something kind of happened, and it was not about being a good student any more. That was secondary. I was an angry young man." Felton would flunk out of Auburn, get drafted, and be sent to Vietnam.

Racial progress was made in at least one area in the spring of 1971. The class-action discrimination suit against Bear Bryant was dismissed after he kept his promise to sign five black players in 1971.

Bryant had told Wilbur Jackson, his first black player, in the fall of 1970 that he didn't know "what was going to happen." But he also told him, "If something does happen, please come to me first so I can try to straighten it out." When junior college transfer John Mitchell arrived at Alabama in the winter of 1971, becoming the Tide's second black player, Bryant was again very direct. "Coach Bryant told me that if I had some problems, to come to him and he'd take care of them," Mitchell said.

Once he was finally in the integration game, Bryant would play to win and treat his black athletes fairly. He would also communicate clearly with his white players. Before Hudson arrived on campus, he spoke to the football team. Then one evening that fall, he led by example when he showed up at the Bryant Hall cafeteria while the residents were eating their late-night "snack" of peanut butter-and-jelly sandwiches and milk. It was Hudson's first week on campus, and he heard a hoarse, coarse voice above him say, "Can I sit with you?" He looked up to see Bryant.

"Yes sir," answered Hudson.

With his players looking on, Bryant sat down. "It was small talk," Hudson said, "but I was trying to choke down that peanut butter and jelly sandwich."

The message was stark. If a fifty-six-year-old white man could eat with an African American—ignoring one of the South's historic taboos—then his players better do likewise.

Chapter 25

Everything Is Everything

Our job was to clear a path to integration out of thorns and coarse weeds with our bare hands for those who followed. We knew that and were reminded of it daily.
— *Thom Gossom*

Harris was elected captain of the Auburn basketball team unanimously by his teammates while recovering from knee surgery. "This sort of surprised me," he told the *Birmingham Post-Herald*. "I know the others will expect me to provide more leadership than before if we want to win. This is a big honor." The possibility of a black American becoming captain of an Auburn or Alabama sports team five years earlier would have been unthinkable. It was a testament to the respect Harris's teammates held for him. Harris, however, was already concerned about how well he would be able to play in six months, saying, "My knee will be a factor in my own game. I'm in a cast right now and will be about six more weeks. But I'll get back to working toward next year just as soon as I can. I know that I have a lot of work to do."

Harris's recovery timetable was put behind schedule when doctors postponed the surgery more than a month after the end of the season to let the swelling subside—a result of the five games Harris played after getting hurt. His mother and sister, Glenda, came to Columbus for the operation, as did Harris's girlfriend, Debra Threatt, and Coach Bill Lynn.

To rehabilitate his knee and take enough academic hours to stay eligible athletically, Harris stayed in Auburn over the summer of 1971. Because he had a spare bed in his room, his youngest brother, Carl, came down from Bessemer and lived with him in Sewell Hall for part of the summer. Six years younger than Harris, Carl was born with a leaky heart valve. "The doctors at Children's Hospital in Birmingham gave him six months to live," said older brother Robert. But Carl fooled the doctors, and Henry admired his spirit and enjoyed being his big brother. Threatt met Carl that summer. "Henry loved him," she said.

Harris was a natural mentor and had become a rock of hope for the black athletes who followed him to Auburn. "Henry was our big brother," James Owens said. "He took care of us. He made us go to class and do things, and we listened to him because we felt he was the old man." Even on days when Harris would not go to class, he'd tell Owens, "Man, go to school. Your life is going to be all right. You better get up and go to class."

Harris also would be a "father figure" to the other four black athletes living in Sewell Hall in the fall of 1971—football players Thom Gossom and Virgil Pearson and basketball players Sylvester Davenport and Albert Johnson. Harris was again living alone in Room 303, the walls and mattress still bare, the heat and lights still on. Davenport and Johnson shared a room in the same suite.

"We got our toughness from Henry," Owens said. "If he didn't complain, why should we complain?" Owens believed complaining would have "just labeled us as complainers, not able to take the pressures." "It would have given way to bitterness and been part of us in our outward appearance," he said. "We would have been mad at our teammates, at our coaches, just mad at Auburn University. And it wouldn't have done any good." Harris and Owens grasped what Jackie and Rachel Robinson had learned two decades earlier, that talking about daily injustices would only sap them of precious energy. "We knew we had to get ready for tomorrow," said Rachel Robinson. "We knew we couldn't carry all that mess into the next day."

The stoicism of Harris and Owens rubbed off on Auburn's younger black athletes. "Nobody ever discussed racial things, but we knew why we were down there," Davenport said. "It was our job, man. It was a job because we had a whole race of people who had to have another way of going into white society, because you have to have somebody in the front. And the ones in the front, in the world of everyday people, was the athlete, somebody that people see every day." Because athletes were supposed to be the tough guys, there was no room in a jock dorm for young men who saw themselves as victims, for that would have meant they weren't men. "As a black man, you feel like you've got to endure," said Henry Ford, a black walk-on freshman football player that fall. "We played the hand we were dealt. That's what Henry did and what James did."

If Harris and the others resembled any group emotionally, it was the black veterans of World War II, who—in the words of author Michele Norris—"woke up every day trying to show America what they could be . . . and what it could be." Black soldiers and sailors compartmentalized their feelings and kept their stories to themselves. Bitterness and victimhood did not fit the narrative they had created for themselves.

Enduring was a role "firsts" had to play across the SEC. "You've got a big responsibility," said Leonard George, who integrated Florida varsity football in 1970 with Willie Jackson, "because there are a lot of people out there in the black community who may never get to the game or may never meet you personally but are depending on you. They've got their hopes and dreams in you." Lester McClain often wanted to leave Tennessee but couldn't. "I knew the next day the headline would say: 'Lester McClain, First Black Athlete, Quits UT.'" The only SEC pioneers to leave early were Vanderbilt's Godfrey Dillard, after being cut from the team because of political activism, and Kentucky's Nate Northington, after his roommate, Greg Page, was killed in a half-speed practice drill.

When Harris wanted to leave Auburn, he usually called Paul Pettway, his high school football coach and the father of his best childhood friend. Coach Pettway once told Thomas Gilmore, the would-be Greene County sheriff, "Henry's ready to leave, got his bags packed." But Harris ended up staying, just like he always did. "Daddy would tell him, 'Just give it time, your day will come,'" said Gary Pettway. "But you have to understand, Daddy was coming from a day when you didn't have that chance at all."

Black Baby Boomers had grown up observing their parents' perseverance against terrible odds, daily indignities, and in-your-face racism. They saw how they rarely spoke of their difficulties and ignored questions about the past, trying desperately not to curse their children with historical trauma and future bitterness. So how could they even grumble quietly? "At my age," Gossom said, "my father was looking at the back of a mule. And you're going to complain about going to class and playing football?" Complaining or even asking questions had gotten black men in trouble in the South, and following integration, an African American male who verbalized mistreatment was labeled an "angry black man" or told to just work harder. The message was: "You're here, so be grateful and shut up," said Gossom.

As first-generation college students, with parents who couldn't understand what they were going through, Harris, Owens, and the rest would parent each other—"we had to encourage ourselves," said Ford—and have fun however they could. They made their greeting for each other a coping mechanism. Whether the question was "How you doing?" or "What's up?", the response was always "everything is everything," a phrase lifted from the barely audible chatter opening Marvin Gaye's classic *What's Going On*, released in 1971. "It was just a slogan that we used that everything was all right," Owens explained. "Everything was going according to the way it's supposed to go. It may not be all right, but it was going—everything was everything. Just go on and do what you need to do. No need in complaining. Just let everything be everything."

Harris, Owens, and Gossom would retreat to their "Clubhouse," the third-floor room shared by Johnson and Davenport, turn on soul music, and let their imaginary band come to life. "I played the guitar," Owens said, "Thomas played the drums. Henry played the trumpet or something. I think Sylvester was playing the bass guitar. We would be listening to music and we were so into it. We had the greatest time just being able to do that." With no one else around, they'd play make-believe instruments, and they'd laugh. "We'd laugh about how Brownie Flournoy said Henry was a gangster. Then Thomas came, and I was the gangster. We used to laugh about those things. About how Henry rode his bike and all the crazy things we did. We just tried to laugh at everything we could laugh about." Even at their own pain sometimes.

"We'd be sitting around on Saturday afternoon at Don Williams' apartment, and Henry would be having a game that night," Gossom remembered. "We might be playing cards or talking. And everybody would razz Henry because he was a good athlete, but he had to play second fiddle to John Mengelt. Just like you had Sullivan-to-Beasley back then [Auburn's All-America passing combo of Pat Sullivan and Terry Beasley], we called it Harris-to-Mengelt, because Henry always ended up feeding Mengelt the whole game. You can be cruel sometimes when you're young." Gossom noticed Harris would never say anything in response to the needling about Mengelt. "I think about that now and that had to eat at him—as good as he was."

As a senior, Harris was still carrying his Dapper Dan gym bag, evidence that he once was one of America's most prized basketball players, but otherwise his appearance had changed in three years. He had an afro and daily wore blue jeans and an old Army jacket, typical attire for the hippie era. "Those last two years, I saw a big change in Henry," said Ralph Foster, owner of Duke's Barber Shop. "He was such a clean-cut young man when he came here. He was well-groomed—'yes sir,' 'no sir,' a very polite young man. His appearance changed. His demeanor changed. He just wasn't the All-American boy after his first two or three years."

Harris was permitted to go to Bremen, Georgia, to visit Sewell Manufacturing Company, owned by Auburn athletics benefactor Roy Sewell, to get free suits, coats, and slacks. It was a rite of passage for Auburn athletes because it meant a player was seen by his coaches as a major contributor. But for Harris, the clothes were just income. "He would sell them," Gossom said. "He sold tennis shoes, he sold pants, he sold suits."

Harris remained a simple man. After getting his first car during the summer, it quit running by fall quarter and sat on the street for weeks before finally being towed off by the university. "He never had a car, but he never complained," Owens said. "You could see he was from a small place from the way he lived. Material things meant nothing to him. He was just Henry. He'd give you the shirt off his back if you asked for it." Harris could always get his friends laughing when he started telling stories about life in Boligee, even if he had to joke about his own poverty. He'd say his family was so poor that it cut off one of the rooms of the house to make firewood. He'd talk about the tiny tavern that sat next to the railroad tracks running through town and recount how a drunk once staggered out into the path of an oncoming train. Ironically, Boligee legend held that a supposedly "uppity" black man was once killed, put on the tracks to cover the crime, and run over by a train.

Owens believed Harris kept "a lot of things to himself and was always trying to find something good to say," but George Smith, who would become president of Auburn's Black Student Union, thought Harris might be using a façade to cope. "Henry always talked about how he loved life, about how he fully enjoyed his life," said Smith, reflecting on all Harris was going through, particularly the knee injury. "He used to say that all the time, all the time. I wondered if he was trying to convince himself."

Hiding feelings was a survival skill for black Americans in the South, and Harris had seen it modeled often in Boligee. "Henry was always smiling," Gossom said. "He could handle it as long as he had to handle it." But the gap between what Harris said and felt was growing wider. Bill Perry, the former team manager, noticed Harris would never say he was unhappy. And if he did admit any displeasure, he'd allude to it being "his own fault," said Perry. Suitemate Johnson noticed that when Harris was around the dorm, he'd "always come in and make a joke about something, say something about me or someone else. He'd act like he was having fun. Sometimes people do that because they've got something else on their mind."

"Henry was not a big complainer," said Dee C. Madison, the black counselor Auburn hired in 1971 in response to the spring march on the president's office. He saw Harris as a "good kid but a little introverted—he liked being by himself an awful lot." But if depression was starting to seize Harris, he self-medicated it with booze, women, and weed and stayed on the run. "He'd just leave and not say anything. You'd look up and he'd be gone," said Johnson. "We'd go over there [to his room] and he wouldn't be there. We'd go back later and he'd be there."

Like most American college campuses at the dawn of the 1970s, marijuana was readily available at Auburn and Sewell Hall. Gossom said Harris had "never gotten high before coming to Auburn" but started smoking marijuana early on. Teammate Bobby York would get on him—"that stuff's bad for you"—but never could get Harris to have a serious conversation about it. Owens thought Harris's use of marijuana use increased after the knee injury, although he did not remember ever seeing Harris drunk—"and with marijuana, he always had a pleasure point he'd get to, and he'd go to jumping around and kidding around," said Owens. Threatt, though, noticed Harris had begun drinking more. "He was always in pain over the leg. He was always complaining about that," she said. "He was in a lot of pain."

Marijuana not only medicated Harris's emotional ache but also his physical pain. He had coped the previous three years under the belief that if he could just avoid making anyone too angry at him, then he could move on to the pros, make some money, and help his family—and it all would have been worthwhile. The knee injury, however, was eating away at his escape plan.

"When he had that knee injury, he was really depressed about that, but I know he fought through it," said Davenport. "I used to practice with him, and his knee wasn't at all getting right. He never could make the moves where he could get away from me like he used to before that knee injury. And I know he tried like hell to rehab the injury." Despite all the rehab Harris had done, he was still hobbling around and wondering. Would he be able to play this season? Could he take a medical redshirt year to allow the knee to heal? Would he ever recover sufficiently to make it to the pros? Would the Dallas Cowboys still have any interest in him? And if he was done athletically, could he still help his mom out financially? Would he be able to graduate?

Harris had long needed a strong male role model at Auburn but never more than now. Larry Chapman and Rudy Davalos were gone, and Bill Lynn was battling alcoholism, fighting for his job, and unable to relate to Harris. "Your coach is supposed to be your leader, not only your basketball leader, but your spiritual leader," said Tim Ash. "He's supposed to set the tone for everybody, and he just couldn't get with it." The contrast between Lynn and Harris, in era and culture, was captured on the cover of Auburn's 1971-72 basketball media guide with a photo that captured the South's past, future, and awkward present. Photographed on a bench in front of Memorial Coliseum, Harris, with a full Afro, wore Auburn's navy-and-white basketball warmup. Lynn wore a blue suit with light blue socks and the trendy black-and-white leather shoes of that era.

Harris was team captain, but that did not spare him from day-to-day life in Auburn. "It was so difficult to be a hero and struggling culturally," Gossom said. To be a hero and a "nobody," to be loved and despised in an instant. "A lot of people saw you on the field or the court but never knew what life was like those other five or six days," said Owens, who once went with Gossom to Burger King and was accosted by a loud white man, who called them "niggers" and challenged them to fight. They resisted their urge to attack him, unsure if they had that much air cover with their coaches and whether black masculinity could be flexed anywhere but the football field or basketball court. They took their bag of burgers and fries back to Sewell Hall.

"To be at Auburn," said Owens, "was a very mental game."

While Owens was watching game film of Tennessee in a football meeting room in September, offensive coordinator Gene Lorendo started talking about Tennessee linebacker Jackie Walker, the first black athlete chosen first-team All-SEC. An All-American as a junior, Walker was a team captain and the defensive play-caller. Lorendo was stressing the need to contain Walker's extraordinary range on the field.

"I guess he forgot I was there," Owens recalled. "He said, 'We got to get that nigger. We got to kill him, we got to kill the nigger.'"

"Then finally, I guess it dawned on him, and everybody is looking at me. What can I say?" asked Owens in 2008, chuckling softly in resignation, his eyes watering with tears. "What are you going to do? Jump up and run out, hollering and screaming? And I know those weren't the only times those words were used, even between the coaches and players. But they hadn't been used around me."

When Lorendo stopped talking, the room was silent. "It got so quiet. I guess he realized after it got so quiet, what he had really said. I guess they [his teammates] were just as shocked as I was. They were looking for a reaction. I went like this," explained Owens, turning his palms out and upward. "What can I say?"

Several teammates came to Owens afterward. "They said, 'Man, you know how Coach Lorendo is, he didn't mean nothing by it.' I even had Coach [Paul] Davis [defensive coordinator] come and say, 'Owens, don't let that bother you. Everything is going to be all right.'"

But as the week wore on and Owens tried to stop replaying the incident in his head, and the more he began to wonder if the whole scenario might have been intentional. "Maybe it was done to see what kind of reaction I would have," he said. "You know, 'He's here and he's never caused any problems, we've never heard him say anything out of the way,' which they never had. Maybe they said, 'We need to test him. I don't know. It happened."

On that Saturday in Knoxville, with Auburn trailing Tennessee 9-3, Owens was on the sideline in the gray steel cavern of Neyland Stadium. Twelve minutes remained in the nationally televised game. Suddenly, he heard Lorendo call his name.

"Owens, get in there."

It was first down and the ball was on Tennessee's two-yard-line. Auburn would have four shots at the potential winning touchdown. Owens lined up as a fullback in the I formation.

"They call the play," he said. "And I fumble the ball."

As Owens was crossing the goal line, the ball rolled down his leg and bounced on the artificial turf of the end zone and a Tennessee defender quickly fell on it. Devastated, Owens ran to the sideline. He knew he had let his teammates and coaches down, but he also knew he had not gotten the handoff cleanly. He headed toward Lorendo.

"Coach, I didn't get the ball."

Lorendo didn't want to hear it.

"Go sit down," he snapped.

Owens did not expect to be believed. "Pat Sullivan was the quarterback—he didn't make mistakes, everything's perfect," he said. (Sullivan would say years later he could not remember the handoff but would go along with Owens's memory of it hitting his thigh.)

Wes Bizilia, the assistant basketball coach, had a sideline pass that day and heard the coaches talking. "He's a blocking back. He can't run the ball. He's a blocking back," they said. Basketball player Dan Kirkland was in the stands. "Folks were saying things that shouldn't have ever been said about someone," he said.

Fortunately for Owens, Sullivan led Auburn eighty-six yards in the final minutes for a touchdown and a 10-9 victory, so the fumble would not cost Auburn the game. Its effect on Owens's life, however, would be enduring, as the fumble played into two racial stereotypes of the era—blacks fumble and blacks can't handle pressure. "I think from that time on, my carrying career as a running back was doomed," Owens said.

The rules were different then. In October, Henley lost three fumbles in the first half at Georgia Tech, and after making him apologize to the team at halftime, Jordan gave him a shot at redemption, starting him in the second half. Auburn came from behind to win.

Despite averaging 5.0 yards per carry, Owens would carry the football only thirty times in 1971. "I couldn't understand it," he said. "They wouldn't let me run the ball, but they let me run back punts." In a mid-November showdown between unbeaten Auburn and unbeaten Georgia, Owens went back to return a punt with Auburn sitting on an eight-point lead late in the fourth quarter on the road. With the Sanford Stadium rabble hollering—"You can drop that ball, boy"—Owens returned the punt sixty yards, enabling Sullivan to throw his fourth touchdown pass of the afternoon and win the Heisman Trophy a dozen days later.

Harris's girlfriend Debra Threatt remembered Harris getting angry only one time. It was evening and he was talking to her from the pay phone in front of the Krystal on Magnolia Street, directly across from campus. "We were talking," Threatt said, "and some white students came by and stopped and yelled the n-word at him and then took off. They called him that. He was so upset. He said, 'Did you hear that? Did you hear what they just called me?' He really freaked out over that. He said, 'Can you believe that, them calling me that.' It took a lot to get him mad." Harris dropped the phone and yelled back. Threatt heard it all. She told him, "Don't do that. They're not even worth it." But the whites had driven off.

"They knew who he was. They were students. And I think that's what hurt him, all them screaming racial slurs," Threatt said. "I think that incident shocked him because he was always so nice to everyone there. He was captain of that team. That really hurt him."

Chapter 26

Wounded Warrior

Harris's senior season finally arrived December 1, 1971. He had made it through three years at Auburn. Only three more months and he could move on to the pros and help his mom. With a black teammate, finally, and blacks on seven of the other nine SEC teams—all but Kentucky and Mississippi State—he would no longer be such a solitary figure on the court. Perry Wallace had his best season as a senior primarily because "after a while I realized I wasn't going to die out on the floor, although I kept getting threats." Harris also should have been relaxed enough to have his best season. He would be playing guard, and John Mengelt was gone, meaning there would be more opportunities to boost his scoring average, an important factor to the NBA. And by his senior season, Harris had adjusted, for better or worse, to the Auburn shuffle.

Thom Gossom believed, for Harris, playing at Auburn wasn't "just about going out to shoot a basketball. If it was that simple, he would have been All-American. It was knowing that if you get the ball off the hoop and run down court real fast and shoot, that's 'n-word ball.' You've got to get it off the hoop and run down and hold it for a while. So everything you've ever been, you have to de-program, and you become programmed all over. So maybe by the time you're a senior, you become relaxed enough you can do something."

But any mental or emotional comfort Harris was feeling as a senior was negated by the physical pain and limitations created by his knee injury. He was still limping when preseason practice began in mid-October, as his left knee was healing slowly. Yet, Coach Lynn did not mention Harris's difficult recovery during a preseason interview with the *Atlanta Constitution's* Richard Hyatt, who knew of Lynn's reputation for not developing players. In a Q&A format, Hyatt asked

Lynn: "As a freshman, Henry Harris showed superstar potential, but thus far he has not reached those heights. Would you classify his career as a disappointment?"

"No," replied Lynn, "because you have to look at Henry's career from all sides. He had an adjustment as our first black athlete and more importantly has been playing out of position at forward for two years. He has had injury problems too. He played the last six games last year with a torn cartilage in his knee, which is hard to believe. In fact, he hurt it in the Alabama game, yet never really rested that day. He's our captain now and having a great preseason. His knee seems strong and in our first scrimmage he hit eleven of twelve from the floor."

Although Lynn continued to call the injury a cartilage tear, it was far worse. Auburn trainer Kenny Howard described Harris's injury as the "unhappy triad," meaning he tore not only the cartilage in his left knee but also the anterior cruciate ligament and the medial collateral ligament. The surgery was done by Jack Hughston, considered one of the top orthopedic surgeons in America, who was based in Columbus, Georgia, and did all of Auburn's surgeries. "If it was just a cartilage injury, Dr. Hughston would not have cut the knee open," said Herbert Waldrup, Auburn's assistant trainer then. "Back then, the surgery itself would have destabilized the knee too much to go in just to fix cartilage."

"Everybody was wondering if he could make it through the season," said assistant coach Larry Phillips. Harris's recovery was so slow he could've been redshirted for medical reasons and received an extra year of eligibility. Howard, who had been Auburn's trainer for a quarter-century, said, "That [redshirting] would be a decision of the coach to say, 'Well we need Henry bad enough at 75 percent that we're going to play him rather than wait for him to be at ninety percent next year.' It would depend on how good your personnel is and whether you can afford to do that."

Lynn's ship was sinking, and he needed all hands on deck. The other four members of Harris's signing class had already left school or the team—debunking the stereotype that black athletes lacked staying power—and the sophomore class was weak, having been signed immediately after the departure of Davalos and Chapman. For two years after signing Harris in 1968, Auburn had failed to recruit additional black players, preferring tokenism over competitiveness when in-state talent was readily available. Now, the cost of that decision was coming due.

"He [Lynn] had to have somebody to play," Howard said in 2011, "and Henry playing at seventy-five percent of his capabilities had to play. At seventy-five percent, he was still better than anybody he [Lynn] had." Howard recalled that redshirting Harris was discussed. "They talked about it. They talked with him. He didn't want to [redshirt]. He wanted to go on and get out of school." So, with his left knee wrapped tightly, Harris returned to battle for Auburn, his teammates, and his race.

Opening the season against South Carolina, the defending ACC champion, Harris again showed the home crowd he would play hard. He took fifteen shots, scored sixteen points, and had nine rebounds. Auburn then reeled off three straight victories but the streak ended in 107-82 blowout loss at Louisiana Tech. By January, Auburn was 4-3 and Harris was back at forward, with sophomore Mike Christian usually teaming with Gary England at guard. "I tried him [Harris] back in the backcourt his senior year," Lynn would try to explain years later, "but we had to get the five best people whom we thought would play the best together, so we had to move him back [to forward]."

The seriousness of Harris's injury was obvious to his teammates. "He was not the same player after that [injury], couldn't have been the same player. His ability to cut and jump was just not the same," said Tim Beavers. "I vividly remember his knee always wrapped, and I remember him icing after games and heat before."

Harris's photo appeared on the cover of the Ole Miss game program January 3, and inside was a profile written by David Housel, a 1969 Auburn graduate who edited the basketball programs. When Housel asked Harris how he'd like to be remembered, he replied as a basketball player "who cares for other people," explaining why he had switched his major to vocational rehabilitation. "It will be a chance to help those less fortunate than I, and there's no greater feeling."

Auburn lost against Ole Miss for the fourth time in five games, and the student section, believing Lynn should have been fired previously, made it clear he would be coaching in front of a tough, albeit small, audience at home. "It was embarrassing to be sitting on the bench with this going on," recalled assistant Wes Bizilia. "It was a tough situation." Between sarcasm in the seats and continuing dissension on the team, Harris, the wounded captain, kept leading on the court in his quiet, strong way. "He would try to get us together," said Albert Johnson, his black teammate. "He'd tell them they needed to do a little better than what they were doing. He'd say, 'You need to guard your man.' He was in a lot of pain. He was a strong person as far as fighting through the pain. I'd see him limping and he'd be in so much pain, but then he'd get out there on the floor and he'd give it his all. Then after the game, he'd be limping again because of the pain." Nothing Harris said could match his leadership by example. "He was very much someone we all looked up to," Beavers said.

Limping or not, Harris had ten rebounds against Georgia and beat the press with his ball-handling during a three-game January winning streak. Against LSU, he had fourteen points, seven rebounds, and six assists, played the entire game, and, as usual, guarded 6-foot-7, 245-pound All-SEC center Al "Apple" Sanders. "Henry could do a number on the big guys," Lynn liked to brag. With Johnson scoring thirteen points at LSU, Auburn's top two scorers were black—a first—but Johnson would play sparingly the rest of the season.

Fifteen years after it integrated its student body under court, LSU finally had a black player, 6-foot-8 Collis Temple Jr. Governor John McKeithen promised Temple his door would be open if he encountered problems, having no idea Louisiana had paid the Michigan State tuition of Collis Temple Sr. just to keep him out of LSU's graduate school. No state had resisted athletic integration more than Louisiana, and Temple Jr. regularly wrestled with the old days. Just three weeks before the Auburn game—during a Christmas Day practice preparing for a game against Houston—LSU coach Press Maravich called Houston's players "jumping jungle bunnies." "He was talking about how they would block shots . . . and they could jump," Temple said. Maravich talked to Temple after practice, saying, "I didn't really mean nothing by that. That wasn't directed at you, and I need you to know that you are a credit to your race," according to Temple. "In other words," Temple said, "your race ain't s---, but you're all right."

A week after playing LSU, Auburn went to Tuscaloosa, and with 12,476 watching on a Saturday night, Coach C. M. Newton got the game he had been building toward for four years. The Alabama sophomores Mengelt had scored sixty on were seniors, and Newton started subbing for them when they were up by twenty-nine points. Alabama won 89-66. Playing on the knee injured there eleven months earlier, Harris had ten points and five rebounds but was only the third best black player on the floor. Wendell Hudson had twenty-four points, sixteen rebounds, eight steals, and six assists. Sophomore guard Raymond Odums made ten of fifteen shots and ignited the running game with steals.

Two nights later, Auburn allowed Georgia to make a school-record 68 percent of its shots, with black guard Ronnie Hogue getting twenty-five points and black center Tim Bassett fifteen points and fifteen rebounds. Auburn then lost at Vanderbilt, as its lone African American, sophomore Bill Ligon, scored twenty-one. The losing streak hit five with losses to Tennessee and Kentucky. Harris had six assists, fourteen points, and six rebounds in thirty-seven minutes against Tennessee and repeatedly kept the Tigers in the Kentucky game, putting them ahead in the second half and making all six of his shots. Auburn then won at Florida and defeated LSU when Harris had seventeen points and nine rebounds and played all forty minutes again. He played twenty-three minutes the next night in a victory over Georgia Tech.

"Henry was probably playing on one leg, and still was able to compete and compete well .That's how good he was," England said. "Athletically, he was the best player on the team. As a teammate and basketball player, he was top-notch. He was very unselfish."

After home games, Harris would dress quickly and escape to the sanctuary of the Windsor Hall Apartments and his black friends. "He would not hang around because inside he was bitter," Gossom said. "He never would say anything, and if any reporters or alumni came up to talk to him, they would think, 'Henry Harris is a good old guy.' But inside, I think it ate him up."

Harris had ice on his knee "even if we were just playing cards," Gossom said. "It was this big round ball thing. It never looked like it went down." Harris had "water on the knee," more formally known as knee effusion, which is the body's natural reaction to ligament or cartilage damage, as synovial fluid surrounds the joint to protect it from further injury.

But for Harris, the swelling never seemed to go down, and his friends could not understand his slow recovery. "It didn't heal," said James Owens. "Henry may have thought he was rehabbing enough. They may not have thought we [blacks] had to work as hard as whites. Or they may not have cared." It was mandatory, however, for athletes to rehab under supervision, according to teammate Dan Kirkland, who had two knee surgeries at Auburn. "We'd be in the training room, any athlete who was injured, working with the coach and team doctor. I'm sure Henry was in there," Kirkland said.

Harris was dealing with a "severe injury," according to trainer Howard, and he could have compounded the damage by continuing to play on the knee before surgery. "He certainly didn't help it any by doing that," Howard said.

Recovering from just the surgery itself was extremely challenging under the best conditions. "Back then, the surgery was almost primitive compared to what it is now," said Kirkland. "You were in a full leg cast for nine weeks, and by the time the cast came off, your leg looked like your arm." Recovery was even more difficult for a basketball player, as the instability created in the knee by the surgery could greatly affect a player's cutting ability.

When Gossom saw Harris start drinking wine and smoking marijuana before Saturday night home games, he felt his friend had become "really depressed." Owens believed Harris's frustration was compounded by the knowledge that he could have scored more the previous two seasons but was not allowed to. "You pick up the paper and it's all about Auburn University and Mengelt. People don't know, but that tears you apart," Owens said. "It begins to wear you down, where you don't have that same focus. All you want to do is get it over with. I think Henry's senior season, that's all that mattered. Just get through with it, and be done with it. He was a hurt young man, really hurt. He'd tell me after a game that he was glad it was over and that he could mark it down as one less game he'd have to play."

Harris hit his limit of pain and frustration two nights after a loss at home to Alabama in the last second. Playing in Mississippi State's bandbox, Auburn was up by two late in the game when Harris missed a free throw. State tied the game, and then the officials called an offensive foul on Harris with a minute to play. State played for the final shot and made it with three seconds left. In the locker room afterward, he told Johnson he was quitting.

"Don't do that," said Johnson. "You got too many people counting on you. There's a lot of people you're going to let down."

Much of Harris's frustration, according to Johnson, was that "I'm giving it everything, but my teammates are not going all out." But it was not as simple as just walking away. How would his scholarship be affected? How would he get a degree without it? What would he tell his mother about not graduating?

"I guess I convinced him," Johnson said. "That next day he said he had changed his mind." He told Johnson, "I've too many people on my side, rooting for me, to quit."

During the final month of the season, *Birmingham News* columnist Clyde Bolton returned to Auburn, two years after describing the huge applause given Harris in his varsity debut. This time he told a different story— "For Henry, Road Has Been Melancholy:"

> ... If you would avoid a sobering sight, don't go to Auburn basketball games. Harris, a smooth leopard when he arrived on the Plain from Boligee nearly four years ago, guts it out in a knee brace now, much of his quickness drained off by a collection of hard calcium. "He would have been a famous basketball player," Coach Bill Lynn said wistfully. "I don't think anybody was as good defensively as Henry was. If he was well, he would be a 20-point man and the best defensive player in the SEC." ...
>
> "He's had sprained ankles, groin pulls and bruises on his thigh," Lynn said. "He's been hurt over half the time here.... He tore the cartilage (in his left knee at Alabama last year) and nobody knows how he continued to play. He started the game the next Monday and played about 10 minutes before we had to take him out. But then he played the rest of the year," Lynn said. "I don't guess anybody ever played on torn cartilage before. He practices about half the time, but I don't think he ever missed a game.
>
> "Henry has never complained about what has happened to him. He never asks for anything. We have to watch him to keep him from practicing when he shouldn't."
>
> Harris will undergo an operation when the season is over.

He could have had surgery before this season, but no one knew the situation would become this serious, complicated by hard calcium in the joint. . . .

"He can't make the move off that leg, and that's the leg a right-handed shooter jumps on. To show you the kind of kid he is, he has learned to jump off his right leg." . . .

There is still a chance for a happy ending to the Henry Harris basketball story. "He would like to play pro," Lynn said, "and he could if the knee gets well. Two or three clubs want him to try. If he doesn't make it, we could use him as a graduate assistant coach here next season. Yes sir, he could have been a fabulous basketball player."

Chapter 27

Hero

*To disregard color even for an instant is
to step away from the old prejudices,
the old hatred. This is not a path
on which many turn back.*

- Roger Kahn

On Friday, February 25, 1972, the day before his final home game, Harris did a telephone interview with the *Atlanta Constitution's* Al Thomy, a veteran sports reporter who was a master at putting interview subjects at ease with softly spoken questions. Thomy was a pro football writer, but he knew all the right questions to ask Harris.

Did he take abuse as Auburn's first black player?

"Abuse? Yes, I took some abuse for being the first black to play. But then there are people who frown upon anybody different, and I just don't mean racially different. Take John Mengelt, who played with us a couple of years. He took some abuse too because he was a little more different than people thought he should have been. Yes, there was some abuse."

Thomy asked Harris to sum up his career.

"I guess I could sum it up by saying my basketball career has been a great experience."

Had he ever regretted his decision to play at Auburn?

Again, Harris evaded the question.

"It was a great experience—that's all I can say."

Thomy was persistent. Would he do it over again?

"I just can't imagine doing it over again," Harris replied.

The article ran the next day in the *Atlanta Constitution* under the headline, "Would Harris Go Again? 'I Just Can't Imagine It.'" It opened with Thomy reviewing Harris' three college choices—Villanova, Alabama, and Auburn. He then wrote:

> He chose Auburn. "Don't know why, really don't. I guess Tuscaloosa was too close to my home. But, on the other hand, Auburn is not that much farther. You might say being the first black athlete at Auburn, knowing I could open some doors, influenced my decision."
>
> At this stage of a Haratio Alger theme, it would be heart-warming to report Henry Harris excelled on the courts of friendly strive, made his marks in the classroom and was given the hero's adulation by the fans and the pro scouts. It didn't work out that way. He suffered two knee injuries. . . . He underwent surgery last April. More cutting is on the agenda. Then too, because of a shortage of forwards, Harris has played a foreign position. "My sophomore and junior years, I played forward," he said, careful not to sound too critical. "Just say it was not the position I originally played. Then I ran into serious knee problems."

The philosophical ending of the article indicated Thomy's grasp of Harris's barrier-shattering experience at Auburn:

> Meanwhile, Henry Harris, his knee heavily bandaged, goes about finishing his basketball career at Auburn. He limps as he goes about it. If he had it to do over again, he doesn't know that he would. He doesn't consider himself a pioneer. He considers himself an academically qualified basketball player who happened to decide to get his education at Auburn. College often can be an education.

In Perry Wallace's farewell interview with the *Nashville Tennessean*, Frank Sutherland had asked him if he would do it again. Wallace responded by saying there was a "thin line between success and failure" and that he would "hate to have to do it again depending on just luck." Within a month, though, Wallace was more definitive, telling interviewer Frye Galliard, "I wouldn't do it again. I couldn't. There is no way." And Steve Martin, the Tulane baseball player who integrated the SEC in 1966, told author Andrew Maraniss before his death in 2013 he would not do it again, despite all the progress that followed.

Only 3,328 people showed up for Harris's final game at Auburn. With 1:18 left to play, he fouled out with ten points, three rebounds, and four assists. Unselfish to the end, he had taken only seven of Auburn's seventy shots. When he walked to the bench with his fifth foul, the crowd rose and began to clap. The ovation did not stop when Harris sat down. It continued. On and on. For a minute and a half. The *Opelika-Auburn Daily News* described the scene in an unsigned column:

> When the proud and tall black man from Boligee, Alabama, left the floor, it took 90 seconds – because that was how long the crowd cheered him. They cheered and clapped and whistled not because it was Henry's last game at home, but because he was simply, Henry Harris. Sure, he was the team captain, a senior and the first black to be signed to a basketball scholarship at Auburn. But more so, he was, as one fan put it: "Gee, that's Henry Harris." Five words can't say it all but somehow they fit.

Harris had given Auburn fans the opportunity to cheer a black man, and he had changed them in the process. Ironically, he had been an Auburn guy all along—he did all the dirty work, the hard stuff, he played tough. He was the ultimate underdog. The ovation proved sport's ability to unify shards of society—perhaps that's why integration was resisted so long. He was the long-feared "other," yet he had buried the myth and forced players and fans to respect him for the size of his heart, demonstrating a resilience and courage that underline the universality of all.

A week after the home finale, Auburn played at Tennessee, which finally had an integrated team four years after signing and then losing Spencer Haywood. Harris gave a regional TV audience an impressive farewell, with sixteen points and fifteen rebounds. "When inspirational leader Henry Harris fouled out with just over four minutes to go, the Vols pulled resolutely away," wrote John Pruett of the *Huntsville Times*.

The Tigers then traveled to Lexington for the final home game of seventy-year-old Coach Adolph Rupp, who would be forced to retire at the end of the season by the university. With Tom Payne having left school early to turn pro, Rupp's final team was as white as the one that lost Texas Western six years earlier. Kentucky beat Auburn, 102-67, and for the first time in his career, Harris failed to score—and on the same court he scored forty-three points as a freshman. When he fouled out, he was applauded by Kentucky's fans. He had made a positive impression. "I remember Henry," said Kentucky co-captain Stan Key, a guard who faced Harris eight times over four years. "He was a little ahead of his day, very confident. We did talk a little during games, and he was a true gentleman. Really a nice guy. You can't say that about everybody."

Three nights later, Harris's career ended in Oxford, Mississippi, where he had played his first SEC opponent as a scared-to-death freshman. But this time his opponent would also have a black player, 6-foot-5 Coolidge Ball, a quiet young man as country as Harris. He would score twenty-three points and lead the Rebels to victory. "Harris, who has played on gimpy knees for the past two years, finished a courageous career with nine [points]," wrote Pruett. Harris, who fouled out of his fourth straight game, told reporters afterward, "Four years . . . it's hard to believe they're over. I only wish we could have won more." In losing its sixth straight game, Auburn finished with a 10-16 record—its worst in twenty-two years but only one loss worse than the previous year's team, which included Mengelt, a second-round NBA draft choice.

When finally given a chance as a black American, Harris had hugged his opportunity. He had never missed a start. Not at Auburn or any of the dark Dixie highways he traveled. He was always there, confronting the past and foreshadowing the future, his simple presence an act of defiance—"Here I am."

On one good leg, he averaged 11.3 points per game, led the team in assists, and was second in rebounds with 6.2 per game. Although his scoring average had dropped each season, his 924 career points placed him eighth on Auburn's all-time scoring list. The media named him third team All-SEC. Three black Americans who had followed Harris to Deep South schools—Wendell Hudson and Raymond Odums of Alabama and Georgia's Ronnie Hogue's—were among the fifteen All-SEC selections.

A hero supposedly suffers for those who follow him, according to Joseph Campbell, the great America chronicler of myth. Henry Harris was a hero. He gave himself to a cause bigger than himself. He played hard, he played hurt, and he kept his mouth shut. He knew what he *had* to do and he did it. He stayed—when all the stereotypes said he wouldn't and common sense said he shouldn't.

Twenty-four-year-old David Housel was one person in Auburn's athletic department who seemed to understand all that. In an article for the Vanderbilt game program—Harris's final home game--Housel, who would become Auburn's athletic director emeritus in 2006, called Harris one of Auburn's greatest competitors ever, in any sport:

> This is a personal opinion.
> Though personal, it is an opinion shared by many both in Auburn and across the Southeast.
> It concerns an Auburn basketball player.
> That player is Henry Harris.
> Henry Harris – that is a common name, nothing in that name to excite crowds and stimulate headline writers. It's just a name, a common, everyday name, Henry Harris. But that's all right. Henry Harris never had to rely on his name – or the color of his skin – to get things done.
> He does them himself, on the basketball court, and herein lies part of the story of the greatness of Henry Harris, but only part. . . .
> To remember Harris as the first man of his race to receive an athletic scholarship to Auburn would be an injustice, especially to Harris. His desire is – always has been – to be "just another basketball player." But to remember Henry Harris as a competitor would not be an injustice. That's what he is, one of the best competitors to ever suit up in an Auburn uniform in any sport.
> This has been a painful year for Henry Harris. Painful in that the team won-loss ratio is no better than it is, and painful in a physical sense because of an aggravated knee ailment.
> A lesser man would have given up the year, possibly the career. But Henry Harris is not an ordinary man, and to consider him a lesser man would be false to all that athletics import. Despite pain bordering on anguish, pain that has robbed Harris' fine black legs of their speed, quickness and maneuverability that once marked him for stardom, he kept on playing, never resting on the court, playing and striving toward the ultimate goal – victory.
> Henry Harris is an athlete's athlete. He is not perfect. He's made mistakes and he's had bad games, but he's always been a competitor. Make no mistake about that. Long after lesser men have acquiesced, Henry Harris is still competing and herein lies Henry Harris' true greatness.

Chapter 28

The Fight We've Been Looking For

Despite what Bill Lynn had told the press and what David Housel wrote weeks earlier, no additional surgery was scheduled on Harris' knee after the season ended. No one could remember why. But Harris's buddy Thom Gossom had an idea.

"When you're through, they're through with you," said Gossom.

Harris would take on the NBA bum knee and all.

The league draft was held Wednesday, April 12, 1972, and it became a long day for Harris. He was finally taken in the eighth round by the Houston Rockets, as their final selection in the eighteen-round draft.

Because of his knee injury, Harris was actually more suited for a backup role in the rival, five-year-old American Basketball Association, but all eleven ABA passed on drafting him.

Harris had told reporter Al Thomy in February he knew he couldn't count on having a pro career, but he dropped out of his spring-quarter classes and began preparing for making the Rockets' roster, playing games wherever he could. However, Harris continued living in Sewell Hall, where he would go through a horrifying experience before leaving for the NBA

Near the end of spring quarter, 6-foot-8 Sylvester Davenport went to the Indianapolis 500 with several white students, and when he returned to Sewell Hall, he was hallucinating from smoking hallucinogenic mushrooms. "I thought I was smoking marijuana and somebody put psychedelic mushrooms in the joint," Davenport said. "I went on a trip that lasted thirty-five days. I didn't think I was going to come down from that trip. I thought I was going to see God. . . . It wasn't any damn joint. It was a space rocket."

James Owens recalled. "We were in the TV room, and he told Brownie Flournoy [the dormitory supervisor] to eat the television."

Not understanding Davenport's behavior and frightened by what might happen if he stayed at the dorm, Owens, Harris, Thom Gossom, and Albert Johnson put him in the backseat of Gossom's car and started driving around Auburn to "cool him down" and figure out what to do. Eventually, during the night, with Johnson, his roommate, talking calmly to him, Davenport allowed himself to be taken out of Sewell Hall in a straightjacket. He would spend the next thirty-five days in a mental health hospital in Columbus, Georgia.

"It was a terrible thing," Owens said. "Here we were, still young men. I had never seen . . . it amazed me. It's amazing all of us didn't lose our minds."

Having grown up in Soddy-Daisy, then a rural hamlet in southeast Tennessee known for moonshine stills and a scant black population, Davenport had attended school with whites most of his life. He was friendly and somewhat naïve because of his country background, and he found Auburn a "real challenge" socially. "I didn't know what part of the university I belonged to," he said in 2016. "See, I had a bunch of friends who had gone down there. When I went to see them, it was different story from Soddy-Daisy, because nobody down there could have black people come into their room and talk to them. There were some very good friends of mine who said, 'You shouldn't call over here.' Well, to put it in real words, it was pure hell for me."

Davenport had his choice of several SEC schools. "Sylvester was an exceptional player, but he was in a backwoods area, outside of Chattanooga," said Auburn assistant coach Larry Phillips. "All of a sudden, boom, everybody in the country came in there. Kentucky came in like gangbusters. Joe B. Hall [Kentucky assistant coach] was there, but I had been working on him [Davenport] for over a year." Like the rural Harris home three years earlier, the Davenports' house became a crossroads for young, hot-shot college coaches, searching the sticks for a star. "His parents were really nice people," Phillips said. "They didn't know a lot about other places and basketball, and recruiting was quite an education for them, because they lived in a pretty poor area. They were nice people, very old, humble people."

Instead of avoiding the Deep South's racism, as many high school prospects did, Davenport's parents wanted to move toward it. "My mother and my daddy and my grandmother said, 'Yeah, you need to go down there because this is the fight we've been looking for.' I didn't know what they were talking about.... Anyway, that's what they said, and I always listened to my mama and daddy," said Davenport, whose family understood racial injustice firsthand—two of his great-grandfathers were lynched. "Remember everything happening in Birmingham and everything happening with the governor. And he had been so restrictive about black people going to major universities in Alabama. That's why my mother and daddy said, 'Well, you need to go somewhere you can make a difference.'"

Another reason Davenport went to Auburn was Harris. He visited Auburn several times and struck an immediate relationship with Harris, although he repeatedly warned Davenport not to come to Auburn. "I guess he had been there long enough to know . . . that I was probably not the right guy for down there," Davenport said. "Henry told me, 'You need to go somewhere else. You don't need to come down here, because your life will be miserable,' which he was right. My life was miserable. He said, 'But you might make a difference,' and I didn't know what he was talking about, so I asked him. He said, 'Oh, you'll make a difference down here, but you never will see it, you never will know it.'"

In the summer of 1972, the Houston Rockets entered a squad of veterans and rookies in the California Summer Pro Basketball League. Games would be played three nights a week at the Cal State–Los Angeles gymnasium. Harris's teammates would include veterans Mike Newlin and Rudy Tomjanovich and rookies Eric McWilliams, James Silas, Wil Robinson, and Paul McCracken.

Harris spent at least half the summer with Loretta Towns Brown, his former high school counselor, who had a two-bedroom apartment in the Crenshaw area of Los Angeles. "Henry called me and asked if he could spend a couple of nights and ended up staying six weeks," she said. Brown was teaching summer school so didn't mind Harris being around. "He told me he was just practicing and trying out. I never saw him that much. I was teaching and he was practicing."

A native of Bessemer, Brown arrived at Greene County Training School in 1965 after completing a master's in school counseling at Indiana University. She was transferred a year later to Carver High

School in Eutaw but stayed in touch with Harris while he was being recruited. She moved to Los Angeles in 1968 to work for Inglewood Public Schools and earn a master's in education from Pepperdine.

Harris showed Brown the 1972 Auburn basketball media guide with his picture on the cover. "He was proud of that," she said. But Brown also noticed how embarrassed Harris was when she took him to dinner. "He would say, 'I should be taking you to dinner.'"

For Brown, it was a bittersweet summer. While Harris was being recruited, she believed he and his mother listened too much to "an old-style principal trying to make history." She thought Harris should go to Villanova. "I told him, 'Henry, you have three schools you can go to—Auburn, Alabama, or Villanova.' I told him. 'You don't have time to make history,'" said Brown, who saw Harris as an "excellent student." "But I knew Auburn was going to be breaking him in. White folks had been trying to hold us back for a long time, so they were not going to let him be the best without a fight. So they weren't going to give him good grades."

Brown was also concerned about Harris's night life. He would quietly leave the house after she went to bed. "He would go out in the middle of the night and then get back before it was time for me to go to school," said Brown, who didn't ask what he was doing, assuming it would only embarrass him further.

Chapter 29

Systematic Lynching

Broken by the Associated Press in August 1972, the story seemed to grow more horrifying each day as additional reporting uncovered more disturbing details of a systematic, undercover, government-funded lynching going on for thirty years in Tuskegee.

In an effort to better understand syphilis, the U.S. government began researching the course of untreated syphilis in African American males in rural Alabama in the early 1940s. Living in the tiny towns and on the dirt roads surrounding Tuskegee, the men—many illiterate and all destitute during the Depression—became test subjects in exchange for "free medical care, free meals on exam days, and burial insurance, a luxury for black Americans in the rural South.

When the study began, no cure existed for syphilis. In 1946, however, penicillin became the standard treatment and cure for syphilis. But for the sake of the research, penicillin was withheld from the study's participants, and the disease continued its course through the bodies of 399 black men. For many, the study ended in death, giving the researchers their most valuable data—autopsy reports.

The men were still coming to the clinic on the grounds of the government's VA Hospital in Tuskegee in 1950, when Henry Harris Sr. was fighting for his life for four days at the hospital. His doctor, George C. Branche Sr., was one of the black physicians the U.S. government used to conduct the study. The test subjects were still coming to the clinic in the late sixties and early seventies when Harris's son was going to Tuskegee searching for a semblance of social life.

The Tuskegee study was still making radio newscasts the late-August morning Virgil Pearson loaded his car and drove from Fairfield to Auburn for preseason football practice.

Pearson was the second black football player given a scholarship, entering Auburn in 1970. A wide receiver who twice won the state 100-yard dash title, he was redshirted in 1971 and did not expect to play the coming season either, because he did not have a good spring practice. But what bothered him the most the previous spring was that "one of the coaches called me a 'black SOB,'" he said. "Now this coach [offensive coordinator Gene Lorendo] would curse everybody, but it seemed like he stayed on me. I don't think it was that loud, but I heard it. That hurt me because he was specific—'you black SOB.'"

The trip back to Auburn had been on Pearson's mind all summer. He kept going back and forth on whether to go back. He was tired of the racism and could see little racial progress since he was in the eighth grade. His first quarter at Auburn he was listening to records with some white players when David Langner, a freshman cornerback from Birmingham's Woodlawn High School, came in the dorm room. "I can't remember all he said," recalled Pearson, "but it was something to the effect of, 'Why have they got this nigger down here?' Or, 'Why do you have to come down here?' And, 'You can go back where you came from.'"

When he arrived at Sewell Hall, he didn't even unload his car. "I just went to my room, and I went to one of the [team] meetings," he said. All the old emotions came flooding back. "I said to myself, 'I'm not going through this.' I just couldn't take it anymore. . . . I just left. I didn't tell anyone."

Assistant coach Jim Hilyer called Pearson later that day. "I told him about the coach who had called me a black SOB. I remember him making the statement, 'You can't be so thin-skinned,'" said Pearson, who had wearied of wearing his skin so thick.

At thirteen, Pearson and some friends decided it might be fun to go to all-white Fairfield Junior High School for a year. It was 1965, and civil rights activists were seeking volunteers to integrate Fairfield's schools. "Once we got down there, we saw this was serious," Pearson said. "The white people didn't want us down there, and people in the black community would say we thought we were white."

Schools were supposed to be the South's great melting pot. Children were to do what most white parents refused to do in their workplace or neighborhood—mix racially.

Pearson and the dozen other blacks came to their new school together in carpools. "We had to stay in the car until the bell would ring. They told us we couldn't stand outside because it was too dangerous," he recalled. Once inside, the blacks were separated, with no more than two students in a classroom. "When we'd sit down, all the [white] kids would just scatter," said Pearson. They'd put their desks around the wall. You'd be sitting in the middle of the class, and then all of a sudden you'd feel a spitball somebody would throw at you. There would be twenty to twenty-five kids and just me, or maybe one other black."

On the last day of school, after nine months of blacks and whites sitting in classrooms together, white students threatened Pearson and the other blacks that "we're going to get you all after school" and were already outside of school when the bell rang "just hollering," said Pearson. "I said, 'I got to get to the car.' And when we got in the car, they all just crowded around the car and weren't going to let us go. The police had to come and make them move."

Pearson was long gone when Harris showed up in Auburn. No one was looking for him, but then one day, there was Henry Harris. Back in Auburn, his NBA career already over.

In hardly a hero's return, Harris had hitchhiked home. A tractor-trailer driver let him out at the Shell station in Boligee, and he walked to Tody Webster's house and borrowed the money for a pay phone to call Rev. Melvin Hodges before going to see Hodges.

Al Young, Harris's high school coach, said Harris told him he was the final player released by the Houston Rockets before they started the regular season, but Harris talked little about the NBA around his friends at Auburn. He told Owens he could not perform at the level he did before his knee injury. "He'd say he was better than a lot of the players, but he couldn't do what he used to be able to do," Owens said. "He always felt he could play in the NBA, but he had to accept that, with that injury and having lost some steps, he couldn't do what he wanted to do." Harris talked so rarely about his time with the Rockets that Thom Gossom wondered if he had actually gotten to try out. (Harris was not mentioned in the *Houston Post's* coverage of the Rockets' rookie camp or preseason camp. Neither the Rockets nor the NBA have a record of player transactions from that era. It's possible Harris was released while playing in the California summer league.)

Harris had returned to Auburn to finish his degree while he could still be on scholarship. Unable to live in Sewell Hall because he had no more athletic eligibility, he moved into Magnolia Hall and enrolled in five classes. He was not back long before Gossom and Owens noticed he had changed. "He was really different," Gossom said. "I think it became obvious to him that he wouldn't play pro. Physically, his body had been used up." That's what Harris told Owens— "Man, they used me, they used me up." "It was like they had taken all that he could give," Owens said. "He was a broken man. That was his dream, to be able to play professional ball, mainly because he wanted to do so much for his family. He didn't make it, and it crushed him. He didn't know what else he could do. He was like a whipped child."

Owens wished Harris would turn more to God, a refuge for him and numerous other southern pioneers. Although Harris regularly attended St. Paul Baptist Church with his family in Boligee and was a Sunday school leader, he did not rely on his faith like Owens did, or Gossom, who went to the local white Catholic church every Sunday for three years although no one spoke to him the whole time. Owens believed going to church regularly was "probably the only thing that kept me sane." "Harris once walked into the room of teammate Albert Johnson, saw him reading the Bible, and said, 'I wish I could sit there and read the Bible.'" Johnson believed Harris was looking for peace but trying to find it with women and by isolating, living on the move, and acting like all was well.

Johnson was one of four black basketball players living in Sewell Hall, the others being Sylvester Davenport, freshman Gary Redding of Atlanta, and junior college transfer Robert Osberry of Birmingham. Harris would play pickup games with them at "The Barn," impressing Redding with his "effort and energy." "I remember a lot of bandages, but he seemed to play fast to me. He played with a passion. His example was, 'I got banged-up knees and all that stuff, but I can still play.' He was no-nonsense on the court," Redding said.

During water breaks, he would tell Redding and Osberry to go to class. "He talked to us about his time at Auburn, encouraging us to just 'keep your nose clean' and go play ball.' He was pretty articulate. He really helped me focus and get my attention the right way, just stay out of trouble and do the things I needed to do," said Redding, who would start 102 games for Auburn over the next four years and graduate. Osberry would also graduate on time.

With preseason basketball practice starting and Owens and Gossom busy with football, Harris spent much of 1972 fall quarter hanging out with Henry Ford, the former football walk-on from Birmingham. Ford, a sophomore, lived in a one-bedroom unit in Windsor Hall Apartments adjacent to campus. "Henry would meet me every day at my apartment," Ford said. "He'd just be there. He almost lived with me. We would eat together. He was trying to teach me a lot of stuff, show me the ropes."

Ford could fix a supper Harris loved, mixing up ground beef patties with onion soup, egg, and crackers and then cook rice and gravy. "I had a stack of those patties in the freezer, that's what would excite Henry so much. He'd be waiting for me. We'd eat those every day," Ford recalled. "Those were good times."

To Ford, Harris did not seem depressed, actually was "sort of upbeat." "He was very optimistic about being a success," Ford said, "and he was very encouraging to those of us who were sort of his understudies, that we were special. I think he felt his role wasn't just about him, it was for the black race, like 'this is my calling.' We talked about that all the time. Like each one of us was a pioneer. It was like we were doing it not just for us but also those coming after us."

Harris realized his visible presence on the basketball team had likely attracted other blacks to Auburn. "He felt like, 'Okay, I started all this. Maybe none of you guys would even be here if it wasn't for me. I owe you guys something,'" Ford said. "I think he felt he owed us something because he was the first. 'Oh, Henry Harris is going to Auburn, and everything seems like it is going pretty good for him, so maybe it's not a bad place to go.'"

Harris had become the mentor he had so desperately needed. "We had no one to tell us, 'Okay, how do you become successful?' What do we actually need to do to make it through," Ford explained. "We had to figure our way. That's what Henry had to do, try to figure his way through. He couldn't ask his mom. Henry saw that we [black students] didn't have anybody, so he was that person for us."

Despite his losses, Harris had retained a positive attitude around others. "Most people would say he was positive almost to the point, 'Oh, he's just faking it.' But it wasn't a fake," Ford said. "Basically, all of us did the same thing. We had to encourage ourselves."

Harris still talked of playing pro basketball. "When he'd talk about the injury and show you his scar, you'd wonder, 'Man, can you really come back from that?' Ford said. "In his mind, once his knee got better, he was going to be able to make it. But as I remember, it didn't seem like the knee was getting much better." Harris may have known that too, for he was apparently starting to consider life without basketball. That's why he was going to classes and giving Ford the same advice, over and over. "Don't leave without that degree. Make sure you take that paper with you. Don't leave without that paper and a career."

Harris gave Ford one other thing to remember that fall. "If ever y'all hear I committed suicide," Harris said, "don't believe it."

Chapter 30

Slashed Tires and Fires

In the fall of 1972, Jackie Robinson died. The heart that burned with such fire on the basepaths of Brooklyn and ignited hope across America had flamed out at fifty-three. He had awakened that morning, realized he was having a heart attack and rushed to Rachel, his wife, confidante, and comrade in social revolution, telling her, "I love you," before collapsing in the kitchen.

The lion was dead.

Robinson may have been only fifty-three but looked seventy-three. His hair was white and his body was wracked with diabetes. He was blind in one eye and losing sight in the other. Both of his strong, marvelous legs were near amputation. That was his cost, in the words of author Chris Lamb, for having to drag America out of the past.

Nine days earlier, October 15, Robinson threw out the first ball at the second game of the World Series in Cincinnati, an honor recognizing the twenty-fifth anniversary of baseball's integration. Baseball previously had done little to nothing to recognize Robinson, as if not to draw attention to earlier sins, and Robinson had kept his distance from baseball hierarchy, convinced it was foot-dragging on black managers. So when given the microphone at the World Series, Robinson said, "I'd like to live long enough to see a black manager."

Robinson had always acted like it did not matter how he was treated—he just played on—but that was the martyr in him. Robinson uplifted thousands of African Americans who would follow his example and spirit in order to walk into their own forms of hell as they busted down racial barriers all over America. "If he could do it, we can do it," thought Elizabeth Eckford, one of the Little Rock Nine who integrated Central High School in 1957.

As Robinson lay in state in Harlem, five hundred people, young and old, passed by per hour. In his eulogy, Jesse Jackson described Robinson's body as a "temple of God."

With quarterback Pat Sullivan moving on to the NFL, Auburn was given little chance of a winning season in 1972. But offensive coordinator Gene Lorendo turned creative and decided to revamp his offense into a run-oriented Power I formation. His goal was to construct an offense so physical that could run the football on anyone, and its cornerstone would be Owens, who was an extraordinary physical specimen at 6-foot-3 and 235 pounds. "And there wasn't any fat," Owens said. "Even during my senior year, I ran a 4.5 forty [yard dash]." Owens was so much faster than Auburn's other running backs the coaches made him run wind sprints with the receivers. But Lorendo saw Owens not as a tailback but a fullback in the Power I—a blocking back. The coaches told him that, because of his size and explosiveness, he was better suited to block for 188-pound tailback Terry Henley than vice-versa.

During spring practice, Owens felt "like a lineman in the backfield," but he accepted his workhorse role. He desperately wanted to feel like a part of the team. For two years he had run on the field and seen the "joy in the faces" of the proud black men of Auburn's buildings and grounds department sitting at the corner of the end zone. "Their hopes were in me," he said, although he felt he had done little to make them, or his race, proud.

In Auburn's season-opening victory over Mississippi State in Jackson, Owens had a beautiful sixteen-yard run for a touchdown, but more ink was given to the ever-quotable Henley. Asked about his own TD run, Henley replied, "Somebody bulldozed a hole and James blacktopped it." Owens would score only one other touchdown all season and average only two carries a game, but his blocking would be the offense's trigger. "That whole team was built on toughness, and Daddy O. [Owens] was the personification of that," said Thom Gossom, a starting wide receiver. "We ran a play called 'Twenty-One Toss' between the guard and the tackle. If James blocked the linebacker, we won that play. If the linebacker beat James, we didn't gain any yards. We ran that play ten times in a row against Tennessee . . .

and we scored on the tenth play."

That was all Auburn needed to beat heavily favored Tennessee 10-6. The September victory would be the turning point of a 10-1 season's and demonstrate how desperately Owens wanted to prove himself. At one point in the huddle, Henley saw tears streaking down Owens's cheeks.

"What's the matter, James?" he asked.

Finally on the field, Owens would not leave the game or even answer Henley, saying only, "Let's go, Terry."

Owens would play hurt rather than abandon his hard-won opportunity and the expectations of his race. The three years of frustration Owens had stuffed at Auburn would ignite explosive blocks that would drive defensive ends to their knees and flip linebackers on their backs. And no matter who scored the touchdowns, Owens was always the first player down the field to congratulate his teammate.

It was a season of great irony and contrast. At the start of the fourth quarter, as at every home game, the crowd rose for the playing of "Dixie" and the lowering of the Confederate flag flying on the same flagpole as the American flag. It was always a moment of great whoop and southern patriotism, and a very uncomfortable and painful time for Owens and Gossom on the sideline. After one home game, Owens and Gossom dressed quickly and hustled to Tuskegee for a party, arriving back at Sewell Hall at 2:30 a.m. Assistant head coach Paul Davis called both in to his office the following week and talked to them about being late and so far from campus. "What are we supposed to do, Coach?" asked Owens, respectful but angry. "There's nothing to do here. Hell, the guys don't want to be with us. There aren't any black women here on campus." Gossom had never seen the "Big O" so mad. "Damn, what do we do?" Owens asked.

Behind Owens's blocks, Henley would lead the SEC in rushing, and when Henley was injured, Owens made backup Chris Linderman look just as good, with 149 yards against a solid Georgia defense.

Two weeks later, Auburn played undefeated, second-ranked Alabama in Birmingham. Trailing 16-3, the Tigers blocked a punt for a touchdown midway through the fourth quarter. Then they blocked another punt for a touchdown. Both times Bill Newton blocked the punts, and David Langner, the frequent antagonist of Gossom and

Virgil Pearson, picked the ball up each time and ran it into the end zone. With Auburn leading 17-16 and 1:34 to play, Langner intercepted a pass to give Alabama its only loss in its forty-four regular-season games between 1971 and 1974 and bestow Auburn with its most revered game in history, known simply by its ensuing bumper sticker, "Punt, Bama, Punt."

The same week Auburn beat Alabama, Eddie McAshan walked into the offices of the Georgia Tech athletic department. Tech's first black athlete, McAshan had been Tech's quarterback for three seasons and was about to play his final regular-season game two days later at Georgia. Tech players were normally allotted four tickets to games, but McAshan wanted six for all his family coming up from Florida. He made his request to a secretary, who said she could not give him six, and an argument arose. Four years of torment began seething out, four years of slashed tires and fires set in his room. The pressure McAshan had lived under finally snapped his cool facade. He skipped practice that day and the next. Coach Bill Fulcher suspended him for the Georgia game, which Tech lost.

Although Freddie Summers, a junior college transfer, had played quarterback for two years at Wake Forest and was All-ACC, the ambidextrous McAshan was the first black quarterback at a major Deep South university and two years ahead of the SEC's initial black quarterbacks. Only a month earlier, McAshan had seen himself hanging in effigy on the pregame bus ride through Auburn's campus.

Life wasn't much easier on his own campus. When he arrived in 1969, cheerleaders were still leading the Yellow Jackets onto the field with a large Rebel flag, but what happened off the field was traumatic. "My personal property was being destroyed. I was shot at. My car was totaled. Even when I'd walk the campus, students would wait until I passed and say little things loud enough for me to hear," said McAshan, who got tired of "going to the coaches with grievances and having them do nothing about them." "They made me feel like I was just trying to get special treatment," he said.

McAshan had kept his mouth shut so often that he was often criticized for being aloof. When he finally showed emotion, he was evicted like a house slave, banished to the fields. Or, in the words of his center, Frank McCloskey, "you are here as long as we want you to be here. You'll do fine if you behave." McCloskey never thought about McAshan having to fit into a mold to make a team and campus comfortable around him. "And I never thought once about him needing to do stuff to pave the way for other black athletes," he said. Only years later would McCloskey begin to realize what McAshan endured. "We were all dealing with the mud and blood at practice every day," McCloskey said, "but Eddie was dealing with shit before he ever came in the door of the locker room, stuff we had no idea about."

Auburn's black students believed "if you ever did anything wrong, you were gone," and after Tech fans and sports writers ripped McAshan for "walking out" on the team the week of the Georgia game, he was suspended for the Liberty Bowl also. *Atlanta Journal* sports columnist Furman Bisher grasped McAshan's plight. "God knows none of us could even conceive the mental extortion he has been suffered to endure these four years. For his consignment as the first black quarterback at an institution heavy in football and southern traditions, he required some of Jackie Robinson's features—a hide as tough as a razorback hog and an artist at cheek-turning," wrote Bisher, who concluded, "What came upon him must have been the climax of an accumulation heaped on in the four years spent under a microscope."

McAshan ended his college career outside the stadium in Memphis with Jesse Jackson and other civil rights leaders by his side. Less safe were Georgia Tech's other five black players, some only eighteen. First-generation college students who feared their scholarships were on the line, they crossed NAACP pickets to enter the Liberty Bowl despite death threats beforehand from the black community and cries of "Uncle Tom" on game night. It was, at last, public exposure of the private squeeze pioneers lived in week to week—despised by whites for being black and denigrated by blacks for not being black enough—and publicly placed the integration of college athletics within the civil rights movement, right where it had been all along.

By the fall of 1972, the desegregation of the SEC was complete, with each of the ten schools having signed at least one black player in football and basketball, but immense growing pains remained for players and coaches and would stretch through the decade.

When Georgia's first five black players showed up for football camp as freshmen in 1971, they found they would have to go through a mock Ku Klux Klan court that had been set up in front of McWhorter Hall, the athletic dormitory, with older players dressed in KKK-like garb.

The KKK, however, even made it on the field in Athens with its Krazy Kickoff Koverage team, an intentional play on the words to foster *esprit de corps*. Future NFL coach Jerry Glanville also had a Krazy Kickoff Koverage team as an assistant at Georgia Tech, naming a weekly Imperial Wizard for the player making a tackle closest to the goal line.

Culture not only out-ranked sensitivity but even competitiveness in the legendary-tough SEC. Although now readily recruiting black stars, Bear Bryant refused to recruit Condredge Holloway as a quarterback, although the slippery Holloway running Alabama's wishbone offense would've been frightening for SEC defenses. Bryant told Holloway he didn't think Alabama fans were "ready," although Holloway was an ideal candidate for being a pioneer. His mother, Dorothy, was the first black employee at NASA's Marshall Space Flight Center in Huntsville, and he had attended an integrated high school. He was also an exceptional athlete. Weeks after graduating in 1971, the Montreal Expos selected him with the No. 4 pick in the major league draft—Coach John Wooden had already contacted him about playing basketball at UCLA. But Holloway turned down the Expos to become an All-SEC quarterback at Tennessee—"I've never seen a quarterback as complete," said Georgia coach Vince Dooley. Holloway went on to Hall of Fame stardom in the Canadian Football League, winning two Grey Cups. Yet he couldn't be a wishbone quarterback in his home state.

Alabama also didn't recruit John Stallworth, who would move from Tuscaloosa High School to the Pro Football Hall of Fame via Alabama A&M and the Pittsburgh Steelers. Stallworth's mother was a maid for the family of Alabama business school dean Paul Garner, who sent Alabama A&M coach Joe Kent a letter congratulating on giving a scholarship "to our young friend, Johnny Stallworth." He sent a copy of the letter to Bryant.

Even more stunning, no SEC school signed Walter Payton in

1971, or even seriously recruited him. Payton's work ethic was already legendary in high school in Columbia, Mississippi, but caution was the order of the day in the post-integration SEC, just as it had been in the major leagues in the years after Jackie Robinson's arrival. The Yankees, Red Sox, and Braves all passed on signing Willie Mays in an era when even marginal white prospects were signed. Payton, arguably the greatest running back of all time, went to Jackson State and signed with the Chicago Bears for $126,000, the highest signing bonus ever offered a college player at that time.

Early black running backs who *were* recruited by SEC schools were often held back from stardom, just as Owens and Harris were. Pioneer Horace King played nine seasons as a Detroit Lions running back but was a wingback at Georgia until his senior season. Florida pioneer Leonard George became the first African American to score a touchdown at Alabama's Denny Stadium as a sophomore but was a cornerback as a junior and senior. Similarly, two other "firsts" starred as running backs on their freshman teams—Kentucky's Nate Northington and Mississippi State's Frank Dowsing—but became cornerbacks on the varsity.

From the way Owens was utilized his initial two years on campus, it appeared Auburn's coaches had signed him either as a token black or to avoid having to try to tackle him in an Alabama crimson jersey. Owens played five different positions on the freshman team. "I was something like an experiment," he said. "They didn't know what to do with me." Then in spring practice, he was never tried on offense despite being a Parade All-American running back and entered his sophomore season as a reserve cornerback. He also would play tight end that year and linebacker that season but never carry the ball. Yet, his 89-yard punt return in a victory at Florida stood as an Auburn record for forty-three years. It was the first Auburn touchdown scored by a black American.

Chapter 31

Leaving Alabama

Harris enrolled in four classes in January 1973—English Literature, Sociology 201, and, because he'd decided to become a teacher, two vocational education courses. He seemed to be turning a corner on the rest of his life. He was making progress toward his degree. During fall quarter, with his focus on graduation and less on the NBA, Harris had the best grade-point average of his fifteen quarters of college work—2.5 on a 3.0 scale. "Henry wasn't dumb," said Thom Gossom. "He'd go through periods where he'd go to class all the time. Then he'd go through periods where he would not go at all. I guess it just depended on how he was feeling in terms of basketball." Upon learning of the uneven class attendance years later, Harris's brother James said, "Sounds like depression to me."

Looking forward to coaching, Harris contacted Larry Chapman, his freshman team coach, about becoming a volunteer assistant coach at Auburn High School. Chapman had coached there since leaving Auburn University with fellow assistant coach Rudy Davalos. Chapman was a strong, supportive male role model and Harris sought him out for help getting started in coaching. "We talked about him coming over and helping me with my team, and he was excited about that. He just wanted to be a volunteer coach," Chapman said. "Henry and I were good friends. We were close." Chapman's instinct was to help a young man he and Davalos had left. "He [Henry] wanted to do it [coach]. I said, 'Heck, yeah.' And then I got everything taken care of with my principal."

But Harris never got to work with Chapman or his players. Bill Lynn threatened to take away his scholarship if he worked with Chapman. "Henry called and he was pretty upset," Chapman remembered. "He said he just couldn't do it, because they [Auburn] weren't going to support him—they were trying to help him graduate. I said, 'Henry, I understand.'"

Lynn still resented Chapman and Rudy Davalos for abandoning him three years earlier. "Coach Lynn was still angry about our resignations," Chapman said. "And the reason I know is because Henry told me." Lynn believed Chapman had tried to undermine him even after they left, and Lynn's son could still talk about his father's hurt four decades later.

"Coach Lynn felt really betrayed by Rudy and Larry," said Wes Bizilia, the assistant coach Lynn hired to replace Davalos. Chapman had played for Lynn, and Auburn was supposedly all about loyalty, but there was more to it psychologically. When Lynn got to drinking, he grew suspicious and resentful—the stories are numerous—which enabled more drinking. In Lynn's mind, Davalos and Chapman had not only gone to the AD Jeff Beard about his alcoholism but also abandoned him on the bench and in recruiting, which, it now appeared, would likely cost him his job. Auburn lost five of its first seven games of the 1972-73 season, only intensifying Lynn's bitterness. If Harris was going to be working with Chapman, that meant, in Lynn's all-or-nothing thinking, he had crossed over to the other side. Chapman and Davalos were the enemy, and the Auburn team captain who had played on one leg just a season earlier evolved into little more than collateral damage.

No one could remember when Harris disappeared. Suddenly, the young man who was so visible, yet so invisible, was gone. And no one at Auburn could remember exactly why he left. His big brother Robert remembered, though. His mom had told him all about it. Willie Pearl said Henry was angry. Harris had played hurt, had accepted a workhorse role, and kept his mouth shut, leaving a legacy that would enable Auburn to recruit more black athletes. Now, he was being told he couldn't finish his degree.

Harris felt used. "He talked to my mother for a long time—she said it was like hours on the phone," Robert remembered. "It was a long talk because he was upset that he didn't have his degree and he needed to get it to be productive. He was crying. He was upset."

Exploiting black athletes physically while thwarting their mental advancement was a common practice at many colleges in the 1960s and 1970s; *Sports Illustrated's* "Black Athlete" series was loaded with examples. But in most of the South, such exploitation summoned a dark time when it was against the law to teach a slave to read or write. And the era of "separate but equal" and "training schools" had similar intentions. Because of that heritage, Lynn could not have picked a more conditioned victim than Harris. If he had taken a scholarship from a white player, someone might have spoken up, expressed the injustice. But Harris grew up under an unjust system, his father was long dead, and his mom was frightened for her son.

Only a year earlier, Harris told writer David Housel, "If I don't make the pros, I think I'll try to get into graduate school here. I want to work in rehabilitation for the mentally retarded." He told a reporter during the final month of his senior season, "Perhaps I'll stay on as a graduate student and help out with the coaching on the side." Harris could have started helping coach the team while finishing his undergraduate degree, but Lynn never asked him to.

Athletes remaining on scholarship until they graduated was the norm at Auburn and throughout the South. "Guys would stay six or seven years on scholarship," said Pat Cowart, Harris's teammate. "A good thing about Coach Lynn," said Carl Shetler, "is that if you needed help, he would help you. If you're having trouble with school work, he'd make sure something happened so that you could get a little help. Nice guy, nice guy." Either Lynn changed, or the rules changed along with integration.

Auburn football coach Shug Jordan told halfback Bobby Hoppe he'd do "anything in his power to fix it where he'd graduate." Hoppe was a fierce blocker and tackler for Jordan's 1957 national championship team, but just weeks before the season, Hoppe was under investigation back home in Chattanooga, Tennessee, for the murder of moonshiner Don Hudson, the former boyfriend of Hoppe's sister. Thirty-one years later, he was indicted for Hudson's murder, but not convicted because of a hung jury. By then, Hoppe had spent a quarter-century as a high school teacher and coach, making a significant contribution to society, all because he had earned a college degree from Auburn—five years after his final game. Jordan was there when he graduated.

Dan Kirkland and several of Harris's teammates were allowed to stay on scholarship to complete their degrees, even Tim Ash, who entered with Harris but quit the team before his senior season after a disagreement with Lynn. "He [Lynn] said he'd keep me on scholarship until I graduated if I didn't cause any problems," recalled Ash. "I said, 'I can't promise you I'm not going to cause any problems because if I see something wrong, I'm going to say something. Your alcohol problem is screwing everybody up here.'"

While Harris was losing his scholarship, across the state four black basketball players were starting for Alabama. During pregame introductions, Kentucky fans booed all four and cheered Alabama's lone white starter. Alabama freshman Leon Douglas was spit on by fans at Mississippi State, just as Vanderbilt freshman Geoffrey Dillard had been in 1967. Georgia's first two black players, Ronnie Hogue and Tim Bassett, were attacked in a game-ending free-for-all at Georgia Tech. With cries of "get that nigger," Hogue was thrown over the scorer's table by Tech football players and fans.

But when the season was over, Alabama pioneer Wendell Hudson had led the SEC in both scoring and rebounding and was voted SEC Player of the Year. When Hudson had signed with Alabama, his mother was convinced he would be killed, but now Willie Pearl Harris was the mother full of fear. Henry wanted to "expose" Auburn, and she had heard of too many young men who spoke up and died. Many of the old ways had vanished in the South, but fear had not. It couldn't; it had been in charge too long. Willie Pearl wanted Henry out of Alabama, telling him to "leave it [Auburn] alone," said Robert. "Willie Pearl told him to get on with his life and get a degree from somewhere else."

This was not the same Willie Pearl who stood up to Boyd Aman rather than take her boys out of school to pick cotton. It was instead the Willie Pearl whom Robert had seen on occasion—apprehensive of trouble that could befall her children in the Black Belt. He had seen it when he told her the white storekeeper was cheating her on her account. He had seen it when he told her the white woman at the post office was throwing away his *Pittsburgh Courier*. "Don't bother that lady. Leave it alone," she told him. And he had seen it as a seven-year-old boy when Willie Pearl and his grandmother came home from the jail and told him Lieutenant Gooden was dead. "You need to investigate that," Robert told them. But they didn't. "Some people don't take risks," Robert said. "I guess they figured they had to do what they had to do to raise kids. She was still the best mama in the world."

Willie Pearl Harris—and all her loving, all her discipline, and all her fear—was a product of her time and place. She had good reason to be frightened. She had grown up in Sumter County, site of seven documented lynchings between 1877 and 1950. The stories were legendary, and even in the sixties, lynching was still the South's enforcer. While dragging rivers and swamps in 1964 searching for the bodies of missing Mississippi civil rights workers James Chaney, Andrew Goodman, and Mickey Schwerner, the FBI discovered the bodies of eight black men.

The lynching Willie Pearl knew about occurred in the Emelle community and killed Esau Robinson, his uncle, two other black men, and a white man who worked with the Robinsons. It happened July 4, 1930, six days before she was born in Emelle, and continued into the next day, until state law officers finally arrived from Montgomery. They arrested Esau's father, Tom Robinson, as well as Esau's two brothers, all of whom had defended their families and homes from the whites attacking them. One white man, Grover Boyd, was killed, and Tom Robinson—a rare major black land owner in the South during the Depression, owning 160 acres—was convicted of his murder, for supposedly "instigating" the violence. In 1931, Tom Robinson was electrocuted at the state prison in south Alabama town of Atmore, forty miles from Monroeville, where author Harper Lee would write *To Kill a Mockingbird* and name the novel's falsely accused black man Tom Robinson.

Whether feeling fear or impotent to stop injustice, Willie Pearl believed she had to get Henry out of Alabama in a hurry. She wanted Henry far away, ideally where Robert could look after him. Robert was teaching in Harrisburg, Pennsylvania, a state that was too far away in 1968, when Villanova was recruiting Harris, but not anymore.

So Harris left Auburn silently, giving his friends little idea of why or of where he was going. "There was the impression that he was done and that was it," said Gossom. "Now go figure your life out."

Henry Harris, like the other pioneers, had been a southern remedy—the medicine the South had to take to build the bridge from Dixie to the Sun Belt. And like a doctor on a house call, when Harris was done, he was gone.

Sylvester Davenport didn't make it through winter quarter either. The 6-foot-8 sophomore was averaging thirteen points and seven rebounds per game for Auburn in mid-February when newspapers reported he was suspended for the season for a training violation. But the truth was Davenport was gone for good, following the discovery of a bag of marijuana in his room.

After playing Monday night, February 12, at Baton Rouge and flying home the next day, Davenport and roommate Gary Redding returned to Sewell Hall to find athletic department officials quickly inside their room. "When we got back, it was strange," Redding remembered. "Somebody came to our room and said, 'Whose closet is this?' Sylvester said, 'This is my closet.' He said, 'Open it.' Sylvester opened it, and they pulled out this bag of marijuana. How in the heck did that get there? I certainly didn't know Sylvester had marijuana in the room. I never saw marijuana in our room. Then the next thing they're saying is he's going to have to go home. He's kicked out of school. I was heartbroken."

"That was a sad day. Somebody set him up," said Robert Osberry, a black teammate in the same suite. "We were there when they raided his room and found it, and they knew exactly where to go to look for it, because we were watching. He was set up. I don't know who it was or why, but we were pretty upset when that happened."

Larry Phillips, the assistant coach who so respected Davenport's proud, humble parents, drove him back to Soddy-Daisy. The four-hour trip seemed to take forever, and Phillips still would not talk about it four decades later. "Silver—that's what I called him—was smart, very polite, a really good kid," he said. "It surprised me, it surprised everybody."

James Owens was the next to go. About a dozen Auburn football players were called in to see their coach on suspicion of using marijuana, and all but three denied it. But when Owens and Gossom were called in separately to Coach Shug Jordan's office, both told the truth, saying they had smoked marijuana. So did their good friend, kicker Chris Wilson, who was called "nigger lover" by some teammates. Owens, Gossom, and Wilson were all thrown off the team and forced to move out of Sewell Hall. As blacks, Owens and Gossom had no one to plead their case.

Jordan, however, eventually realized he had been lied to and reinstated all three players out of respect for their honesty, but they had already moved out of Sewell to much-disparaged Magnolia Hall, the only other male dormitory on campus. Gossom and Wilson would be allowed to move back in Sewell at the start of spring quarter, but by then, Owens would be gone. The ferocious fullback with so much speed, power, and work ethic, would leave Auburn as Harris did, humiliated and angry. He had taken all he could. "I was physically and mentally drained from Auburn." he said. ". . . I had become sick of it. I couldn't stand it. I just wanted to get away and see if another chapter of my life would begin."

Owens had attended Auburn for three and a half years but still needed at least two more years of coursework to graduate with a degree in vocational education—with his hardest classes still ahead of him. He had managed to stay eligible through the tutoring he received from other black students and his eventual wife, Gloria. "We scheduled enough dummy courses to stay eligible," Owens said. "We had people [advisors] who told us what to take. We didn't have a choice. We took all these courses that we didn't need until after our senior season, and then they say, 'Well, it's on you now,' and I've got most of my major courses staring me in the eye."

Feeling the shame of being booted from Sewell Hall and with minimal hope of graduating, Owens packed to go home to Fairfield. "My life was in disarray." he said, breaking down as he recalled that time in 2008. "I didn't know what to do. I didn't think I had given what I had wanted to Auburn or that Auburn had given to me."

As a junior, Owens had asked his coaches for a car, after noticing other players had new cars. He got a car too—a used one. Everything is everything. The coaches explained to Owens the car had to look like a car his parents could afford, to allay any suspicion by the NCAA. But Owens was repulsed by the hand-me-down, second-class feel of the gray 1966 Ford Falcon, so he called it the "family car," left the key in it, and let "anybody and everybody" use it. "Most black students at Auburn didn't have cars, and if they wanted to use it to go to the grocery store or somewhere, I'd say, 'Hey, it's the family car, so go ahead.'"

With his bags packed and the NFL ahead of him, Owens left the "family car"— with the fall-away steering wheel and back doors that had to be tied shut—on the street. Auburn gave it to him used, he used it, and then he left it. "I left it sitting right in front of Magnolia Hall," he said. "I was leaving for good."

Now, Harris, Davenport, and Owens were all gone, departing Auburn within a month of each other in the winter of 1973. They were three of the first four black athletes to sign Auburn scholarships. The fourth, Virgil Pearson, had packed up six months earlier.

Once Owens was back in Fairfield, he gathered up all his clothes with "Auburn" on them and put them in a pile. Then, he got rid of them. Turned out he and Harris had been trespassing all along.

Chapter 32

Summer in Harrisburg

Harris got a call from Thom Gossom in March. Gossom had some news for him.

"Debra is getting ready to get married," he said.

Gossom was referring to Debra Threatt, Harris's former girlfriend. He knew how much Harris had liked her, and he had just read of her engagement in the *Opelika-Auburn Daily News*.

Harris couldn't believe it. He was stunned.

"Henry called and called and asked me to give him another chance," Threatt said. Harris told her that he had always assumed they would be married one day, although their yearlong relationship had cooled considerably during the eighteen months since she left Auburn High School for Alabama State in the fall of 1971.

Harris could tell he wasn't making any headway with Threatt and was running out of time—she planned to marry in May. He decided to go back to Auburn to plead for a second chance. "He stayed for a while," recalled Threatt.

The two talked and talked. Harris said he couldn't stand the thought of another man being with her. Threatt knew she had loved Harris at one time, and probably still did, but with women coming on to him all the time, she didn't think she could trust him. Threatt didn't change her mind about getting married, but she did remember one statement he made in asking for more time and a second chance. He told her, "I'm trying to get things together."

Harris went to Harrisburg, Pennsylvania, hoping for a change in luck. "It made sense that my mother sent Henry to Harrisburg, because Robert had always sort of played the father-brother role," said Harris's brother James. When Robert graduated from Alabama

A&M in 1970, he mailed out nearly fifty resumes for teaching positions and decided he would take the best financial offer regardless of location. He had student loans to pay off, despite working all through college, and he wanted to send money to his mother. His best offer was $6,900 annually from Harrisburg, so he took a northbound Greyhound, found an apartment, and walked ten blocks to school every day to teach industrial technology. When Henry arrived, Robert got him a job as a hall monitor at a junior high school.

In mid-April, Harris finally caught a break when the University of Wisconsin at Milwaukee selected Rudy Davalos as its new basketball coach. One of Davalos's first moves was to offer Larry Chapman an assistant coaching position. Chapman turned him down but mentioned Harris as a possible graduate assistant coach.

"Rudy, Henry Harris would be awesome with you," Chapman told him. "Henry Harris is a great, great person. You can't get a better guy."

Chapman called Harris. "I told him Rudy was interested, and then Rudy called him." The details were quickly worked out. Assistantships were usually given to graduate students, but Harris would be finishing his undergraduate degree and coach the junior varsity and help with the varsity. It seemed an ideal situation.

Because the coaching position did not start until mid-August, Harris would remain in Harrisburg for the next four months, living downtown a block from the Susquehanna River in a large house divided into apartments and owned by one of Robert's fraternity brothers. Harris took a clerical job at nearby New Cumberland Army Depot, the repair site for Chinook helicopters used in Vietnam. He was soon joined in Harrisburg by his brother James, who was on an academic scholarship at the University of Pennsylvania and had landed a summer internship with Pennsylvania's state government. With three of Willie Pearl's sons in Harrisburg, it became a summer for re-bonding for the brothers who had rarely been together since Henry left for Auburn and the rest of the family moved to Bessemer. "The good times were when we were talking about our family," Robert said. "The good times were when we were just sitting around, whether we were drinking a beer or playing one-on-one. We would remember when we would shoot [a basketball] against a tree. We still had the dream of doing something good for our mother."

Harris also invited his friend Don Williams, the first black in the Auburn band, to join him in Harrisburg. Williams drove his Volkswagen up from Auburn and took a typist's job at New Cumberland Army Depot, giving Harris a ride and a party buddy. James recalled Harris and Williams having an "array of women going and coming." He also remembered Harris having two white puppies that summer. "They were remarkably white, and he spent a lot of time playing with those dogs," James said. "Wherever Henry was, those two puppies were right there."

This was the carefree brother James knew growing up. But James, Robert, and Williams all saw a more serious side of Harris that summer too. "Anything about Auburn would set him off," Robert said. "He told me he was mistreated playing basketball, but he could deal with that. Not finishing his degree bothered him after getting cut [by the NBA]. His mother wanted him to get his degree. He wanted his degree. His eligibility had run out, so he was saying they wouldn't give him any more money." The few times Harris mentioned Auburn to James, "you could hear the anger, the hurt, the resentment, the pain," he said. "Henry seemed like he was dealing with stuff. But he wasn't one to talk about it." Instead, Harris continued to self-medicate his emotions. Robert once saw him smoking marijuana and asked him, "Why you smoking that? Leave that stuff alone," Robert recalled. "He said, 'Why you say that?' But if he didn't tell you [he was using], you wouldn't know it."

Harris read *The Autobiography of Malcolm X* during the summer. "He subscribed very strongly to the notions of Malcolm X," James said. "Those concepts were new to me. It was enough to make me start reading it. A lot of that stuff wasn't that different from what our mother had taught us, and some of it may have just resonated with Henry because of that." "Henry loved Malcolm X," recalled Owens. "He talked about the things he would say and how he witnessed with his life what he was going through, but he wasn't outspoken about it."

Harris told James he was writing a book about his college experiences and asked him to edit the introduction. "That book occupied a lot of his time that summer. He talked about it a lot, and he was determined to do that book," James said. "I cannot recall the content much. I did not see the entire book. I do remember he had a strong resentment against Coach Lynn."

Harris never showed the manuscript to Williams, but he remembered it. "Something would hit him and he'd grab that pad and go to writing. He kept it with him all the time," Williams said. "He'd work on it, work on it, work on it. He didn't want anybody to read it until he was finished. He'd talk about how he was going to make all this money, how he was going to get them back for how they did him." Williams said Harris told him his knees would "never be any good because instead of giving him the operation he needed, they just kept sticking him, sticking him [with shots]." "He had a bunch of stuff that he was writing about the coaches. He also talked about money changing hands, with him not getting any," Williams said.

Fully away from Auburn for the first time in five years, Harris used writing to process his experience and long-buried feelings. Time also opened the hatch of hindsight that other black college "firsts" would descend into. Should he have spoken up more? Would it have made any difference? That's what Duke's first black athlete, C. B. Claiborne, kept wondering while working on a master's at Dartmouth and a doctorate at Virginia Tech. He regretted having gone to Duke while understanding he "had to go." "I probably was much too compliant and didn't push the system enough to make more happen," Claiborne told author Barry Jacobs. Billy Jones, one of two players to integrate Maryland's basketball team, told Jacobs, "We didn't challenge. We didn't test authority." Black athletes knew they couldn't fail, too many people were counting on them. "'You just tell me how hard, and I'll do it, Coach.' That's who we were," Jones said. "We were gullible. I wish I had been more challenging to authority. Probably would have gotten thrown off the team, but I wish I had been."

Harris had been Auburn's battering ram, and its emotional toll became palpable in Harrisburg. "From what I recall, it [Auburn] was just a bitter, bitter experience for him, and he felt like he got the short end of the stick. And it seems like that book was his way of voicing it," James said. "He just wasn't a confrontational type person, which is just the opposite of me and my mother. We would swallow, swallow, swallow, but we'd reach a point and very vocally express a position. Henry took a lot, he swallowed a lot, but he dealt with it in a different way. He was a happy-go-lucky fellow. I just think that's who he was. Maybe he used sports to sublimate some of that. He could have used sports to deal with his depression, deal with his anger."

Athletic competition was no longer a consistent outlet for Harris. Neither was mentoring and encouraging young black men. "I remember one thing Henry did that I guess I will remember the remainder of my life," said James, who was going through an admitted "rough spot" that summer. "He [Henry] grabbed me, he hugged me, he laid my head on his shoulder and told me, 'You're my brother,' and then something similar to what my mother used to say, 'You'll always have a shoulder to cry on, and I love you regardless.' He was a caring guy, but that was uncharacteristically caring."

While Harris was wrestling the past in Harrisburg, James Owens was trying to make his pro football dream come true. Although he was an eleventh-round draft choice of the New Orleans Saints because of his lack of ball carrying at Auburn, Owens was making such a good impression on the Saints' coaches that during the last round of player cuts, they told him to get an apartment. Coach J. D. Roberts had decided to keep him on the taxi squad while his knee healed from surgery. However, after losing his first four preseason games, Roberts was fired the week before the start of the season and replaced by backfield coach John North, who felt he needed to win quickly. "North said he needed to get somebody in who would be able to perform that year," said Owens, "so he brought in somebody else."

Owens went home to Fairfield for the second time in six months. "I felt my whole world had . . . ," said Owens, unable to complete the sentence nearly four decades later.

Living game to game for years, athletes are often only as good as their last one, so when the games are over and the last one ends in defeat—not drafted, released, cut—it can seem catastrophic. Owens believed he was "the biggest failure that had ever come through." He sat with his depression for weeks. "For days at a time, I'd just go out and sit by myself. There was a place called Edgewater [near Fairfield], and there was a lake out there, and a lot of places where you could just go sit and gaze out into the water or the woods," he said.

Owens's sense of failure was magnified by the expectations that he had sensed from others and then internalized. "When people put things on you, we try to live up to that," he said, "and that adds even more to the hurt that you are a failure."

Owens did not call Harris during those dark days. And Harris did not call him. Long distance phone calls were expensive, and the two men who best understood what the other was going through remained isolated from each other. Neither was adept at talking about emotions anyway, or feelings of failure. It was too painful, too discouraging. Although Owens admitted to "a lot of crying together" when Harris returned from his NBA tryout, both young men had tried to focus on the positive as a survival strategy.

"I think Henry and James felt like, 'If I just can survive these four years, then I can make the pros and it'll be over,'" Gossom said. But when it was over, neither had made the pros and they were eight hundred miles apart, dealing with their grief the best they knew how.

"Never give up and sit down and grieve," said Satchel Paige, the great Negro Leagues pitcher from Alabama, who was not allowed in the major leagues until he was forty-two years old and his really *fast*ball had slowed with age. He said, "Find another way," and that's what Harris had done. The guy who lived on the move at Auburn was now headed to Milwaukee, looking forward to completing his degree. "We all lived to please our mother," James said, "so I think that was something important for him to do." At the same time, Harris planned to keep rehabbing his knee. "He told me he still wanted to make the pros," said Robert, who told him to go for it. "He and I were the same type people—'Do it. Do it. You can do it.'"

Chapter 33

Milwaukee

*Hold fast to your dreams
For if dreams die,
Life is a broken winged bird
That cannot fly*

*- Langston Hughes
'Dreams'*

Harris arrived in Milwaukee on Thursday, August 16. It was a day he had anticipated since being hired in April and was noticeably excited about his new opportunity. Coach Rudy Davalos sent his young assistant coach, Tom Sager, to pick Harris up at the airport. The two young men struck up a quick relationship as Sager showed Harris around the city and campus. "He was a very soft-spoken, very respectful kid, really nice," Sager said. Harris told Sager that he thought Milwaukee was "his second favorite place in the world." He had been in town only a couple of hours.

The University of Wisconsin-Milwaukee campus was north of downtown, bounded by Lake Michigan on the east and a declining commercial area on the west. Sager dropped Harris off at Sandburg Residence Halls, a three-tower dormitory complex honoring poet Carl Sandburg, a former Milwaukee newspaper reporter and biographer of Abraham Lincoln. Completed in 1970, the towers were the tallest buildings in Milwaukee and emblematic of UWM's fifteen-year progression from a commuter school of 6,000 to an enrollment of 23,000 students on a tight, bustling campus spread over three square city blocks. Harris was assigned Room S-1720C, a single room in a three-room suite on the seventeenth floor of the twenty-story South tower.

During his first week, Harris ate a couple of meals with Davalos.

It was a nice reunion; the two had not been together during the three years Davalos coached the University of the South in Sewanee, Tennessee, his 23-4 record the previous season leading to the UWM job. But if Harris was excited about his new opportunity in a new city, Davalos was feeling frustrated after only four months on the job. He believed UWM athletic director Tom Rosandich had made him promises he wasn't keeping, particularly related to upgrading facilities. Baker Fieldhouse was built in the 1930s for the then teachers college and was the "last place" a coach would show recruits. "It was a lousy place to play—it had a cinder track going around the court," Davalos said. In an interview with the *Milwaukee Journal*, he had even referred to UWM as a "mirage university." "Rudy felt he had been told of all these things that weren't there," said Glenn Brady, the UWM football coach, who saw the conflict was a "battle of egos." "Rudy could not get along with Rosandich, but Rosandich clashed with everyone."

Davalos had spent the summer working at basketball camps run by the NBA's Milwaukee Bucks, and while working with kids, had met Tom Nissalke, the former Bucks assistant and Seattle SuperSonics head coach. After Nissalke was selected in late June as coach of the San Antonio Spurs of the American Basketball Association, he offered Davalos an assistant's position. Coaching professional basketball would be another rung up the ladder for Davalos and provide an exit from what increasingly looked like a dead-end job. For a man turned away from San Antonio's public swimming pools growing up because of his Mexican ethnicity, returning home at basketball's highest level was a golden opportunity, he felt. "I was ready to go back to Texas," he said. "I had been gone thirteen years."

Five days after Harris's arrival, Davalos turned in a letter of resignation, writing:

> San Antonio, Texas, is my hometown and also that of my wife. Most of our family relatives and friends live in the area. The opportunity to come "home" with a professional basketball team is too good to turn down.... Only a professional position in my hometown makes me leave at his this time of the year. An opportunity like this does not come often and I must act accordingly.

Davalos thought the UWM position would still work for Harris "because it would give him a chance to get his degree and get into college coaching," he said. Davalos wanted to help Harris "get on the right road," Sager said, "but when things weren't going well with Rudy and the administration, he jumped ship." Davalos was the only person Harris knew in a large city a long way from Alabama, and he now faced the future without a mentor. He had lost yet another male role model. Perhaps sensing the vacuum, Davalos told the thirty-one-year-old Sager: "Make sure you take care of Henry."

Davalos had recommended Sager become the new coach, but that did not sway Rosandich, who apparently wanted someone with college experience. Sager, a very successful Milwaukee high school coach, had applied for the UWM head coaching job in April and ended up being hired by Davalos as his assistant. Sager and Harris faced an awkward time as they waited for Rosandich to hire a new coach. "I am sure a coach coming in would like to have the people he knows with him," Sager said. "I'm sure Henry was insecure. Both of us had talked about it, and it was not a good situation."

With only seven weeks before practice started, Rosandich moved quickly by returning to his April finalists list and hired Bill Klucas, an assistant coach at the University of Minnesota under Bill Musselman. A hot coaching property since 1972, when he won Minnesota's first Big Ten title in a half-century. Musselman had installed a very physical and oft-criticized approach to college basketball, with a game against Ohio State erupting into a brawl that put Buckeye center Luke Witte in the hospital. "Musselman was a fiery, jump-down-your-throat coach. Klucas was an exact opposite. He would try to level things off after the fact," said Bobby Nix, the Auburn transfer who was the point guard on Minnesota's championship team.

Only thirty-two, Klucas believed the UWM job was "a way to make a name for yourself rather quickly." "We had great success at Minnesota," he said, "and your ego gets away from you and you say, 'Well, I had a lot to do with that, I must know something.'"

Klucas, however, had never been a head coach at any level.

Harris was working out in the gym when he and Klucas met. "He had tremendous work ethic," said Klucas, who would soon be impressed by Harris's coaching ability too. "Even though I inherited

Henry, he was what I would have hoped to have hired. He required very little guidance. He related well to the kids. He just knew how to work with them."

Coaching, though, would be only part of Harris's assignment at UWM. To earn his $4,000 salary, he had to also take fifteen academic hours, serve as a residential assistant in Sandburg Hall, and help run the intramural basketball program even during basketball season. Rosandich like to make all his coaches be involved in the "little stuff" involved in running an athletic department that also included intramurals, recreation programs, and club sports. Harris took his responsibilities seriously and earned the respect of his co-workers. "Henry was just outstanding," said intramurals coordinator Daniel Harris.

As junior varsity coach, Harris worked with freshmen and sophomores not ready for varsity competition. He also worked with the guards during varsity practice. The junior varsity had its own schedule of games, and if they didn't create conflicts, Harris would help recruit and make road trips with the varsity, assisting Klucas and Sager on the bench. And the UWM varsity was on the road often. To make his budget work, Rosandich scheduled fifteen of UWM's twenty-six games on the road, receiving financial guarantees for playing more prestigious programs. During the season's first month, Klucas faced Memphis State, the 1973 NCAA runner-up, and Florida State, the 1972 NCAA runner-up. "It doesn't take long to realize that you could be an assistant for thirty-four years and it's not like that first year as a head coach," Klucas said. "There's a big difference between making a suggestion and a decision."

Klucas's inexperience would affect a veteran team that was 18-8 the previous season. "It was tough transitional year for us, we had higher hopes as a team," said Richard Cox, the team captain. "But Henry was someone we all liked. He was someone we all related very well with. He was an easy-going guy. A good guy. Honest man, straightforward, had a good demeanor about him. Very, very well liked by the team."

Harris met with Klucas, and Sager early every morning in their offices at Baker Fieldhouse, so they would have the rest of the day free to coach and recruit. Harris was never late. "We always had to figure out our days," Klucas recalled. "If we wanted Henry to help us recruit, we had to sit down and say, 'You have to do this,' and Henry would say, 'Well, they don't need me this day.' He had a busy schedule, but I thought he was thriving on it. He had it pretty darn well organized. He was a well-poised, smart guy, very motivated and hard working." The three coaches developed a rapport carried them through their meetings and coaching. "Henry had a kind of a sense of humor that you really like, you could kid him," Klucas said. "I remember kidding him about his knee. He'd try to do something [on the court], and I'd say, 'I bet you didn't have any problem doing that a couple of years ago.' You know, the usual give-and-take. I didn't know anyone who didn't like him."

Harris made friends within the athletic department, particularly with the young football coaches. One of them was Bill Nunn, who was a couple of years older than Harris and one of the first black football players at the University of Tulsa and the first to graduate, even earning a graduate degree before leaving. Harris and Nunn were both resident assistants in Sandburg and UWM's only African American coaches. They developed a close friendship. "I have one image of Henry, standing in the office and talking to Bill," said defensive coordinator Gary Wynveen, who shared an office with Nunn. "He [Harris] was an extremely well-mannered guy. He was a gentleman. He handled himself so well." When the football staff would have a party on the weekend, Harris would go if he could.

By December, Harris had started dating Susan Loritz, a junior from Mantiwoc, Wisconsin, who also lived in Sandburg's south tower. Loritz was white, but on UWM's liberal urban campus, interracial dating was not particularly unusual in 1974. "We had inter-racial dating and marriage with players and students in Milwaukee then," said Brady, the head football coach. Interracial dating was not "a big deal at all," said Cox, the team captain and one of several black UWM players who dated whites. "Henry dating a white girl wouldn't have been anything that stuck out. You could have said that about a bunch of people on that campus in 1974." Klucas said he didn't even know Harris had a white girlfriend. "He was a discreet guy. He didn't walk around throwing his social life in people's faces."

After the New Year, Harris went by Sager's house before they left on a recruiting trip. Harris had been there before to eat dinner, and with his twenty-fourth birthday on January 2, the family decided to make him a cake—"we all really liked Henry," said Sager. "When Harris saw the cake, "I thought he was going to cry."

But less than ten days later, Harris received crushing news. Rosandich and the athletic board decided not to renew his assistantship for the next academic year. For Harris, this was Auburn all over again, exactly a year later, summoning a pain still unhealed. He knew he had to have a degree to coach.

With seemingly scarce time for studying between coaching and running intramurals on nights and weekends, Harris had bombed out academically the fall semester. He took four three-hour courses and a three-hour independent study and didn't pass any of them. He drew "Incompletes" in the History of Modern Philosophy, the Cultural Foundations of Education, and Social Services for the Aged. Because of the academic record he brought with him from Auburn, UWM admitted Harris on probation and therefore put him on "academic cancellation" after only one semester.

Harris's struggles were hardly noticed in the turmoil reigning in the Wisconsin-Milwaukee athletic department. "It was very much in chaos," Brady said. "They had a beer pocketbook and champagne aspirations."

Rosandich started laying the groundwork for his financial needs in the fall when the state Board of Regents announced it was eliminating its support of athletics at state schools. He said UWM would lose $70,000 in state funding in July and would have to depend solely on student activity fees and ticket sales for support. "This will have a horrendous effect," he said. ". . . The program, as known today, can no longer exist."

Then in January during the NCAA's annual convention, UWM moved up to Division I, although "they had no realistic idea of what it was going to cost," according to Klucas. "It was a smalltime program trying to go bigtime," said Ray Nykaza, one of Harris's junior varsity players.

As AD, Rosandich oversaw nineteen men's and women's intercollegiate and club sports, but he was also burdened with an unrealistic university administration that chafed under the shadow of Marquette, a perennial basketball power that would make the NCAA finals in 1974.

Rosandich, however, had his own particular agenda at UWM. He was a track coach who resented the high cost of football—he would eliminate the program later in 1974—and saw basketball as a money-maker that could support other sports. He believed UWM could become a national power in both track and soccer, although the latter was then a speck on America's sports landscape. A Type-A personality who could rub people the wrong way, Rosandich enjoyed running the athletic department like the Marine he was His memos were exacting. "He wanted to control the horizontal, the vertical, everything," said Brady.

A Wisconsin native and skilled self-promoter, Rosandich was extremely focused on the U.S. Sports Academy, which he created when he came to Milwaukee in 1972 following five years as AD at Wisconsin-Parkside. As a career Marine officer, he had been an athletics ambassador for the U.S. State Department, working in athletic programs all over the world and helping train national teams for the 1960, 1964, and 1968 Olympics. His international experience would become the foundation of his academy at a time when there was interest in making coaching more academic by providing certification. "He had gotten tied up with some money from Saudi Arabia. Some of the sheiks were putting big dollars in. And he was doing sports clinics [internationally] and he was getting infusions," Brady said. "Tom was more concerned about U.S. Sports Academy than he was with being athletic director at UWM."

By March, Klucas was advocating dissolving the junior varsity program, saying that was a "growing trend" among major universities. With freshmen now eligible to play on the varsity, he said the developmental program no longer justified its $2,500 cost. He told reporter Dennis Marsolek he was uncertain if Harris would be retained, saying it was "a personnel matter for the athletic board." Harris expressed little reaction or emotion, saying he had known that dropping the JV program was possible.

"When Coach Davalos left, that was not good for Henry," Sager said. "Bill had no allegiance to Henry." Davalos would have stood up to Rosandich and, according to Sager, prevented Rosandich from "fragmenting" Harris's job and thereby making it so difficult for him to succeed academically. Sager and assistant athletic director Jerome Fishbain tried to save Harris and his position. "The point Tom Sager and I made was that we had brought Henry in here in a tough situation, and we probably were obligated to renew his contract," Fishbain said. "But that idea was thrown out."

With a college degree again in limbo, finding a way to play pro basketball grew critical for Harris if he wanted to help his mother. He still had a "giant scar" on his knee but had worked out hard since arriving in Milwaukee. "Henry had a tremendous year working out. He worked out all the time," Klucas said. "We'd give him a hard time. We knew he worked hard, but we were always pushing him to work harder because no one wanted him to succeed more than we did."

Harris was succeeding as a coach. He was good at it and worked hard. Basketball officials repeatedly told Fishbain "what a fine job Henry had done in all respects." Everyone seemed impressed. "The thing I admired in him [Harris] was the way he could handle the kids—what he said went," said UWM sports information director Tom Skibosh.

Marsolek, the student sports writer, had asked Harris what he'd do if he lost his job. Assuming his Auburn veneer, he said that was the "least of his worries." "It did not seem to bother him," Marsolek wrote later. Harris told him he planned to stay at UWM regardless and complete his degree. He gave no indication how he planned to do so.

Chapter 34

Swept Away

*It did not really matter what we expected from life
but rather what life expected from us.*
                                       - *Viktor Frankl*

On a southern spring night in early April 1974, a black man from Alabama named Henry—his quick wrists made strong by picking cotton and batting cross-handed and his nerves made icy for all he had endured since—hit his 715th home run in the major leagues, breaking Babe Ruth's career homer record. He then made it around the bases without being shot.

If Jackie Robinson broke baseball's very visible color line, Henry Aaron shattered an invisible American boundary designed to keep black people out. It was a numbers barrier that supposedly indicated greatness over time. That's why it came at such a cost. His daughter was under FBI protection in college for two years following a kidnapping threat aimed at making Aaron stop his chase of the Babe. For two years, he received an average of one hundred pounds of mail a day. More than half of it was negative, if not also racist and threatening. The hate mail poured in from all over the United States—it was a truly American phenomenon.

For too many Americans, Aaron was a threatening black man, a threat to their belief in white superiority. Some could accept equal treatment under the law easier than they could black success. They saw blacks' progress advancing at their expense—"they are coming to get our stuff."

Aaron was forty years old and the Atlanta Braves' right fielder when he broke the record April 8 against Robinson's old team, the Dodgers. The quest for greatness, however, started at age eighteen, when Aaron got on a train in Mobile, two sandwiches in a sack and two dollars in his pocket, and went to play professional baseball in 1952. The Braves would send him to play for the Eau Claire Bears in northwest Wisconsin, which was not unlike Harris going to Auburn in 1968. "Here I was," Aaron said, "just a little black kid with no experience. I had never played with white players. I stayed at the YMCA because there were no other blacks up there. There was nothing to do." So Aaron sat in his room and listened to big-league baseball games on the radio. Then one day he called his mother and said he was coming back to Alabama. His older brother, Herbert Aaron Jr., got on the phone and told him he would be crazy to give up such an opportunity. So the kid stayed, and kept hitting.

The next year Aaron played at Jacksonville, Florida, where, at nineteen, he was one of five blacks integrating the South Atlantic (Sally) League and traveling highways through South Carolina, Georgia, and Alabama. "We had a terrible time the first couple of months. Really, it was a bad situation," he said. "A lot of the stuff we went through, we thought it was the law of the land." The worst fans were in Jacksonville. "They just couldn't understand why they wanted to have blacks and whites play together." By July, Aaron's bat had silenced their hatred. By September, he was the Sally League's most valuable player. "Hank made Christians of those people," said league president Dick Butler.

Aaron was noticeably quiet when he reached Milwaukee and the major leagues and had to convince media he was not "just a simple colored boy." He became a young star, and Braves executive Donald Davidson changed his baseball name to "Hank" so he wouldn't seem like "just another Henry," then a common African American name. When the Braves won the World Series, he was the toast of Beer City, but he repeatedly encountered racism buying a house and then living in the city's suburbs. Again, he said little.

"There was too much at stake for us to screw it up," he said years later. "Black people had been crying out for opportunity in this country for two centuries and finally we had it. Our mission—and that's the only thing to call it—was to do something with the chance we had." Aaron got his race lessons from Jackie Robinson and his black Brooklyn teammates as the Braves and Dodgers traveled north together for the start of the season, playing exhibition games along the way. The older players' message was: "Either I could forget I was black and just smile and go along, or I could never forget I was black."

The record meant so much to black America. Not the record itself but how Aaron had blown up so many myths breaking it—showing up every day, being steely consistent, never attracting attention to himself. A grandson of slaves had stepped on a stair with white America's most beloved sports icon and then climbed beyond him. It was proof of the greatness African Americans could achieve—if given a chance.

April in Milwaukee found Henry Harris awaiting a special "re-entry" draft being held by the American Basketball Association. The league was in its seventh season and, in facing its possible demise, doing all it could to compete with the NBA. The April 17 draft would enable ABA teams to select any player already out of college, whether they were already on NBA teams or had never played professionally. With no degree and his assistantship gone, Harris saw the draft as his salvation. He hoped Rudy Davalos could get the San Antonio Spurs to draft him or else land him a contract to play in Europe. Harris was still clinging to the dream. Two years after his college career ended, he still wanted to play basketball. "He loved it so much," said James Owens, "and that was the best way he could help his family."

Harris wrote Davalos, seeking help. "He wrote a long letter," Davalos recalled, "just saying he'd like to give it a shot." He also called Davalos. "I told him it would really be difficult to make it, after being off and with his knee and everything. He was just asking, 'If by chance, this and that.' He wasn't the kind to beg."

Bill Klucas, having scouted part-time for the NBA, believed Harris had recuperated enough to earn a roster spot with a team, particularly in the ABA. "There was a demand for guys who could be no less than good roster players. With two leagues, he certainly could have played for a while," Klucas said. And if he could play two or three years, he could help his mother, Klucas thought. "Henry was the kind of guy who did not treat money lightly. Henry was not the kind to go through his paycheck. My thought was that Henry would make the most of those two or three years."

After that, in Klucas's mind, Harris would become a "tremendous coach." "Although we weren't sure Henry was going to be a great pro player, we knew Henry was going to be a great person, and I had no doubts he was going to be a great coach," Klucas said. "He was really well poised. He was a smart guy. He did with the freshmen [junior varsity] what we wanted done. I thought down the line that Henry could have written his own ticket—especially knowing which way the world was going [racially]—that Henry, with the way he could coach, would end up being one of the leaders. I just knew Henry wasn't going to end up in some steel mill in Bessemer."

Klucas's optimism about Harris's future, however, blinded him to Harris's past and present. He had never even asked him about his experience at Auburn and in the SEC.

While Harris was enduring a Wisconsin winter and Milwaukee's third worst snowfall ever—twenty-three inches—life was finally changing at Auburn. In February, its black athletes staged a walkout over rules regarding facial hair. Appropriately, they crowded into Room 303 at Sewell Hall to talk over their decision beforehand, the same room where Harris lived so long by himself. Auburn capitulated quickly, and the walkout ended, but not before freshman Eddie Johnson told a reporter, "I would never advise any black to come here." But Johnson, a quick, 6-foot-2 guard, was not suspended or even benched. He was allowed to play on and finished the season leading the SEC in scoring. His black freshman teammate, Pepto Bolden, led the league in rebounding, both playing in the wake left by Harris's skill and commitment.

The entire South was changing. With southern high schools desegregated for at least four years, college coaches were recruiting more blacks. Twenty-six percent of the SEC's football signees in 1974 were African Americans, and more than half of the SEC's basketball signees were black.

Thursday evening, April 11, 1974, Harris and Susan Loritz, his girlfriend, ate dinner together in the Green Commons cafeteria in the Sandburg complex. It would be the last time they would see each other for more than a week. Easter was Sunday, and UWM would be on spring break the following week. Loritz and some friends were leaving for Florida. The Student Union was sponsoring a bus trip for students to Daytona Beach. Harris was upset that she was leaving, but he didn't try to stop her from going.

It became a long weekend for Harris. Basketball season was over so he had a lot of time to think. In his seventeenth-floor room, he smoked marijuana, putting the butts in the deflated basketball he used as an ashtray. He wrote of his loneliness with Loritz gone.

Monday, with the ABA draft two days away, Harris grew anxious. "I remember him getting depressed and concerned leading up to the draft, because Rudy hadn't talked to him," Klucas said. "I know he came in to use the phone in the basketball office to try to reach him. I let him use my office, and I went down the hall. I let him do that a couple of times maybe a month before the draft." Klucas saw Harris was depressed—"because he thought there would be some reassurances about the draft and I don't think he got that."

Tuesday, Harris went back to the athletic offices, where he saw Tom Rosandich, the athletic director. With a pro career in jeopardy, Harris was making a plea to get his degree and start coaching. He wanted a chance to stay at UWM. Rosandich stressed to Harris the importance of completing his education. He told him he could be a real asset in a community or educational program but had to finish his degree. He gave Harris no hope of that happening at UWM.

The older white men in Milwaukee didn't get it or, at worst, didn't want to. For southern blacks, education was armor, armor against racism, armor against white supremacy. The risk taken in the Great Migration was driven by parents' hope for a better life for their children. And education was the vehicle of hope, particularly for Willie Pearl, who so wanted her children to surpass her own education and level of success. Both Davalos and Larry Chapman had tried to help Harris get a degree only to see their efforts backfire.

It had been a difficult two years for Harris. Just as he had lost his father and uncle before he was two and Lieutenant Gooden before he was six, Harris had now lost a chance for a college degree not once, but twice. He had lost Debra Threatt to another man. He had lost his shot at the NBA and now, apparently, a shot at the ABA. He had lost Davalos and Chapman at Auburn, and then lost Davalos again in Milwaukee. And he had lost his basketball future to a horrific knee injury and a lack of caring.

By Tuesday night, Harris was despondent, his hope seemingly gone. He saw Jerry Willis, a black UWM basketball player, in the fifth-floor hall of the south tower around 1 a.m. He told Willis, "I feel empty, empty like a shell, and I want to die."

Draft day arrived Wednesday. Despite Harris's pain less than nine hours earlier, his friend Tom Sager could not detect any anxiety or depression when he saw Harris at 10:30. "We were really recruiting hard at that time, and we were all going in different directions," Sager said. "I think he thought he was going to be picked up by somebody."

Harris spent the rest of the day awaiting a call from Davalos or anyone with the ABA. But a call never came, and the news he finally got was not good. He was not selected by the Spurs or anyone else during the draft's ten rounds.

Around 11 p.m. Wednesday Harris talked by phone with George Tandy, a black UWM player. He gave Tandy no indication of any personal problems. It had been a traumatic day, but Harris was so practiced at masking his feelings he couldn't let his guard drop even when he was in his greatest pain.

Harris's story had always been one of a determined young warrior moving relentlessly forward despite obstacles. He had met everyone's fears, suspicions, and prejudices head on and survived the ordeal. He had overcome so much, but this was yet another body blow and it staggered him. "That was our life, that was our dream, and all of a sudden that's not there anymore," said Owens.

Harris and Owens often talked about life after Auburn. "We talked about getting married and having kids and finding out what we wanted to do," Owens said. "Henry would always say he wanted to have plenty of children. He wanted to be involved with kids in sports and activities, and even go back home to Boligee and build a recreation center. That was his dream, to go back home and do something for his home in Boligee. That [Boligee] was his love."

But that dream was not alive late Wednesday as midnight came and went. Harris could not reframe the picture that kept staring back at him on a cold, gray April night in Milwaukee. He could not see that final ovation he received at Auburn or all the black athletes he had knocked down the door for. That was a goal he had achieved, but there was no solace in it, not this night. The tunnel he was seeing the future through was completely dark.

Harris was supposed to go to Chicago on a recruiting trip the next day and had told his aunt and uncle he would visit them. Alice Horn loved his visits and would fix his favorite meal—ribs and greens—whenever he came. "He was a smart and energetic person and an intelligent person," she said. "He was a people person, because he loved people. And he always kept a smile."

But Harris didn't make it to Chicago the next day, and he didn't get to the ABA or NBA either. He never got to coach again, never got to teach. He never made it back to Auburn or Boligee, and he never finished his book. The strong, brave young man who was the hope of so many had finally lost hope himself. The encourager could not encourage himself one more time. Drawn to the river of a revolution ripping through America, he was ultimately swept away. As he had done so many times at Auburn, he simply disappeared, vanishing into the darkness.

Chapter 35

Big Chill

Brother, brother, brother,
There's far too many of you dying
   - Marvin Gaye
   'What's Going On'

Al Young was driving his car late Thursday afternoon when he heard someone on the radio mention Henry Harris. He turned it up. The man said something about Henry Harris being dead. Young didn't believe it. How could that be right? How could he be dead? He had talked to Harris just a couple of weeks earlier.

Young drove home and turned on his TV, sat down and waited for the local evening news out of Birmingham. The newsman confirmed Young's fears. He said the same thing the man on the radio had said. Henry Harris was dead, and apparently from suicide. Sadness overpowered Young, and he was suddenly confused. He couldn't understand what could have happened. How could things have gone so wrong since they had talked no more than two weeks earlier? Harris had called his high school coach, seemingly just to talk. He had seemed "kind of down," and Young had tried to lift him up. "Go on and get your degree," Young told him.

Thom Gossom was walking into the TV room in Sewell Hall to watch a late-night NBA game. The eleven o'clock local news was still on, and the sports guy was talking. Before he ever sat down, Gossom began hearing bits of what he was saying.

" . . . died . . . suicide . . . depressed . . . "

" . . . Auburn's first black athlete . . . "

Gossom glanced at the screen and saw a photo of his friend

staring back at him. The newscaster kept saying Harris was dead. It seemed he was saying it over and over. How could that be? Things were finally turning around for him. He wouldn't commit suicide.

"God, no!" he screamed.

Gossom left the room quickly. "I didn't want anyone to see my reaction, so I got up and went to my room and just cried," he said.

Harris had called Gossom periodically from Milwaukee, waking him up in the middle of the night. "I'm coming back [to Auburn], and I'm going to let people know what it was like," Harris would say. "I'm going to write a book," but Gossom could never get a good sense of how things were going for Harris. "He felt like he was overdue, he had never gotten a break, he'd always had to work for everything he got, and he was going to hit it big. And once he hit it big, he was going to come down to Auburn and tell everyone what it had been like for him."

"There's no way Henry would kill himself," Gossom told himself.

The bad chill reverberating through Alabama eventually reached East Lansing, Michigan. Gary Pettway's mom called him. "Have you heard?" she asked.

"Heard what?"

"Henry died."

Within an instant, Pettway was lonely. He felt he had lost something. He felt a void. He cried. "You can't believe it. It didn't happen. Anybody else but not him," said Pettway.

Pettway thought about Harris's phone call just two weeks earlier. It was the first time the two childhood best friends had talked in five years. Harris told Pettway about "all these great things that were happening in his life." "Henry didn't sound like a person who was about to do kill himself," Pettway thought. "He didn't talk about drinking or drugging or partying. He talked like a person who had matured."

Pettway was still at Michigan State, getting a graduate degree in biology, and didn't even known Harris was in Milwaukee. Harris told Pettway he would come see him in a couple of weeks and he'd stay a week. "I'm going to be happy to get over there and see you, we've been separated for a while, but now we've got some time," Harris told him.

Pettway began to replay their hour-long conversation in his mind. He thought Harris sounded good. He didn't sound like he was "high or anything of that nature." He talked like "life was looking up." He told Pettway how good he felt about his job, that he thought he had the possibility of having a real good career. He said he was looking forward to the next season, that he thought he would have a pretty good team."

Harris did not tell Pettway, Gossom, or Young about how his life was really going—whether out of shame, the belief that he had let those closest to him down, or some other rationalization. But over and over, he was trying to connect, reaching out without saying what he needed to say, crying out for help with silence.

He also called Loretta Brown, the high school counselor he had stayed six weeks with in Los Angeles. It was one night about a month before he died, and he didn't say anything about any problems he was having. But Brown's boyfriend was there and wanted her to get off the phone with Harris, so she told him she would call him back. But she never did—her boyfriend didn't want her talking to Harris. "I hate that I did not call him back. That has bothered me," Brown said in 2018. "I don't know, but I think he wanted to ask me something or for something. That tore me up. I wondered what I could've done."

Bill Klucas arrived in Bessemer about suppertime. He went to 2931 North Tenth Avenue, to the corner house that Willie Pearl Harris shared with her sister, Mary Alice Sipp. Still not knowing what to say some six hours after learning of Harris's death, Klucas knocked on the door. The family had just heard the news on TV. "I think it was Channel 42, and this man was the sportscaster there for years," said Harris's sister, Glenda. "He started to read it, and then he stopped, like it shocked him. About the same time he did that, the man was knocking at the door to come tell us."

"Walking into that house and facing that family . . .," said Klucas, his voice trailing off many years later. "I had to go down there and answer questions I could not answer."

"What happened?" Willie Pearl asked him.

Klucas felt he had no adequate response. "How do you explain suicide?" he said.

Late Thursday night, more than an hour past midnight, a twenty-one-year-old African American student walked into UWM's campus police station. He identified himself as Stephen A. Parks and handed a wallet to Darryl Coons, the officer on duty. Inside the wallet was Harris's university ID card, his Wisconsin driver's license, and Sandburg Hall meal tickets.

"Where did you get this?" Coons asked.

Parks replied that just ten minutes earlier a female student had brought it to his room on the sixth floor of Sandburg Hall's south tower. She told him she had found the wallet on the sidewalk going from the dormitory to North Maryland Avenue.

"Who was she?" Coons asked.

Parks said he didn't know her but had seen her around the dorm.

"Why did she bring it to you?"

Parks replied she may have felt he was a "good friend" of Harris.

Later Thursday night, just after 4 a.m., another UWM police officer, Kenneth Nieman, went to the Sandburg front desk in Green Commons to interview nineteen-year-old David Bigelow, who was in the middle of his overnight shift. Nieman asked Bigelow if he remembered anything unusual happening the night before. Bigelow replied he had heard a loud thump between 2:30 and 3:00 a.m. He said the noise came from the overhang above the walkway between the south tower and Green Commons. He said he thought it was the wind and didn't investigate.

Susan Loritz walked into the UWM police station Friday morning around 9:30. She said, "I'm Henry Harris's girlfriend."

A twenty-one-year-old junior, Loritz told Richard Sroka, the lead detective on the case, she had returned to Milwaukee from Florida as soon as she heard the news. She said she and Harris had dated for four months, seeing each other almost nightly. She stated they were "very close" and that Harris "confided in her." She told Sroka he smoked marijuana and drank beer and wine.

Loritz said she had last seen Harris eight days earlier, when they ate dinner on Thursday night, April 11, before she left with friends for Florida on spring break. She said he was "very upset" about her leaving but did not try to stop her or indicate he was suicidal. In the writings found in his room, Harris expressed his loneliness with Loritz gone. Sroka asked if Harris had ever talked of suicide. Loritz said only once and just briefly. She said he told her that when he was thirteen or fourteen, he took an overdose of sleeping pills to take his life because he thought he was in trouble with the police over a petty theft. He knew going to jail had cost Lieutenant Gooden his life.

In the medical examiner's office downtown early Friday morning, assistant medical examiner Warren Hill received a call from Sroka's partner, detective Robert Kowalski, who said he still had not interviewed any basketball players, that they still were "in mourning" late Thursday. Several players had tears in their eyes when police attempted to question them earlier Thursday, and most still did not want to talk, so Kowalski did not press them. Kowalski also told Hill he had returned to Harris's room searching for any pills other than the decongestant and penicillin from the infirmary discovered initially but had found none. Toxicologist Robert Eberhardt of the medical examiner's office had already confirmed for Hill that the greenish tobacco in the plastic bags found in Harris's room was marijuana, as were the butts in the deflated basketball. He would later report that Harris's blood contained neither alcohol nor barbiturates.

When Harris's body had arrived downtown Thursday at the county morgue, Paul D. Danko of the medical examiner's office conducted the exam, searching and undressing the body in the presence of ambulance attendants John Skipchak and Greg Kamens. Danko found compound fractures of the upper left arm and a fracture of the left leg below the knee. He found no gunshot wounds or other indicators of foul play, writing, "Nothing to indicate foul play has been revealed."

An autopsy was not performed—they were not mandatory in Wisconsin until 1987. Harris's self-report of depression to UWM player Jerry Willis less than thirty hours before his death was sufficient to rule suicide. Hill had made that ruling Thursday but continued collecting information. He added Kowalski's call to the medical examiner's report as well as the discovery of the wallet, which police believed was ejected from Harris's pocket on impact. Hill also noted the Milwaukee's city police department had no record on Harris.

Throughout Friday, Milwaukeeans read of "the life of a complex young man" who died tragically a very long way from home.

"The aftermath of sorrow and dismay and confusion that the apparent suicide of Henry Harris, 24, assistant basketball coach, has left in the tight little circle of the athletic department at UWM is deep and wide reaching," wrote the *Milwaukee Journal's* Bill Dwyre.

Dwyre had interviewed Tom Rosandich, Jerry Fishbain, and Tom Sager. He cited unnamed "other reports" in writing Harris had attempted suicide after his knee injury at Auburn. Dwyre also mentioned Davalos's departure, writing: "Harris was left in a town and situation totally new and strange to him—and without the person who had hired him and would be most available to help and advise him." Then, after reporting Harris had academic difficulty, Dwyre wrote:

> At this point the story becomes as jumbled and complex as the young man's personality.
> Rosandich said he had talked to Harris as recently as Tuesday about the importance of continuing his education and of his potential worth in a future community educational program. Rosandich said he had spent quite a bit of time trying to get financial aid for Harris for the upcoming year for Harris to further this pursuit. . . .
> Another aspect of the case was that Harris's contract to coach next season had been turned down by Rosandich and the athletic board.

The *Milwaukee Sentinel* reported sadly that Davalos thought he had found Harris an opportunity to play professionally in Europe. Davalos said he had talked to "other basketball officials" while in New York for Wednesday's ABA draft, according to the *Sentinel*, "and returned to San Antonio Wednesday night convinced that Harris would be able to play basketball in Europe." No further details were reported.

"I feel like I have lost a son or brother," Davalos said.

"Maybe if I had been in Milwaukee . . . ," he said without completing the sentence.

Klucas told the *Sentinel* Harris had "ups and downs" but he had never heard him talk of suicide. "The tragedy is that here was young man who would have made a contribution to society simply because he was a good person," he said.

At 10:55 a.m. Friday, Hill received a phone call he was awaiting. Harris's older brother Robert was calling from Harrisburg. He said he would come to Milwaukee the next day with his uncle from Chicago to identify the body.

Hill quickly began asking questions.

Robert said he had never heard Harris threaten his own life. He said Harris could "give good advice but didn't take it." He said his brother "always appeared happy outwardly" but there had been "a great deal of pressure on him."

"What kind of pressure? Hill asked.

Robert mentioned the stress placed on education by their mother and the stress of being the first black athlete at Auburn. He told Hill that Harris had played four years at Auburn but had not graduated, that he had hoped to play pro basketball and had been drafted by the Houston Rockets but had been unable to make the team because of the knee injury he sustained at Auburn. Robert said Harris had spent the summer in Harrisburg and had a good job, earning as much as $200 a week, but that he had to pay for Harris's transportation to Milwaukee.

Robert was talking rapidly, and Hill scribbled notes furiously: "Came from a very poor environment and also a black environment. He decided to join white society to get ahead, for he felt that no matter what education you had, it meant less than 'who you know,' especially if you were black. His 'joining' of the white culture undoubtedly put pressure on him. He started to 'make it' as the first black player at Auburn, but things evidently started to fall apart on him. He never underwent psychiatric treatment."

Robert next booked a flight to Chicago, having already sent James, now a sophomore at Penn, to Bessemer to be with their mother, brother, and sister. The following morning, he rode to Milwaukee with his uncle, Willie Horn, Willie Pearl's brother. They had to identify the body, but they also wanted to learn more about Harris's death. "My uncle was working part-time as a security guard or an auxiliary policeman, but he knew a little about detective work," he said. Their first stop was the UWM campus.

"Some people took us to his dormitory. We looked around the room, and there was a security guard there answering any questions he could. We tried to call the police department to come over there and tell us what went down, but nobody came," Robert said. "We left and went over to the medical examiner, and that's when we saw Henry. My uncle went and looked at him. I couldn't. I froze. I lost it."

A shocked Bill Lynn told the Associated Press Harris was "a fierce competitor . . . He was very unselfish, a terrific team player." He told the *Auburn Plainsman* that Harris "always seemed to handle his own problems his own ways and never appeared in a state to do something as drastic as this."

In Milwaukee, Dennis Marsolek, the student sports writer who covered Harris's junior varsity team, was hit hard by the suicide, having interviewed Harris several times. "He was such a nice guy, he was so forthcoming," he said.

On the day Harris was buried in Bessemer, Marsolek published a column in the *UWM Post,* opening with: "Most people on this campus didn't know Henry Harris existed until it was too late." After describing Harris's ups and downs, he concluded:

> When Henry Harris died, many people lost the chance to meet a good man, the kind of man that made the world worth living in. The few who had met him and came to know him well lost a small part of themselves when Henry Harris died, and probably lost a big part of their hope for mankind after seeing what can happen to a man who did nothing but good. Henry Harris was a man with the ability to do great things, but got many bad breaks in return for his hard work. He deserved a hell of a lot more than that.

Chapter 36

A Black Prince Comes Home

... So boy, don't you turn back.
Don't you set down on the steps
'Cause you finds it's kinder hard.
Don't you fall now—
For I'se still goin', honey,
I'se still climbin',
And life for me ain't been no crystal stair.
― Langston Hughes
'Mother to Son'

The morning was already turning hot when the people started arriving at New Zion Missionary Baptist Church in downtown Bessemer on Tuesday, April 23. It had been six days since Harris's body was discovered eight hundred miles away. A black prince dead too soon, Harris was back home in a pine box that wasn't even long enough for his 6-foot-3 frame. "A community sends a kid off to college, you expect great things from him," said Dee Cee Madison, the black Auburn counselor. "Maybe the pressure on him was too great."

A blue collar suburb southwest of Birmingham, Bessemer was home to the Ku Klux Klan klavern that bombed the Sixteenth Street Baptist Church in 1963 and then, unarrested and undaunted, killed voting rights activist Viola Liuso in 1965 on the highway between Selma and Montgomery. Between those attacks, on July 5, 1964, four days after passage of the Civil Rights Act, nine black male high school students, wanting to try out the new law, sat down at the lunch counter in McLellan's dime store in downtown Bessemer and were attacked by men rushing into the store with bats. Ten years later and only a few blocks away, Bessemer would be the homegoing site for a young man who tried to live out the Civil Rights Act. Legislation changed laws, and brave black Americans made the laws a reality.

Willie Pearl Harris and her three youngest children had lived in Bessemer since they moved from Boligee when Harris left for Auburn. Willie Pearl was a regular usher at Mount Zion, the two-story brick church in the center of Bessemer, just six blocks from the house she and her kids shared with her sister Mary Alice.

James Owens and Thom Gossom were pallbearers for their "big brother" who always told them things would get better. Among the dozens of people who drove up from Greene County that morning were Harris's teachers, coaches, classmates, and townspeople whose dreams he carried. Bill Lynn was there and so was Bill Klucas and Bill Nunn, the UWM black assistant football coach and Harris's good friend. Auburn teammates Jimmy Walker, Pat Cowart, and Ralph Smith came together, all having been made better men simply by being around Harris, who blew away stereotypes so they could thrive in an integrated America. "I know my life was enhanced by my friendship with Henry," Walker said.

The sanctuary was packed and hot. The balcony was running over. "Hundreds and hundreds of people came," said Glenda Harris, Henry's sister. The casket was draped with a navy blue Auburn blanket, the school's orange "AU" logo in its center. Auburn sent it, along with an orange floral arrangement in the shape of an "A."

"It was a typical black funeral," Madison said. "Lot of emotion. Lot of people hurt. It was a hard funeral." The choir opened the service with *Amazing Grace*, and the church's pastor, the Revered Wilson Fallin Jr., a thirty-one-year-old graduate of Colgate-Rochester Divinity School, gave the eulogy. He did not know Harris so he made his remarks general—"God has the power to help us through this." He did not mention suicide because of the black church's view of suicide then—you will go to hell if you kill yourself. But Fallin didn't need to mention suicide. Its dark cloud already hung over the sanctuary, making a tragically sad service heartbreaking. "It was terrible. The wailing. It was so sad that a friend, a teammate, had died," said Gary England, an Auburn teammate.

When Fallin finished, he invited the mourners to view the casket, but Larry Chapman kept his seat. The former Auburn assistant coach learned of Harris's death from athletic director Lee Hayley, who wanted Willie Pearl's phone number so he could call her. Ever since, what-ifs had cascaded through Chapman's mind. What if he had not tried to help Harris by allowing him to be a volunteer high school coach, prompting Lynn to take him off scholarship? What if he had not tried to help Harris by recommending Davalos hire him? What if Harris had never gone to Milwaukee? What if Davalos had never left? What if they had stayed in touch more? "I got really pissed," Chapman said.

But now in the packed sanctuary, Chapman was overcome with grief. "I had all kind of mixed emotions about how Henry got from Boligee to the bottom of that high-rise," he said. "I cried."

After the service, Harris's body was taken to a black cemetery, Pine Hills, located at the end of a dirt road on the south end of Bessemer, a tombstone to the segregation Harris had broken. The young man who gave his life for the integration of Alabama would be buried on a hillside among men and women who lived and died in the Jim Crow South, and among World War II veterans who died trying to prove blacks were Americans too and fit for the fight. It was hardly appropriate for them or Harris, or anyone else. "It just seemed to be a barren, spotty-grass, red clay cemetery," Klucas said. "I remember thinking if someone could have just planted some grass and flowers."

Glenda had passed out while viewing the casket. Then, as Harris's body was being lowered into Alabama earth, Harris's brother Carl, also a high school senior, passed out.

Following the funeral, Klucas, Nunn, and others went by the Harris home. Klucas left after a while, but Nunn stayed. "It was really important to Bill to spend some time with the family. I was glad he did because I was out of answers and out of trying to pretend to have answers. They were all very respectful to me. Bill was doing a lot more for that family than I was at that time," Klucas said.

Albert Johnson also went to the house. Auburn's second black basketball player, the 6-foot-7 Johnson wanted to talk to Willie Pearl. "I remember so many people at the house," Glenda said, "and there was one guy—Johnson. I don't know why he stands out, but I remember him being there talking to my mother, trying to comfort and console my mother, out of all these people who were there." Johnson had delivered a message to Willie Pearl from Henry.

In the fall of 1972, Johnson was in his Sewell Hall room when he got a call well past midnight from Harris, who was back in school after being released by the Rockets. It was around two o'clock. Harris told Johnson he had just taken "a whole bottle of sleeping pills."

"I'm dying," he said.

Johnson attempted to get as much information as he possibly could but could not persuade Harris to tell him where he was. Johnson feared if he went looking for him, he might not find him and Harris might die in the meantime. So he stayed on the phone and kept talking to Harris, for an hour or so. Johnson only hung up when he knew Harris's girlfriend had returned and was there with him. "I think the young lady had gone out and he had gotten a little upset about it. He said he couldn't find her, didn't know where she was," Johnson said.

When Johnson had seen Harris a day or two later, he asked him how he was doing, and Harris replied that he was doing better. But Harris said little else, and Johnson didn't pry. Johnson was quiet by nature, and Harris knew he could be trusted not to tell anyone. "He [Johnson] was laid-back, he was sensible," said Robert Osberry, his roommate. "Very mature," said Gary Redding, a suitemate.

This was the autumn Harris regularly ate dinner at Henry Ford's apartment, the autumn Harris, seemingly out of nowhere, told Ford: "If you ever hear that I committed suicide, don't believe it."

The message Johnson had for Willie Pearl was straight from Harris himself. He had called Johnson in the middle of the night to give him a specific instruction. "If I don't make it through the night," he said, "then tell my mother I tried."

Chapter 37

Doubt

When Henry Ford heard Harris had committed suicide, he didn't believe it. "It was like, 'Wow, he told us,'" Ford said. Less than eighteen months earlier, Harris had told Ford not to believe it if he ever heard he killed himself, so Ford didn't. "All of us close to him in college thought it had to be some sort of hanky-panky. We just couldn't see him committing suicide," Ford said. "Of course, we didn't ever hear from him once he left."

The first reaction was disbelief. Then doubt. "There's no way Henry Harris could have committed suicide," his friends said back in Auburn. "Milwaukee? What was he doing way up there? That can't be right." In Greene County, where life was finally improving, "everybody was shocked," said Boligee's Severe Strode, "wondering what had happened."

Newspapers in Alabama and across the South reported Harris's death mostly in four or five paragraphs sent by the wire services, with no mention that Harris had lost his assistantship. The lack of information fostered doubt, and how Harris died spawned suspicion, as some lynching victims were forced to leap from or were thrown from bridges.

"The black community had very few suicides back then, because we always knew there could be things that would stop us from accomplishing our goals. We had major problems, but suicide was not an option," said Dee C. Madison, the first black counselor at Auburn. "I know it was called suicide, but I don't believe Henry was suicidal. He was there by himself, or so we think, in that room when he jumped. We don't know. Was there a note left? No. . . . It appeared to be suicide, but we don't know. We don't think he was the type of person to commit suicide."

Alice Horn, Harris's aunt in Chicago, didn't believe Harris killed himself because if he had, "he would have done it a long time before that," she said. "He had lived in a home with holes in the floor. It's hard to believe that you could rise above poverty and have more in your life, and then you commit suicide. He had never shown that side. He was always so happy. I never saw him without a smile. He and Robert knew that they could call us collect if they ever needed anything."

The trip to Milwaukee by Robert and Horn's husband, Willie, fostered the family's suspicion the death might have been a murder. Not getting to talk to the investigators prompted Robert to wonder "maybe this guy is trying to cover up something." "And my uncle was upset with Henry because a lot of times when he came to Chicago, he had this white girl with him." Robert and Willie Horn concluded Harris could have been murdered for one of two reasons—his white girlfriend or the book he was writing on Auburn. "He was very disgruntled about leaving school without getting his degree. He was threatening to expose something, and we didn't know what it was," Robert said.

Mourners at the funeral had cried in pain that Harris was murdered—a logical assumption in a black community that had endured so much white-on-black violence. Loretta Brown, whom Harris had stayed with in Los Angeles, thought the only way Harris would have jumped out of a building would be if "someone had a gun and said, 'You better jump.'"

Gary Pettway, Harris's childhood friend, and Dianne Kirksey, Harris's onetime-girlfriend in Greene County, both believed his romantic interests could have killed him. "If you think in terms of Henry and women, it could have been anybody [who killed him]," Pettway said. Kirksey felt suicide was a rarity among blacks and would not have been an option for Harris. "Look at all he had already been through in Greene County," she said. "The more believable scenario was that his girlfriend was out of town and he hit on somebody else's girlfriend, and somebody didn't like that and there was a fight. That would make more sense to me." After considering the possibility of suicide again, Kirksey said, "If Henry committed suicide, it was because he thought he wasn't going to get a degree."

Others in Greene County and Auburn assumed drugs must have gotten Harris killed. Bill Lynn Jr. was among those surprised to learn marijuana was found in Harris's room. "Nobody ever knew Henry to do drugs," he said. "The story finally settled on was that he must have gotten up there and got in with some bad drug dealers and must have gotten pushed, or got on drugs. I can't see him going up there and getting depressed and just jumping."

UWM coach Bill Klucas said Harris's drinking and social life never interfered with his job performance. "I never saw him drunk," Klucas said. "We had early staff meetings, and he never missed one or looked like he was hung over. It was never a problem for him preparing for or doing his duties. And I never heard anything about marijuana use period." Klucas said he wasn't even aware Harris had a white girlfriend. Assistant coach Tom Sager said he never saw Harris high "or even a starry look in his eyes."

Team captain Richard Cox said the entire team was shocked when they heard the news. "You never know what is going in someone's life completely, but he was very well liked, very well respected, and it was really a blow to everybody when it happened, it really was," he said. "It was a tough day."

No one on the team thought it was murder, however, according to Cox. "None of us would have thought that at all. No. To the contrary, he was a physical specimen, and there was no one that would have thought there was someone who would have thrown him out of Sandburg Hall. That was not even a thought by anybody who knew him well," Cox said. "Henry wasn't someone who invited trouble, and people wouldn't look to start trouble with him, especially in the dorms. The dorms at that time here weren't a rowdy place. They weren't as open as things are now, and in my opinion it would have been difficult for an outsider to come in to start something or assault someone. That doesn't sound likely in Sandburg Hall, just doesn't."

Neither Klucas nor Sager ever suspected foul play either. "I don't think there's any question [it was suicide]," Sager said. "He snapped. That's why his death was so violent."

Sager had not seen depression in Harris during his final days. "With someone as quiet as he was, you might not have known. I didn't." "He handled himself so well," said assistant football coach

Gary Wynveen. "That's why what happened was so surprising, but that's the way it is sometimes. People are so nice on the outside, but they are repressing so many feelings on the inside." Sager wondered if his friend "might have acquired [his good attitude] to survive."

Bill Perry, the basketball manager and part-time roommate, saw Harris as a more complex person than most did at Auburn. He thought Harris was an "emotional person" who "had a way of keeping himself bottled up around us." "There was a lot more there than was coming out. He kept himself under control," he said. "I thought he was complex. I felt like he had a lot of things going through his head, and he was kind of intense. And I guess his death proved it."

Larry Chapman thought Harris's "respectful" and "obedient" nature may have masked his emotions. "Externally, Henry was a strong black man," Chapman said. "Internally, he was no different from me or you or anyone else. When our head hits that pillow at night and all we can hear is that motor on the refrigerator, truth of that day and truth of our life and truth of our past and the fear of the future all wax in on us. Henry was very sensitive. That's why he was who he was. His sensitivity spoke volumes about his ability to cope and handle that environment. He had just a sweet nature about him, and who's to say how much pain he experienced."

"I mean to tell you," said Wes Bizilia, another Auburn assistant, "Henry was an awfully nice person." Bizilia understood what was going on during those three hours after midnight on April 17, 1974 in that eight-by-twelve-foot room on the north side of Milwaukee. "There's only so many times you can get knocked down until you don't want to get back up. Henry got knocked down too many times. Too many things happened that weren't supposed to happen to him. Gosh, he had a tough road. It was tough, tough road," Bizilia said. "What happened to Henry shouldn't have happened. But somebody had to break the ice. He opened the door, but it was a doggone tough door."

Debra Threatt, whom Harris had tried to marry a year earlier, got the news in a letter while she was living in Belgium with her soldier husband. "My mom sent me a newspaper clipping of him taking his life, which to this day I will never believe. That really shattered me. I looked at the paper in disbelief because I knew how he felt about his mother and his brothers, and that was just so out of character."

Tim Ash was back home in Indiana, working on a job, when his mother came and found him. Someone from Auburn had called the house. "It broke my heart when I heard it. He was a good guy. He didn't deserve that," Ash said. "He was a helluva athlete. He could have played football, he could've played baseball, he could've done whatever he wanted to do. I never believed he intended to kill himself. He loved life too much. There were still too many women to chase and too many beers to drink for him to kill himself." Greg Austin, who entered Auburn with Ash and Harris, couldn't get "anyone to tell me anything" when he heard the news. "At one point I was so sad about it," he said, "I just tried to wipe it from my memory."

Four decades later, the details remain sketchy, creating wiggle room for doubt. No one wants to think their teammate killed himself or that they didn't see his pain. His teammates know little of Harris's circumstances in Milwaukee. "Even to this day, I don't know what happened," said Pat Cowart, who roomed with Harris in the summer of 1969. "It's bad when you don't want to know."

"Henry was usually smiling, talking, and cutting up. Just trying to make a joke out of things," said Bobby York. "It might've been that his depression was so great, but I didn't think anything about it at the time. For me, we were all on the same team, and we were just trying to treat him like everyone else. We were all white boys in a mostly white university, and he was the only black kid. I probably didn't understand the pressure he was going through."

"We'll never know what Henry's inner feelings were, what his thoughts were," said Dan Jacobs, the student manager when Harris was a freshman. "There are so many unanswered questions, but what impact did [integrating Auburn] have leading up to his death?"

Tim Beavers, who shared a suite with Harris for two years, said, "Henry was not the kind of guy who would sit with us and tell us what he was going through. I think we all knew it—he was part of us and very much someone we all looked up to. We saw what he was going through. He didn't bring it up, and we didn't bring it up, because we were very supportive of him and he knew that."

James Owens eventually understood why so many of Harris's friends couldn't see the possibility that he killed himself. "I didn't see it, and I don't see it now," Owens said in 2008. "But then, we don't want to see it."

Harris's friends and teammates didn't see Harris's depression in his final days. They didn't know about the loss of role models in Boligee or the loss of his scholarship at Auburn. And they didn't know about his attempted suicide at Auburn eighteen months earlier, a previous attempt being a leading predictor of suicide. Like Bizilia said, "If Henry had a problem, he kept it to himself. He didn't complain, at least not to me. But then again, he wasn't part of the family."

The suicide attempt Susan Loritz described to detectives sounded like a combination of Harris's attempted overdose on aspirin at Auburn and an incident that occurred in Boligee when he was around "ten or twelve."

"Henry was a bright young man, and his mom and grandmom had high expectations in relation to his behavior," said Eunice Outland, a neighbor who owned a small store with her husband. "One day, Henry came down and snitched a cinnamon roll. My husband saw him. He said, 'You can have the cinnamon roll but I'm going to take you home and tell your mother what you did, because I know she wouldn't approve of that.' My husband said when he got there and told her what Henry had done, he was sorry he had told her because she gave him such a whipping that Henry dropped the cinnamon roll and didn't want to eat it. She thought she was doing the right thing."

Harris's brother Robert saw Willie Pearl go in the house and get a belt or switch and come back out. "She beat Henry until that man [Outland] started crying and said that he hated that he told her. That's the way my mother was. She said, 'We'll work to get it, or we don't get it,'" said Robert. "Later in life, she recanted. She said that she shouldn't have beat us. She said that was a slavery thing, but she didn't know any better." Harris's younger brother James said Willie Pearl learned other ways to discipline children from early-childhood teachers she got to work with. "You could tell she had changed by the way she disciplined her grandchildren, compared with how she had disciplined us," he said.

James said it would have been extremely unlikely Henry could have taken an overdose of aspirin without his three brothers knowing about it, as they all shared a bedroom with him.

The men who investigated Harris's death had not forgotten it some forty years later. "It's sad anytime some young man like that takes his life—over what seems senseless to us, but it must have seemed pretty big to him," said lead detective Richard Sroka. His partner, UWM detective Robert Kowalski, said, "I can still see him lying on the roof." Both men could accurately recall circumstances of the case. "It seemed to me there was some report of him being depressed or an injury that kept him from progressing along the professional route of basketball," Sroka said. Kowalski remembered other details—"I think there were some drugs or marijuana in the room, and I think there was some relation with the coach [Davalos] and with some female [Loritz]."

Warren Hill, the assistant medical examiner for Milwaukee County, also remembered Harris's death. He said an autopsy would not have been required then to rule a death a suicide—depression and personal problems would have been sufficient. "He was having personal problems and there was a history of depression, and at that time that would have been enough for the medical examiner [to rule it suicide]," Hill said. In 1974, Hill already had a decade of experience in the medical examiner's office and would work there another quarter-century.

Sroka and Kowalski retired after long careers as UWM detectives. Their chief in 1974, William Harvey, who recognized Harris's body on the rooftop, became head of the Wisconsin State Patrol.

Sroka said there was no indication of homicide or fighting. "No, not at all," he said.

Any possibility someone threw Harris off the roof and later pushed the screen out? "No, no," he said.

Sroka called Harris's death a "classic" suicide. "Believe it or not, we had quite a few jumpers during my thirty years. It was classic."

Chapter 38

The Weight

Calvin Patterson and Ernest Cook were expected to integrate the Florida State University football program in the fall of 1968, just as Harris was entering Auburn and integrating athletics. Patterson, a running back from Miami, and Cook, a fullback from Daytona Beach, were can't-miss prospects, but not long after signing, both began receiving letters replete with racism and threats not to come to Tallahassee. "It wasn't like a caution light came on. We're seventeen-year-old kids who had no idea that kind of hatred existed," said Patterson's good friend Javan Ferguson. "We would laugh, thinking these people were crazy." Cook's parents didn't laugh, though. They suggested their son visit some northern schools.

Cook never made it to Tallahassee, accepting a scholarship to Minnesota instead. Patterson could have gone to Southern Cal or Notre Dame but ignored the warnings of relatives and went on to FSU, which did not belong to a conference at that time and had already integrated its basketball and baseball teams.

On the freshman team that fall, Patterson carried the ball only six times. The coaches wanted to switch him to defense in spring practice, but he refused. He never got in the spring intra-squad game but never removed his helmet on the sideline, telling a coach he didn't want his teammates to see his tears. Patterson was redshirted as a sophomore, and whenever he walked the mile to Florida A&M, the students there told him he should be playing for the Rattlers and not going to a "white kids" school. Black students at FSU, meanwhile ostracized him for dating a white student.

Patterson began struggling academically and eventually stopped going to classes. "He had the IQ," said T. K. Wetherell, an academic advisor for the athletic department who became FSU's president years later. By the end of two years at FSU, Patterson was ruled academically ineligible for the 1970 season and dropped out of school. Instead of going home to face friends and five younger siblings in Liberty City, where he was hailed a hero for integrating FSU football, he stayed in Tallahassee for the next two years.

In the spring of 1972, Patterson moved in with FSU history instructor Craig Ammerman, telling him and others that he was going to Tallahassee Junior College to regain his eligibility for football, as he had one season of eligibility remaining, but he actually never enrolled. In mid-August, he called a friend in Miami and told her he had been wounded as a bystander in a failed robbery at a convenience store. He assured her he would be able to recover but probably could not play football again. But there was no robbery, and Patterson was not wounded. That night, he told Ammerman, "What's so hard is trying to act so happy when you're so sad." Ammerman asked him if he was planning to run away.

The following day, Patterson shot himself in the stomach with a .38 revolver. He somehow managed to call the police immediately afterward. The bullet, however, had punctured his aorta. When the first officer arrived, Patterson asked him to hold his hand. He bled to death in the ambulance taking him to the hospital.

The death was listed as an "apparent suicide," but Ammerman and other friends believe Patterson was trying to only injure himself sufficiently to create a cover for not playing football. Like Harris, Patterson was a victim of the shame of unrealized expectations, and like Harris, he hid his pain well, being described by friends as "not a big complainer."

No FSU coaches or university administrators attended Patterson's funeral in Tallahassee, only a handful of players. Among them were four African Americans who had followed Patterson to FSU and ended up as his pallbearers. FSU coaches had told their players not to attend the funeral, and thus began a three-decade campaign—conscious or unconscious—to erase a black suicide victim from FSU's corporate memory.

One of the black players who attended the funeral was J. T. Thomas, who would win four Super Bowl rings with the Pittsburgh Steelers. When Thomas was listed as FSU's first black player on a souvenir cup at a game in the 1990s, former FSU quarterback Tommy Warren was so angered that he spent the next decade trying to persuade the university to honor Patterson. As an FSU quarterback, Warren had befriended the younger Patterson and become his roommate, their friendship inspiring him to become a civil rights attorney. "People don't like to talk about those times," Thomas told reporter Mark Schlabach in 2008. "They like to think things have always been the way they are now."

In 2004, thirty-six years after Patterson entered FSU, the school did the right thing, inviting more than two dozen family members to Tallahassee for a dinner and recognizing Patterson in a ceremony during a game. Warren and his wife later donated $100,000 to endow a scholarship in Patterson's name at FSU's law school. His portrait hangs in the law school rotunda.

Cook, the other FSU signee whom Patterson and his buddy Ferguson had laughed about "bailing out," became an All-Big Ten fullback and then went on to Minnesota's medical school. He was able to go back home to Daytona Beach as a doctor.

John Westbrook dreamed of becoming the first black player at Baylor University. The son of a minister and ordained himself as a minister at fifteen, he liked Baylor's Baptist heritage and knew it had the psychology and religion courses he was seeking. Westbrook believed an integrated school would prepare him for a rapidly changing world. Both an idealist and an optimist, Westbrook was salutatorian of his class, a musician, and an outstanding debater and public speaker. He wanted to be president of the United States.

When Westbrook entered Baylor in 1965 and "walked on" the freshman football team without a scholarship, he was just one of seven African Americans on a campus of 7,000. The freshman team's coach, "Catfish" Smith, called him "Sambo" and played him only three minutes all season. Although disappointed, Westbrook was heartened when he thought of his parents and a family friend who came to freshman practices, fed Westbrook on weekends, and urged him to "keep going, don't quit." So Westbrook showed up for spring practice and in his initial scrimmage with the varsity, ran for sixty yards on his first carry. Baylor coach John Bridgers, who had coached blacks in the NFL, gave Westbrook a scholarship after spring practice—despite protests from assistant coaches.

On September 10, 1966, he became the first African American to compete for a Southwest Conference varsity football team during a nationally televised game against Syracuse. When he entered the game, the Baylor public address announcer proclaimed, "Colored football for color TV."

Westbrook was averaging five yards a carry at midseason before a TCU player tackled him, injured his knee, and ended his season. The torn cartilage was removed, but the knee was slow to heal and Westbrook played rarely in 1967 before a concussion during a midseason practice sidelined him for the rest of the season.

Depression followed, and Westbrook swallowed a handful of aspirin at one point, later calling the act his "psychological suicide." Then one summer night in 1968, he drove his 1953 Studebaker to Lake Waco, thinking he could drive it into the water and end his pain. Once he got there, though, he decided he wanted to live and hurriedly left.

Believing he would play rarely as a senior and concerned about the long-term health risk to his knee, Westbrook met with Bridgers, who urged him not to quit, that he had come too far. Westbrook played little but, with two younger teammates, integrated LSU's Tiger Stadium that season. Then, in Baylor's final game, Bridgers sent him in with four minutes remaining, and he carried the ball five times for twenty-five yards and a game-clinching touchdown.

After Westbrook graduated, two NFL teams talked to him about a tryout until they examined his knee. So he earned a master's degree in English instead, went to seminary for a while, and worked for the Fellowship of Christian Athletes and the Southern Baptist Convention. In 1974, he came home to Texas and started preaching. His speaking ability and personality made him a natural for public office, and with a campaign fund of only $10,000, he ran for lieutenant governor of Texas in 1978 and finished second to incumbent Houston millionaire Bill Hobby in the Democratic primary. That same year he was called to pastor Houston's historic black Antioch Baptist Church and developed a socially active ministry there.

In 1982, Westbrook told Baylor students, "You can't have both racism and Christianity." By then, his health was failing. Unable to exercise because of his knee injury, he gained weight and developed high blood pressure. In 1983, he collapsed and died of a blood clot in his lungs. He lived only fifteen years after deciding not to kill himself, yet his impact on others during that time was so great that both Governor Mark White and Houston mayor Kathy Whitmire attended his funeral.

Jerry LeVias played his first game in the Southwest Conference a week after Westbrook did. He would find much more success on the field and, as a result, endure more racial hatred. No football "first" anywhere likely endured more. LeVias was a marked man who survived on SMU coach Hayden Fry's constant counseling and his grandmother's enormous faith, wearing "23" at her request for Psalms 23. On the back of the door of his single dorm room, he taped the Serenity Prayer—"God grant me the serenity to accept the things I cannot change and the courage to change the things I can . . ." There were death threats, late hits, and opponents spitting in his face, but no one ever questioned his courage. LeVias—five-foot-eight and 170 pounds—always showed up for the next kickoff, knowing he was playing to improve the lives of black Americans.

LeVias led the NFL in punt returns as a rookie and played for six seasons before deciding the game was no fun anymore. Not much was. He had used his SMU academic background to become a successful businessman in Houston and kept moving forward. The past couldn't catch up with him until 2007, when he was diagnosed with post-traumatic depression. LeVias had never hated white people before going to SMU but realized in hindsight he had survived SMU and the Southwest Conference by internalizing his hate. He said his legendary 1968 punt return against TCU as a senior was "fueled" entirely by hate.

In the fourth quarter of a tie game, a TCU linebacker knocked LeVias down, spit in his face, and said, "Go home, nigger." Incensed, LeVias took himself out of the game, slung his helmet to the ground, and shouted, "I quit!" He sat down on the bench and cried. When SMU's defense forced a TCU punt, Fry started searching for another punt returner, but by the time he found one, LeVias was running onto the field and turning back to tell Fry he was going to run the punt back for a touchdown. Catching the ball on his eleven-yard-line, LeVias zig-zagged across the field and eluded eleven TCU tacklers on his way to the end zone. Fry called it "one of the most inspirational things ever to happen in sports." But LeVias would eventually realize the same hatred that carried him eighty-nine yards against TCU had "crippled" him.

"That hate changed my personality," said LeVias, who would rarely talk about his experiences. "I shut down my emotions so much that I couldn't feel anything. I became remote, unable to experience intimacy, alone." His sleep was tormented; he would slap out at the darkness with his fists. He did not start healing until forty-five years after his gauntlet ended. Counseling gave him an opportunity to process and release the emotions he repressed at SMU to push onward—"I had to learn not to feel sorry for myself or I'd cry". He forgave those who hurt him and threatened to kill him, and after forty years, finally took pride in what he achieved for others.

Like LeVias and Westbrook, Darrell Brown was a courageous freshman football player in the Southwest Conference in 1965. He was the walk-on at Arkansas who was used for tackling practice as he returned kickoffs against eleven defenders with no blockers. Arkansas coaches hoped "I would go away, just quit," he said. "But I kept thinking, 'No, not today.'" Only after receiving two injuries that trainers refused to treat as a sophomore, did Brown say to himself, "Let's refocus. Let me get into something where I can make a difference. . . . Let me go to law school."

Brown graduated from the University of Arkansas law school and became an outstanding trial lawyer in Little Rock. He tried to block out his college ordeal and cheered for any team playing the Razorbacks. That worked for two decades, until the track coach at Arkansas started recruiting his daughter. Brown had to decide if he could forgive enough to allow her to attend his alma mater. He eventually determined that even if he could not forget, he could forgive. His daughter became a track All-American at Arkansas and only there did she fully learn all her dad endured just to be a Razorback. She asked him why he had not told her the whole story. Sounding like black World War II veterans who didn't want to embitter the next generation, he said he didn't want to scar her, and besides, he still couldn't tell his story without crying. The trauma wouldn't go away. He couldn't understand how so many adults could be so cruel to a kid.

Years afterward, Brown introduced himself to Frank Broyles, the Hall of Fame coach who oversaw practices and later became Arkansas athletic director and a longtime ABC commentator for college games. Broyles told Brown he didn't remember him.

Virgil Pearson wouldn't talk about Auburn. After walking out at the start of preseason practice in 1972, Pearson enrolled at Jacksonville State, played well, and became the first black football player to receive a degree there. But if anyone brought up his two years at Auburn, he changed the subject.

"I bet it was twenty years before I really could sit down and talk about it. The experiences down there really had a negative effect on me," said Pearson, who disguised his depression, just as Harris did. "I was always just a happy-go-lucky guy, but deep within me, I was hurting for a long time." He never sought counseling. "At that time, depression and things like that weren't really talked about. But I knew it was abnormal to have something bother me like that for that long a period of time." Like other black athletes in Sewell Hall, he didn't talk about his feelings. "If a man is hurting on the inside, he doesn't want to express it to another man. I kept my feelings to myself."

For more than a dozen years, Pearson had nightmares about being back at Auburn. Most of them ended the same way—"I'd wake up thinking it's time to go to practice." During his second year at Auburn, as his depression increased, Pearson would retreat to Sewell Hall after classes and sleep before football practice. "I would stay in the bed for two or three hours. When it was about time to go, I would just get so anxious. I dreaded it, just dreaded it," he said. ". . . .So later on, I'd go to sleep at night, and I'd wake up and think it was time to go to practice." (Recurrence of trauma, like nightmares, and avoidance, such as not talking about the trauma, are two of the four clinical indicators of post-traumatic stress disorder.)

As Auburn's second black scholarship football player, Pearson did not feel the pressure Harris and James Owens did to "stick it out," but in the years afterward, feeling like a failure in the integration game tormented him. "It was like I ran away, I left," he said. A potential employer once pointed out his lack of confidence during a job interview. "I was just never the same after I left Auburn. It just seems like I couldn't get past it," Pearson said. "Sometimes I look back and say, 'I probably should have stayed, or could have.' But I think I was better off leaving—I know I was mentally."

Pearson was aided in his healing by running into his former high school quarterback, David White. "I was working for UPS and making deliveries," Pearson said. "He [White] owned a roofing company and was up on a roof. And he came down, and we got to talking."

"I want to apologize to you for the way we acted," White told him. "I've always admired you all [blacks] because there is no way I could have taken what we did to you. I don't see how y'all took that."

"I guess," replied Pearson, "that was just the way it was back then."

For forty-five years, Nate Northington refused to talk about being the SEC's first African American football player. It was just too painful. He dodged interviews or if a reporter caught him unaware on the phone, he would hang up. He just couldn't reopen that wound.

Northington and Greg Page signed scholarships with Kentucky and were roommates, but then Page died in a non-contact practice drill and Northington had to integrate the league by himself. He played against Ole Miss and Auburn, but it all eventually became too much—the grief, the loneliness, the empty room, the constant reminders Page was not there, the lack of understanding by coaches. Northington left Lexington, transferred to Western Kentucky, graduated, and became a longtime administrator for the Louisville Housing Authority. In the late 1990s, he was called to the ministry.

With age, Northington began to appreciate the magnitude of what he and Page had achieved. "I realized I needed to share that with others," he said. In 2013, he finally told his story in *Still Running*, his autobiography. "There was a lot of pain with what transpired with Greg," he explained in the introduction. "For a long time I just didn't want to go back to that." Talking about those dark days made him sad and revisited the shame he had felt for so long about leaving Kentucky. The headline on October 23, 1967 blared "Northington Quits UK, Football Team," but the article omitted the back story—

the meal ticket taken away, the loneliness of a single room, the shoulder not repaired, the punishing nighttime practice after Page's funeral.

As Northington began telling his story, he saw it as a way for people "to remember Greg Page." He grew convinced that "God wants it told."

Even Perry Wallace, integration's ideal candidate, felt he was close to a nervous breakdown at times. "They weren't the worst four years any black person had ever encountered, but they were difficult years," said Wallace, the SEC's first black basketball player. "I had to figure out how I was going to deal with the pain, the confusion." He had no one to talk to about what he was going through. "People either didn't understand or didn't care, or it really scared them. Stuff like that scares people because they hate to have to realize that stuff like that existed," said Wallace, whose body could go icy cold with fear just thinking about an upcoming road trip a week or two away. "Oh god," he'd think, "I have to go to Ole Miss again."

Wallace started the healing process the day after his final game at Vanderbilt by speaking his truth to the *Nashville Tennessean*, the consequences be damned. "I was the only one who knew how harmful that sort of experience could be to a young person," he said. Wallace left Vanderbilt two months later with a degree in engineering mathematics and electrical engineering but realized quickly he'd need to work hard to ensure the experience did not permanently scar him. "The danger of being a pioneer is not in the immediate experience, but reconciling the experience for the rest of your life," he told the *Nashville Tennesseean* in 1973. He later said that process could take "anywhere from a few years to forever."

During Wallace's three years at Columbia Law School, he consciously processed the emotions he carried out of the SEC, opening up "feelings that you had to block out to survive." "I could have been consumed by fear and pain, but I fought to overcome that," he said. "I was spending time making sure I didn't turn into the ugly person an experience like that can make a person. . . . You have to understand that during those four years I learned exactly how things were. I had to face the naked truth and deal with it day by day." Wallace even had to spend time to "get a good sense" of whether what he did was beneficial. "After I had some time to reflect on it, it became quite clear to me that I had done something that was useful, that was needed," he said.

While at Columbia, Wallace heard of Harris's death. He had a visceral reaction. "I thought to myself, 'Wait a minute. I know that guy. I played against him.' It just dredged up all those old feelings," recalled Wallace, who could not imagine what Auburn was like for Harris. "Going to Auburn back then was like going to hell. Going straight to hell. I know what it was like for me and I can only imagine what he must have endured down there." The two times Wallace played at the cramped Sports Arena, he asked his coaches not to take him out of the game so he would not be assaulted with abuse from fans directly behind the bench. "Auburn was a rough, rough place in those days," he said.

As an attorney for the U.S. Department of Justice, Wallace—seemingly providentially—ran into Godfrey Dillard, his black freshman teammate, who was also working for the Justice Department after graduating from the University of Michigan law school. Dillard had gone to Vanderbilt to be part of the civil rights movement, despite his grandmother begging him not to go into the South. But Dillard's father had been a Tuskegee Airman and Dillard wanted to play his part by integrating the SEC.

Wallace, meanwhile, became a law professor in the 1980s, first at the University of Baltimore and then at George Washington University, where only an occasional student would even know he once played college basketball, much less changed history.

Tom Payne grew up on integrated U.S. military bases across Europe and America, moving every year or two, rarely making friends and often being ridiculed for being so tall. When he was fifteen and nearly seven feet tall, his father, one of Airborne's top black sergeants, retired and bought a house in his wife's hometown of Louisville, Kentucky, just blocks from Muhammad Ali's parents on the west side.

Payne had never played basketball, but that wouldn't last in Kentucky. He worked hard and the game came easy, as he went from not being able to dunk as a sophomore to all-state as a junior and all the friends he could want. As a 7-foot-2 senior, he had more than three hundred scholarship offers, but the Paynes knew little of recruiting and even less of the University Kentucky's long racist reputation. Payne's father, a Korean War veteran, believed integrating Kentucky would be noble, and both parents were protective enough to want their firstborn close to home. Payne knew Kentucky's team was all-white but believed he'd be seen like everyone else. He would soon come to believe Kentucky wanted to sign an African American more than it wanted one on its roster.

"It was a cultural and social shock," said Payne in 1980. "I had always been treated as a human being. My mama raised me to be proud of myself. Most of the people I had been around in my life had been positive. They weren't big people, but they were good people."

Payne's initial surprise was learning his roommate was a black baseball player—he asked why he wasn't rooming with a basketball player. So began two years of threatening calls, broken car windows, distant teammates, and a head coach who was rarely helpful. Payne wanted to transfer. His father, the sergeant, said no. Tough it out, be a man. "But I wasn't a man," Payne remembered. "I was a big boy—a lanky, dumb kid." Like Harris, he found refuge off campus. "Socially and culturally, I just dealt with the black side of Lexington."

Six games into his varsity career, Payne was booed by Kentucky fans after the Wildcats lost in the finals of their own holiday tournament and he did not play well. "When I made the all-tournament team, they bombasted me with a whole bunch of boos and things. I was a pretty sensitive guy at that time. . . . My family was there, and they had to do a whole lot of talking to keep me from losing it," he said. *Basketball Weekly's* Mike Tierney wrote: "Tom Payne has taken more abuse than any college player I've ever seen. And remarkably, most of the criticism has come from so-called UK fans."

Jack Perry, Kentucky's assistant sports publicist, saw Payne as "withdrawn and untrusting" and "treated badly by opponents." Payne's hurt was still palpable a decade later when he talked about a 1971 trip to Knoxville to play Tennessee. "I remember they had a sign that said, 'Nigger Tom Payne,' or something to that extent," he said. The sign was in the locker room after the game, and the incident was recalled by Rupp in 1976. "Someone had written, 'Payne—just a nigger,' on a blackboard in our dressing room," Rupp said.

Payne was ejected from at least two games, saying, "It was my way of fighting back. I was an emotional individual at that time, and there were certain things I couldn't tolerate," he said. By season's end, he was "a total wreck inside. I had to disguise the fact that I started hating white folk."

Again ready to transfer, Payne got an exit ramp out of the SEC when the NBA created a "financial hardship" provision for college undergraduates—in response to a lawsuit by Spencer Haywood, the 1968 Olympic hero who grew up hungry in the Delta. The racial abuse Payne's family received when he left was intense. "Basically, they said I was an ungrateful nigger who they had allowed to go to their school," he recalled.

Payne received a five-year, $750,000 contract from the Atlanta Hawks but was only twenty and no more ready for the lifestyle of pro sports than he was for Kentucky. He tried to keep Kentucky "out of my mind," but his emotions could not be compartmentalized and some of his Lexington habits followed him to Atlanta. He had married his first high school girlfriend while at Kentucky and had a daughter, but he still acted single.

Whereas Harris, Patterson, and other pioneers turned their anger inward and injured themselves with depression, Payne turned his anger outward and hurt others. Just eighteen months after becoming Kentucky's first black basketball player, he was arrested for rape in Atlanta in the spring of 1972 and quickly became a suspect in several more rapes in metro Atlanta and Kentucky. All the victims were white.

He was convicted in Atlanta and sentenced to two years, perhaps the lightest sentence ever given a black man in the South for raping a white woman. But when he went to suburban Cobb County, the prosecution sought the death penalty and an all-white jury gave him ten years. He was sent to Georgia's infamous Reidsville prison—a 1970s racial war zone—and spent a year there in solitary confinement.

In 1977, a Kentucky jury convicted Payne of raping a Louisville woman in 1971, although she initially said her attacker was 6-foot-1 or 6-foot-2. He was offered a plea deal of ten years but, with his family's support, maintained his innocence and turned down the deal. He got life. Paroled out of Georgia, Payne became a model inmate in Kentucky, as well as the only one serving life for rape. He received a parole from the governor in 1983 after six years. Only thirty-three, he began boxing professionally and acting in Hollywood.

In 1986, however, Payne was arrested as he was raping a white woman in a Hollywood parking garage. In the California prison system, he finally admitted he had a problem and received years of counseling and psychiatric evaluations. He was surprised by his therapists' conclusion that he was expressing his rage against whites by raping white women. "That's what was given to me as to why these things happened. I don't have a reason not to believe it," Payne said in a 2000 interview with reporter Tierney. Although he was taking full responsibility for his crimes, Payne asked Tierney: "How much hate is a person supposed to take before they respond? For 18 years I didn't do anything wrong. No juvenile record. Then I made one mistake and picked the University of Kentucky. We know I went through *something* there."

After fourteen years in California prisons—six years longer than stipulated by law because of an error made in his sentencing—Payne was ready to start life anew at fifty. But the state of Kentucky said it wasn't through with him. He had violated his Kentucky parole with the California conviction, so the Kentucky parole board gave him another fifteen years, although he had already served nearly that much in California. He was returned to the Kentucky Reformatory. In 2016, the parole board deferred his request for parole until December 2018.

When Payne was finally released thirty-two years after the California rape, he told a reporter he regretted hiding the anger and resentment he felt in college. "If you're seen as a Superman, you don't feel you can talk and emote like other people. You won't go to other people for help," he said. "I just held it in, you know. I just held it in and held it in."

Chapter 39

Left Behind

In the weeks after her son's death, Willie Pearl Harris wore a path around the circumference of her large side yard on the corner of Tenth Avenue in Bessemer. "My mother would just walk around the yard, just wailing, like a crazy woman," said her son James. "I think a piece of my mother was forever lost at that point."

Inside, Willie Pearl would sit in her living room chair and stare at Henry's trophies on the dining room sideboard. "Mama just basically stopped functioning," said her daughter, Glenda. "She'd sit and look at that sideboard and just cry. If she wasn't doing that, she'd go out and walk, and just cry and pray, cry and pray. To me, she was trying to get some understanding, some acceptance. That went on for months."

Willie Pearl had always "kept her appearance up" although she didn't wear makeup, but she became "unkempt," according to James "Just walking relentlessly in that back yard, wailing." "She was greatly depressed," said Wilson Fallin, her pastor.

As part of her grief cycle, she had to wrestle the demons of guilt, like any parent would, wondering, "What could I have done differently?" "She was always guilt-ridden," recalled James. "I think to this day she felt responsible for Henry's death."

In the weeks and then months after Harris's death, his eighteen-year-old brother Carl repeatedly disappeared. He'd be at the house one moment, and then he'd be gone. When it was time for dinner, Willie Pearl would send James to get him. After a while, James knew where to look—Chambers Funeral Home.

"He would go to the funeral home for several months afterward. You'd look for him, couldn't find him. You'd go up there, and he'd be sitting on the steps at the funeral home," James said.

Only six blocks from the house, Chambers Funeral Home was Carl's refuge. It was where he had first seen his big brother's body. Until he saw the body, "he would not accept that Henry was dead," said Glenda. "He kept saying, 'What's wrong with y'all? He's not dead.'" When he passed out at the cemetery, Glenda said, "He just completely lost it when they went to lower that casket down in the hole. I guess reality finally sunk in."

Just three years earlier, Carl had spent part of his summer at Auburn with Henry, his hero. In an article a few months afterward, Harris acknowledged Carl for playing "against me day in and day out," even though Carl was six years younger and offered Henry little competition. For Carl, just weeks away from graduating from high school in the top fifteen of his class, the death of his brother was unfathomable. "Being the youngest, we looked up to Henry," said Glenda, also a senior, "and being children that young, you don't understand why things happen."

In the days immediately following Harris's death, James kept asking the same question—"Where is his book?" Nine months earlier, James saw the start of the manuscript in Harrisburg. "He had that book if he didn't have anything else," he said. "Where was it? Wherever he was, it would have been with him." The only item Glenda remembered coming back from Milwaukee was the black Dapper Dan gym bag, the one Henry carried all through Auburn and then to Pennsylvania and Wisconsin, as if it still held his dreams. James never got an answer to his questions. Robert had not seen the manuscript when he went in Henry's room two days after his death. Investigators had entered several times by then, and police had given Harris's girlfriend, Susan Loritz, a stack of his papers when she came to the station after his death.

To Glenda, Harris's death "just didn't make sense." "I remember my uncle in Chicago and Robert going up there [Milwaukee] and how quickly the case was closed," she said. But Willie Pearl told Glenda to "let it go." "The only thing I ever heard my mother say was to accept it and leave it alone. In other words, once you go to probing into it, it will probably end up hurting her more in the long run," Glenda said. "I think someone contacted our pastor because he even talked to Mother and convinced her not to try to have an investigation, just accept it as what they were telling her had happened and let it go."

Having talked to Albert Johnson after the funeral, Willie Pearl knew her son attempted suicide in the fall of 1972, but she did not tell her children about the attempt. Without that knowledge, murder seemed more believable. "Foul play would have been the expectation of blacks rather than suicide, especially for our family," said Glenda.

Harris's burial so stretched Willie Pearl financially that she couldn't afford a grave marker and certainly not an independent investigation. "My sister-in-law didn't have any money, and she said, 'Just let it be,'" said Alice Horn, Harris's aunt in Chicago. Horn's husband, Willie, had sent "an NAACP man and a Wisconsin peace officer" to Milwaukee to look into Harris's death, according to Robert. Afterward, Robert went to Chicago to meet with them. "This guy told me, 'You don't have enough money to find out what happened to Henry,' but he didn't think he committed suicide," said Robert, who was left with questions that would torture him for thirteen years.

Robert left Harrisburg at the end of the school year and came home to help care for his mom and siblings. "I knew in my soul from the killings that happened in Boligee that I needed to help my Mom, so I moved back to Alabama," he said. But he couldn't land a teaching job. "I had a madness in me because I didn't know what happened to my brother. I would put in for jobs to teach, and I guess I had an attitude." So Robert started managing a shoe store in Demopolis, a half-hour from Boligee. "I kept a job, I drank, I worked two jobs. I was a functioning alcoholic for thirteen years," he said. "I didn't know what had happened to my brother, and I didn't know how to turn it loose."

James also came home after his brother's death. He completed his sophomore year, took a job in Birmingham, and never went back to Penn. He enrolled in a local seminary, did well, but didn't finish there either. "I dealt with my depression in different ways. I was never into drugs and alcohol, but if there was a party and hanging out with the crowd, I was in it—just reckless," he said. "I think at some level I was trying to destroy myself or some part of me."

Joe Gilliam Sr. was a black college All-America quarterback in 1948, but the Green Bay Packers told him if he wanted to play in the NFL he would need to move to another position. Gilliam chose to coach instead and eventually became the defensive coordinator at

Tennessee State in the 1960s, creating the "nickel defense" by using five defensive backs to stop the passing offenses prevalent in black college football. Then he conceived "bump-and-run" pass coverage by coaching his cornerbacks to stiff-arm receivers just past the line of scrimmage. Both innovations would become staples of NFL defenses, and Gilliam's son, Joe Jr., would become the second black quarterback in the NFL in 1974. But the star of the family was Gilliam's daughter, Sonia, who was smart, musically gifted, and listed in *Who's Who* of college students. But as a student at Tennessee State, Sonia became clinically depressed, and despite counseling and even hospitalization, eventually committed suicide, falling from her sixth-floor dormitory window. Already overcome with grief, Gilliam and his wife were told by their pastor that their church could not hold a funeral for someone who had killed herself. Two more churches told them the same thing.

"You've taken your life. There is no chance for you to repent. That was a fairly strong belief," explained the Rev. Wilson Fallin, who presided over Harris's funeral.

"For blacks—going way, way back—there was a great stigma to suicide, particularly because of our strong religious orientation, where suicide in many churches is seen as sin," said Alvin Poussaint, author of *Lay My Burden Down* on black suicide. A psychiatrist at Harvard Medical School, Poussaint said the shame of suicide was so great that black families would often deny it. "If they [family] don't tell you a person hung themselves or did this or that, it's going to be put down as a heart attack." Black communities would "play down" suicides, according to Poussaint, "to the point blacks even believed they didn't commit suicide." That belief has occasionally bordered absurdity. Psychiatrist William B. Lawson once went to the Washington, D.C., coroner's office to examine the body of a young man who had a bullet hole in his head. "They said someone had shot him and then put a gun in his hand," said Lawson, who asked if there were any witnesses. "They said, 'Well, no, but we know black people don't commit suicide.'"

"You don't want to believe that your family committed suicide," Robert said. "No one wants to believe it, but it happens. It happens all over the country every day. But no one wants to believe it initially."

The façade was that African Americans were strong and able to handle anything, even slavery and segregation, or that it is cowardly or even sinful to admit any weakness of spirit. Suicide's precursor, depression, was therefore also seen as an indicator of a lack of strength, inhibiting blacks from admitting unexplainable sadness or seeking help for it.

Growing up in Birmingham in the 1960s, Condoleezza Rice was repeatedly told there could be no victims. "There was nothing worse than being a helpless victim of your circumstances. That was a sin to consider yourself victimized or not able to control your destiny, or your fate—that was a cardinal sin in our community," said Rice, the former Secretary of State whose great-grandfather grew up in western Greene County, near Boligee, before leaving to go to college and become a minister. "You may not have been able to control the circumstances, but you could control how you reacted to your circumstances."

Southern college teams delayed so long in integrating that their "firsts" found themselves in the midst of the Black Power movement and flung into a sort of no-man's land. "The Black Power movement and whole idea that African Americans were just as good anyone else created additional pressure not to show any weakness, not to show intra-psychic problems, not to show depression," said Lawson, past president of Black Psychiatrists of America and emeritus professor at Howard University Medical School. "So the tendency would be much stronger to hide depression feelings. Several prominent people committed suicide during that time."

Poussaint, who participated in the Mississippi civil rights movement as a medical volunteer in 1965, called the emotional and mental landscape faced by African American pioneers a "psychological disaster—no black people to relate to, just alone and not feeling connected." "All the blacks who were integrating southern schools at that time—not just athletes—had that burden on them. They had to prove how smart they were. They had to deal with all the hostile, angry, black-rejecting stereotypes. And this wasn't just coming from the kids, it was coming from the teachers, which made it worse. You tend to think adult white people wouldn't believe such awful things."

The first black athletes, according to Poussaint, would've felt "culture shock—everyone talking differently, dressing differently, having different styles"—but also rejection. "This was a place you knew they didn't really want you, not as a person. Then, you were leaving a place where most of the people were black that gave you a sense of belonging, of who you were, a sense of identity that was suddenly yanked out of you. And you were put in a hostile, foreign environment with the burden of "now prove yourself" and the feeling you had to prove yourself for all those blacks you left behind, who said, 'This university has never accepted us.'"

"And then," said Lawson, "who can you talk to about your fear that one mistake can be catastrophic. It takes a tremendous toll because that means the person is under constant vigilance and cannot have a period where he can relax and be like everybody else. That creates persistent anxiety and additional stress." And if you think you should be happy because you are so much better off than parents, you "disown your pain," according to Lawson. "We have to put on a façade that we can handle anything and we're strong. So when someone thinks you should be in miserable condition, you say, 'I'm fine.'"

In the years after Harris's death, James Owens occasionally visited Willie Pearl Harris. "She was the type lady that never showed her real emotions," he said. "Whenever I'd go around them, they were the happiest people you could ever be around." James Harris believed his mother held herself accountable for Henry's death. "She was always guilt-ridden," he said. "And I still think she felt responsible for Henry's death." Harris often told reporters going to Auburn made his mother happy, and his despair over having to leave Auburn and then Wisconsin-Milwaukee without a degree was largely driven by the belief he would be disappointing his mother. But Henry had already beaten extraordinary odds, and Willie Pearl was filled with pride over his achievements, with or without a degree. "She was so proud of what her son had accomplished and how he had been accepted at a white school," said her sister-in-law, Alice Horn.

Willie Pearl became a supervisor in a Bessemer high school cafeteria, but she had higher goals before Henry died. Before his death, she had completed her Graduate Equivalency Diploma [GED] and planned to get an associate degree. "When she got her GED, she was so happy," Robert recalled. "When Henry died, she was just getting ready to enroll in Lawson State College. She didn't do it. She kept telling me, 'Robert, you don't understand, that was my child. You just don't understand.' She aged about twenty years in the next five years."

Willie Pearl's goal in returning to school was to work with children. "Before she left Boligee, she worked one summer with some type of enrichment program for small school children," James recalled. "My mother was always friends with a lot of the teachers, and one of them pulled strings for my mother to get this job. My mother was just flushed with life that summer. She often said that she learned so much that summer about child rearing and wished she'd had that knowledge to raise her own children. Her approach to child rearing changed after that. You could see how she had disciplined us and then how she disciplined her grandchildren, how she talked to them."

James, Robert, and their sister, Glenda, all tried to assure Willie Pearl she had done "what she was supposed to do" in rearing them, but they were never sure she heard them. "Mama wanted so much more out of life for all of us," Glenda said. "And she felt it was her job to make it happen, although we were all grown. It was up to us. She felt, 'I need to make sure this happens, and she didn't have the control to do that.'"

Willie Pearl developed a particularly close relationship with Glenda's son, Tony, her grandson. But after graduating from college, Tony was killed in a wreck in Birmingham at twenty-three, a year younger than Henry was when he died. "He was riding in a vehicle that an eighteen-wheeler hit, and he was the only person killed," James said. "After that, my mother lost her will to live. I think those experiences really took the life out of my mother."

Willie Pearl would suffer a series of strokes that led to her death in 2002. She was only seventy-two.

The torment of suicide created a heaviness that hung over the family for years. It was never part of the conversation but often not far from mind. So much went unspoken. Discussing feelings was still not in vogue, and life was challenging enough already—everyone had some sort of pain or oppression to cope with—without talking about a tragedy they couldn't change. James and Glenda felt every member of the family struggled with depression for years.

"Depression is hereditary," James said. "My mother definitely wouldn't acknowledge it, but there is certainly, as far as I can see, a strong line of depression in our family. Definitely with my mother. I've struggled with depression. My brother Robert deals with depression. We've dealt with it in different ways. I'm not sure how Henry dealt with it, maybe through sports."

Henry's youngest brother, Carl, never recovered from his death. "Carl was very smart in high school, very meticulous, and all that changed," Glenda said. "It was like he made a 360-degree turn." After graduating among the top dozen students in his class, Carl dropped out of college and successfully taught himself everything from auto mechanics to home repair. He also began using drugs. "Carl was the straight one, straight and narrow, quiet, solid," James said. "But he admitted to me later on that no one knew he started drinking in high school, and it led to other drugs, cocaine and stuff like that. It was obvious he was addicted to crack cocaine. He dealt with depression with drugs, which eventually killed him." Carl died of an overdose in 2006. He was fifty. "I think the thing that pushed him over the edge was Henry's death. He was really close to Henry."

Robert got sober in the late 1980s. His healing from Henry's death started the day his mother gave him "a box of Henry's things." "I was going through it," he remembered. "I was looking at his student ID at Milwaukee and a lot of other little things, and I just sat down started crying like a baby." Robert realized he could not grieve any more. "To go forward, I had to turn that loose." He entered counseling. "We got into the idea that to grow, you can't hold a grudge. To grow, you have to realize you are going to die tomorrow. Tomorrow could be the next day or fifty years from now. That's where I was."

In 1999, some of Harris's teammates persuaded the Auburn basketball program to recognize Harris at the halftime of a game and arranged for the framing of a blue Auburn jersey with Harris's number 25 and name on it. They wanted to present the jersey and a plaque to Harris's mom, but Willie Pearl declined to return to Auburn, so Robert represented the family. The long-overdue recognition was a curative, validating salve for Robert, who was humbled and heartened to hear his former teammates talk about how much they liked Henry. John Mengelt told him, "Your brother was good. If it was not for his knee, the sky would have been the limit." For Robert, it was as if Henry's memory had been resurrected from the darkness of suicide.

For James and other family members, Henry's death had seemed like nothing more than a "senseless death" for decades. Because neither Auburn nor anyone else was recognizing his memory or achievement, they could not see him for the civil rights hero he had become.

James did not seek counseling until two decades after Henry's death. "It's kind of hard going back and dealing with some of this stuff," he said. "I hadn't dealt with any of it. Everything was repressed. I coped by blocking and running. I had not dealt with any of the feelings associated with a loss like that." James left Alabama to work out West and later completed a psychology degree at the University of Montana. He worked up to second in charge of the Montana governor's office and had nearly completed a master's in public administration when he came home to care for Willie Pearl in her final weeks. After watching the caring a student nurse showed his mother and stirred by the need for quality medical care in America, James returned to college to earn a degree in nursing. He had planned to be a physician when he entered Penn, but that dream disappeared with Henry's death. In the past fifteen years, he has worked across America in hospitals in need of high-skilled nursing.

When James graduated from nursing school, big brother Robert was at the ceremony, bursting with pride. "There were about thirty people in the class, and eighty percent of them were white," Robert recalled, "But the whole group voted him the most outstanding student. I couldn't believe that. I sat there and cried."

Chapter 40

The Lion in Winter

*Be assured that we will wear you down by our capacity to suffer. . . .
We will not only win freedom for ourselves, we will so appeal to your
heart and conscience that we will win you in the process.*
                                            - Martin Luther King Jr.

On a splendid late Sunday afternoon in April, James Owens was drained from a day of preaching. He had taken off his suitcoat and tie and was sitting in his living room, three miles from Jordan-Hare Stadium. He was talking about how two of his 1972 teammates—Steve Wilson and team captain Mac Lorendo, the coach's son—thought enough of him to invite him to go out for a beer after practice.

"They said, 'Are you going with us to The Supper Club?'" recalled Owens, referring to a popular bar for Auburn players. "We walked in, and there were only two guys in the club. One of the guys owned the club, I guess, and was behind the bar, and the other guy was sitting there talking to him. He told Mac or Steve to go get a table." After they took a seat, one of his teammates went back up to the bar to place their order. "Then he came back and said, 'We got to leave. They don't want to serve us.' So we just got up . . . ," Owens paused. ". . . and left, you know. The comment I made at that time was, 'They can come and watch us run, jump and play but we can't . . . '"

Again, Owens paused, trying to compose himself. The large man who had preached a sermon was at a loss for words. A tear glistened on his upper cheek. After twenty seconds, he got up. "I need to take a break," he said, leaving the room.

More than five minutes later, Owens returned and sat back down. "I'm okay. I try not to think about this too much, because it hurts a whole lot," he said, his voice cracking again.

Owens then turned the conversation toward Harris, whom he once called "my greatest hero," saying, "He came when no one else was here. He stood, and he stayed." Owens said he had long regretted not talking to Harris after they both fled Auburn in shame in the winter of 1973. "I knew he was a broken man, but I didn't see that [suicide] in him the last time I saw him. I saw there was still something he wanted to prove, and he was trying to go about it the best way he could. And it might have been coaching, since he couldn't play anymore. If I had reached out more, things could have been better."

After Harris's death, Owens became the living embodiment of Harris, a symbol of his sacrifice and the best source for what college must have been like for Harris. He became a minister at forty-five as a result of the relationship he cemented with God at Auburn. "People don't believe it, but every day for the four years I was there, I was ready to quit—every day," said Owens. "But I had a praying mama and daddy that kept telling me, 'Everything is going to be all right. Just go on and endure it.' And we stayed, and we stayed, and we stayed."

Owens came to believe leaving Auburn was not God's will for him. "When Virgil [Pearson] left—he was from the same high school—it was close for me to pick up my stuff and leave also. But God's purpose was that it wasn't about me. It was about all the young Bo Jacksons and all those guys that were coming on behind, who wouldn't be labeled and thought to be quitters. If Virgil quit and then I quit, the first thing they'd say is 'black players can't stay here. They don't have that staying power, that long suffering.' So the Lord said, 'Stay, this is where you are supposed to be.' And every day, 'Lord, do I go home today?' He said, 'No. Stay where you are,'" recalled Owens, laughing and imitating his daily conversation with God. "Get up the next day and say, 'Lord, is this when . . . ?' 'Stay!'"

Going to college, it turned out, had prepared Owens not for pro football but for the ministry. "Auburn," Owens said simply, "taught me about handling adversity and building character."

Prior to the ministry, Owens had lived out the prophecy of the white teachers at Fairfield High School who told him he had no business going to college. "Just go on and graduate and go to work at U.S. Steel [in Fairfield] because that's as far you're going," they would say.

After his pro football dreams died, Owens did work at U.S. Steel, operating a crane for eight years. When the plant shut down, he couldn't find another job. "You can imagine, being James Owens, Auburn's first black football player, and there's supposed to be all sorts of Auburn alumni around that really could help," said his wife, Gloria. "But there were no offers." So Owens contacted Auburn coach Pat Dye and became a student assistant coach so he could complete his degree. "I passed the courses. I enjoyed going [to classes] and I enjoyed the coaching," Owens said. As a coach, he was able to see the fruit of his sacrifice. "I used to walk around and say, 'Is this Auburn? I just can't believe all you [black] guys are here.' You're walking among them, and you've lived long enough to see this change. It was a great thrill."

Bo Jackson played for Auburn those two seasons, starting a Heisman Trophy–winning college career exactly a decade after Owens's final season as an all-world blocking back. Jackson and the rest had questions for Owens. "They were amazed at how things were back then," recalled Owens. "A lot them said they didn't think they could have done that." But Owens's assistantship ended after Auburn's 1983 SEC championship season. "The NCAA said you could only be a student coach for so long." If anyone from Auburn stood up and pushed back against the NCAA, it did not do any good. Owens was crushed. He felt rejected again by Auburn and did not speak its name for years.

He became a security guard at historically black Miles College in Birmingham and eventually coached the football team for three years. He then took a machinist's job with a paper company and loved it. "I could be just myself without any pressures of anybody knowing who I was," he said. But Owens didn't like raising his two daughters in the city, and because Gloria grew up in Opelika, they returned to the Auburn area, and Owens became a custodian at Tuskegee, the college he had visited for a social life. "We were in charge of keeping the academic buildings clean," he said. "That's where I got my training." He left a decade later to go home—to Auburn. "I was the assistant to the head lady over Buildings and Services, so I was making sure the [custodian] supervisors did their job." Ironically, Buildings and Grounds was the only department where black males worked when Owens came to Auburn.

Owens entered fulltime ministry in 2001, when he was called to pastor Pleasant Ridge Missionary Baptist in Dadeville, forty miles away. "Saving souls, that was his ministry. He always talked positive and encouraged, especially the young people," said his wife, Gloria. "He wanted people to know that they've got God on their side and mountains could be moved."

In the spring of 2000, Owens received a tearful apology from Gene Lorendo, his old offensive coordinator. It meant the world to him. "We were at a banquet in Birmingham—Terry Henley was being inducted into the Alabama Sports Hall of Fame and had invited the entire 1972 team," Owens said. "He [Lorendo] came up to me and began to weep and cry and apologized to me for all the things he had done." Owens believed Lorendo was talking about his reaction to Owens's fumble in the Tennessee end zone twenty-nine years earlier and for not fully using his skills.

The 1972 team got together again for a thirtieth reunion in 2002, and with the evolution of race relations, some of Owens's teammates finally started to figure out what Auburn had been like for him. Like Lorendo, with hindsight, they realized what had happened. On a team built on toughness, no one personified it more than the black guy, and they knew it. "No matter how hot it was or how tired we were, he never complained," said Henley, the All-SEC tailback Owens cleared lanes for. Having seen Owens live a sermon for years, his teammates began to turn to him in spiritual need—an unimaginable possibility three decades earlier. He became close to teammate Rhett Davis, son of Paul Davis, the associate head coach whom Shug Jordan had used to counsel Owens and Thom Gossom. When Coach Davis died, Owens performed his funeral.

Owens and Gossom maintained a friendship over the decades. They occasionally talked about Harris and wondered what his life would be like if he were still alive. Owens told Gossom, "He'd be proud of you." The constant encouragement of Harris and Owens to go to class enabled Gossom to become the first black athlete to attend Auburn four years and graduate. Then, while building a successful business career in Birmingham, Gossom began acting in local theater productions. By thirty-two, he was living in California and a member of the Screen Actors Guild. His movie credits would eventually include *Fight Club* and, ironically, *Miss Evers' Boys*, the story of the Tuskegee syphilis victims. On TV, he played a recurring role in *In the Heat of the Night* and acted in episodes of *NYPD Blue*, *The West Wing*, and *Jack and Bobby*. He also wrote and starred in the one-man play *Speak of Me as I Am*, the story of nine black men who gather every Saturday at a Birmingham barber shop to tell stories, recite poetry, and share dreams.

Despite success, Gossom did not go back to Auburn until 2002. It was just too painful. And the only reason he went then was the 1972 team's thirtieth reunion. During the final half-hour of his drive back to Auburn, Gossom found himself suddenly crying. He could hardly explain his feelings, but he knew they revealed old wounds and pain he had still not shaken. But when Gossom got to the reunion, all his teammates shook hands with him, even David Langner, whom he once fought with daily at practice over racial slurs.

With his healing begun, Gossom eventually moved on to one of his life goals, writing a book about being a black walk-on at Auburn in the early 1970s. When *Walk-On: My Reluctant Journey to Integration at Auburn University* was published in 2008, he called it a tribute to Harris and Owens, whom he referred to as "heroes in my house." Of Harris, he wrote:

> He gave to me and every Auburn University black athlete, and every black athlete since in the state of Alabama, a chance to play ball on a level that had been denied before he accepted the challenge of integration. His star shined intermittently at Auburn. There were good days and bad ones but not many happy ones. The burdens he carried, representing all the black people and those white people who wanted and who needed the social experiment to succeed, were a daily load. But he bore it for those of us who followed. Those of us who remember, who understand what he did for us, will never forget.

Owens and Gossom always vowed to keep Harris's "memory alive" as long they were alive. Neither had thought Harris could have committed suicide, but in 2011, a depressed Owens admitted to Gossom that he finally understood how Harris could've killed himself.

Owens battled depression, along with Type II diabetes, two back surgeries for compressed vertebrae, and a heart attack. Believing he had "shortchanged" his family, he once said, "I regret every day of my life that I did not graduate." Even at fifty-seven, he talked of somehow completing his degree despite needing another year and a half of classes. "I want to go ahead and finish school. I really want to," he said. He re-enrolled in Auburn three times to take classes. When he was working for Buildings and Grounds, he worked at night and went to class during the day.

"I didn't have a great educational background," he explained. "So when I get to Auburn, it's a struggle. You're in class with students, and you're sitting there, the only black in the class, and they're raising hands and asking questions, and you have no idea what is happening. And the English teacher says go over to the library and use the Dewey Decimal System and do such and such. I had no idea what the Dewey Decimal System was. We [athletes] had study halls, but what can I tell you I need help on when I don't know what I need?' We scheduled enough dummy courses to stay eligible. We had people [advisors] who told us what to take. We didn't have a choice. I thought I was doing good, but I wasn't taking anything. We took all these courses that we didn't need until after our senior season, and then they say, 'Well, it's on you now,' and I've got most of my major courses staring me in the eye."

Growing up, Owens saw "there was a thing the white race was trying to teach us, that we were inferior," but he believed that attitude made Auburn's black students want to succeed even more. "We felt, we can succeed no matter how they treat us."

By 2012, the big man with a huge heart needed a new one. The news broke that Owens was in serious condition and needed a heart transplant. He underwent six weeks of tests at the University of Alabama at Birmingham hospital to see if he qualified for a transplant. His teeth were extracted to avoid the risk of infection after surgery. An x-ray showed a spot on his lungs, so part of the lung was removed, causing a painful recovery. Owens met all protocols until one final exam discovered he had a form of neuropathy, nerve damage that can lead to loss of movement and sensation. Because the drugs necessary for a heart transplant can accelerate neuropathy, leading to amputation or paralysis, Owens did not meet transplant eligibility. If a doctor or prominent Auburn alumnus tried to intervene on Owens's behalf, it didn't help. He turned to Emory University Hospital in Atlanta but was rejected there too. Doctors implanted a defibrillator and pacemaker in his chest to maintain an electrical impulse in his heart and possibly buy him some time.

Owens returned to his Auburn home. Although it was just three miles from Jordan-Hare Stadium, Owens had rarely ventured onto campus since resigning his custodial position. He knew he had changed Auburn's history and trajectory, but he still felt apart. But he also knew where he belonged. He had long lingered in the neighborhood, as if waiting for the separation to end.

Owens had waited and waited, as patient as always, and with him now near death, Gossom, Henley, and others believed it was time for Auburn to truly welcome him into the family. They convinced the athletic department to create a James Owens Courage Award. The first award was presented at the 2012 home opener, and Owens was the recipient. In his typical unselfish style, he invited any of his former high school or college teammates to stand with him on the field during the presentation. Dozens did so as Owens received a standing ovation.

With his saga finally freed from the closet of time, sports writers began asking what it had been like. "Fear was the greatest thing about it all," Owens said, "not really knowing what was going to happen." To another writer, he admitted, "Many times I wished I had gone to Grambling. Now, after seeing what I went through and the person it made me, I am proud of what I did."

Then in December 2012, Auburn did the right thing. During graduation ceremonies, Owens received an honorary bachelor's degree—Auburn's first ever. He was finally part of the family.

Two years later, *Quiet Courage: The James Curtis Owens Story* aired on Alabama Public Television. Produced and written by Gossom, the documentary created a lasting memory of Owens in the state where he helped change life for black and white Americans alike. "James Owens, Auburn University's first African American football player, loved his university," wrote Gossom. "She learned to love him back."

David Housel, the athletic director emeritus, told Gossom that Owens "should not have been on an island by himself," that another black should have been signed with him. "Everyone was doing the best they could, but they really didn't know how," Housel said. He described the late sixties and early seventies as a time that "good men remained silent, and that's because of the way life had always been."

Gossom pointed out in the film that Auburn missed an opportunity to atone for its earlier academic missteps by not acting proactively when the NCAA limited how long Owens could be a student assistant. Gossom said Owens academic difficulty stemmed from several factors—a lack of academic support, the lure of the NFL, loneliness, and unspoken bitterness, in addition to nine years of segregated, inferior education that left him unprepared for Auburn.

Owens said in the film he believed "things were forced" on Coach Shug Jordan, rather than Jordan "being ready to accept" integration. He felt Jordan signed him only because "he knew he would have to integrate sooner or later." As for himself, Owens said, "I never knew what I was getting into."

At the end of the film, Owens looked at the camera and stated, "I was selected by God. I was trained by parents to give and not take. . . . God had groomed me—whatever comes, we can endure."

By January 2016, Owens's heart had given out. Experiencing both heart and kidney failure, he started home hospice care. Reporter, Jeff Shearer, knowing his condition, interviewed him for one more article. Owens talked about his arrival at Auburn at eighteen. "When my parents dropped me off, I realized I was here all by myself," he said. "When my teammates left the field, they were going home. I was never home." He also recalled his first varsity game. "You would have thought there was a parade. Those black people [in the bleachers] cheered and hollered. . . . I was their hero, and they were my heroes. I realized I was there for more than James Owens. I was there for a nation, and people were depending on me to succeed."

Owens died two months later—at his home in Auburn. He was sixty-five. Forty-four years after his final game, two dozen white teammates attended the funeral at Pleasant Grove Missionary Baptist Church, along with eight African American players who followed him to Auburn and understood how he transformed their lives. It was a sunny Saturday in early April. The crowd filled the downstairs and spilled into the balcony. By then, Owens was a much-loved Auburn legend. He was easy to love, humble and genuine, a big man with a deep voice and a big laugh. As Gossom, one of his eulogizers, said, "If you did not love James Owens, you did not know James Owens."

Owens was a blocker, clearing a path for Terry Henley or whomever was lucky enough to run behind him. He was also a path-clearer for generations, knocking down obstacles and blowing up the stereotypes like he did linebackers, getting coaches and southern white boys accustomed to being around blacks. Like Gossom said, "Our job was to clear a path to integration out of thorns and coarse weeds with our bare hands." Owens also cleared a path for Auburn. Where would it be today without black football players? He made it okay for African Americans to come to Auburn, whether they were Bo Jackson or Cam Newton or the hundreds of other black Auburn players who have made it to the NFL or just have become better men by being able to play football at Auburn University.

Having been the hub of the Auburn offense in the 1972 "Punt, Bama, Punt" game, Owens lived long enough to see his nephew, LaDarius Owens, get to play in the only game to rival it in Auburn lore. It was the 2013 "Kick Six" game that denied Alabama a shot at a third straight national title. With a second left in the game, Alabama missed a field goal that Chris Davis caught in the end zone and ran 108 yards for a touchdown. It is considered the most famous play in Auburn football history, and, there, helping lead Davis down the field was LaDarius Owens, protecting him to midfield, from where he would sprint easily into the end zone. Another year, another Owens, clearing a path for Auburn.

Chapter 41

Dream Deferred

*The great force of history comes from the fact we carry it within us,
are unconsciously controlled by it in many ways,
and history is literally present in all we do.*
- James Baldwin

Within just four years of the winter of 1973, when Henry Harris and James Owens left Auburn in shame and disgust, Auburn's football roster included three black running backs who would go on to All-Pro NFL careers—William Andrews, James Brooks, and Joe Cribbs.

Change had occurred that quickly.

Then in 1982, just ten years after Owens season as a blocking black, Bo Jackson arrived and rushed for 829 yards. He would win the Heisman Trophy three years later. By the end of 2018, four of the SEC's five black Heisman winners had played for Auburn or Alabama. But for any of this to happen, Harris had to bravely show up at Auburn and integrate major college athletics in Alabama

After becoming fully integrated in the 1970s and 1980s, the SEC has enjoyed unparalleled success in the twenty-first century, winning seven straight national football championships from 2006-12. And in the ensuing six years, Alabama, Florida State, and Clemson have combined for five of the six national titles—Clemson and FSU being Deep South schools that did not integrate their varsity football teams until after Harris enrolled at Auburn. Even in the 2016 Olympics, athletes who had competed for SEC members won fifteen gold or silver medals in track and field. During the 2017-2018 academic year alone, the SEC distributed more than $600 million in revenue sharing to its members.

What had everyone been so scared of anyway?

In the wide lens of the U.S. civil rights struggle, the role of sports has been historically ignored or minimized. Just by showing up every day, Harris became part of the movement, part of a revolution in a country founded on revolution. The rebelling has been missed because it was so nonviolent and occurred within an existing societal system.

If sport grew into a social hoist for equality and justice during the final half of the twentieth century, nowhere was that more true than in the South, where it became a powerful tool for change because it had been part of the resistance so long, part of the maintenance system protecting white superiority. Southern blacks had no other ramp into mainstream society—accession avenues used by other American minorities, like a decent education and labor unions, were off-limits in the South. So, after stonewalling so long, the South's colleges, ironically, propelled integration forward, even if unintentionally.

Black and white athletes taught southerners how to unite with each other for a common cause, how to live together. Unlike the workplace or classroom, the football field and basketball court provided a very visible and measurable model of cooperation. "You were all playing together as a unit, all with a single purpose in mind. Fans responded to productivity and they saw productivity," said Vince Dooley, Georgia's football coach at the time. "Once you put a uniform on, you were playing for a particular school, and it didn't matter what color you were beneath the uniform," As Nike claims, sports can "can unite us." Wilford Bailey, who had been Auburn's president before becoming the NCAA's president in 1987, told author Charles H. Martin he believed athletic integration to be "the single greatest contributor to racial progress and development in the South."

Harris had lived his life off stage, obscure and overlooked in the Black Belt. Then in 1968, he stepped into the middle of a great American drama, only to disappear again when his part was done, dead at twenty-four.

"Henry took a heck of a risk coming to Auburn," Thom Gossom said. "I can't imagine being there alone."

Harris was not the person you would expect to change history. He was one of the people who, according to newscaster Dan Rather, came forward and "were quickly forgotten" but were the strength of the movement." Harris was a poor country boy but he was entrusted to advance human rights in America and did so for four years. He was just eighteen but he was brave. And generous. He planted trees he would never sit under, just as so many athletic pioneers did. Those who are still alive can gaze back and, like 1968 Olympic sprinter John Carlos, say, "I did my part in my life and time, and I prize that more than any medal they can give me. Not everyone who walks the earth can say that."

The South's black college athletes stand on shoulders of giants, but they have little, if any, idea who they are. Their contribution has been lost in the progress and prosperity and the embarrassment over the past. Rather than wrestling with history, southern athletic programs have more often forfeited the match rather than get to close to it and possibly offend older fans or remind new ones even college games were once part of a dark, painful time. Appropriate recognition of athletic pioneers is difficult to find at many Deep South universities, where their courage was so necessary and their footprint is so indelible.

But how we understand the past affects how we understand now, and without history, our perspective grows as short as a text message. History is race in America and it cannot be avoided, but the SEC and its members at times seem to prefer to fast-forward as if the league was always integrated, and one big happy family.

To its credit, the conference recognized Tulane's Steve Martin, the first black athlete in any sport, at the SEC baseball tournament in 2015, the fiftieth anniversary of his season on Tulane's freshman team. Unfortunately, the honor came two years after his death. The SEC saluted Wallace and Nate Northington at its 2017 football championship showcase on the fiftieth anniversary of their first varsity season but, again, came up tardy. Wallace—the model pioneer who had waited a half-century for the SEC to say thanks—was cancer-stricken and died the day before the ceremony.

Conference members have done little better. Each year they are able to cite two former athletes, one basketball and one football, as "SEC Legends," to be celebrated during post-season play. Less than twenty percent of the schools' "firsts" in both sports have been selected, although it would be difficult to believe anyone has cast a longer shadow. A region with a long history of building monuments and markers to bravery and sacrifice would appear to have a few more to construct.

Major league baseball moved like a sloth in recognizing Jackie Robinson, but at the fiftieth anniversary of April 15, 1947, it finally grasped the swath of his influence and retired his number "42" at every big league stadium in America. Colleges throughout the United States have failed to follow the lead. Among SEC schools, Wallace is apparently the only "first" to have a retired number—25, the same number Harris wore at Auburn—and it only happened because Vanderbilt students signed petitions and demanded it of their administration. "When the first black basketball player in the SEC went to your school and nobody knows about it, this is something that needs to be done," said Zach Thomas, one of the organizers.

Kentucky's statue of Greg Page, Nate Northington, Houston Hogg, and Wilbur Hackett—the fiftieth anniversary of Page's death and Northington's SEC debut—was driven by a teammate, Paul Karem, just as suicide victim Calvin Patterson was finally recognized by Florida State only because of teammate Tommy Warren's efforts.

Similarly, if Auburn ever recognizes Harris, the impetus will likely need to come from students, former teammates, current athletes, or former athletes who have found fame only because Harris walked daringly into Auburn in 1968.

If Harris's life had been a rock flung into a pond, the ripples would still be rising from the bottom. Yet, in the summer of 2019, fifty years after his first varsity season, there was no memory of Harris on the campus he forever changed. Harris changed Auburn and the state of Alabama and helped change the South. He made his life matter, and his disappearance from history should matter.

"Henry deserves a lot of credit for doing what he did. He had so many things going on that we didn't even know about," said Gossom, who made a promise with James Owens decades ago that they would keep Harris's memory alive for as long as they lived. Owens is gone now, but Harris lives on with Gossom and in the minds of those who saw him play, were encouraged by him, or laughed out loud at his stories.

Many thought about him when Auburn made its marvelous run

to the Final Four in 2019, playing ten players every game, all of them African Americans. Gossom was asked how he thought Harris would have reacted if he were still alive.

"He'd be proud of the basketball team. He'd also tell you how much better he was than the current players," Gossom said. Then, after thinking for a second, Gossom added, "And he would be right."

"If he [Harris] was playing today, they'd all want him. He'd be one of the top ten guards in America," said Larry Chapman, his freshman coach.

If Harris was indeed alive, his teammates believe he'd be a coach, a teacher, or a principal, probably in the Black Belt. His buddies know he would be proud of the progress he started at Auburn and elsewhere. But with a choice he made on a long night that must have seemed like it would never end, Harris denied himself the opportunity to see his life tape play out, to grow old and gray, to receive the thanks of young and old. At the point of his greatest despair, he removed himself from not only a possible solution but also the payback from the investment he had made and had caused him such pain.

Harris was not unlike Larry Doby, who followed Jackie Robinson into the major leagues by eleven weeks but does not get an ounce of the credit Robinson rightly receives, even though Doby received much less preparation and guidance.

Yet, in integrating the American League, Cleveland's Doby had to play in St. Louis and Philadelphia, just like Robinson, as well as in Washington and Detroit. His face wore the age lines to prove it.

The real mark against Harris's legacy, though, is how he died. Suicide lands its victims in the penalty box of history and, with Harris, has circumscribed the memory of an otherwise resilient, courageous American. Although we now understand more about the plague of suicide and disease of depression, we seem stuck using the same lens Harris was judged under a half-century ago. He did not knock down a door and flee. He stayed. And stayed. And stayed, completing his mission. But the focus remains more on one miserable night in Milwaukee—when darkness overtook him—than the thousand-plus he spent in Auburn. We cannot seem to hold in each hand that a hero with the perseverance to change history could also somehow kill himself.

Sport's universal appeal is the remarkable arena it crafts for drama, imitating life itself. Anything can happen. Favorites don't always win, and lives sometimes end in seeming defeat.

With the perspective of time, Harris's saga is due for reframing. Auburn can be deservedly proud that it was ahead of everyone in the Deep South in signing a black American. But that's also why things went so wrong—Harris became a teenage guinea pig in southern integration. "Don't eat here. Don't sit near me. Don't make waves." How could it have gone any way but badly? `Harris coped the best he knew how, but burying his pain in silence and self-medicating it with prolonged marijuana use eventually compounded his depression. Still, his travail could have conceivably happened at any Deep South university trying to escape the vise of segregation. He wasn't even the only southern pioneer to kill himself.

Yet, Auburn could not have had a better pioneer. "It took somebody that was not hung up on himself to be the first black athlete at Auburn University, because there was so much at stake," said Owens. Calling Harris a "stepping stone for all that goes on in the Auburn athletic department today," Chapman said, "For Auburn University to be integrated with Henry Harris was God's work. God sent him to that program. Who's to say it wasn't supposed to happen that way."

Auburn is not same provincial college Harris enrolled in, but he remains the child living under Auburn's steps into the New South. Auburn now operates a big tent, as they say. It has sent six astronauts into space and another alumnus runs the richest company in the world—Apple CEO Tim Cook. Surely, somewhere under the tent is room for Harris's memory, because Auburn owes him decades of gratitude. He came when others wouldn't.

Bud Stallworth's retired number hangs in the University of Kansas's historic Allen Fieldhouse because, one, he was a great player and, two, he chose not to risk his career, social life, and possibly his safety by going to Alabama or Auburn. Both were marvelous black athletes and valedictorians discovered in their home state's primitive "training schools." Stallworth was able to score a lot of points in college; Harris got to redirect the future.

That's why Thomas Gilmore—the black Greene County sheriff

who saw a Hollywood film made of his improbable life story—suggested after the Auburn Arena opened in 2010 that it be named after his longtime hero, maybe something like Harris Hall.

Hanging from the rafters of the Auburn Arena in 2019 were the retired numbers of nine former Auburn men's and women's basketball players. Seven of them were black Americans who got to play for Auburn only after Harris cleared the debris from the entranceway.

If the past asks anything of the present, it's "don't forget me." But a half-century after he took the high road to Auburn and set the SEC on a higher road, Harris is as forgotten and invisible as he was growing up dirt poor in the Black Belt. Even when he died, Harris was buried in an unmarked grave, like many of the estimated six million enslaved Americans who lived and died before the Civil War—and like Georgia-born Josh Gibson, the Negro Leagues slugger who hit some eight hundred home runs but was born too early and died eighty-four days before Robinson's first major league game. Gibson's grave received a small plaque three decades later. Harris's is still unmarked, somewhere on a rocky hillside of an unkempt black cemetery on the backside of Bessemer.

In some ways, Harris was no different than all the other Americans who were born at the twentieth century's midpoint of 1950 and went off to college amid the turbulence of 1968. They all came and, eventually, they all went, usually silently, leaving a space for someone else. The only difference was that Harris transformed his space into a gate, and the sound of footsteps marching through it still echo through time.

Higher Dreams

What happens to the dreams of warriors who fall early on the battlefield?
Uncommon courage conveyed them to the front wielding standards
Soaring skyward, stretching to touch the hems of justice, truth.
But first flags swiftly falter, cut down by determined defiance.
First fighters often stumble, sacrificed to leaden aspirations,
Accumulated hope laden on the soft shoulders of youth.

Some hopes soar beyond the reach of dreams.
Some dreams soar beyond the reach of hope.

What happens to the brave promises of young soldiers who faint,
Weary from forcing mere fissures in deep-rooted fortifications?
They do not know arising armies will later flow through tiny breaches,
Flying proud pennants high, hailing heroes to wide acclaim,
Mounting up like eagle wings, bearing them home on shoulders strong,
Forgetting a few lost battles, left behind in a flicker of victory's flame.

Some victories soar below the reach of fame.
Some fame soars below the reach of victory.

What happens to the hopes of defeated warriors denied redemption?
Their higher dreams unsettle our sleep like ghosts refusing to rest in peace.
They cried out to us back then; they call out to us still.
We must summon the armies of a new generation
To find their battered banners and hold them high.
To the battlefields, we must return to gather the bones.
On shoulders sage and sound, we shall carry them home,
Carry them home.

                                                    - Dub Taft

Henry Harris at Auburn with his mom, Willie Pearl Harris, and Coach Bill Lynn.

Epilogue

Wes Bizilia's voice was weak. He could barely speak. He was in the hospital recovering from surgery. Cancer had forced doctors to remove part of a lung the day before. He was seventy-one, retired, and living in Fairhope, Alabama. The evening before, his wife, Patsy, received a call at home from an author researching a book on Henry Harris and seeking an interview with Bizilia. She explained he was hospitalized, and the writer said he would call back in a couple of weeks. But Patsy called back the next day from the hospital. "Hold on," she said, "Wes really wants to talk to you."

Bizilia's voice was soft and crackling. "I think it's a fantastic enterprise, what you're doing," he whispered. Then he pushed on through the emotion that was overwhelming him. "I think it needs to be done. I really do."

Henry Harris's story could make grown men cry.

* * *

It was the Martin Luther King Holiday and Larry Chapman was back in Auburn. He was hesitant to tell an interviewer why Harris did not become a volunteer coach for him in 1973.

"Something happened, and he didn't come," he said evasively.

What happened?

A long pause. "I'd rather not say."

After more questioning, Chapman said, "I hesitate to tell you because I don't want to make Coach Lynn look bad." Finally, he explained that Harris told him Lynn had threatened to take away his scholarship if he worked with Chapman.

Then he said, "But I've gotten through all that now."

How?

"Just prayed and asked the Lord to put all that behind me. I mean, I wasn't the reason all those things happened. I didn't feel like that was something I contributed to. I loved Henry, and Rudy too. We made an extension out towards Henry that reached to help him. I didn't know his emotions at all." Chapman said he and Lynn patched their differences, that he wrote Lynn a long letter thanking him for his support over the years and that Lynn kept it in his office, showing it to visitors.

Chapman was a college head coach for forty years, thirty-seven at Auburn-Montgomery. He won 705 games, one of them against Auburn at Memorial Coliseum, and ranked among the top forty all-time winningest college coaches and fifth among NAIA coaches when he retired in 2014.

Chapman estimated ninety percent of his college players were black Americans. "And Henry Harris was the first," he said proudly, still recalling the excitement of recruiting Harris. "We were ahead of everybody in the Deep South. It was exciting to me to coach Henry. It was exciting going up to York that night to see him play [in high school]." Harris changed Chapman, just like he changed teammates. "I came out of an environment of prejudiced white in Ludowici, Georgia," said Chapman. "Believe me, I had to get through all that."

* * *

Rudy Davalos asked the interviewer if the Harris family was angry at him. He admitted he battled guilt in the years after Harris's death. "I have thought at times that maybe if I had stayed, that [Harris's death] would not have happened. I can go down the guilt road like anyone else," he said. "But I have not taken blame for his death. I was trying to help him. I felt this [UWM position] was one way of trying to fulfill the obligation I made to him when I recruited him. I feel good that I tried to help him get his education."

After abruptly leaving Wisconsin-Milwaukee, Davalos stayed with the San Antonio Spurs for three seasons as assistant coach and director of player personnel. In 1976, he became athletic director at the University of Texas at San Antonio and then moved to the University of Houston as AD in 1987. Six years later, he became athletic director at the University of New Mexico, serving in that capacity for thirteen years before retiring in 2005. He was a member of the prestigious selection committee for the NCAA Division I men's basketball tournament in the 1990s and New Mexico's basketball practice facility is the Rudy Davalos Basketball Center.

"Henry had lots of guts to do what he did, to come to Auburn, at that time, the 1960s," Davalos said. "I don't think he had a bad experience there. He was a great, great kid, had a great smile. I loved the kid. He was a precious young man."

* * *

Grief over Harris's death chased Auburn coach Bill Lynn deeper into alcoholism. "Daddy was just sick when Henry died. He was really upset," said Bill Lynn Jr. "I can remember my mother saying, 'Just come on out of there and leave your daddy alone. He's really upset about Henry Harris.' He just couldn't believe it, and he was just adamant somebody pushed him. When someone would bring it up, he'd say, 'Someone did something to Henry.' Daddy always thought Henry wouldn't do drugs. He was really sick." Lynn's alcoholism worsened significantly in the mid-seventies. "It was after his coaching days were over that he got bad," his son said.

Lynn retired as administrative assistant to Auburn athletic director in 1980 and turned his part-time contractor's business into a fulltime job. When interviewed that year about Harris's death, he said, "I tell you, that hurt me a lot. He was such a good kid. If he changed, I don't know what happened. He was such a good kid. He wanted to play in the NBA bad, and he could have played had he not gotten hurt." Lynn said he did not believe Harris could have killed himself. "Henry liked to live. He was a strong person. His overall mental toughness is what made him." Three years later, Lynn told the *Los Angeles Times*, "Henry was a good boy. He was team captain his senior year. I don't know how tough school was for him. I suppose it was tough, but he never said anything [to me]."

Lynn quit drinking in 1985—this time for good. "He just finally figured it out," his son said. "A man at church worked with him." He stopped smoking six months later, but it was too late to stop a massive heart attack that killed two-thirds of his heart less than a year later. "He lived the last eight years with a third of a heart. He didn't smoke or drink those eight years. He had eight good years with his grandkids. A lot of good things happened the last eight years of his life." Bizilia got to see the change—"Bill had dried out and was the nicest person."

"He was a good man, a very good man," said Bill Jr. "Alcoholism is not what I think about when I think about him." "Bill Lynn was a good guy," agreed longtime Auburn black businessman Ralph Foster, owner of Duke's Barber Shop. "He defied all odds by bringing Henry in. But like a lot of things during that era, it just didn't work out."

* * *

"Henry Harris? Oh, my."

The name out of his past shocked Bill Klucas. He sighed heavily over the phone and was briefly speechless, his mind racing backward. "It's such a tragedy. I don't have any words for you. It's such a tragedy," he said.

The former UWM head coach termed Harris's suicide "one of the mysteries of my life." "Who can ever anticipate something like this," he said. "You have to examine yourself. You have to look at yourself and say, 'Could I have done something about this? Could I have seen this?'" But Klucas wanted to talk more about not understanding why Davalos and the Spurs did not draft Harris than he did about how Harris fell through the cracks of the UWM athletic department *after* Davalos left. He said he couldn't recall the details of Harris losing his assistantship.

Klucas was fired a year later, after his second UWM team went 8-18. "In retrospect, I probably wouldn't have done it again facing the same circumstances," he said of going to UWM. Klucas spent the rest of his career scouting for NBA teams and coaching minor league basketball in the Continental Basketball Association for fifteen seasons. He also became a political consultant and campaign manager in Minnesota, working on state and national races. He died of cancer in 2014 at seventy-two.

* * *

Tom Rosandich achieved his dream—in Alabama. He resigned as UWM athletic director two years after Harris died, moved his United States Sports Academy to Mobile, and directed it for the next forty years, collecting honors all along the way.

In a 2015 interview, the eighty-four-year-old Rosandich said he had no recall of Harris. "I'm sorry I can't help you, I would if I could," he said. "I just don't remember." Then, after reading a 1974 article describing the circumstances around his death, Rosandich said he did recall Davalos introducing him to Harris upon his arrival but no other details. "He was a very polite, well-mannered young man. That's the only time I ever talked with him. And obviously the rest of it is tragedy. It all came back when I looked at the article," he said. When asked about meeting with Harris the day before he died and urging him to finish his degree, Rosandich said, "My whole career has been education, and I could have well said that, but to be very, very honest, I don't remember." Then later, he added, "The only thing I can say is that I try to find a way to get people through programs, and of course, that's the history here at the academy."

Rosandich described the sports academy as "very successful." "Thousands and thousands of people have graduated from the academy," he said. "It's the largest doctoral program in the world."

One of the finalists Rosandich passed over in 1973 when he selected Davalos and then Klucas as UWM coach was twenty-eight-year-old Larry Riley, who was UWM's assistant coach the previous three seasons. Riley became general manager of the Golden State Warriors in 2009, then refused to trade the seventh pick in that year's draft, and then selected Steph Curry, who would become the centerpiece of one of the NBA's great dynasties.

* * *

Wendell Hudson became an assistant coach at Ole Miss a decade after the vicious verbal attacks he received as a freshman there. Perhaps because he had grown up on Birmingham's Dynamite Hill, Hudson came to Alabama expecting the worst. "It was a difficult experience at times, but a positive one. I'm a better person for having done it," he said. "If I had to do it over again, I would without a doubt." In Tuscaloosa, Hudson found a lifelong mentor in C. M. Newton, who brought him back as a student assistant coach when a knee injury abruptly ended his pro career. "I gave Wendell a job because I wanted him around. He was a good person," said Newton, who launched Hudson on a thirty-four-year college coaching career. Hudson returned to Alabama in 2003 as associate athletic director.

Similarly, John Mitchell, the junior college transfer who became the first black Alabama football player to enter a game in 1971, was brought back by Bear Bryant in 1973 as a student coach. He would coach the next forty-five years, becoming the SEC's first black defensive coordinator at LSU in 1990 and concluding a seventeen-year NFL coaching career as the assistant head coach of the Pittsburgh Steelers.

Wilbur Jackson, Alabama's first black scholarship football player in 1970, played nine years in the NFL, winning a Super Bowl ring and eventually going home to Ozark, Alabama.

Bryant promised attorney U. W. Clemon and Alabama's black students he would have at least five blacks in his 1971 recruiting class. One of them was Sylvester Croom, who became the SEC's first black head football coach at Mississippi State in 2004. Clemon, meanwhile, became Alabama's first black federal judge in 1980.

In 1974, Bryant signed Ozzie Newsome, whom he would call Alabama's greatest end ever, better than even his own teammate, the great Don Hutson. Newsome would catch more passes than any NFL tight end ever, be chosen NFL Man of the Year for community service, and become the NFL's first black general manager. He would run the Baltimore Ravens for sixteen seasons, winning the Super Bowl in 2013.

In 1979, the nephew of Vivian Malone—one of the two black students escorted past Governor Wallace at Alabama's Foster Auditorium in 1963—signed a scholarship to play basketball for Mississippi State, the school that refused to play Harris just a decade earlier. Jeff Malone would be a three-year All-SEC selection and score 19.0 points per game over thirteen years in the NBA.

* * *

Steve Martin, the Tulane baseball player who became the SEC's first black varsity athlete in any sport in 1966, earned a degree in Latin from Tulane in 1968 and after serving in the Army, received an MBA from Tulane. He retired as chief financial officer of Tuskegee University in 2012 and died a year later of cancer. He is buried in Georgia National Cemetery.

Godfrey Dillard, the Detroit guard who entered Vanderbilt with Perry Wallace only to be cut from the team two years later because of his student activism, graduated from the University of Michigan Law School, built a successful career as a civil rights lawyer, arguing before the U.S. Supreme Court, and was named a "Champion of Justice" by the State Bar. He served as U.S. ambassador to the Democratic Republic of the Congo and won the Democratic nomination for attorney general of Michigan in 2016.

In 1968, when Kentucky's Wilbur Hackett and Houston Hogg and Tennessee's Lester McClain became the first blacks to play an entire football season in the SEC, it would have been unimaginable to think then that an African American might one day be enforcing the rules on an SEC field of play. But Hackett, a chainsaw of a linebacker, refereed SEC football games for fifteen seasons. After Greg Page was killed, Hackett was one of three black Kentucky freshmen who Nate Northington told, before leaving, to stick it out or integration would fail.

Jackie Walker, Tennessee's black All-American linebacker whom no one could block, Alabama triple-teamed, and Gene Lorendo ranted about in a film session, was released by the San Francisco 49ers in training camp because, he said, they learned he was gay. Walker moved to Atlanta, worked in the city recreation department, and died of AIDS in 2002, still tied for the NCAA career record for most interception touchdowns—and he had two more called back in a single game because of penalties.

Frank Dowsing—who integrated Mississippi State athletics with Robert Bell in 1969 and became an All-SEC cornerback and Mr. Mississippi State—attended medical school for three years before going into management with Bell Telephone. He too died of AIDS, in 1994. Fifteen years later, an ex-teammate finally got him inducted into the Mississippi Sports Hall of Fame.

LSU's first black basketball player, Collis Temple Jr., whose father was barred from attending LSU graduate school, earned a graduate degree from LSU. His sons, Garrett and Collis III, realizing the sacrifice of their father and grandfather, chose to play basketball for LSU.

Willie Jackson—who integrated Florida varsity football with Leonard George but said he "could have given it up any time" after the excitement wore off—also saw his two sons, Willie Jr. and Terry, follow him to his alma mater before going on to NFL careers.

Miami's first black athlete, Ray Bellamy, who received death threats when he played at Auburn, was elected president of the Miami student body after his football career ended in a near-fatal car crash. He credited his mentor, university president Henry King Stanford, with teaching him how to handle his situation at Miami, saying Stanford "stood up for me when it wasn't popular to stand up for African American men." The son of Florida migrant farmers who grew up in a tent, Bellamy earned two degrees from Miami and later a master's and became an academic advisor at Florida A&M.

Robert Grant, one of the two Wake Forest football players who became the first blacks to play at Auburn in 1966, made it to two Super Bowls but called integration his greatest achievement. "What we did was absolutely worth it. Forget the Super Bowls, forget the NFL. That was the best thing I ever did," he said. When Grant was inducted into the Wake Forest sports hall of fame, he was introduced by William H. Smith, his freshman teammate who was suspended from the team because he was seen hugging a white woman from his nearby Baha'i congregation before a game at Clemson. Smith dropped out of school that year, became a civil rights organizer and then a decorated medic in Vietnam, and later earned a doctorate from the University of Massachusetts. In 2000, he produced the acclaimed documentary *Invisible Soldiers: Unheard Voices*, which spurred Congress to establish the Day of Honor to acknowledge the contribution of U.S. minorities in World War II.

Casey Manning, South Carolina's first black basketball player and a graduate of its law school, became a Circuit Court judge in Columbia and the radio color analyst for South Carolina games.

* * *

Joseph "Pete" Peterson, Auburn's first black walk-on football player as a freshman in 1967, became the first African American to complete four years of Air Force ROTC at Auburn. He was so accomplished as a pilot that he was chosen as for the Thunderbirds, the Air Force's air demonstration squadron. He died in the 1982 Diamond Crash in the Nevada desert.

George Smith, the Black Student Union president who climbed a flagpole to take down the Confederate flag flying over Cliff Hare Stadium in 1974, became a member of Auburn's National Alumni Board.

Don Cole, one of the eight black student protestors expelled from Ole Miss in 1971, became the university's assistant provost.

Arthur Dunning, one the Alabama Five who integrated Alabama football as walk-ons in 1967, earned a Ph.D from Alabama and eventually became its vice chancellor for international programs and outreach. He retired in 2018 as president of Albany State University.

Maxie Foster, the African American given a conditional track scholarship in Georgia's initial, tentative step toward athletic integration in 1968, became a college professor. And Harold Black, the early

UGA black student whose room was set afire and who saw the university pool drained after he got out, became the Smith Professor of Finance at Tennessee.

* * *

Thomas Gilmore, who ended the reign of Big Bill Lee, was Greene County sheriff for a dozen years before turning to fulltime preaching. He was so influenced by the principle of nonviolence that he became known as "the sheriff without a gun" and inspired the movie *He Who Walks Alone*, in which Louis Gossett Jr. played a civil rights worker returning from California and running for sheriff against a segregationist incumbent, just as Gilmore did. "You get in the white world and it's a lot. It's more than a lot," said Gilmore, who died in 2015. "I don't think Henry knew the enormity of it. There's no way he could have. For a pioneer, it can become so much of your life. It can take over and push you in so many directions."

Gilmore's mentor, William McKinley Branch, the teacher-turned-activist who went to the U.S. Supreme Court to win an election taken from him, became the first black elected probate judge in America, served for eighteen years, preached for sixty, and met every president from John Kennedy to Bill Clinton.

The secretary of Harris's high school class, Earlean Williams Isaac—one of fifteen children of a sharecropper family—served as Greene County's probate judge for twenty-seven years, working in the Judge William McKinley Branch Courthouse. Her husband, Johnny Isaac, was sheriff of Greene County, and his brother Sam, one of Harris's teammates, was a deputy for thirty-five years. Their brother Charlie Isaac had been shot and killed in 1969 by a white man who was never arrested.

Dianne Kirksey, Harris's girlfriend from Greene County who told coaches she would never encourage a black to come to Alabama, was chosen one of the university's forty most influential pioneers during its fortieth anniversary commemoration of integration. She became an actress and director in New York.

Debra Threatt, Harris's onetime girlfriend, divorced the man she married despite Harris's protests. She earned a master's and Ph.D and worked for the CDC in Atlanta for a quarter-century. Although saying Harris "kept a lot of things in, you could tell he was troubled at times," she still did not believe in 2014 that he had killed himself. "He would do nothing to hurt his mom. He loved her," she said.

* * *

In 2007, police in Minneapolis had to identify the body of another onetime promising African American high school basketball star from the Deep South. The body was discovered early one morning in an alley, badly beaten, and comatose. Howard Porter would not be identified for more than twenty-four hours. He would die a week later.

George Raveling, who worked so hard to recruit Harris, recruited Porter from Sarasota to Villanova, where he was a three-time All-American and MVP of the 1971 Final Four. Villanova had to forfeit its national runner-up trophy, however, because Porter, the son of a domestic, signed with a professional agent during the season. He was the NBA's top draft pick but never achieved the success expected of him. He played seven seasons and then retreated to Florida, struggling with the shame of disappointing his college teammates and struggling in the NBA. "If you feel bad about yourself, you find a way to medicate yourself," he said. "My medication was cocaine."

But Porter got clean at Minnesota's Hazelden Clinic, stayed in recovery, got married, and became a probation officer, counseling troubled men with truth and inspiration. His funeral in St. Paul drew 2,000 people. The line into the church ran nonstop for three hours.

The year after recruiting Harris, Raveling moved on to Maryland, becoming the first black assistant coach in the Atlantic Coast Conference or any of the three major southern conferences. In 1972, he went to Washington State as the first black head basketball coach in one of America's six major conferences. He later coached Iowa and Southern Cal, became Nike's director of international basketball, and is now in the Naismith Memorial Basketball Hall of Fame.

C. M. Newton, the other coach who couldn't land Harris, is also in the Basketball Hall of Fame. When he left Alabama in 1980 for Vanderbilt, Newton had beaten Auburn eighteen straight times. He eventually became athletic director at Kentucky and in 1997 hired the school's first black men's basketball coach, Tubby Smith, who won the national championship ten months later.

Newton and Raveling, as well as Joby Wright, were assistants to Bobby Knight in the 1984 Olympics. Newton would take a major role in USA Basketball, putting together America's first Olympic Dream Team and, as a member of the NCAA rules committee, bringing the three-point shot to college basketball, having watched its effect internationally. Newton went into the Hall of Fame as a "contributor." He invited Hudson to his induction, listing him on the guest list as "family." "Had he [Hudson] failed, I don't think there would have been a Wilbur Jackson or a John Mitchell," Newton said. ". . . It was not a courageous effort for us to offer Wendell Hudson a scholarship. It was a tremendous act for him to accept it."

Spencer Haywood made it to the Hall of Fame as well, all the way from Mississippi Delta poverty. Albert Davis, the running back who also did not have test scores to enter Tennessee in 1967 due to the SEC's "750 rule," received a master's from Tennessee and became a high school administrator.

Brooklyn basketball star Bernard King signed with Tennessee the spring Harris died and then survived the racism of SEC fans and Knoxville cops, as well as alcoholism, to become the SEC's first superstar in basketball or football. He would enter the Hall of Fame as one of the NBA's most prolific and hard-working scorers ever.

Charles Barkley is of course in the Hall of Fame, his path through Auburn cleared by Harris. And Frank Thomas, the Auburn slugger, is already in Cooperstown. Bo Jackson might be there too, or in the Pro Football Hall of Fame, if he had devoted himself to one sport, or maybe in both if injury had not betrayed him in his prime. But Jackson kept his promise to his mother and finally graduated from Auburn in 1995, ten years after winning the Heisman Trophy. In 2009, he was selected to give the university commencement address, likening Auburn's warmth to a "bowl of chicken soup" and boiling its spirit into four words—"You are always family."

* * *

For the three black Americans who joined Harris in integrating the Alabama high school all-star game in 1968, college and life afterward worked out well.

Travis Grant won the Joe Lapchick Trophy in 1972 as college basketball's player of the year, averaging 39.5 points per game *without* a three-point line—with it, he would have averaged fifty The 6-foot-7 forward from Barbour County Training School chose historically black Kentucky State, which employed the same running game he played in high school, and became the centerpiece of its offense, free to shoot the ball, which he did frequently, making 63 percent of his shots. He led Kentucky State to three straight NAIA national championships, and his 4,045 career points are still the most in the history of college basketball—NAIA or NCAA. A first-round NBA choice, Grant bought a car with his signing bonus and then drove it "back home and took my mother uptown and paid off all her bills." Then he bought her a new home and remodeled it for her. "I guess I've been inducted into five halls of fame, but the thing that meant the most to me was being able to go back and make my mother's situation better," said Grant, who earned two advanced education degrees and worked for thirty years as a teacher, coach, and principal in Atlanta.

Bud Stallworth was the Big Eight Conference's player of the year at Kansas in 1972, averaging 25.3 points per game and scoring fifty in his final home game. A first-round draft pick, he played five years in the NBA and then worked for his alma mater for twenty-seven years, retiring as the financial manager of all design and construction.

Stallworth was an Academic All-American, as was Scottsboro's Sam McCamey, who needed tutoring from his English teacher three nights a week to become eligible to go to college. McCamey, the son of a sharecropper mother, became a bank analyst in California after starring at Oral Roberts University. Like Grant, he still played masters-level basketball nationally and internationally in his mid-sixties.

Joby Wright, the initial black player recruited by Auburn, captained Bobby Knight's first Indiana team in 1972, was All-Big Ten, and averaged twenty points per game. A second-round draft pick, he played five years professionally and then went back to Indiana, completed his degree, earned a master's in counseling, and coached for Knight for a decade, assisting him in the 1984 Olympics. He later served as head coach of Miami of Ohio and Wyoming.

* * *

John Mengelt played ten seasons in the NBA, mostly with the Detroit Pistons and Chicago Bulls. Upon retirement, he settled in Chicago and became a radio/TV color analyst for Bulls, Pistons, and DePaul games. He also started a successful executive search firm that has included Auburn among its clients.

Henry Ford thinks about Harris when he and his wife do mission work in the Black Belt. "We take a team of doctors and nurses down there and give free medical care. We feed them and give clothes away. We go to Greene County. We know how people are living—it's Third World. Some of the kids are just like Henry Harris." Because Harris told him in the fall of 1972 not to believe it if he ever heard he had committed suicide, Ford doesn't think he killed himself. "I got some good memories of Henry," he said. "I guess I'm going to keep my good memories. I don't want to think he committed suicide."

* * *

Sylvester Davenport—after being thrown out of Auburn in 1973 when marijuana was found in his room—became captain of the Tennessee-Chattanooga basketball team. But a few days before Christmas during the 1974-1975 season, Davenport was indicted by a Chattanooga grand jury and arrested on a felony charge of selling drugs. He would eventually play professionally in Belgium but has worked mostly as a carpenter since returning home to Tennessee. In 2016, Davenport still referred to Harris as "like a surrogate father." "I'm sixty-three years old," he said. "I don't know why Henry didn't hang around for that. I don't know why he jumped off that building."

While Harris was "trying to go to the pros," Davenport said, "I was just trying to make a difference in black people's lives. We got it started. All we were supposed to do was push the button and get it started. We done that forty-five years ago, and it's still working today."

Davenport wanted to follow Harris because "he was the first." "I knew if I could follow him, maybe good things could happen to me too," he said. "But good things didn't follow for him and good things didn't follow for me either. But that's what we had to go through back then. It's not what the result was [then], it's what the result is now. Fifteen years later, we got Charles Barkley down there—he's on TV every night. Somebody had to build the foundation. That's what I've been doing for the past forty years, building buildings, and you can't build a building without a foundation."

March 13, 1968: Henry Harris on the day he signed with Auburn.

Acknowledgements

I was fortunate to see Henry Harris play basketball for the first time when I was eighteen years old—Henry had turned nineteen six days earlier. I grew interested in his story that evening, particularly after I read he had graduated from Greene County Training School. I had never heard of a "training school." I began to grow fascinated with his story a decade later when I visited the converted store where Henry and his family lived in Boligee, Alabama.

That was in 1980. Since then, I have shared my idea of writing a book on Henry Harris with dozens of people. The number of them who have given me encouragement may be in three figures by now, and the value of their encouragement has been immeasurable. As I look back over the winding path to publication, I see those encouragers all along the way.

The one person who has been by my side all that time is Pat Heys, my wife and partner in life, and she has been a constant in her support of Henry's story, my writing, and my research, much of it gathered on our trips across the South. She remains the best proofreader I have ever known.

During the past dozen years, more than a hundred people have stopped their lives long enough to allow me to interview them. Their help and generosity of time have been essential in telling Henry's story. Whether they were his Auburn teammates or his friends, teachers, or coaches in Boligee, all were concerned by the lack of recognition Henry has received and wanted to help preserve his memory.

The most important interviews, however, were with Henry's brothers, Robert Raymond and James Harris, and his sister, Glenda Harris Dunn. They were extremely open, gracious, and helpful from the start, and I came to know Henry through them.

I am particularly indebted to Susan Boyan and Dub Taft, who have supported me in this project for a long time. Early on, both believed in the importance of telling Henry's story, and they have propelled me forward not only with encouragement but also with wonderful ideas, many of which are now part of the manuscript. I will always appreciate Dub writing his wonderful poem *Higher Dreams* and sharing it with us all (see page 305).

Special thanks also goes out to Jim Barber and Steve Yount. Jim came to my aid this year after the publication of his novel *Plowed Fields* and has been invaluable and diligent as an advisor on the publishing process and a copy editor. As a good friend, Steve has listened to me discuss Henry Harris for years, always offering a good idea and a helpful word, and was one of the book's first editors. Roscoe Nance, another former newspaper coworker, was an early reader too and provided valuable insight.

Gary Davis and Mark Lunceford moved my writing forward simply by asking about the book's progress. Both also proved to be very valuable proofreaders when book needed some fresh eyes on it.

I am also very appreciative of Christine Horner, who came in at the end of the process to create a wonderful cover design that captures Henry's hope and optimism in the face of a changing America.

I want to thank Amoi Geter and Elena Mappus for their long belief in Henry's story; Jenni Nichols for her endurance in transcribing interviews; and researcher Lori Miller for chasing down the World War II service record of Henry Harris Sr. at the National Archives and Records Administration in St. Louis.

I am thankful Spencer McCallie III opened my eyes to a world much wider than his eleventh-grade English class and to a southern landscape at war with change. And I remember the late Warren Newman, a journalist and coworker who decades ago helped ignite my curiosity about the young men who integrated the SEC.

I would have been unable to recapture the details and mood of southern campuses in the midst of the final stages of the civil rights movement without the assistance of countless reference librarians. I never ceased to be amazed at their helpfulness, resourcefulness, and patience. They were always willing to look "one more place" for what I was seeking. I am particularly grateful to John Varner, Joyce Hicks, and rest of the extremely helpful staff of Special Collections and Archives at Auburn's Draughon Library. Auburn is fortunate to have such a great repository of its rich history.

I also appreciate of the research assistance I received at the Golda Meir Library at the University of Wisconsin at Milwaukee, the William T. Young Library at the University of Kentucky, the J. D. Williams Library at the University of Mississippi, and the Paul W. Bryant Museum at the University of Alabama.

I could not have successfully researched the Army service of Henry's father and uncle, Thomas Edmonds, without the generous aid of Rich Baker at the U.S. Army Heritage and Education Center in Carlisle, Pennsylvania, and Luther Hanson at the U.S. Quartermaster Museum at Ft. Lee, Virginia.

Thom Gossom and the late James Owens committed long ago to keep their good friend's memory alive for as long as they were alive. Their support, time, and encouragement has been essential in completing this project.

I also will always owe a debt of gratitude to the late Perry Wallace, who got SEC integration started. I first interviewed Perry in 1980, and he was so open and generous that I began to understand the significance of what the "firsts" had achieved for the South. He was the person who helped me see the importance of Henry's story. "I played against Henry Harris," he told me, and he wondered what had happened to Henry. I had no answers but would soon set out to look for some.

I regret that both Perry and James Owens won't get to read this book, but their inspiration runs through it.

With his injured knee heavily taped as a senior, Henry Harris drives inside against 6-foot-7, 245-pound senior center, Al "Apple" Sanders (31). In his "workhorse" role, the 6-foot-3 Harris defended Sanders whenever Auburn and LSU played.

Endnotes

Abbreviations: **AADA**-Auburn Athletic Department Archives, located in Special Collections and Archives, Draughon Library, Auburn University. **OADN**-*Opelika-Auburn Daily News*, **Plainsman**-*Auburn Plainsman*, **SI**-*Sports Illustrated*, **NYT**-*New York Times*, **AJC**-*Atlanta Journal-Constitution*, **AP**-*Associated Press*,

Chapter 1

1 police investigation: Richard A. Sroka, "Offense Report," UWM Police Department, April 18, 1974 (in possession of author); Richard Sroka, interview, December 5, 2016; Robert Kowalski, interview, September 30, 2009; Martin Studenec, interview, September 30, 2009

1 "outside my window": UWM Police Department, handwritten notes, April 18, 1974

1 weather conditions: weatherunderground.com

2 medical examiner investigation: Warren Hill and Paul Danko, Milwaukee County Medical Examiner's Report, April 18, 1974; Warren Hill, interview, September 22, 2009

2 Harvey friend of Klucas: Richard Sroka, interview, December 5, 2016

Chapter 2

6 Bizilia's recruiting trip: Wes Bizilia, interview, May 30, 2008

7 "rural, dark…": Jason Sokol, *There Goes My Everything*, 264

8 Boligee racial ratio: Ida Colgrove, interview, July 9, 2009

8 sixth poorest in U.S.: Sokol, *"There Goes My Everything,"* 259

8 reasons for poverty: *Ibid.*; Robert Brown, interview, June 28, 2008

8 a sticky clay, black dots on map: Charles W. Eagles, *Outside Agitator*, 91

8 Chapman's recruiting trip: Larry Chapman, interview, January 21, 2008

Chapter 3

11 Harris's Army service, hospitalization: "Application for Headstone or Marker," for Henry Harris Sr., Department of Veteran Affairs, October 30, 1950

11 one million blacks: *The African Americans: Many Rivers to Cross with Henry Louis Games*, PBS, 2013

11 truck driver: Thennie Mae Branch, interview, May 13, 2008

12 hopes of black soldiers: Part 1, *Eyes on the Prize*, PBS, 1987

12 "Those of us…": Michele Norris, *The Grace of Silence*, 84

13 "table of victory": Part 1, *Jackie Robinson*, documentary, PBS, 2016

13 seventy-five percent: Richard Gergel, *Unexampled Courage*, 3

12 "attacks, spells": Willie Saxton, interviews, circa July 1984; Johnny Snoddy, interview, circa July 1984

12 ambulance trip: "Certificate of Delivery of Patients," Tuskegee VA Hospital

12 Branche background: "Deaths," Journal of the National Medical Association, March 1958, p139; Dan T. Carter, *Scottsboro*, 45

12 hospitalization, death: "Certificate of Death," Henry Harris Sr., Alabama Center for Health Statistics, October 16, 1950

13 Edmonds' background, Army service: "Service Record," Thomas J. Edmonds, National Archives and Records Administration, St. Louis, Missouri; "Application for Headstone or Marker" for Thomas Edmonds, Department of Veteran Affairs, December 10, 1951

13 four killed: Laura Wexler, *Fire in a Canebreak*

13 Woodard's blinding: Christine Myers, "Civil Rights Historians...," AP, May 28, 2018
13 Snipes death: Dan Barry, "Killing and Segregated...," *NYT*, March 18, 2007
14 Edmonds family: Ernest Edmonds, interview, July 28, 2007
14 early part of day: Tommie Mae Edmonds, interview, July 28, 2008
15 "They hired old men...": A. L. Lavender, interview, September 22, 2009
15 "He'd just sit there ...": Eunice Outland, interview, May 25, 2008
15 attempted arrest of Edmonds: Harry Collins, interview, circa Summer 2009
15 "They got to fighting...": Ernest Edmonds interview, July 28, 2007
15 "Edmonds took...": James Cox, interview, July 11, 2009
15 "Why y'all kill...": Tommie Mae Edmonds interview, July 26, 2008
16 shooter was a logger: Lavender interview, September 22, 2009
16 "They knew...": Lulu Cooks, interview, September 30, 2009
16 cause of death: "Certificate of Death," Thomas J. Edmonds, Alabama Center for Health Statistics, July 21, 1951
16 details of wreck, arrest: Cox interview, July 11, 2009
16 "The water was up...": Colgrove, interview, July 9, 2009
17 fear of jail: Part 3, *Eyes on the Prize*, PBS, 1987
17 visits to jail: Robert Raymond, interview, June 11, 2007
17 possibly hanged: William Branch, interview, May 13, 2008; Robert Brown, interview, May 18, 2008
17 cause of death: "Certificate of Death," Lieutenant Gooden, Alabama Center for Health Statistics, November 17, 1955

Chapter 4

18 road trip: Al Young, interviews, February 8, 2008 and October 6, 2012
18 "Which one is Henry?": Young interview, October 6, 2012
18 "He came over there...": James Patrick, interview, December 21, 2016
19 Raveling background: George Raveling, interview, January 8, 2001; Seth Davis, "Pioneering Coach...": *Sports Illustrated*, January 9, 2015
19 Porter's recruitment: Raveling interview, January 8, 2001; Dick Weiss, "Remembering Howard Porter," *New York Daily News*, May 28, 2007
19 King's speech: Douglas Brinkley, "Guardian of the Dream," *Time*, August 28, 2003; Tom Hoffarth, "MLK Dream...," *LA Daily News*, August 27, 2013
20 "Once the whistle...": Hoffarth, "MLK Dream Never Dies..."
20 Raveling's scholarship offer: Young interview, February 8, 2008
20 Tuskegee superintendent: Jean Howard, interview, circa 2001
20 Davalos background: Rudy Davalos, interview, November 16, 2007; Cleon Walfoort, "Davalos UWM Coach," *Milwaukee Journal*, April 19, 1973
21 decision to recruit blacks: Chapman interview, January 21, 2008
21 conversation with Philpott: Bizilia interview, May 30, 2008
22 letter to Bryant: Young interview, February 8, 2008,
22 "Here was a young man ...": Bob Andrews, interview, September 22, 2009
22 All-American boy: Henry Harris, "Auburn Sports Publicity Questionnaire," AADA; "School Activities, Honors...," Harris scrapbook, owned by Al Young
23 "You just enjoyed...": James Harris, interview, January 14, 2008
23 Bryant-Riley conversation: Andrews interview, September 22, 2009
23 "Alabama got into a frenzy...": Young interview, circa 1984
23 asking Kirksey for help: Andrews interview, September 22, 2009Dianne
23 Boyd Aman's visit: *Ibid.*

Chapter 5

24 confrontation with Aman: James Harris, interview, February 24, 2008

24	Aman leased fields, house: Colgrove interview, July 9, 2009
24	"Just stay out there…": Raymond interview, June 11, 2007
25	"I guess you'll have to move.": *Ibid.*
25	"Well, I can fix that.": *Ibid.*
25	background on Snoddys: *Ibid.*, Severe Strode, interview, February 11, 2008
25	"She didn't have no place…": Snoddy interview, circa July 1984
25	Willie Pearl background, income: Raymond interview, June 11, 2007
26	"We were extremely poor…": James Harris, interview, February 24, 2008
26	stopped smoking: *Ibid.*
26	Davalos in Australia: Walfoort, "Davalos…," *Milwaukee Journal*, April 19, 1973
26	warmth of Davalos: James Harris interview, February 24, 2008
26	"I resented …": James Harris, interview, January 14, 2008
26	boxes of steaks: James Harris interview, February 24, 2008
27	offer of new car: Raymond interview, June 11, 2007
27	"We're staying in this hellhole…": *Ibid.*
27	1956 legislative act: William Warren Rogers, Robert David Ward, Leah Rawls Atkins, Wayne Flynt, *Alabama: The History of a Deep South State*, 547
27	1963 state integration: *Ibid.*
27	integration in Greene: Susan Yougblood Ashmore, *Carry It On*, 95-96
27	threatened firing: Robert Brown, interview, June 28, 20008
27	"I carried a bunch of colored…": Marshall Frady, "Nightwatch in Greene…," *Newsweek*, May 16, 1966
28	swimming pool incident: Brown interview, June 28, 20008
28	"I would go in:…": Davalos interview, November 16, 2007
28	Voting Rights Act significance: Sokol, *There Goes My Everything*, 259
28	SNCC in Greene County: Ashmore, *Carry It On*, 134-35
28	SCLC in Greene: Frye Galliard, *Cradle of Freedom*, 319
28	historic homes: "History," pamphlet, Greene County Historical Society, undated
28	crosses burned: Brown interview, June 28, 2008
28	Wallace's injunction: UPI, "Suit Filed to Halt…," *NYT*, August 28, 1965
28	economic boycott: Brown interview, May 18, 2008
29	SNCC's registration push: Ashmore, *Carry It On*,143
29	voting examiners: John Herbers, "12 More Counties…," *NYT*, October 30, 1965
29	"it seemed like…": "Black Power in Greene County," *Time*, May 11. 1981
29	Tishobee tent city: Brown interview, June 28, 2008
29	black panther symbol: "Negro Voters Double," *NYT*, January 23, 1966
29	Black Panthers' origin: Part 1, *Black America Since MLK*, PBS, 2016
29	"When I talk…": Stokely Carmichael, *Face the Nation*, CBS, June 19, 1966
30	voting day: Ashmore, *Carry It On*, 181
30	Gilmore background: Galliard, *Cradle of Freedom*, 313-315
30	"cotton patch nigger…": *Ibid.*, 318
30	sheriff by birth: Sokol, *There Goes My Everything*, 260
30	prison commissioner: Wayne Greenhaw, *Fighting the Devil in Dixie*, 187,189
30	no gun or uniform: Martin Waldron, "Alabama Blacks Seek…," *NYT*, July 27, 1969
30	Lee's football career: Lee bio, Alabama Sports Hall of Fame program
30	"I don't think…": Frady, "Nightwatch in Greene County"
31	blacks outnumbered whites: Sokol, *There Goes My Everything*, 261
31	"It would be hard…": Frady, "Nightwatch in Greene County"

31	King's visit: "Dr. King Bids Alabama Negroes...," *NYT*, April 30, 1966
31	"We are not Bill Lee's...": Frady, "Nightwatch in Greene County
31	federal observers: Gene Roberts, "Alabama Negroes...," *NYT*, May 3, 1966
31	since Reconstruction: David J Garrow, *Bearing the Cross*, 471
31	ballots of illiterates: Roy Reid, "U.S. Observers...," *NYT*, May 7, 1966
31	rolls not purged: "Black Power in Greene County," *Time*, May 11. 1981
31	Gilmore ahead: Galliard, *Cradle of Freedom*, 320
31	absentee ballot box: Sokol, *There Goes My Everything*, 261
31	1867 KKK indictments: Frady, "Nightwatch in Greene County"
31	only one of 200 votes: Sokol, *There Goes My Everything*, 261

Chapter 6

32	Harris practicing as kid: Benny Marshall, "A Little Boy...," *Birmingham News*, March 15, 1968
32	bicycle rim: Jerry Brown, interview, circa 2001
32	"He always had ...": James Harris, interview, January 14, 2008
32	summers in gym: Gary Pettway, interview, circa 1984
32	high school statistics: "School Activities...," scrapbook, owned by Al Young
32	Harris's seriousness: Jerome Roberts, interview, May 13, 2008; Young interview, circa 1984
33	trustees meeting: Harry Philpott, oral history, July 20, 1990, Special Collections and Archives, Draughon Library, Auburn University, 244
33	black custodian Auburn: Dan Jacobs, interview, March 13, 2017
33	Harris at reception: Bill Perry, interview, circa Fall 1984
34	"Just get the youngsters: C. M. Newton, interview, circa Fall 2007
34	"Look, we need to ...": *Ibid.*
34	Newton's impression of Harris: *Ibid.*
34	Escelera as teammate: Andrew Maraniss, "How C. M. Newton Changed the Face of the SEC," www.theundefeated.com, May 26, 2016
34	signing day: Andrews interview, September 22, 2009; Bizilia interview, May 30, 2008
34	going out window: Bill Lynn Jr., interview, May 27, 2008
35	"I guess this wasn't really legal...": Bizilia interview, May 30, 2008
35	"Coach, there's no place...": *Ibid.*
35	"Wimp was running all over...": Young interview, February 8, 2008
35	Bizilia-Sanderson interchange: *Ibid.*
35	"Yes I did...": Bizilia interview, May 30, 2008
36	"first Deep South...": Jim Minter, "Auburn Signs...," *Atlanta Journal*, March 14, 1968
36	"He's just the kind of boy...": Benny Marshall, "A Little Boy..."
36	"confused youngster": Dennis Smitherman, "Recruit the Best...," *Mobile Press*, March 17, 1968
37	Dapper Dan: game program, newspaper articles, owned by Al Young
37	"I was able to sell them...": Raveling interview, January 8, 2001
37	Iowa's scholarship offer: Young interview, February 8, 2008
37	"Why would Henry...": Chapman interview, January 21, 2008
38	"I think Henry felt...": Davalos, interview, November 16. 2007
38	coaching in Australia: Walfoort, "Davalos UWM Coach"
38	"We aggressively recruited him...": Raveling interview, January 8, 2001
38	wouldn't leave state: Newton interview, circa Fall 2007
38	"close under hand": James Harris, interview, February 24, 2008
39	new clothes: Andrews interview, September 22, 2009

39	taking family to Meridian: Frank Morrow, interview, May 13, 2008
39	"The man was...": Outland interview, May 25, 2008
39	"We didn't have...": Glenda Harris Dunn, interview, April 8, 2009
39	"Knowing my mother...": James Harris, interview, January 14, 2008
39	"Maybe someone...": Raymond interview, June 11, 2007
40	advice from principal: James Harris, interview, January 14, 2008
40	Springbok comparison: *Invictus*, film, 2009
40	impact of Wallace's stand: Brown interview, June 28, 2008
40	Bryant on TV: Sam Heys, "It's a Whole New Ball Game," *Atlanta Weekly, Atlanta Journal-Constitution,* February 21, 1982, 25
40	*Look* magazine: *Three Days at Foster,* 2013

Chapter 7

41	"We were ignorant...": Rosie Carpenter, interview, February 28, 2008
41	MLK's week of travel: Garrow, *Bearing the Cross,* 605-6; Taylor Branch, *At Canaan's Edge,* 721
41	Eutaw speech text: www.thekingcenter.org/archive/document/mlk-address-mass-meting-eutaw-alabama
41	ride with Gilmore: Gaillard, *Cradle of Freedom,* 322-3
41	Johnnie Coleman case: Thomas Gilmore, interview, November 14, 2011; 42 Wayne Greenhaw, *Fighting the Devil in Dixie,* 187-90; Coleman v. State, 1964, Supreme Court of Alabama Decisions, Alabama Case Law, law.justia.com/cases/alabama/supreme-court/1964/164-so-2d-704-1.html
42	"Everyone was jubilant...": Gilmore interview, November 28, 2011
43	rioting in 110 cities: Clay Risen, *A Nation on Fire*
43	"Negro living conditions": "Rights Panel Finds...," *NYT,* May 5, 1968
43	costly labor system, cashless society: Rogers et al., *Alabama...,* 112, 237
43	most lasting scar: Bryan Stephenson, *PBS Newshour,* December 19, 2016
44	"It was just like slavery...": Carpenter interview, February 28, 2008
44	"It would've been more...": Leah Rawls Atkins, interview, April 28, 2008
44	"We didn't own anything...": Pettway interview, circa Fall 1984
44	role of black teachers: Pamela Grundy, "A Special Type of Discipline," *Sport and Color Line,* 105
44	Branch fired: "Black Power in Greene County," *Time,* May 11. 1981
44	"That was the worst thing...": Young interview, circa 1984
45	Brown in WWII, registering to vote: Brown interview, May 18, 2008
45	'She made sure...': Eunice Outland, interview, May 25, 2008
45	"We were raised...": James Harris, interview, February 24, 2008
45	"I am the Lord...": Exodus 6:6
45	"He has sent me...": Luke 4:18–19
46	biblical in undertones: Diane McWhorter, *Carry Me Home,* 17
46	preparing for integration: David Margolick, *Elizabeth and Hazel,* 85
46	student Freedom Riders: Part 2, *Eyes on the Prize,* PBS, 1987
46	"It was like a wave...": *Freedom Riders,* PBS, 2010
46	"We signed our...": *Hope & Fury,* NBC, March 24, 2018
46	their Egypt: *Freedom's Children,* 85
46	waving U.S. flags. *Hope & Fury...,* NBC, 2018
46	2,000 arrested: Part 3, *Eyes on the Prize,* PBS, 1987
46	Audrey Faye Hendricks: *Freedom's Children,* 78-79
47	"I appeal to all of you...": John Lewis, speech, March on Washington for Jobs and Freedom, Washington, D.C., August 27, 1963
47	Robert taken to jail: Raymond interview, June 11, 2007

47	"the year that rocked...": Mark Kurlansky, *1968: Year That Rocked the World*
47	"We choose to go to the moon...": John F. Kennedy, speech, Rice University, Houston, Texas, September 12, 1962
48	"It was jubilation...": Strode interview, February 11, 2008
48	"a great influence on Henry": Jerome Roberts interview, May 13, 2008
48	history as identity: Charles Reagan Wilson, panel remarks, Atlanta History Center, October 28, 2017
48	"No one ever had this opportunity...": Jacobs, *Across the Line*, 55
48	"You have to go...": Tom Graham and Rachel Graham Cody, *Getting Open*
48	"There are those...": McWhorter, *Carry Me Home*, 585
50	"It's so cold up there...": Robert Brown interview, June 28, 2008
50	Willie Pearl chose not to move: Vinnie Smoot, interview, July 9, 2009
50	"hope in the face of difficulty...": Barrack Obama, _____

Chapter 8

51	Owens background: William J. Baker, *Jesse Owens: An American Life*
51	Louis background: Sam Heys, "Louis Journey...," *Atlanta Constitution*, April 16, 1981; William Wiggins, "Joe Louis: America Folk Hero," *Sport and the Color Line*, 127
52	Robinson background: Jonathan Eig, *Opening Day: The Story of Jackie Robinson's First Season*; Jackie Robinson, *I Never Had It Made*
52	Train 58: "Cairo," *AJC*, June 2, 2007
52	"Earl Mann...": Nat Peeples, interview, circa August 1985
52	"It thought it was time...": Earl Mann, interview, circa August 1985
53	Robinson plays in Atlanta: Richard Hyatt, "Races Were Separate...," *Atlanta Constitution*, February 7, 1972
53	175 cities and towns: Bruce Adelson, *Brushing Back Jim Crow*, 5
53	1951 integration of two Class D leagues: *Ibid*.
53	Dave Hoskins, Texas League: *Ibid*.
53	Cotton States League: Adelson, *Bushing Back Jim Crow*, 108
53	Peeples saga: Peeples interview, circa August 1985
54	league pressure: Sam Heys, "South's Jackie...," *AJC*, September 1, 1985
54	Southern Association folds: *Ibid*.
54	Willie McCovey saga: *Ibid*.
54	Montgomery exhibitions: Jim Tocco and Jesse Goldberg-Strassler, "When Montgomery Met the Majors," *Montgomery Biscuits Magazine*, 2006
54	graduate students sent out of state: Samuel Freedman, *Breaking the Line*, 8-9;
55	Stanley Hill saga: David Wharton, "A Sporting Gesture...," *LA Times*, March 17, 2001
56	"old master's wife: Oriard, *Bowled Over*, 80
56	massive Confederate flag: Charles Martin, *Benching Jim Crow*, 282
56	passed out small flags: *Ibid*.
56	poor, lost war, practiced inequality: Charles Regan Wilson, panel remarks, Atlanta History Center, October 28, 2014
56	Clegg Starks: Patrick Garbin, "About Them Dawgs! Blawg"
57	J. M. Forgey: "'Dummy' Forgey, Veteran UT...," *Knoxville News-Sentinel*, July 26, 1941; "Dummy Forgey Dies...," *Knoxville News-Sentinel*, August 1, 1941
57	"Blind Jim" Ivey: Charles W. Eagles, *The Price of Defiance*, 44-49
57	"mean, angry, ...": "Celebrating Courage," *Georgia Magazine*, March 2011
58	"for their own protection": Rebecca McCarthy, "40 Years Ago ...," *AJC*, January 7, 2001
58	Barnett's halftime speech: *Breaking the Huddle*, documentary, HBO, 2008

58	"Segregation today…": McWhorter, *Carry Me Home*, 311
58	federalized troops: Douglas Martin, "Vivian Malone Jones, 63…," *NYT*, October 14, 2005
58	Kennedy's TV address: Rogers *et al.*, *Alabama: The History of a Deep South…*
59	harassment at Denny Stadium: Archie Wade, interview, September 23, 2011
59	program after program: Peter Wallenstein, *Higher Education and the Civil Rights Movement*
60	SEC's 750 rule: Charles H. Martin, *Benching Jim Crow*, 219
60	ACC's 750 and 800 rules: *Ibid.*, 123
60	not discussed at SEC meeting: Charles H. Martin, *Benching Jim Crow*, 219
60	got rid of blacks 1891: Part 1, *Jackie Robinson*, documentary
61	Mobile game moved: George Ross, "Integration Bowl," *Oakland Tribune*, August 21, 1963; AP, "Grid Game…," *Saratogan*, August 23, 1963
61	chicken wire: Ray Glier, "Birmingham Ballpark…," *NYT*, August 16, 2010
61	Peachtree Street parade: Sandy Tolan, *Me and Hank*
62	eleven Jackson State players: Roscoe Nance, "Black Schools Adjusting," *Jackson Clarion-Ledger*, May 12, 1980
62	final citadel: Sam Heys, "The Man Who Integrated the SEC," *Atlanta Constitution*, January 12, 1988
62	five students at Texas: Charles H. Martin, *Benching Jim Crow*, 205
62	Holmes and football: Charlayne Hunter-Gault, *To the Mountaintop*, 84
62	Darrell Brown saga: Rus Bradburd, *Forty Minutes of Hel*; Dan Wetzel, "Brown Recognized as Arkansas…," Yahoo! Sports, October 7, 2011

Chapter 9

64	Aaron's teammates: Hank Aaron and Lonnie Wheeler, *I Had a Hammer*, 54
64	Wright's background, recruitment: Joby Wright, interviews, February 23, 2016 and March 16, 2016; Chapman interview, January 21, 2008; Larry Chapman, letter to Joby Wright, AADA
65	"The Hole": Thom Gossom, *Walkon*, 143;
65	"We would have…": Joe B. Hall, interview, November 7, 2016
65	Stallworth's background, recruitment: Bud Stallworth, interview, December 4, 2015; Bud Stallworth, Oral History Project, Endacott Society, circa 2011, University of Kansas Library
66	voted "outstanding players": Ray Holliman, "Harris Leads South…," *Montgomery Advertiser*, August 9, 1968
67	merger of AIAA, AHSAA: Charles Land, "New Tide Era Ahead," *Tuscaloosa News*, March 1968; AHSAA website, History/Mission Statement,
67	Grant's background: Travis Grant, interview, December 8, 2015; Guy Curtright, "A Scoring Machine," *AJC*, January 23, 2000
67	McCamey's background and education: Sam McCamey, interview, December 7, 2015
68	"I can't see…": Mark Shoemaker, "No Problem Seen by First Tiger Negro," *Birmingham Post-Herald*, circa August 1968
68	"My mother…": *Ibid.*
68	Kerner Commission: Charles Kaiser, *1968 in America*, 141-2
68	hate mail to signees: John Wallace, interview, circa Spring 1980; Maraniss, *Strong Inside*, 66
68	"The desire to win…": Charles H. Martin, *Benching Jim Crow*, 226
68	"typical, stupid…": Rudy Davalos, interview, November 16, 2007
68	Coleman hate mail: "Orange Park's Ron Coleman…," *Florida Times-Union*, August 16, 2008

69 "They were the meanest...": Alexander Wolff, "Ground Breakers," *SI*, November 7, 2005
69 Cook's decision: *Ibid.*; Mark Schlabach, "Teammates Work...," ESPN.com, February 15, 2008,
69 Aug. 19 and Sept 2 letters: Bill Lynn, to Henry Harris, August 19, 1968 and September 2, 1968, AADA, Box 19, Folder 9
69 specificity atypical: Chapman interview, January 21, 2008
70 move to Bessemer: Raymond interview, June 11, 2007; James Harris interview, February 24, 2008
70 suspicion over move: Morrow interview, May 13, 2008; Dianne Kirksey, interview, July 15 2009; Al Young, interview, October 6, 2012
70 stayed for Henry to graduate: David Housel, "Henry Harris," AU basketball game program, January 3, 1972, ADAA
70 kept her business to herself: Vinnie Smoot, interview, July 9, 2009
70 worked at grill: Glenda Harris Dunn, interview, April 8, 2009
70 better opportunity: James Harris, interview, February 24, 2008
71 the American way: *Freedom Riders*, PBS, 2011
71 pushed Americans forward: Barrack Obama, acceptance speech, Democratic national convention, Charlotte, North Carolina, September 6, 2012
71 "He and the boss...": *Time*, September 22, 1947

Chapter 10

72 Page family background: Robert Page, interview, May 23, 1980
72 decade ahead: Frank Fitzpatrick, *And the Walls Came Tumbling Down*, 145
72 threats against Unseld: Fitzpatrick, *And the Walls Came Tumbling Down*, 144
72 Rupp's sincerity: Mike Littwin, "Playing in Pain...," *LA Times*, March 13, 1983
73 Beard's recruitment: Maraniss, *Strong Inside*, 90
73 Oswald background, message: Russell Rice, *Kentucky Football*, 113
73 Bradshaw background: *Ibid.*, 108-109; Morton Sharnik, "The New Rage to Win," *SI*, October 8, 1962
73 NCAA trouble: Mike Sullivan, "UK's Past...," *Louisville Courier-Journal*, December 20, 1976
73 fifty-eight players left: Rice, *Kentucky Football*, 110
73 lifetime contract: David Wharton, "Great Barrier," *LA Times*, September 3, 2004; Russell Rice, "Bradshaw Resigned...," *Cats' Pause*, December 15, 2007
73 "contract of indeterminate length...": Rice, *Kentucky Football*, 121
73 "a position of equal standing...": Rice, "Bradshaw Resigned..."
73 "immediate all-out...": Fitzpatrick, *And the Walls Came Tumbling Down*, 135-6
73 son of a domestic: Nathaniel Northington, *Still Running*, 20-21
73 not alone: Sarah M. Kazadi, "SEC Integrated," cbssports.com, February 17, 2015
73 Northington signing: "UK Signs...," *Lexington Herald*, December 20, 1965
74 competing for playing time: Rick Bailey, "Page in Critical Condition with Severe Neck Injury," *Lexington Herald*, August 23, 1967
74 description of drill: *Ibid.*, Charlie Bradshaw, interview, circa Spring 1980
74 extent of injury: Bill Pugh, "Early Reports...," *Lexington Leader*, August 23, 1967; Rick Bailey, "Football Injury...," *Lexington Herald*, September 30, 1967
74 Bradshaw's visits: John McGill, "Time Out," *Lexington Herald*, October 4, 1967
74 speaking at practice: *Ibid.*, Bradshaw interview, circa Spring 1980
74 "Greg was coming...": Bradshaw interview, circa Spring 1980
75 "He told us...": Robert Page interview, May 23, 1980
75 uncertainty on nature of injury: McGill, "Time Out," October 4, 1967

75 services for Page: John McGill, "Mourners Bestow…," *Lexington Herald*, October 4, 1967; "Fund Set…," *Lexington Leader*, October 2, 1967
75 Wallace background: Wallace interviews, circa May 1980 and January 5, 1988
75 thousands of squats: Andrew Maraniss, *Strong Inside*, 18
76 assurances from Vanderbilt: Wallace interview, January 5, 1988
76 parents hid hate mail: Maraniss, *Strong Inside*, 66
76 ignored pioneering: Wallace interview, circa May 1980
76 "I felt, 'Well…'": Heys, "It's a Whole New Ballgame"
76 "it was going to be nice…": Wallace interview, circa May 1980
76 rebuke at church: *Ibid.*
76 "I was in a world…": Heys, "It's a Whole New Ballgame"
76 Ole Miss cancellation: Wallace interview, circa May 1980
76 Dillard background: Godfrey Dillard, interview, circa January 1988
76 Dillard's father: Maraniss, *Strong Inside*, 107
77 Mississippi State game: Sam Heys, "The Man Who Integrated SEC Basketball," *Atlanta Constitution*, January 12, 1988
77 spit and Coke: Dillard interview, circa January 1988
77 "The business they…": Wallace interview, circa May 1980
77 held hands: Heys, "Man Who Integrated…," January 12, 1988
77 "We're going to…": Perry Wallace, interview, January 8, 1988
77 Hall's performance: Steve Clark, "Hall First to Show 'Blackie' Can Play," *Atlanta Constitution*, February 8, 1972
77 "The Klan sent…": Lennie Hall, interview, circa Spring 1980
77 integration by independents: Charles H. Martin, "Jim Crow in the Gymnasium," *Sport and the Color Line*, 241
78 Steve Martin: Tammy Nunez, "Tulane's Stephen…," nola.com, May 16, 2013
78 "He was good enough…": Joe B. Hall interview, November 7, 2016

Chapter 11

79 "We walk…": Elizabeth Alexander, Inaugural Poem, January 20, 2009
79 "Can you imagine…": Chapman interview, January 21, 2008
79 football players as ringleaders: Thom Gossom, interview, January 21, 2014
79 "I thought there was…": Tim Ash, interview, July 6, 2017
80 "I got to the dorm…": Bobby York, interview, November 3, 2011
80 "Henry had a…": Greg Austin, interview, June 20, 2017
80 "My recollection…": Dan Jacobs, interview, March 13, 2017
81 Bell applies: "API School Gets…," *Birmingham News*, February 15, 1948
81 paying Israel: Brandon Evans, "Breaking Down the Walls…," *Plainsman*, February 22, 2001; Clare Harp, "Following the Leader:…," master's thesis, Auburn University, December 5, 2013, https://clareharp.weebly.com
81 "nervous attack": "Negro Withdraws," *Montgomery Advertiser*, April 22, 1948
81 Draughon told not to integrate: Evans, "Breaking Down the Walls…"
81 denying black applicants: Craig Darch, *From Brooklyn to the Olympics*, 100-101
81 JFK telegram: Kristen Oliver, "Draughon…," *OADN*, November 23, 2013
81 "less than bad than others": Charles R. Martin, *Benching Jim Crow*, 225
81 ruling on Franklin: "Federal Judge Orders…," *OADN*, November 6, 1963
82 stadium meeting: "President Draughon…," *This Is Auburn*, December 1963
82 "You young people…": "Suggested Remarks…," December 3, 1963, Civil Rights folder, Draughon file, Special Collections and Archives, Draughon Library, Auburn University
82 troopers: Bob Ingram, "Negro…," *Montgomery Advertiser*, January 5, 1964
82 Draughon asked Wallace: Evans, "Breaking Down the Walls…"

82	housing Franklin: Bob Hess, "House Negro…," *Montgomery Advertiser*, January 4, 1964
82	"whole wing…": Harold Franklin, "Dialogue on Race, Integration, and Education," "Commemorating 50 Years of Integration…," January 21, 2014
82	firearm ban lifted: Gossom, *Walk-On*, 39
82	"You can legislate…": Willie Wyatt, "Dialogue on…," January 21, 2014
83	Meredith's dorm room: William Doyle, *An American Insurrection:*
83	Black's saga: Harold A. Black, "The First Day," *Georgia Magazine*, March 2011, 22
83	"We had our own little…": Anthony Lee, Dialogue on…," January 21, 2014
83	"I was very proud…": *Ibid.*
83	black enrollment: Office of Inclusion and Diversity, Auburn University
83	Harris's class schedule: Henry Harris transcript, in possession of author
83	"The guy…": Charles Smith, interview, September 22, 2009
84	"When you've got…": Don Williams, interview, May 31, 2008
84	all flunked: Charles Smith interview, September 22, 2009
84	aisle seats: "First Black Players…," *Augusta Chronicle*, May 22, 2005
84	"It was pretty rough…": Butch Henry, interview, circa Spring 1980
84	Northington at Auburn: Northington, *Still Running*, 164-166
85	"And we heard the n-word…": *Turning the Page*, documentary, 2012
85	Fry background: Richard Pennington, *Breaking the Ice*, 178-179
85	LeVias background: *Ibid.*, 80-110; *Breaking the Huddle,* HBO, 2008
86	"I'm not worried…": Pennington, *Breaking the Ice*, 107
86	"There was all this legal…": *Ibid.*, 107
86	busted lip: Pennington, *Breaking the Ice*, 108
87	"Henry has not…": Bill Lynn, letter to Al Young, AADA, Box 19, Folder 9
87	"Henry had never …": Fred Hughes, interview, July 6, 2008
87	"on a large area…": Roberts interview, May 13, 2008
87	"Henry, I…": Bill Lynn, letter to Henry Harris, August 19, 1968, AADA
87	"Both of those guys…": Wright, interview, March 15, 2016
88	"We didn't cut Henry…": Jimmy Walker, interview, November 3, 2011
88	attacks on hippies: James Thornton, "Assailants Attack Students in Front of Noble Hall," *Plainsman*, November 27, 1968
88	spying on students: "Alabama Spied on…," *AJC*, undated
88	"No matter what town …": Ralph Foster, interview, July 10, 2007
88	Lynn's asked Foster to call Harris: *Ibid.*

Chapter 12

89	"Recruited into…": Jack Olsen, *SI*, circa Summer 1968
89	a stud: Pat Cowart, interview, March 9, 2009
89	"Even though he…": Dan Jacobs interview, March 13, 2017
89	"Many were trying to find fault…": Chapman interview, January 21, 2008
90	Tommie Smith background, quotes: *Return to Mexico City*, ESPN, February 7, 2009; Amy Bass, *Silent Gesture*
90	Olympic Project for Human Rights: *Ibid.*
90	*Time* cover, *Newsweek* article: Frye Galliard, "Crumbling Segregation in the Southeastern Conference," Race Relations Information Center, Nashville, Tennessee, (formerly Southern Education Reporting Service), August 1970
91	"Everyone is looking…": Harry Edwards, interview, January 9, 2018
91	Wallace as symbol of backlash: Part 1, *Black America Since MLK*, PBS, 2016
91	"Our nation is moving…": "Kerner Commission Report…," history.com,
92	Haywood background: Scott Ostler, *Spencer Haywood*, Amistad Press, 1992

92	positive thinking: *Ibid.*, 82
92	SEC forbade tutoring: Charles H. Martin, *Benching Jim Crow*, 239
93	early-morning practices: Parks Jones, interview, November 22, 2014
93	"The only thing …:" Chapman interview, January 21, 2008
94	Baton Rouge restaurant incident: Houston Hogg, interview, October 17, 2017; Wilbur Hackett, interview, October 14, 2017
94	Charlie Scott at Atlanta restaurant: Art Chansky, *Game Changers*, 133
94	playing Dixie at Tech: Jim Joanos, "In the Center of the Storm…," *Garnet and Old*, February 2, 2003
95	"The first six…": Ed Ruzic, "Henry Was …," *Plainsman*, January 30, 1969
96	"If you come to Auburn…": Bill Lynn, letter to Joby Wright, August 15, 1967, AADA, Box 18, Folder 7

Chapter 13

96	"kind of like a victory…": Chapman interview, January 21, 2008
96	Smith not taken to Ole Miss: Charles Smith interview, September 22, 2009
96	Williams protected at Jackson: *Ibid.*
97	rocks, empty beer cans: Charles H. Martin, *Benching Jim Crow*, 284
97	Wallace at Ole Miss: Wallace interviews, January 5, 1988 and circa Spring 1980
97	shooting of James Meredith: Eagles, *Price of Defiance*, 434
98	"Nigger, get out…": Parks Jones interview,
98	"I've got to hate…": *Black Magic,* documentary
98	"It wasn't minorities…": McWhorter, *Carry Me Home, 476*
98	"scared to death": Bill Lynn, interview, circa July 1980
98	"nigger-lovers": Gordon, "Basketball's Color Line"
98	"I sat down on the bench…": Austin interview, June 20, 2017
99	integration of UGA: Rebecca McCarthy, "40 Years Ago …," *AJC*, January 7, 2001; Celebrating Courage, *Georgia Magazine*, March 2011
99	"I would've given…": "Whatever Happened..," *AJC*, undated
99	Don Adams saga: Richard Hyatt, "Blacks Look…," *Atlanta Constitution*, February 9, 1972
100	"We were just cautious…": Patrick Garbin, "About Them Dawgs! Blawg: Five Pioneers," undated
100	not recruiting blacks: David Hall, interview, October 19, 2016; Wright interview, February 13, 2016
100	"an alumni discussion…": Blake Giles, "Foster Was One of Us…," *Athens Banner-Herald*, October 3, 1991
100	locker room blocked: Patricia Heys, *Red & Black*, 1997
100	"They were quite open…": Maxie Foster, interview, circa May 1980
100	protected by Towns: Charles H. Martin, *Benching Jim Crow*, 230
100	"We were running…": Bob Bowen, interview, November 28, 2007
101	Ray Bellamy saga: Richard Lapchick, *100 Pioneers, 2008,* 305-7
102	parental anxiety: *Jackie Robinson*, Part 1, Ken Burns documentary, 2016
102	first Greyhound driver: Eig, *Opening Day*, 87
102	posing with megaphone: Ruzic, "Henry Was Cheered"
102	"It's not rare…": Ruzic, "Henry Was Cheered"
103	"Young Harris…": Paul Cox, "Henry…," *Columbus Enquirer*, circa January 1969
103	"He's a good ball-handler…";Clyde Bolton, "Harris Is…," *Birmingham News*, circa January 1969
103	"The last thing…": Fitzpatrick, *And The Walls Came Tumbling Down*, 236
103	"I don't think they noticed me.": Ruzic, "Henry Was Cheered"

Chapter 14

104 racial hostility at Kentucky: Tim Beavers, interview, June 22, 2017; Ash interview, July 6, 2017
104 defense designed to stop Shuffle: "Balanced Kittens...," *Lexington Leader*, February 4, 1969
104 jumpers and layups: John McGill Jr., "Kittens Win...," *Lexington Herald*, February 4, 1969
105 "Henry was a flow ...": Chapman interview, circa Winter 2001
105 injured kneecaps: Clyde Bolton, "For Henry...," *Birmingham News*, circa February 1972
105 Harris's shooting statistics: "Auburn Star Scores 43...," *Louisville Courier-Journal*, February 4, 1969
105 "Harris is an excellent...": "Balanced Kittens...,"
105 "He's a good ballplayer...": McGill., "Kittens Win..."
105 Rupp and banning of dunk: Jacobs, *Across the Line*, 46
105 Wallace dunking on Issel: Wallace interview, circa Spring 1980
106 "I never got called...": Wright interview, February 23, 2016
106 "I can't take this...": Michael Oriard, *Bowled Over*, 2009, 79
106 "I just couldn't...": Rick Bailey, "Northington Quits UK...," *Lexington Herald*, October 23, 1967
106 "I know I'm letting...": *Ibid*.
106 "Houston, Albert, and...": *Turning the Page*, documentary, 2013
106 Northington's farewell message: Hackett interview, October 14, 2016
106 "I don't believe anyone...": *Ibid*.
106 "I don't know if it was an accident...": Hogg interview, October 17, 2016
106 "Nobody would ever talk...": Chris Patrick, interview, June 21, 2017
107 reputation for brutality, racism: Oriard, *Bowled Over*, 78
107 Kindred's account of injury: Mark Story, "UK's Northington and Page...," *Lexington Herald-Leader*, October 5, 2013
107 injury, "scholastic difficulty": Bailey, "Northington Quits UK...",
107 meal ticket: Northington, *Still Running*, 169
107 three-hour nighttime practice: Oriard, *Bowled Over*, 78-79
108 "There was a lot of bigotry...": Ash interview, July 6, 1017
108 Maravich press conference: Wayne Federman and Marshall Terrill, *Pete Maravich*, 2006, 96
108 Butler possible walk-on: "John Sibley Butler," *LSU Magazine*, Summer 1997
108 Claiborne at Alabama: Charles H. Martin, *Benching Jim Crow*, 159
109 "Never make...": *Hope & Fury*, NBC, 2018
109 showing anger was weakness: Tolan, *Me and Hank*
109 moral issues: Eric Foner, remarks, Atlanta History Center, October 28, 2014
109 "A lot of...": Ivan Maisel, "Dr. King...," espn.com, February 21, 2014
109 Tinker incident: Maraniss, *Strong Inside*, 226, 228
110 "You had to walk a very fine line...": Wallace interview, January 8, 1988
110 "Am I crazy?": Wallace interview, January 8, 1988
111 "I think if anyone...": Chapman, interview, January 21, 2008
111 "I don't really remember...": York interview, November 3, 2011
111 "Hey, you're not crazy...": Wallace interview, circa Spring 1980

Chapter 15

113 lawsuit: court transcript, Paul W. Bryant Museum, University of Alabama
113 "What we are contending...": Galliard, "Crumbling Segregation...."
113 "It's quite unrealistic...": *Ibid*.

113 Clemon background: U. W. Clemon, speech, Auburn University integration 50th anniversary program; *STAND! Untold Stories of the Civil Rights Movement*, Alabama Public Television, 2014
114 Kirksey helped write charter: Dianne Kirksey, interview, July 15, 2009
114 lawsuit threatened in 1967: Michael Oriard, *Bowled Over*, 62
115 summer coursework: transcript of Henry Harris, in possession of author
115 "Commies Incite Nigras...": *Plainsman*, April 1, 1969
115 "I was walking...": Charles Smith interview, September 22, 2009
115 no effort by university: Gossom, *Walk-On*, 46
116 no escort: Anna Claire Stamps, "Auburn's First Black...," *Plainsman*, undated
116 separation bred ignorance: Kenny Howard, interview, May 24, 2011
116 "We got along real good...": Willie Pitts, interview, June 28, 2017
116 "The child is expected...": David Margolick, *Elizabeth and Hazel*, 293
116 "I knew it was going to be difficult...": *Ibid.*, 137
117 "The culture shock...": Leah Rawls Atkins, interview, April 28, 2008
117 Harris shaving: Jimmy Walker, interview. November 3, 2011
117 "Henry may have left...": Pat Cowart interview, March 9, 2009
117 sleeping with lights on: *Ibid.*
117 racist incidents at Wake Forest: Lapchick, *100 Pioneers*, 296
117 sleeping at Bryant Hall: Pettway interview, April 27, 2017
118 "improved more than...": Bill Lynn, letter to John Mengelt, August 21, 1969, AADA, Box 21, File 3
118 "Henry would come over...": Bill Lynn Jr. interview, May 27, 2008
118 "We had a dog that didn't let anybody...": *Ibid.*
118 election background: "Black Power in Greene County," *Time*, May 11. 1981
119 1968-1969 elections: Sokol, *There Goes My Everything*, 261-2
119 "unthinkable ...": *Ibid.*, 266

Chapter 16

120 room assignments: Bill Lynn, letter to Mengelt, August 21, 1969, AADA
120 "There was a bunch...": Ash interview, July 6, 2017
120 "There was nothing sinister...": Bill Perry, interview, June 27, 2008
121 "I went in his room...": Dan Kirkland, interview, May 27, 2014
121 Owens background: James Owens, interviews, April 27, 2008 and May 27, 2008
122 "They'd say, 'Whatever you...": Virgil Pearson, interview, April 9, 2009
122 handshake with Bear Bryant: Gossom interview, December 10, 2012
122 why Owens chose Auburn: Gossom interview, December 19, 2016
122 "If Henry had not...": James Owens, interview, circa July 1980
123 Jordan's complaint to Philpott: Martin, *Benching Jim Crow*, 264
123 "He was just cautious...": Harry Philpott, oral history, Special Collections and Archives, Draughon Library, Auburn University
123 Jordan's warning to Hillyer: *Quiet Courage*, documentary produced by Thom Gossom, Alabama Public Television, 2015
123 Jordan background: Auburn football media guide, 1973, 51
124 "Auburn would...": Craig Darch, *From Brooklyn to the Olympics,* 2014
124 HEW visit: Charles F. Simmons, letter to Willard F. Gray, Philpott Papers, Special Collections and Archives, Draughon Library, Auburn University
125 "colored employees": Sewell Dining Hall Daily Meal Attendance Report, September 30, 1969, G. W. Beard files, AADA
125 Hawks, Bulls in Auburn: Gary England, interview, June 29, 2008
125 Auburn's decision on Hudson: Wes Bizilia, interview, May 8, 2008

126 Alabama's decision on Hudson: Newton interview, circa Fall 2007
126 "Wendell was the most unsung…": Gordon, "Basketball's Color Line"
126 Hudson's background: Wendell Hudson, interview, circa Spring 1980
126 hate mail: Christopher Walsh, "From Pioneer…," *Tuscaloosa News*, February 23, 2008
126 "If you want to play…": Hudson interview, Spring 1980
126 "I walked through the door…": Walsh, "From Pioneer…"
127 walked out of history class: Gordon, "Basketball's Color Line"

Chapter 17

129 Robinson looking in mirror: Part 1, *Jackie Robinson*, PBS, 2016
129 game-opening scene: Clyde Bolton, "The Spotlight…" *Birmingham News*, December 4, 1969
130 "Playing an unfamiliar…": *Ibid.*
130 "We feel like…": Roy Riley, "Lynn Plans…," *OADN*, December 3, 1969
131 Clemson students fled campus: Charles H. Martin, *Benching Jim Crow*, 170
131 Darryl Hill at Clemson: Steve Hummer, "Breaking the Color Barrier," *AJC*, August 29, 2010
131 "He might have scored thirty or forty…": Kent Mitchell, "Henry Blushes Maroon," *Atlanta Journal*, December 16, 1969
131 "Henry Harris…": Tom Dial, "LSU's a Problem…," *Atlanta Constitution*, January 9, 1970
132 "It put some things…": Dan Kirkland, interview, May 27. 2014
132 "if he had hit Henry…": Roy Riley, "Lienhard 'Axed' Mengelt…," *Opelika-Auburn News*, January 26, 1970
132 Lienhard running: Tom Brennan, interview, June 25, 2016
133 cover story: Arlie W. Schardt, "Secrets of Auburn's…," *SI*, December 11, 1961
133 opponents understood shuffle: Cowart interview, March 9, 2009
133 "It was just a constant…": Bobby Nix, interview, December 17, 2016
133 "As talented…": Parks Jones interview, November 22, 2014
133 "plow on a racehorse…": York interview, November 11, 2011
133 "The guy was out of…": John Mengelt, interview, circa Summer 1980
133 "He kind of needed…": …": *Ibid.*
133 preferred SEC's slower pace: *Ibid.*
133 football at Notre Dame: Bizilia interview, May 30, 2008
134 "It would've been…": Carl Shetler, interview, November 15, 2011
134 "They were different…": Chapman interview, January 21, 2008
134 "He didn't get along…": Ash interview, July 6, 2017
134 "John was so cocky…": Bizilia interview, May 30, 2008
134 "You got the impression…": Perry interview, circa Spring 1984
134 technical fouls: Roy Riley, "Unbeaten N.C. State…," *OADN*, December 18, 1969
134 "He was mean…": Tom Brennan, interview, June 25, 2016
135 "John had fifty-eight…": Perry interview, June 27, 2008
135 "You can have one more…": Clyde Bolton, "Auburn Runs by Bama," *Birmingham News*, February 15, 1970
136 "I got really upset…": Chapman interview, January 21, 2008
136 applauded loudly: Roy Riley, "Wildcats Weep…," *OADN*, March 3, 1970
136 "I may have played eight minutes…": Gordon, "Basketball's Color Line"
136 "I'm sitting on…": *Courage Matters*, SEC Sports Network, 2017
136 "a hell of a lot…": C. M. Newton and Billy Reed, *Newton's Laws*, 104

136 Hudson stopping bus: Newton interview, circa Fall 2007
136 "Henry and I...": Greg Austin interview, June 20, 2017
136 "no one man can handle": Lynn letter to Mengelt, August 21, 1969, AADA
136 "There's only one ball.": Newton interview, circa Fall 2007
137 "Henry did very well...": Shetler interview, November 15, 2011
137 "Henry's never been...": Charles Land, "Henry Harris Is...," *Tuscaloosa News*, circa 1970
137 "definitely be a guard next season.": *Ibid.*
137 "I think we had a good year...": John Pruett, "Lynn for Time...," *Huntsville Times*, March 10, 1970

Chapter 18
138 "We had a lack...": Davalos interview, November 16, 2007
138 "Rudy was a big influence...": Chapman interview, January 21, 2008
138 Davalos background: Auburn basketball media guide, 1969-70, 6
138 "He was a climber...": Perry interview, circa Fall 1984
139 "He'd do or say...": Tom Bardin, interview, February 2, 2002
139 "A lot of people...": Walker interview, November 3, 2011
139 "What do we do?": Perry interview, circa Fall 1984
139 "Rudy did everything...": Shetler interview, November 15, 2011
139 government car: Bill Lynn Jr. interview, May 27, 2008
139 Lynn's background: Auburn basketball media guide, 1971-2, 4; Bill Lynn Jr. interview, May 27, 2008
139 "I knew Alabama...": Chapman interview, January 21, 2008
141 fallen asleep: *Ibid.*
141 "My dad did have a drinking...": Bill Lynn Jr. interview, May 27, 2008
141 "periodic": *Ibid.*
141 "a mom and pop...": Richard Hyatt, interview, September 17, 2017
141 bourbon in Coke: Gossom interview, circa Summer 1984
141 smelled alcohol: Vince Dooley, interview, circa 2016; York interview, November 3, 2011; Perry interview, June 17, 2008
142 manager had to drive bus: Jacobs interview, March 13, 2017
142 LSU motel incident: York interview, November 3, 2011; Walker, interview, November 3, 2011
142 incident on plane: Walker interview, November 3, 2011; Shetler interview, November 15, 2011
142 incident at Tennessee: Walker interview, November 3, 2011; Chapman interview, January 21, 2008
143 meeting with Beard: Chapman interview, January 21, 2008
143 "He hooked me up...": Hyatt interview, September 27, 2016
143 issuing news release...: Chapman interview, January 21, 2008
143 Beard's announcement: Roy Riley, "Davalos...," *OADN*, circa March 1970
143 seen as a revolt: Paul Cox, "The Revolt," *OADN*, February 25, 1973
144 "Coach, I can't do this...": Chapman interview, January 21, 2008
144 "We asked Coach Beard...": York interview, November 3, 2011
144 "I just packed up...": Nix interview, December 17, 2016
144 "They ended up getting fired...": Kirkland interview, May 17, 2014

Chapter 19
145 Wallace achievements: Wallace interview, circa Spring 1980
145 "It is ironic...": Frank Sutherland, "Lonely Four Years...," *Nashville Tennesseean*, March 9, 1970
145 ticket out of town: Wallace interview, circa Spring 1980

145 like Lewis and Clark: Andrew Maraniss, speech, Decatur Library, Decatur, Georgia, February 4, 2015
146 "An institution…": Wallace interview, circa Spring 1980
146 talk to Human Relations Council: Maraniss, *Strong Inside*, 305
146 "fitting in": Kirksey interview, July 15, 2009
146 Bama Belle, homecoming voting: *Ibid.*
147 "I remember him…": York interview, November 3, 2011
147 "From an interaction…": Jacobs interview, March 13, 2017
147 "Henry would come…": Kirkland, interview, May 27, 2014
147 "Henry didn't stay there…": Perry interview, circa Fall 1984
148 not calling attention: Norris, *The Grace of Silence*, 134
148 "You didn't see much of Henry…": Bizilia interview, May 30, 2008
148 "a loner…": Tim Ash, interview, July 6, 2017
148 "It was like he was scared…": Shetler interview, November 15, 2011
148 "get much sense": Gossom interview, circa Summer 1984
148 "He went off on his own…": England interview, June 29, 2008
148 Harris's bicycle: Pettway interview, circa Fall 1984
148 "You're watching white guys…": Owens interview, May 27, 2008
148 "It's probably very difficult…": Mengelt interview, circa Summer 1980
148 "He came on this side of town…": Rush Tanner, interview, June 21, 2017
149 bootleg whiskey: *Ibid.*
149 "looked like someone…": Gossom interview, circa Summer 1984
149 "He said, 'Don't send your child…": Fred Gray, speech, "Dialogue on Race, Integration, and Education," Auburn, Alabama, January 21, 2014
149 Samuel Younge's death: Encyclopedia of Alabama, www.encyclopediaofalabama.org/article/h-1669
149 Claiborne bought meal ticket: Jacobs, *Across the Line*, 69
150 "not black enough": Gossom interview, December 19, 2016
150 "white nigger": Richard Pennington, *Breaking the Ice*
150 "On one hand…": Wallace interview, circa 1980

Chapter 20

151 FBI tracks Bryant case: Jay Reeves, "FBI Tracked…," AP, August 21, 2010
151 Hoover's approval: *Ibid.*
151 time recruiting Harris: court transcript, Bryant Museum
151 Pernell's scholarship: Galliard, "Crumbling Segregation in the SEC"
151 July 20 meeting: Galliard," Crumbling Segregation in the SEC"
151 Clemon's quotes: *Ibid.*
152 "damn sure wouldn't stand":
152 Aderhold blamed alumni: Charles H. Martin, *Benching Jim Crow*, 289
152 Barnett's request of Kennedy: "Aug. 18, 1963, James Meredith Graduates," Learning Network, August 18, 2011
152 Wallace posturing: John Hayman, *Bitter Harvest*, 191
153 "Coach Bryant had to work through…": Newton interview, circa Fall 2007
153 housing projects: *Breaking the Huddle*, HBO, 2008
153 game was a rationale, not catalyst: Oriard, *Bowled Over*, 62
153 both hero and victim:
154 Vaught "joking" with writers: Maraniss, *Strong Inside*, 114-115
154 Purnell saga: J. T. Purnell, interview, October 9, 2018; "Ole Miss Adds Black Footballer," *Daily Mississippian*, May 6, 1969; "Negro Athlete…," *Daily Mississippian*, May 7, 1969
155 best won-loss record: Galliard," Crumbling Segregation in the SEC"

155 NAACP complaints: Charles H. Martin, *Benching Jim Crow*, 272
155 "People had a hard time...": Buddy Martin, *The Boys From Old Florida*
155 "When I got there...": Doug Dickey, interview, circa Spring 1980
155 Supreme Court over desegregation: Lindsay Taulbee, "Gainesville in the '70s," *Gainesville Sun*, February 2006
156 King to Minnesota: Sam Heys, *Atlanta Constitution*, circa September 1970; Vince Dooley, interview, circa Summer 1980

Chapter 21

157 not discouraged from signing blacks: Davalos interview, November 16, 2007
157 "You didn't hear much...": Bizilia interview, May 30, 2008
157 Pearson in single room: Pearson interview, April 9, 2009
157 "I thought I was special...": Owens interview, April 27, 2008
158 Reggie Jackson in Birmingham: Bob Nightengale, "For Jackson, a Rise That Symbolized His Generation," *USA Today*, December 15, 2010
158 "Yeah, I went to bed...": Hogg interview, October 17, 2016
158 scholarship offer to Mitchell: anonymous source
158 "We want someone...": Roger Mitchell, interview, April 2, 2016
158 "bad influence": Gossom interview, December 10, 2012
159 Myrdal study: Jonathan Eig, *Opening Day*, 45-46
159 Junior Coffey benched: Pennington, *Breaking the Ice*, 9
159 message to Bubba Smith: *Breaking the Huddle*, HBO
159 warning to Westbrook: Pennington, *Breaking the Ice*, 56
159 William Smith suspended: "First Black Players at Death Valley...," *Augusta Chronicle*, May 22, 2005
159 Ray Bellamy saga: Lapchick, *100 Pioneers*, 307
159 Susan Warley background: Susan Warley Hales, interview, December 4, 2015
159 "I really had a crush on him...": *Ibid.*
160 "He was beautiful...": Kirksey interview, July 15, 2009
160 "Henry didn't go with...": Pettway interview, circa Fall 1984
160 "He had a way...": Ash interview, July 6, 2017
160 two black freshman females: Charles Smith interview, September 22, 2009
160 "kept it under control": Gossom interview, circa 1984
160 "He dated white girls...": Shetler interview, December 15, 2011
160 block party: Debra Threatt, interview, February 18, 2014
161 "He'd say...": Debra Threatt, interview, February 20, 2014
161 "complete black power": Sokol, *There Goes My Everything*, 262-3
161 "We thought we had...": *Ibid.*, 263

Chapter 22

162 "I need you here...": Bizilia interview, May 30, 2008
162 most hostile arena: Jacobs, *Across the Line*, 257
162 Charlie Scott at Columbia: Chansky, *Game Changers*, 139-140
162 parading Confederate flag: Charles H. Martin, *Benching Jim Crow*, 175
163 description of Heartley: Al Heartley, interview, circa Spring 1980; Jacobs, *Across the Line*, 214
163 "Walker was probably...": Roy Riley, *OADN*
163 "You've got a black kid out here...": Bizilia interview, May 30, 2008
163 'things that were pretty shocking": Beavers interview, June 22, 2017
164 "Both of us had traveled...": Hudson interview, circa Spring 1980
164 adequate ball-handler: Mengelt interview, circa Summer 1980
164 only pioneer point guard: Barry Jacobs, *Across the Line*
164 "black athletes...": Wallace interview, circa Spring 1980

164 reeked of racism: Pettway interview, circa Fall 1984
164 "He could get you...": Kirkland interview, May 27, 2014
165 a defensive coach: Bill Lynn Jr., interview, May 27, 2008
165 "Henry is a fabulous...": Land, "Henry Harris...,"
165 "His passion...": Chapman interview, January 21, 2008
166 "We are really struggling...": Larry Phillips, letter to Bob Jones, February 3, 1971, AADA
166 sports columnists: Roy Riley, "Auburn Will Be Back," *OADN*, undated; Paul Cox, "Better Days Are Coming...," *Columbus Enquirer*, March 10, 1971
166 "Mengelt was a one-man...": Walker interview, November 3, 2011
166 "We told them about...": Ash interview, July 6, 2017
167 "I thought a lot...": Jimmy Walker, email to author, December 12, 2016
167 double-dating, Chevelle: Walker interview, November 3, 201
167 "would and could rap about anything...": Thom Gossom, "I Knew Henry," *Plainsman*, April 25, 1974
167 "around us Henry wanted to be...": Cowart interview, March 9, 2009
167 back of the bus: Pennington, *Breaking the Ice*, 146
168 "a little place along the side...": Austin interview, June 20, 2017
168 Florida's Williams in Baton Rouge: Jacobs, *Across the Line*, 315
168 Coleman in Tuscaloosa: "Orange Park's Ron Coleman...," jacksonville.com/tu-online, August 16, 2008

Chapter 23

169 make game physical: Bizilia interview, May 30 2008
169 "I was not popular...": C. M. Newton, interview, circa 2002
169 new contract: Newton and Reed, *Newton's Laws*, 105
170 "Hey, Bill...": Bizilia interview, May 30 2008
170 "Bill, what's the matter?": *Ibid.*
170 "They had some very physical...": Larry Phillips, interview, May 25, 2016
170 larger player fell on Harris: Henry Ford, interview, November 12, 2012
170 "I remember when...": Threatt interview, February 18, 2014
170 "He's down, he's down.": *Ibid.*, February 20, 2014
170 dust rising from floor: Ray Mears, interview, circa Spring 1980
171 "You just can't imagine...": David Housel, "Tigers Miss Harris," *OADN*, February 16, 1971
171 "highly doubtful": Mike McKenzie, "Harris...," *Huntsville Times*, February 19, 1971
171 "He told me...": Robert Owsley, "Hoosier...," *OADN*, February 21, 1971
171 "Maybe it was...": Roy Riley, "Kentucky Horses...," *OADN*, March 2, 1971
171 "Any player would...": Beavers interview, June 22, 2016
172 taped so tightly: Thom Gossom, *Walk-On*, 46
172 "Henry was motivated...": Walker interview, November 3, 2011
172 "He'd hurt after...": Richard Hyatt, "Balance Succeeds John Mengelt," *Atlanta Constitution*, November 18, 1971
172 "He said he'd go...": Ford interview, November 12, 2012

Chapter 24

173 "Jim McDaniels...": Joe B. Hall, interview, November 7, 2016
173 "He would've played a lot...": Raveling interview, January 8, 2001
174 "nigger corner": Gossom, *Walk-On*,
174 "we didn't have...": Owens interview, April 27, 2008
174 had not pursued blacks: Martin T. Oliff, "The Post-War Years," AU Digital Library diglib.auburn.edu/auburnhistory/ralphdraughon.htm

174 left Haley Center: Owens interview, April 27, 2008
175 "We don't do things like that": *Ibid.*
175 "When you were a black athlete…": Gossom interview,
175 arrests, withdrawals at Florida: Lindsay Taulbee, "Gainesville in the '70s," *Gainesville Sun*, circa February 2006
175 "there's got to be…": Mike DiRocco, "Generations of Inspiration," espn.com, February 24, 2012
175 eight expelled: "Ole Miss Athlete . . .," hottytoddy.com, December 5, 2013
175 "We all were…": Charles Smith, interview, September 22, 2009
176 students attacked: "Football Players…," *Red & Black*, February 11, 1971
176 "My freshman year…": *Courage Matters*, SEC Sports Network, 2017
176 "A normal course load…": Rufus Felton, interview, May 27, 2008
177 "I don't know…": Paul W. Bryant, interview by Earnest Reese, *Atlanta Constitution*, circa Spring 1980
177 "Coach Bryant told me…": John Mitchell, interview, Spring 1980
177 spoke to team: Newton and Reed, *Newton's Laws*, 104
177 "It was small talk…": Christopher Walsh, "From Pioneer to Powerful,"

Chapter 25

178 "This sort of…": Roy Riley, "Harris Is Captain," *Birmingham Post-Herald*, circa spring 1972
178 late-spring surgery: "Auburn…," *Columbus Enquirer*, February 26, 1972
179 Carl Harris staying in Auburn: Threatt interview, February 18, 2014
179 "The doctors gave him…": Raymond interview, June 11, 2007
179 "Henry was our big brother.…": Owens interview, April 27, 2008
179 "Nobody ever…": Sylvester Davenport, interview, May 23, 2016
179 "We knew we had to…": William C. Rhoden, "A Way to Mark…," *NYT*, January 25, 2009
179 "Nobody ever discussed…": Sylvester Davenport, interview, May 23, 2016
180 "As a black man…": Ford interview, November 12, 2012
180 "woke up every day…": Michele Norris, *On Race and the Grace of Silence*
180 did not fit narrative: *Ibid.*, 124
180 "You've got a big…": Leonard George, interview, circa Spring 1980
180 "I knew the next day…": Charles H. Martin, *Benching Jim Crow*, 263
180 "Henry's ready…": Thomas Gilmore, interview,
180 "Daddy would tell…": Pettway interview, circa Fall 1984
181 "At my age…": Gossom, interview, December 10, 2012
181 "angry black man": Frank McCloskey, interview, December 8, 2009
181 "you're here, so…": Gossom interview, December 10, 2012
181 "We'd be sitting around…": Gossom interview, circa Summer 1984
182 "I think about that now…": Thom Gossom, interview, January 21, 2014
182 Dapper Dan gym bag: Gossom interview, circa Summer 1984
182 jeans and Army jacket: *Ibid.*
182 "Those last two years…": Foster interview, July 10, 2007
182 Sewell Manufacturing: Gossom interview, circa Summer 1984
182 Harris's old car: *Ibid.*
182 telling jokes about Boligee: *Ibid.*
183 legend about railroad tracks: Outland interview, May 25, 2008
183 "Henry was always…": George Smith, interview, May 27, 2008
183 "He was always smiling…": Gossom interview, circa Summer 1984
183 "his own fault": Perry interview, circa Fall 1984
183 "always come in…": Albert Johnson, interview, July 11, 2009

183	"Henry was not….": Dee C. Madison, interview, circa 1984
183	"He'd just leave…": Albert Johnson interview, July 11, 2009
183	never gotten high: Gossom interview, December 10, 2012
183	"that stuff's bad for you": York interview, November 3, 2011
184	not make anyone too angry: Gossom interview, circa Summer 1980
184	"Your coach…" Ash interview, July 6, 2017
184	photo of Lynn and Harris: "Auburn Basketball Media Guide, 1971-72"
185	"It was so difficult…": Gossom interview, December 19, 2016
185	hero or nobody: Perry Wallace, *Morning Joe*, MSNBC, February 4, 2015
185	loved and despised: Fitzpatrick, *The Walls Came Tumbling Down*, 53-54
185	"A lot of people saw you…": Gordon, "Basketball's Color Line"
185	Burger King incident: Gossom, *Walk-On*, 69
185	"To be at Auburn…": Gordon, "Basketball's Color Line"
186	"Owens, get in…": Owens interview, April 27, 2008
186	"Coach, I didn't get…": *Ibid*.
186	"He's a blocking…": Bizilia interview, May 30, 2008
186	"Folks were saying…": Kirkland interview, May 27, 2014
187	apology for fumbles: Terry Henley, interview, November 27, 2012
187	Krystal incident: Threatt interview, February 20, 2014

Chapter 26

188	"after a while…": Wallace interview, circa Spring 1980
188	"just about going to shoot…": Gossom interview, circa Summer 1984
188	reputation of not developing players: Hyatt interview, September 27, 2016
188	"No, because…": Hyatt, "Balance Succeeds John Mengelt,"
189	"unhappy triad": Howard interview, May 24, 2011
189	"Dr. Hughston…": Herbert Waldrup, interview, My 24, 2011
189	"Everybody was wondering…": Phillips interview, May 25, 2016
189	"That would be a decision…": Howard interview, May 24, 2011
190	"He had to have somebody to play…": *Ibid*.
190	"I tried him…": Lynn interview, circa July 1980
190	"He was not the same…": Beavers interview June 22, 2016
190	"who cares for other people": David Housel, "Henry Harris," AU basketball game program, January 3, 1972, ADAA
190	students riding Lynn: Paul Cox, *Columbus Enquirer*, circa Winter 1972
191	"It was embarrassing…": Bizilia interview, May 30, 2008
191	"He'd try to get us together…": Albert Johnson interview, July 11, 2009
191	"Henry could do a number…": Lynn interview, circa July 1980
191	play sparingly: Johnson interview, July 11, 2009
191	Temple background: Collis Temple, interview, circa Spring 1980
191	Maravich's remarks about Houston: Marc J. Spears, "Inside Collis Temple's…," theundefeated.com, February 8, 2017
191	"In other words…": *Ibid*.
192	"Henry was probably playing…": England interview, June 29, 2008
192	"He would not hang around…": Gossom interview, circa Summer 1984
193	"water on the knee": Howard interview, May 24, 2011
193	"It didn't heal…": Owens interview, May 27, 2008
193	"We'd be in the training…": Kirkland interview, May 27, 2008
193	"He certainly didn't help it…": Howard interview, May 24, 2011
193	"really depressed": Gossom interview, December 10, 2012
194	conversation about quitting: Albert Johnson interview, July 11, 2009
194	"If you would…": Clyde Bolton, "For Henry, Road Has Been Melancholy,"

Birmingham News, circa February 1972

Chapter 27

196 interview with Harris: Al Thomy, "Would Harris Go Again?...," *Atlanta Constitution*, February 26, 1972
197 "went the wrong...": Sutherland, "Lonely Four Years...," *Nashville Tennessean*, March 9, 1970
197 "I wouldn't do it...": Galliard, "Crumbling Segregation..."
197 Steve Martin interview: Maraniss, *Strong Inside*, 219
198 description of ovation: "The Last Hurrah," *OADN*, February 27, 1972
198 "When inspirational leader Henry...": John Pruett, "Auburn Ploy...," *Huntsville Times*, March 5, 1972
198 Rupp forced to retire: Fitzpatrick, *And the Walls Came Tumbling Down*, 222
198 applause at Kentucky: "Kentucky Mauls...," *OADN*, March 7, 1972
198 "I remember Henry...": Stan Key, interview, June 28, 2017
199 "Harris who has played...": John Pruett, "Auburn Ends...," *Huntsville Times*, March 10, 1972
200 Housel's farewell to Harris: David Housel, "A Salute to a Competitor," AU basketball game program, February 26, 1972, ADAA

Chapter 28

201 "When you're through...": Gossom interview, December 19, 2016
201 "I thought I was smoking...": Davenport interview, May 23, 2016
201 "We were in the TV room...": Owens interview, April 27, 2008
202 talked calmly: Albert Johnson interview, July 11, 2009
202 Davenport background: Davenport interview, May 23, 2016
202 "Sylvester was an exceptional...": Phillips interview, May 25, 2016
203 great-grandfathers lynched: Davenport interview, May 23, 2016
203 Davenport warned: Davenport interview, May 23, 2016
203 "Henry called me...": Loretta Towns Brown, interview, May 10, 2018
203 Loretta Towns Brown background: *Ibid.*

Chapter 29

206 Pearson background: Virgil Pearson, interviews, March 11, 2009 and April 9, 2009
206 "black SOB": *Ibid.*, March 11, 2009
207 hitchhiked home: Tody Webster, interview, July 8, 2009
207 called Melvin Hodges: *Ibid.*
207 last player cut: Young interview, February 8, 2008
207 "He'd say he was...": Owens interview, April 27, 2008
208 five classes: Henry Harris transcript
208 "He was really different...": Gossom interview, circa Summer 1984
208 rely more on faith: Owens interview, April 27, 2008
208 "I wish I could sit there...": Albert Johnson interview, July 11, 2009
208 "effort and energy": Gary Redding, interview, January 12, 2017
209 "Henry would meet me...": Ford interview, November 12, 2012
210 "If ever y'all hear I committed...": *Ibid.*

Chapter 30

212 Owens was centerpiece: Kenneth Wayne Ringer, *Lorendo*, 181
212 ran with receivers: Owens interview, May 27, 2008
212 Owens blocking for Henley: Gossom, *Walk-On*, 112
212 "I felt like...": *Quiet Courage,* documentary by Thom Gossom, 2014
212 "We ran a play called..." Tom Green, "Trailblazing James Owens...," OADN, March 27, 2016

213   conversation in huddle: Henley interview, November 27, 2012
213   playing "Dixie": Gossom, *Walk-On*, 142-3
213   "What are we supposed to do...": Owens interview, April 27, 2008
214   conflict over tickets: Earnest Reese, "McAshan Unscarred...," *Atlanta Constitution*, undated
214   McAshan hanging in effigy: Ford interview, November 12, 2012
214   "My personal property...": Reese, "McAshan Unscarred..."
214   "you're here as long as...": McCloskey interview, December 8, 2009
215   "if you ever did...": Henry Ford, interview, circa Summer 1984
215   "God knows none of us...": Oriard, *Bowled Over*, 87
215   Liberty Bowl scene: *Ibid.*, 86-87
217   KKK mock court: Emily Giambalvo, "1971: How One Year and Five Men...," *Red & Black*, February 23, 2017
217   Tech's KKK team: Dave Beavin, interview, January 29, 2018
217   "I've never seen...": Simon Henderson, *Sidelined*, 173

Chapter 31

218   winter-quarter classes, fall-quarter grades: Harris transcript
218   "Henry wasn't dumb...": Gossom interview, circa Summer 1984
218   "Sounds like depression...": James Harris interview, February 24, 2008
218   contacted Chapman: Chapman interview, January 21, 2008
218   would no longer pay tuition: *Ibid.*
219   "Coach Lynn was still angry...": *Ibid.*
219   felt betrayed: Bill Lynn Jr. interview, May 27, 2008
219   "Coach Lynn felt...": Bizilia interview, May 30, 2008
219   suspicion, resentment: *Ibid.*; Dan Kirkland, interview, May 27, 2014
219   Henry was angry: Raymond interview, June 11, 2007
219   "He talked to my mother...": *Ibid.*
220   "If I don't make the pros...": David Housel, "Henry Harris"
220   "Perhaps I'll stay on...": Al Thomy, "Would Harris Go Again?...,"
220   "Guys would stay...": Cowart interview, March 9, 2009
220   "A good thing about Coach Lynn...": Shetler interview, December 15, 2011
220   Bobby Hoppe saga: Sam Heys, "Tackling Decades-Old Mystery...," *AJC*, March 18, 1988
220   "anything in his power...": Sherry Lee Hoppe, *A Matter of Conscience*
221   "He said he would keep me...": Ash interview, July 6, 2017
221   starting four blacks: Newton and Reed, *Newton's Laws*, 107
221   Douglas spit on: Scarbinsky, "The University of Alabama...,"
221   Hogue, Basset attacked: David Muia, interview, October 24, 2016; Jacobs, *Across the Line*, 225
221   "expose" Auburn: Raymond interview, June 11, 2007
221   "leave it [Auburn] alone": *Ibid.*
221   cheating storekeeper, white woman at post office: *Ibid.*
222   "You need to investigate that...": *Ibid.*
222   get Henry out of Alabama: *Ibid.*
223   "There was the impression...": Gossom interview, December 19, 2016
223   suspension reported: AP, circa February 14, 1973
223   "When we got back...": Redding interview, January 12, 2017
223   "That was a sad day...": Robert Osberry, interview, December 17, 2016
223   driving Davenport home: Phillips interview, May 25, 2016
224   thrown out of dormitory: Gossom, *Walk-On*, 170-174
224   "nigger-lover": *Ibid.*, 176

224	"I was physically…": Owens interview, April 27, 2008
224	needed two more years: Owens interview, May 27, 2008
224	"My life was in disarray…": *Quiet Courage*, 2014
224	Owens asked for car: Pearson interview, April 9, 2009
224	Owens given a car: anonymous source
224	"I was leaving for good…": *Quiet Courage*, 2014
227	Auburn clothes: Owens interview, May 27, 2008

Chapter 32

226	call from Gossom: Threatt interview, February 18, 2014
226	Harris returns to Auburn: Threatt interview, February 18, 2014
227	"It made sense…": James Harris, interview, February 24, 2008
227	Harrisburg teaching offer: Raymond interview, June 11, 2007
227	hall monitor: Raymond interview, June 11, 2007
227	"Rudy, Henry Harris…": Chapman interview, January 21, 2008
227	house downtown: James Harris interview, February 24, 2008; Raymond interview, June 11, 2007
227	New Cumberland Army Depot: Don Williams interview, May 31, 2008
229	"I probably was…": Jacobs, *Across the Line*, 65
229	"We didn't challenge…": *Ibid.*, 19-20
230	Saints training camp: Owens interview, May 27, 2008
230	no phone calls: *Ibid.*
230	"I think Henry and James…": Gossom interview, circa Summer 1980

Chapter 33

Background on the UWM Athletic Department was researched in athletic department archives held at Golda Meir Library at the University of Wisconsin at Milwaukee.

232	date of arrival: "University Housing registration form," Department of Housing, University of Wisconsin-Milwaukee
232	noticeably excited: Tom Sager, interview, September 22, 2009
232	"his second favorite…": Sager interview, circa 1980
232	couple of meals: Davalos interview, November 16, 2007
233	promises not met: *Ibid.*; Bill Dwyre, "UWM Aide's Tangled…," *Milwaukee Journal*, April 19, 1974
233	Baker Fieldhouse: Dennis Marsolek, interview, February 8, 2017
233	"last place": Bill Klucas, interview, September 22, 2009
233	"mirage university": Glenn Brady, interview, September 30, 2009
233	turned away from pools: Davalos interview, November 16, 2007
234	"Make sure you take care…": Davalos interview, November 16, 2007
234	"I am sure…": Sager interview, circa 1980
234	"Mussleman was a fiery…": Nix interview, December 17, 2016
235	long hours and weekends: Dwyre, "UWM Aide's Tangled…"
235	"Henry was just…": "Break Too Late…," *Milwaukee Sentinel*, April 19, 1974
235	"It was a tough…": Richard Cox, interview, February 17, 2017
235	morning meetings: Klucas interview, September 22, 2009
236	"Nunn's background: Mike Nunn, interview, circa 2009
236	"I have one image…": Gary Wynveen, interview, October 1, 2009
236	started dating Loritz: memo detailing interview of Susan Loritz, Richard A. Sroka, "Offense Report," UWM Police Department, April 19, 1974
236	liberal school: Marsolek interview, February 8, 2017
237	"When Henry saw it…": Sager interview, September 22, 2009
237	decided not to renew assistantship: Bill Dwyre, "UWM Aide's Tangled Life Ends Abruptly," *Milwaukee Journal*, April 19, 1974

237 fall-quarter grades: Henry Harris transcript, UWM
237 "This will have a horrendous...": Jeff Huth, Budget Cuts Threaten Sports," UWM Post, circa Fall 1973
237 "It was a smalltime...": Ray Nykaza, interview, January 18, 2017
238 dissolving junior varsity: Dennis Marsolek, "Klucas Advises Dropping JV," UWM Post, March 1, 1974
238 Rosandich's vision for UWM athletics: Brady interview, September 30, 2009; Marsolek interview, February 8, 2017
239 lack of allegiance to Harris: Sager interview, September 22, 2009
239 tried to save Harris's position: Dwyre, "UWM Aide's Tangled..."
239 "giant scar": Klucas interview, September 22, 2009
239 "what a fine job Henry...": : Dwyre, "UWM Aide's Tangled..."
239 "The thing I admired in him...": "Break Too Late..."
239 "least of his worries": Dennis Marsolek, "Wrong Reason to Remember Harris," UWM Post, April 23, 1974
239 "It did not seem..." Ibid.
239 planned to stay at UWM, complete degree: Dennis Marsolek, "Klucas Advises Dropping JV," UWM Post, March 1, 1974

Chapter 34

241 two sandwiches in a sack: Hank Aaron, interview, circa January 1982
241 "Here I was...": Sam Heys, "Lonely Kid Didn't Quit, Kept Swinging," Atlanta Constitution, circa January 1982
241 "We had a terrible time...": Aaron interview, circa January 1982
241 "Hank made Christians...": Aaron and Wheeler, I Had a Hammer, 80
241 "just a simple colored boy...": Ibid., 132
241 changed name to Hank: Donald Davidson, Caught Short
241 "There was too much at stake...": Wheeler, I Had a Hammer Ibid., 121
242 "Either I could...": Ibid., 120
242 special draft: AP, "ABA to Draft...," Columbus Enquirer, April 15, 1974
242 "He love it so much...": Owens interview, April 27, 2008
242 "He wrote a long letter...": Davalos interview, circa Spring 1980
243 twenty-three inches of snow: UWM Post, February 8, 1974
243 ate dinner together: Sroka, "Offense Report," UWM Police Department, April 19, 1974
243 black athlete walkout at Auburn: Gossom, Walk-On
243 percentage of SEC black signees: Sam Heys, series of articles on SEC, ACC integration, Atlanta Constitution, unpublished, 1980
244 Student Union bus trip: UWM Post; Marsolek interview, February 8, 2017
244 wrote of loneliness: Sroka, "Offense Report," April 19, 1974
244 "I remember him...": Klucas interview, September 22, 2009
244 meeting with Rosandich: Bill Dwyre, "UWM Aide's Tangled..."
244 education as armor: Condoleezza Rice, "Morning Edition," NPR, October 13, 2010
245 "I feel empty...": Sroka, "Offense Report," April 19, 1974
245 Sager noticed no depression: Sroka, "Offense Report," April 18, 1974
245 Tandy didn't notice any problems: Ibid.
246 trip to Chicago: Alice Horn, interview, November 28, 2007
246 his favorite meal: Ibid.

Chapter 35

247 Young's reaction: Young interview, February 12, 2008
247 "He was kind of down...": Ibid.

248 "God, no!": Gossom, Walk-On, 208-209
248 "I didn't want…": Scarbinsky, "Remember Henry Harris"
248 "I'm coming back…": Gossom interview, circa Summer 1984
249 Pettway's reaction: Pettway interview, circa Fall 1984
249 had planned to visit Pettway: Ibid.
249 called Loretta Brown: Brown interview, May 10, 2018
249 Klucas goes to Bessemer: Klucas interview, September 22, 2009
249 "I think it was…": Glenda Harris Dunn interview, April 8, 2009
250 conversation between Coons and Parks: Darryl G. Koons Jr., "Offense Report," UWM Police Department, April 19, 1974
250 Nieman's interview of Bigelow: Kenneth A. Nieman, "Offense Report," UWM Police Department, April 19, 1974
250 Sroka's interview of Loritz: Richard A. Sroka, "Offense Report," UWM Police Department, April 19, 1974
251 Kowalski's call to Hill: Warren Hill and Paul Danko, Milwaukee County Medical Examiner's Report, April 18, 1974
251 Eberhardt confirms marijuana in bag: Ibid.
251 no alcohol or barbiturate: Robert D. Eberhardt, memo to file, Office of Medical Examiner, Milwaukee County, May 1, 1974
251 examination of body: Ibid.; Warren Hill, interview, September 22, 2009
251 autopsy not mandatory: Warren Hill, interview, September 22, 2009
251 Willis's report of depression sufficient: Ibid.
252 "the life of a complex…": Bill Dwyre, "UWM Aide's Tangled Life Ends Abruptly," *Milwaukee Journal*, April 19, 1974
252 "I feel like…": "Break Too Late…," *Milwaukee Sentinel*, April 19, 1974
253 Robert's call: Hill and Danko, Medical Examiner's Report, April 18, 1974
253 Robert's call to James: Raymond interview, June 11, 2007
254 "a fierce competitor…": AP, "Former AU Star…," OADN, April 19, 1974
254 "always seemed…": Gossom, "I Remember…," *Plainsman*, April 25, 1974
254 "He was such…": Dennis Marsolek, interview, February 8, 2017
254 "Most people on this campus…": Dennis Marsolek, "Wrong Reason to Remember Harris," *UWM Post*, April 23, 1974

Chapter 36

255 "A community sends…": Dee C. Madison, interview, May 9, 2008
255 Bessemer KKK: McWhorter, *Carry Me Home*
255 McClellan's attack: John Schuppe, "Attack During Alabama Sit-In," nbcnews.com, June 30, 2014,
256 "I know my life…": Jimmy Walker, email to author, August 21, 2019
256 "Hundreds and hundreds…": Glenda Harris Dunn interview, April 8, 2009
256 Auburn blanket: Young interview, February 12, 2008
256 orange flowers: Dunn interview, April 8, 2009
256 "It was a typical…": Madison interview, May 9 , 2008
256 opening hymn: Order of Service, in possession of author
256 Fallin's background: Wilson Fallin, interview, July 15, 2009
256 content of Fallin's remarks: Ibid.
256 "It was terrible…": England interview, June 29, 2008
257 "I had all kind of mixed…": Chapman interview, January 21, 2008
257 Glenda and Carl passed out: Dunn interview, April 8, 2009
258 description of suicide attempt: Albert Johnson interviews, March 11, 2009 and July 11, 2009
258 "I'm dying…": Albert Johnson interview, March 11, 2009

258 Johnson's quiet nature: Gossom interview, December 10, 2012
258 "he was laid-back…": Osberry, interview, December 17, 2016
258 "very mature": Redding, interview, January 12, 2017
258 "If you ever hear…": Ford interview, November 12, 2012
258 "If I don't make it…": Albert Johnson interview, March 11, 2009

Chapter 37

259 "It was like, 'Wow,' he told us…": Ford interview, November 12, 2012
259 "It was disbelief…": Strode interview, February 11, 2008
259 "The black community…": Madison interview, May 9, 2008
260 "he would've done it…": Horn interview, November 28, 2007
260 girlfriend or book as cause of death: Raymond interview, June 11, 2007
260 "someone had a gun:" Brown interview, May 10, 2018
260 "If you think in terms…": Pettway interview, circa Fall 1984
260 "Look at all he had been through…": Kirksey interview, July 15, 2009
261 "Nobody ever knew…": Bill Lynn Jr. interview, May 27, 2008
261 "I never saw him drunk…": Klucas interview, September 22, 2009
261 "Henry dating a…": Richard Cox interview, February 17, 2017
261 "None of us would…": *Ibid.*
261 "I don't think there's any question…": Sager interview, September 22, 2009
262 "He handled himself so well…": Wynveen interview, October 1, 2009
262 "emotional person": Perry interview, June 27, 2008
262 "respectful," "obedient": Chapman interview, January 21, 2008
262 "I mean to tell you…": Bizilia interview, May 30, 2008
263 "My mom sent…": Threatt interview, February 18, 2014
263 "It broke my…": Ash interview, July 6, 2017
263 "anyone to tell meanything": Austin interview, June 20, 2017
263 "Even to this day…": Cowart interview, March 9, 2009
263 "Henry was usually smiling…": York interview, November 3, 2011
263 "We'll never know…": Dan Jacobs interview, March 13, 2017
263 "Henry was not the kind…": Beavers interview, June 22, 2017
264 "I didn't see it…": Owens interview, April 27, 2008
264 "Henry was a bright…": Outland interview, May 25, 2008
265 "You could tell she'd changed…": James Harris interview, February 24, 2008
265 "It's sad anytime a young man…": Sroka interview, December 5, 2016
265 "I can still…": Robert Kowalski, interview, September 30, 2009
265 "He was having personal…": Hill interview, September 22, 2009
265 Hill background: *Ibid.*

Chapter 39

279 "My mother would just walk…": James Harris interview, February 24, 2008
279 "Mama just basically…": Glenda Harris Dunn interview, April 8, 2009
280 "against me day in and day out…": Housel, "Henry Harris"
280 "Where is his book?": James Harris interview, February 24, 2008
280 Dapper Dan bag: Dunn interview, April 8, 2009
280 Loritz given papers: Sroka, "Offense Report," UWM Police, April 19, 1974
281 did not tell children of previous attempt: Dunn interview, April 8, 2009; Harris interview, February 24, 2008; Raymond interview, June 11, 2007
284 "She was the type lady…": Owens interview, May 27, 2008
284 "She was so proud…": Horn interview, November 28, 2007
284 cafeteria supervisor: James Harris interview, February 24, 2008
285 completed GED: Raymond interview, June 11, 2007
285 Tony's death: James Harris interview, February 24, 2008

286 depression within family: Dunn interview, April 8, 2009; James Harris interview, February 24, 2008
286 Carl's death from overdose: Raymond interview, June 11, 2007
286 1999 recognition: Jimmy Walker interview, November 3, 2011
287 "Your brother was good...": Raymond interview, June 11, 2007
287 "senseless death": James Harris interview, February 24, 2008

Chapter 40
Unless noted, Owens quotes are from author interviews April 24, 2008 and May 24, 2008
290 "The NCAA said...": *Quiet Courage*, documentary, 2014
293 "I regret every day...": *Ibid.*
294 "I was selected by God...": *Ibid.*
294 "When my parents...": Jeff Shearer, "James Owens, Auburn Trailblazer...," auburntigers.com, January 17, 2016
294 "You would have thought...": *Ibid.*
295 "If you did not love James Owens...": Thom Gossom, Eulogy, James Owens funeral service, April 2, 2016, Auburn, Alabama

Chapter 41
298 after stonewalling so long: Simon Henderson, *Sidelined*, 150-151, 170
298 "You were all playing...": Vince Dooley, interview by Patricia Heys, *Red & Black*, circa 1997
298 "the single greatest contributor...": Charles H. Martin, *Benching Jim Crow*, 304
298 "Henry took a heck of a risk...": Gossom interview, December 10, 2012
299 "I did my part in my life...": *Return to Mexico City*, ESPN, February 7, 2009
300 Vanderbilt students: Matt Pulle, "Class Action," *Nashville Scene*, February 26, 2004
300 "When the first black basketball player...": *Ibid.*
300 "Henry deserves...": Gossom interview, December 19, 2016
301 "He'd be proud of...": Thom Gossom, email to author, April 4, 2019
301 "If he was playing today...": Chapman interview, January 21, 2008
301 Lary Doby's forgotten legacy: Thomas Stinson, "Courage Unrecognized," *AJC*, June 22, 2003
302 "It took somebody...": *Quiet Courage*, 2014
302 naming arena for Harris: Gilmore interview, circa November 2011
302 richest company: Dana Hanson, "The 20 Richest Companies in the World in 2019," moneyinc.com., circa April 2019

Henry Harris was the only African American on Auburn's 1968-69 freshman basketball team. (Coach Larry Chapman is on the back left.)

As a junior on the 1970-71 varsity, Harris was still the only black in the Auburn basketball program. (Other players include John Mengelt (15), Jimmy Walker (20), Gary England (22), Dan Kirkland (33), Pat Cowart (12), Tim Ash (31).

Bibliography

Charles H. Martin, *Benching Jim Crow: The Rise and Fall of the Color Line in Southern College Sports 1890-1980* (Urbana, Illinois 2010) University of Illinois Press

Andrew Maraniss, *Strong Inside: Perry Wallace and the Collision of Race and Sports in the South* (Nashville 2014) Vanderbilt University Press

Thom Gossom Jr., *Walk-On: My Reluctant Journey to Integration at Auburn University* (Ann Arbor 2008) State Street Press

Barry Jacobs, *Across the Line: Profiles in Basketball Courage,* Lyons Press, 2008

Michael Oriard, *Bowled Over: Big-Time College Football from the Sixties to the BCS Era* (Chapel Hill 2009), University of North Carolina Press

Susan Youngblood Ashmore, *Carry It On: The War on Poverty and the Civil Rights Movement in Alabama 1964-1972,* (Athens, Georgia 2008) UGA Press

Jason Sokol, *There Goes My Everything: White Southerners in the Age of Civil Rights, 1945-1975* (New York: 2006)

Frye Gaillard, *Cradle of Freedom: Alabama and the Movement that Changed America,* (Tuscaloosa 2004) University of Alabama Press

Sandy Tolan, *Me and Hank: A Boy and His Hero, Twenty-Five Years Later* (New York 2000), Touchstone

Bruce Adelson, *Brushing Back Jim Crow: The Integration of Minor-League Baseball in the South* (Charlottesville 1999), University Press of Virginia

Charles W. Eagles, *Outside Agitator: Jon Daniels and the Civil Rights Movement in Alabama,* (Chapel Hill 1993)

Veronica L. Womack, *Abandonment in Dixie: Underdevelopment in the Black Belt* (Macon 2013) Mercer University Press

William Warren Rogers, Robert David Ward, Leah Rawls Atkins, Wayne Flynt, *Alabama: The History of a Deep South State,* University of Alabama Press, 1994

Wayne Greenhaw, *Fighting the Devil in Dixie: How Civil Rights Activists Took on the Ku Klux Klan in Alabama* (Chicago 2011) Lawrence Hill Books

David J, Garrow, *Bearing the Cross: Martin Luther King Jr. and the Southern Christian Leadership Conference,* (New York 1986) Random House

Taylor Branch, *At Canaan's Edge: America in the King Years 1965-68,* Simon & Schuster, 2006

Taylor Branch, *Pillar of Fire: America in the King Years 1963-65,* Simon &Schuster, 1998

Spencer Crew, *Field to Factory: Afro-American Migration 1915-1940,* 1987

Dan T. Carter, *Scottsboro: A Tragedy of the American South,* LSU Press, 1969

Jordana Y. Shakoor, *A Civil Rights Childhood* (Jackson, Mississippi 1999)

Clay Risen, *A Nation on Fire* (Hoboken, New Jersey 2009)

Condoleezza Rice, *Extraordinary Ordinary People: A Memoir of Family* (New York 2010)

Tom Graham and Rachel Graham Cody, *Getting Open: The Unknown Story of Bill Garrett and the Integration of College Basketball* (Bloomington, Indiana 2006)

Catherine M. Lewis, *"Don't Ask What I Shot": How Eisenhower's Love of Golf Hewlped Shape 1950 America* (New York 2007), McGraw Hill

David Margolick, *Elizabeth and Hazel: Two Women of Little Rock* (New Haven 2011), Yale University Press

Art Chansky, *Game Changers: Dean Smith. Charlie Scott and the Era That Transfored a Southern College Town* (Chapel Hill 2016)

Jonathan Eig, *Opening Day: The Story of Jackie Robinson's First Season* (New York 2007)

Jackie Robinson, *I Never Had It Made* (New York 1972)

William J. Baker, *Jesse Owens: An American Life* (New York 1986)

Charlayne Hunter-Gault, *To the Mountaintop: My Journey Through the Civil Rights Movement* (New York 2012)

Patrick B. Miller and David K. Wiggins, *Sport and the Color Line: Black Athletes and Race Relations in Twentieth Century,* (New York 2004)

Samuel Freedman, *Breaking the Line* (New York 2013)

John Klima, *Willie's Boys: The 1948 Birmingham Black Barons, the Last Negro League World Series, and the Making of a Baseball Legend* (Hoboken 2009)

Peter Wallenstein, *Higher Education and the Civil Rights Movement: White Supremacy, Black Southerners and College Campuses,* (Gainesville: 2008)

Frank Fitzpatrick, *And the Walls Came Tumbling Down: Kentucky, Texas Western, and the Game That Changed American Sports* (New York 1999)

Russell Rice, *Kentucky Football: Graveyard or Sleeping Giant? A Personal History* (2013)

Charles W. Eagles, *The Price of Defiance: James Meredith and the Integration of Ole Miss* (Chapel Hill 2009), 94-95

Craig Darch, *From Brooklyn to the Olympics: The Hall of Fame Career of Auburn University Track Coach Mel Rosen* (Montgomery 2014) New South Books

C. M. Newton and Billy Reed, *Newton's Laws* (Lexington, Kentucky 2000)

Sherry Lee Hoppe, *A Matter of Conscience: Redemption of a Hometown Hero, Bobby Hoppe* (Nashville 2010), Wakestone Press

Wayne Federman and Marshall Terrill, *Pete Maravich: The Authorized Biography of Pistol Pete.* (Carroll Stream, Illinois: 2006)

John Hayman, *Bitter Harvest: Richmond Flowers and the Civil Rights Revolution* (Montgomery, Alabama 1996)

Art Chansky, *The Dean's List: A Celebration of Tar Heel Basketball and Dean Smith* (New York 1996)

Tommie Smith, *Silent Gesture: The Autobiography of Tommie Smith*, Temple University Press, 2007

Interviews

Greene County: Jerry Brown, Loretta Towns Brown, Robert Brown, Judge William McKinley Branch, Thennie Mae Edmonds Branch, Addene Byrd, Rosie Carpenter, Ida Colgrove, Harry Collins, Lulu Cooks, James Cox, Glenda Harris Dunn, Ernest Edmonds, Tommie Mae Edmonds, Thomas Gilmore, Spiver Gordon, James Harris, Fred Hughes, Earlean Isaac, Sam Isaac, Dianne Kirksey, A. L Lavender, Frank Morrow, Eunice Outland, Gary Pettway, Robert Raymond, Jerome Roberts, Willie Saxton, Iris Sermon, Vinnie Smoot, Gladys Smothers, Johnny Snoddy, Severe Strode, Tody Webster, Al Young, Bernice Young

Auburn: Tim Ash, Greg Austin, Tom Bardin, Tim Beavers, Wes Bizilia, Larry Chapman, Pat Cowart, Rudy Davalos, Sylvester Davenport, Rufus Felton, Henry Ford, Gary England, Rufus Felton, Ralph Foster, Thom Gossom, Keenan Greenell, Susan Warley Hales, Terry Henley, Eugene Harris, Kenny Howard, Dan Jacobs, Parks Jones, Albert Johnson, Dan Kirkland, Bill Lynn Sr, Billy Lynn Jr., Dee C. Madison, John Mengelt, Roger Mitchell, Bobby Nix, Robert Osberry, James

Owens, Virgil Pearson, Bill Perry, Larry Phillips, Willie Pitts, Gary Redding, Mel Rosen, Carl Shetler, Charles Smith, George Smith, Rush Tanner, Debra Threatt, Herbert Waldrup, Jimmy Walker, Donald Williams, Bobby York

Milwaukee: Glenn Brady, Richard Cox, Jerry Fishbain, Lucy Harvey, Warren Hill, Pamela Hoderman, Bill Klucas, Robert Kowalski, Dennis Marsolek, Mike Nunn, Ray Nykaza, Tom Rosandich, Tom Sager, Richard Sroka, Martin Studenec, Gary Wynveen

Racial Pioneers: Robert Bell, Jackie Brown, Coolidge Ball, Karl Binns, Chuck Claiborne, Godfrey Dillard, Frank Dowsing, Maxie Foster, Leonard George, Robert Grant, Wilbur Hackett, Lennie Hall, Al Heartley, Kenneth "Butch," Henry, Darryl Hill, Lora Hinton, Ronnie Hogue, Houston Hogg, Wendell Hudson, James Hurley, Ernie Jackson, Wilbur Jackson, Willie Jackson, Billy Jones, Horace King, Chuck Kinnebrew, Casey Manning, Lester McClain, John Mitchell, Tom Payne, Clarence Pope, James Reed, Marion Reeves, Freddie Summers, Collis Temple, Perry Wallace

Coaches: Bob Andrews, Charlie Bradshaw, Tom Brennan, Bill Curry, Doug Dickey, Paul Dietzel, Vince Dooley, Hugh Durham, Rob Evans, Joe B. Hall, C. M. Newton, George Raveling, Wimp Sanderson, Roy Skinner

Others: Willie Anderson, Leah Atkins, Rich Baker, Dave Beavin, Marty Blake, Bob Bowen, John Sibley Butler, J. C. Caroline, Albert Davis, ,Harry Edwards, Lonnie Edwards, Claude English, Wilson Fallin, Ralph Foster, Harvey Glance, Travis Grant, David Hall, Luther Hanson, Alice Horn, Jean Howard, Richard Hyatt, Thomas Joiner, Stan Key. William Lawson, Ken Mayfield, Sam McCamey, Frank McCloskey, David Muia, Robert Page, Chris Patrick, James Patrick, Alvin Pouissant, J. T. Purnell, Bud Stallworth, Norman Towns, Archie Wade, John Wallace, Joby Wright

About the Author

Sam Heys covered the integration of the Southeastern Conference as a reporter for the *Atlanta Constitution* and *Columbus Enquirer* in the 1970s and 1980s. Heys is author or co-author of three nonfiction books, including *The Winecoff Fire: The Untold Story of America's Deadliest Hotel Fire* and *Big Bets: Decisions and Leaders That Shaped Southern Company*. He holds master's and specialist degrees in professional counseling and is a licensed mental health counselor.

Made in the
USA
Lexington, KY